CRITICAL PERSPECTIVES ON WORK AND E

MW00512333

Series editors
Irena Grugulis, Leeds University Business School, UK
Chris Smith, Royal Holloway University of London School of Management, UK
Chris Warhurst, University of Warwick Business School, UK

Critical Perspectives on Work and Employment combines the best empirical research with leading edge, critical debate on key issues and developments in the field of work and employment. Extremely well regarded and popular, the series has links to the highly successful International Labour Process Conference.

Formerly edited by David Knights, Hugh Willmott, Chris Smith and Paul Thompson, each volume in the series includes contributions from a range of disciplines, including the sociology of work and employment, business and management studies, human resources management, industrial relations, and organizational analysis.

Further details of the International Labour Process Conference can be found at www. ilpc.org.uk

More details of the publications in this series can be found at www.palgrave.com/business/cpwe

Critical Perspectives on Work and Employment Series
Series Standing Order ISBN 978–0–230–23017–0

You can receive future titles in this series as they are published by placing a standing order. Please contact your bookseller or, in the case of difficulty, write to us at the address below with your name and address, the title of the series and the ISBN quoted above.

Customer Services Department, Macmillan Distribution Ltd, Houndmills, Basingstoke, Hampshire, RG21 6XS, UK

China at Work

A Labour Process Perspective on the Transformation of Work and Employment in China

Edited by
Mingwei Liu

Chris Smith

 palgrave

© Mingwei Liu and Chris Smith 2016
Individual chapters © Contributors 2016

First published 2016 by
PALGRAVE

Palgrave in the UK is an imprint of Macmillan Publishers Limited, registered in England, company number 785998, of 4 Crinan Street, London, N1 9XW.

Palgrave Macmillan in the US is a division of St Martin's Press LLC, 175 Fifth Avenue, New York, NY 10010.

Palgrave is a global imprint of the above companies and is represented throughout the world.

Palgrave® and Macmillan® are registered trademarks in the United States, the United Kingdom, Europe and other countries.

ISBN 978–1–137–43331–2 hardback
ISBN 978–1–137–43328–2 paperback

This book is printed on paper suitable for recycling and made from fully managed and sustained forest sources. Logging, pulping and manufacturing processes are expected to conform to the environmental regulations of the country of origin.

A catalogue record for this book is available from the British Library.

A catalog record for this book is available from the Library of Congress.

Printed and bound by CPI Group UK Ltd, Croydon, CR0 4YY

Contents

Part II   Labour Market Institutions: Unions and Collective Bargaining

Part III   Strikes and Labour Activism

Part IV   Work and Employment in the Overseas Chinese Firm

List of Illustrations

Figures

Acknowledgements

The editors would like to thank all of the contributors, many of whom participated in a special stream, entitled *Work, Labour and Employment in China*, at the 2013 *International Labour Process Conference* at Rutgers University, New Jersey. From the 25 presentations at this stream, we have selected many of the chapters that appear in this volume. The lively debate that took place in the conference special stream has hopefully been captured in the content of the chapters that appear here.

Mingwei Liu and Chris Smith

Notes on Contributors

Rutvica Andrijasevic is a senior lecturer of management at the School of Economics, Finance and Management at the University of Bristol, UK. She has published widely on the impact of migration on labour relations and citizenship. Her monograph *Agency, Migration and Citizenship in Sex Trafficking* (Palgrave, 2010) interrogates the link between migration, gendered organization of labour markets, and citizenship in enlarged Europe. Her most recent project investigates global firms and the rise of China and studies the ways in which 'Chinese' modes of production and management are impacting on work and employment relations in Europe. Rutvica is a member of the editorial collective *Feminist Review* and an editorial board member of the *Anti-Trafficking Review*.

Chris King-Chi Chan is an associate professor in the Department of Applied Social Sciences at the City University of Hong Kong. He has published widely on Chinese labour, including the book *The Challenge of Labour in China* (Routledge, 2010) and articles in many journals, such as *Industrial Relations Journal; Journal of Industrial Relations; British Journal of Industrial Relations; International Labor Review; International Labor and Working Class History; Development and Change; Journal of Contemporary Asia*, and *China Quarterly*.

Yunxue Deng is a PhD student in the Department of Sociology at the University of Hong Kong. Her research interests include migrant workers, labour protests, and trade unions in China. She is currently researching the trade union reform and protests of workers in the Chinese automobile industry.

Lulu Fan is a PhD candidate in the Department of Applied Social Sciences at the Hong Kong Polytechnic University, Hong Kong. Her research interests include informal employment, labour protest, state-owned enterprise reform, and occupational disease problems in China.

Elaine Sio-ieng Hui is a post-doctoral fellow in the Department of Applied Social Sciences in the City University of Hong Kong. Her research interests include critical state theories, legal theories, class consciousness, civil society, social welfare, and labour relations in China. She has published in peer-reviewed journals such as *British Journal of Industrial Relations; Journal of Contemporary Asia; Journal of Industrial Relations; China Quarterly*, and *International Labour Review*.

Wenjuan Jia is a post-doctoral fellow at the Department of Sociology of Shanghai University. She received her PhD from Sun Yat-sen University in Guangzhou, China. Since 2005 she has conducted research on labour–management relations in private firms, the subcontracting system in the Chinese construction industry, and the changing labour process in Chinese state-owned enterprises.

Jaesok Kim is an assistant professor in the Department of Anthropology, University of Pennsylvania. His research interests include transnational corporations and globalization, management and labour discipline, governmentality and post-socialism, and ethnicity and nationalism in East Asia. He is the author of *Chinese Labour in a Korean Factory: Class, Ethnicity, and Productivity on the shop floor in Globalizing China* (Stanford, 2013). His recent research appears in journals such as *Anthropological Quarterly*.

Chunyun Li is an assistant professor at the Department of Management of London School of Economics and Political Science. Her research focuses primarily on Chinese industrial relations and collective bargaining, trade unions, labour NGOs, rural migrant workers, and working conditions in Chinese suppliers in global value chains. She is currently engaged in fieldwork in China, studying labour NGOs and striking workers. Her dissertation examines how Chinese labour NGOs utilize collective bargaining to help workers coordinate sustained and successful collective action. She has published her research in *British Journal of Industrial Relations* as well as edited books.

Lefeng Lin is a PhD candidate in the Department of Sociology at the University of Wisconsin-Madison. His research interests include labour movements, global cities, and third-world development. He is currently working on his dissertation about China's trade-union reform and labour insurgency.

Mingwei Liu is an associate professor of Labour Studies and Employment Relations at Rutgers University. His research interests fall into three broad areas. The first is comparative employment relations with a focus on Chinese employment relations, trade unions, human resource management, and skill development. The second is high-performance work practices in different industries and national contexts. The third is international labour standards and corporate social responsibility in global value chains. His publications appear in journals such as *Industrial and Labour Relations Review*; *British Journal of Industrial Relations*; and numerous edited books. His research has won several prestigious national and international awards such as the John T. Dunlop Scholar Award of the Labour and Employment Relations Association (2014) and the Early Career Research Award of the W.E. Upjohn Institute for Employment Research (2014). In 2015 he was selected as one of the thirteen Chancellor's Scholars at Rutgers.

Xiangmin (Helen) Liu is an assistant professor of Human Resource Management in the School of Labor and Employment Relations at Pennsylvania State University, USA. She is also an affiliate faculty of the Department of Asian Studies. Her research focuses on strategic human resource management, contingent work, and employment relations in Asian countries such as China and Vietnam. She has published in *Industrial and Labor Relations Review*; *Journal of Management*; *Personnel Psychology*; *Advances in Industrial & Labor Relations*; *Journal of Labor Research* and *Relations Industrielles/Industrial Relations*.

Mengjie Lu is a post-doctoral fellow in the Centre of Social Research at Peking University. She obtained her PhD in Labour Economics from Renmin University of China in 2015. From 2012 to 2014, she worked as a visiting scholar in the Institute of Social Research at the University of Michigan, Ann Arbor. She is interested in using both qualitative and quantitative approaches to study Chinese labour relations. She is currently working on a project examining union effects on wages and benefits in China.

Pun Ngai is a professor in the Department of Applied Social Sciences at the Hong Kong Polytechnic University and director of the China Research and Development Network, Hong Kong Polytechnic University. Her research interests include labour, gender, socialist theory, and history. Her first book *Made in China: Women Factory Workers in a Global Workplace* (Duke University Press, 2005) received the C. Wright Mills Award of 2006. Her new book *Labour in China: A Great Transformation* (Polity Press) will be published March 2016.

Can Ouyang is a PhD student in the School of Industrial and Labor Relations (ILR) at Cornell University, USA. His current research interest is in strategic human resource management, exploring the impact of regional institutions, labour-market conditions, and specific organizational features on human resource decisions in Chinese domestic enterprises.

Devi Sacchetto is an associate professor of Sociology of Labour at the Department of Philosophy, Sociology, Education and Applied Psychology at the University of Padua, Italy. He has published widely on migration and labour processes. He has participated in national and international research on issues of social inequality, changes in labour and migration processes. He has focused particularly on changes in Eastern Europe where he has conducted longitudinal and ethnographic research. Among his publications are *Fabbriche galleggianti. Solitudine e sfruttamento dei nuovi marinai* (2009) (On Changing Conditions of Work of Seafarers); 'The Shifting Maelstrom: From Plantations to Assembly-Lines' (with F. Gambino, 2013) in M. van der Linden, K. H. Roth (eds.), *Beyond Marx*; *International Migration and Labour Turnover: Workers' Agency in the Construction Sector of Russia and Italy* (with C. Morrison, O. Cretu, 2014).

Chris Smith is professor of Organisation Studies and Comparative Management, School of Management, Royal Holloway, University of London and has research interests in labour process theory, knowledge transfer through the transnational firm, comparative analysis of work and employment, and professional labour. He has written extensively on work organization and HRM in the Japanese overseas company. He is currently researching the organization of the labour process in Chinese factories and the 'Chinese Business Model' abroad. He has been active in the International Labour Process Conference for many years. He has published in *Journal of Management Studies*; *Organization Studies*; *Human Relations*; *Work, Employment and Society*; *International Journal of Human Resource Management*; *Sociology*; *Economy and Society* among others. Recent book publications include: *Working Life Renewing Labour Process Analysis* with Paul Thompson (Palgrave, 2010); *Creative Labour – Working in the Creative Industries* with Alan Mckinlay, (Palgrave, 2009); *Remaking Management: Between Global and Local* with Brendan McSweeney and Robert Fitzgerald (Cambridge University Press, 2008); and *Assembling Work: Remaking Factory Regimes in Japanese Multinational Companies in Britain* with Tony Elger (Oxford University Press, 2005).

Fuxi Wang is a doctoral candidate at the School of Management and Labour Relations of Rutgers University. Her research interests include labour relations and human resources in China with a particular focus on collective bargaining and democratic management, contingent work, dispute resolution, strategic human resources management, employee participation, and career development.

Hao Zhang is a PhD student in the International and Comparative Labour department at Cornell University's School of Industrial and Labour Relations. His primary research focus is labour and employment relations, with special attention to China, and he has ongoing interests in globalization, development, political economy, skill formation, production, and work. He is currently working on two research projects. In one he looks into the collective bargaining system in China, especially the development of centralized bargaining and informal bargaining and coordination. He has also started a research project on skill formation systems in which he examines different regional models of skill formation in China and their implications for workers. He is a co-author of *Beyond the Iron Rice Bowl: Regimes of Production and Industrial Relations in China* (Campus Verlag, 2013). He has also published in the peer-reviewed journal *Management and Organization Review* and several edited volumes.

Yu Zheng is a lecturer in Asian Business and International Human Resource Management at Royal Holloway, University of London. She has published *Managing Human Resources in China: The View from Inside Multinationals* (Cambridge University Press, 2013) and papers with academic journals such as the *International Journal of HRM*; *Journal of Asia Pacific Management*; and *International Journal of Entrepreneurial Behaviour & Research*. Her research interests include: multinational companies (MNCs) and cross-country transfer of employment practices, employment relations in global R&D centres in China, human resource management in Japanese MNCs, and human resource management strategy and employment practices of Chinese MNCs. She is an active member of the Euro-Asia Management Studies Association and holds close research link with the National University of Singapore, Ritsumeikan University, Japan and the School of Business Economics and Law, Göteborg University, Sweden. Her research has been funded by the Sanwa Foundation and the Japan Foundation.

Preface

Pun Ngai

> The term 'working class,' properly understood, never designated a specific body of people, but rather an expression for an ongoing social process.
>
> Harry Braverman, *Labor and Monopoly Capital*, 1974 (1998):17

Cast by the editors of *China at Work* as a member of the new generation of Chinese labour scholars, I feel very honoured to provide a preface and hope that I have the capability to liven things up. Labour studies in China were booming in recent years because of the great transformation of the country that not only reshaped its 'socialist' path but also the neoliberal global economy and the birth of the new Chinese working class that helped affect the future of world labour. Bringing in a labour process perspective is a timely project to which the editors and the authors of this volume contribute, reconnecting the abundant and divergent empirical studies of Chinese labour with a Marxist theoretical tradition. Re-examining Harry Braverman and Michael Burawoy's work, this volume calls to a standpoint of Marxist labour process theory or sociology of work.

While Harry Braverman's *Labor and Monopoly Capital* (1974) was largely neglected in the field of China's labour studies, Michael Burawoy's various works are very influential and popular in the studies by the new generation of Chinese scholars. The contribution of Burawoy has been depicted in detail in the introduction of this volume. But one interesting change in Burawoy's work that has not been pointed out in this volume is that he has re-directed his analysis from Karl Marx to Karl Polanyi who emphasized market instead of capital, commodification instead of exploitation, and counter movement instead of class struggle. By introducing a third-wave marketization scheme to discern the neoliberal turn of global capitalism, Burawoy's attitude towards Marxist labour process theory and class struggle of labour is now ambivalent.

Equally problematic is the fact that Burawoy prioritizes 'nature' (and perhaps knowledge) over labour in the twenty-first-century struggles against third-wave marketization. Looking at most of the studies in this volume, it is clear that both nature and labour are at the root of global capital accumulation. Hence, the faster the process of capital accumulation the more extensive the scale of expropriation of both nature and labour. Surprisingly, the concept of class in relation to capital seems lacking in his discussion of the third-wave marketization. Yet in the absence of an analysis of class, can there be an emancipatory labour movement whether at local, national, or global levels? Can a moral appeal to humanity and a universal call to civil/labour rights be an effective substitute for a class-oriented movement, often narrowly understood, of course?[1]

Indeed, labour and class itself is virtually missing from Burawoy's advocacy of an unspecified global counter movement to the third-wave marketization that he perceives emerging from the oil crisis and subsequent neoliberalism that has gained momentum since the 1970s. Given Burawoy's insightful critique of Polanyi's thesis which 'shifts from exploitation to commodification, from production to markets, and from classes to society' (2010: 301), it is surprising that Burawoy himself appears to have moved from an analysis rooted in class. He failed, in other words to show how the life experience of commodification in the market, both as a seller of labour power and a consumer, can be linked and synergized with that of the exploitation of workers in the production sphere.

Could two Karls, Karl Marx and Karl Polyani, meet? We can put this interesting question not only to Michael Burawoy but also to everybody. What is the nature of labour actions that most of the authors of this volume studied, market-oriented or class-based? To our view, these labour actions or struggles on the ground are anxiously awaiting to be connected to Marxist labour process and class tradition. By lingering on Polanyi's concept of commodification and counter movement, Burawoy, without suggesting a new direction for labour struggles, reaffirms Antonio Gramsci's call for 'pessimism of the intellect' and 'optimism of the will' (Burawoy 2010; 2011). Fierce as the debate has been, we found it unhelpful for gauging the struggle of China's embattled workers which the authors present here through the lens of a constellation of commodification and market forces spearheaded by Karl Polanyi. China's new working class, comprised overwhelmingly of rural migrant workers, face distinctive forms of exploitation on the frontline of a class struggle with important implications for Chinese and international workers. What are the implications for world labour and labour resistance when a wave of protests, riots, and strikes occur in their wake? Michael Burawoy's 'uncompromising pessimism' (2011) about a current third wave of marketization in the context of Polanyi's counter movement offers neither a theoretical analysis nor a compelling approach grounded in life-world struggle of the workers compared to his important insights in his earlier research on South African, Hungarian, and Russian workers. We miss old Burawoy, just like we miss old Marx.

To sum up, Chinese labour studies with a labour process perspective should bring class back into the centrality of analysis. In China, it was particularly difficult because of the negation of socialist experience, the U-turn to neoliberal capitalism and the subsumption of class discourse. Class analysis had to be eradicated in order to prepare for the new age of reform and opening to come. This negation of class, followed up by change of socialist production relations, the pouring in of foreign capital, the rebirth of private capital, and last but not the least, the birth of a new Chinese working class, all attest to the foundation for the inevitable renewal of class relations. The negation is the prerequisite for the rebirth of class.

The rise of China as the 'world's workshop' in the age of globalization and the accompanying new working class comprising several hundred million provide us with a class perspective to understand the importance of labouring subjects and their class in shaping the transformed space of global capitalism. The richly and vividly lived experience of the new working class in terms of work organization, dormitory labour life, feeling of class, and collective action is the key to understanding the change of work and employment in China. Unlike most post-modern literature which denounces the importance of Karl Marx's class, class is still the central concept for providing an effective analytical weapon to discern the lives of the working class under the major contradictions of contemporary capitalism.

This volume excels in providing comparative labour studies between China and the world, is compelled to a mission-impossible project of new labour internationalism only because we now live in the neoliberal capitalism of the twenty-first century. This century calls more to the 'end of history', than to the creation of new labouring subjects that could challenge this history and potentially create a new one. The struggle to create this new labouring class by itself and for itself nevertheless reshapes the future of class relations and their struggles not only in China, but the world. Class struggle is a matter of fact and a matter of time.

Note

1 Most people, including labour scholars, often narrowly or 'radically' consider 'class' actions as political struggles taken up by an organized working class to overhaul a capitalist system. A question to us is: why is a group of workers, small or large, fighting for their economic interests at the point of production not considered class action? Are these actions not driven by class conflicts occurring at the sphere of production or reproduction?

REFERENCES

Braverman, H. (1974) *Labor and Monopoly Capital*, New York: Monthly Review Press.

Burawoy, M. (2010) From Polanyi to Pollyanna: The False Optimism of Global Labor Studies. *Global Labour Journal*, 1(2) 301–313.

Burawoy, M. (2011) On Uncompromising Pessimism: Response to My Critics. *Global Labour Journal*, 2(1) 73–77.

In Search of the Labour Process Perspective in China

Chris Smith and Mingwei Liu

Introduction

A chemical explosion in Tianjin, China on 12 August 2015, killed 161 people and at least 12 people remained missing, presumed dead, at the time of writing (early September 2015), with many more in hospital and thousands unable to return to their homes. This disaster highlights several things about the current state of labour and employment relations in China. Firstly, the slow release of the death toll; this was because so many firefighters and workers on the site of the chemical store were temporary or agency workers, so that the authorities did not have an accurate record of who was actually working on that night. If you are a temporary worker in China, you are more or less invisible. Secondly, while much has been made in the media about the proximity of housing to the chemical store – breaking the one kilometre law on housing adjacent to industrial sites – very little was said about the migrant workers' dormitories that were proximate to the store and totally flattened by the explosion. If you're a migrant worker, your living conditions are disregarded. Thirdly, Chinese enterprise-based firefighters such as those employed by the Tianjin Port are on performance bonuses.[1] While regulations state that with chemical fires workers should be at least one kilometre away when fighting the fire to avoid hazardous explosions, this rule was flagrantly breached as the performance bonus firefighters received was based on the property they managed to save, which incentivized approaching the fire to better tackle the blaze to reduce damage to property. If you're a poor worker, you need to work under dangerous additional pressure to make money. Fourthly, the chemical store was illegally warehousing excessive amounts of dangerous chemicals, and because of this the firefighters were not aware of the problems they were tackling – instead of using foam that would have suppressed the initial fire, they used water which produced catastrophic fireballs, and major loss of life. If you're a temporary migrant worker you are kept in the dark about your working conditions, which can have fatal results. Finally, while firefighters in the West often have strong unions to represent their interests, the Tianjin Port union obviously failed to monitor workplace safety on behalf of its members. If you are a worker in China, you cannot count on your union to protect your rights and interests.

China is the world's second biggest economy and has grown in an unprecedented way to become the world's assembly line. China's economic reform, now in its fourth decade, has gradually transformed the country from a Communist planned economy to a mixed economy with elements of both market and central planning. Not only has unprecedented economic growth been generated by this transformation, but work and employment in the Chinese workplace have been fundamentally reshaped. In particular, the highly rigid and centralized 'iron rice bowl' system in which state workers enjoyed lifetime employment; standard, stable, and egalitarian wages and 'cradle-to-grave' welfare has been gradually replaced by a labour contract system characterized by high managerial autonomy, employment flexibility, and contributory social insurance schemes. China is now home to many business models; has been penetrated by significant foreign direct investment (and hence produces a greater diversity to employment forms); but it remains a transitional developing economy with internal divisions between state socialist and capitalist political economies. Nevertheless, given the importance of China on the world stage, we need to know more about the nature of current labour process practices, which this book aims to provide.

The transition from state socialism to capitalism in China has been accompanied by many attempts to isolate the nature of work and employment within China. Approaches to frame a unique way of managing have used values and culture; institutions and history; different ownerships and nationality of capital; and space and regional differentiation in economic development across China. There has also been a strong focus assigned to the way labour is attached to employment and organizations, with special attention to migrant workers, the internal passport (*hukou*) system, and the recent casualization or informalization of labour contracts, a radical shift from former long-term bonds between worker and workplace.

The outcome of some 30 years of theorizing and empirical engagement with reform and transformation has been mixed. Some divide Chinese workplaces into 'sunrise' and 'sunset' industries – each with their own labour management regimes, labour supply, and working class politics (Lee, 2007). Others see in China a dominant form of 'bloody Taylorism', epitomized by one reading of the work regime enunciated by the Taiwanese contractor firm Foxconn – military discipline and ideology, task simplification, and intensive work combining production and reproduction of labour power in huge industrial compounds that function like enclosed cities (Chan and Pun, 2012). But Foxconn is one story. Huawei – with longer-term relations between workers, more innovation, more investment in skills and training, and shared ownership between workers and firm – tells another story. Which represents the Chinese labour process? Is there a single or dominant labour process? Having been in a state of flux and transition for over 30 years, can we now say with confidence that there is a settled and agreed way of attaching labour to the firm, or does diversity and fragmentation persist?

The changing face of workers, trade unions, labour NGOs, employers, governments (central and local), labour processes, employment practices, workplace democracy, and labour-management relations have to some extent been documented by the growing literature of China labour studies. However, the Chinese workers, employers, and local governments are much more diversified and the interactions and relationships among the three actors are much more complicated than the existing scholarship has revealed. An illustrative example is that while Honda workers in Guangdong went on strikes in 2010 asking for higher wages, their counterparts in Hubei gained significant wage increase through union-led collective consultation. Moreover, the Chinese labour-market institutions and workplace relations have been constantly changing. For instance, since 2007 China has enacted several important labour laws such as the Labour Contract Law, the Labour Dispute Mediation and Arbitration Law, and the Social Insurance Law, the effects of which on employment practices and workplace dynamics have not been systematically examined or even explored. In addition, China has experienced another wave of strikes since 2010, the causes, processes, and outcomes of which have not been well studied.

This book therefore aims to capture some of the diversity that is the Chinese workplace today, bringing in different types of industry, ownerships, and regions and the growing role that labour institutions have for mobilizing actors and opinions from below. The 15 chapters in this book are separated into four sections, reflecting these themes: (i) work & employment by sector and firm – which covers the impact of reforms of state-owned enterprises (SOEs) on labour process organization and employment relations, as well as labour relations in MNCs in China and within SMEs and worker-organized units of production; (ii) labour market institutions: unions and collective bargaining; (iii) strikes and labour activism; and (iv) work and employment in the overseas Chinese firm. The aim of this introduction is to give a sense of the writing of Chinese and non-Chinese researchers on the labour process and labour agency in China, and what we currently know about the Chinese workplace and the social character of actors at work, especially institutional and class actors.

The Labour Process in One Country?

The themes of temporary and migrant work; workplace status divisions and tensions, and the authoritarianism of management pervade the chapters of this book, which is the first in the Palgrave *Critical Perspectives on Work and Employment* series to focus on labour processes in one country. Country-centred research is important, especially in the case of China, given its size and its dramatic entry into global capitalism, unique in terms of timing, the heritage it brings and scale of its economy. We need to know about working in this giant economy and ancient civilization. China is a capitalist society that retains socialist ideology while bonding with global capitalism through an export-driven industrialization strategy and membership of the WTO. China retains one-party politics, enormous censorship, state run-trade unions, powerful state-run industries, weak rule of law, weak civil society institutions such as autonomous professions (journalists, lawyers, academics, etc.), and an ideology of socialism that continues to influence, albeit rhetorically, the organization of some of the workplaces and labour processes in the country.

But there are also problems with country-specific books on the labour process, especially those which separate one country from others, reinforcing, in the case of China, the idea of country 'exceptionalism' which has strong parallels with American exceptionalism (see Chan, 2015). We need to start with the statement that all countries have exceptional features to some degree. While pointing these out is important, making them tell the whole story is deficient because foreign or outside forces play a role in the home story, and globalization within capitalism

ensures that it is interaction not comparative differences between societies that becomes imperative in the new world economy. Equally, trying
to frame China against other 'types' of capitalism *à la* the Varieties of
Capitalism (VoC) school (Hall and Soskice, 2001) is unhelpful. Lüthje
(2015) notes China's correspondence to patterns of corporatism (as in
Germany and Japan) under the VoC framework; but others (Liu et al.,
2015) note liberal market capitalism elements within China, immediately highlighting the futility of a forced choice between two static
models within what is a highly dynamic and contradictory landscape –
see Peck and Zhang (2013) and Zhang and Peck (2014) for a discussion
of the problems of this way of framing China.

The VoC framework projects the myth of integrated economies
which is ahistorical, and particularly hopeless for trying to capture
something as large, diversified, dynamic, and fluid as the political economy of China (Peck and Zhang, 2013; Smith, 2005). It is also hopeless
from a labour process perspective, which builds bottom-up from the
workplace to more macro pieces of social structure, stressing dynamism
and innovation within production, and constant forming and reforming of social relations between capital and labour that characterize this
abode of capitalist rationality. In a labour process approach, social structure speaks; it is fluid, has agency and changes, whereas isolating a set
of institutional factors (at a point in time) is unable to provide an adequate explanation for what remains a rapidly shifting social structure,
and an innovative workplace.

Breaking China down into different regional sub-economies has some
merits (see chapter by Smith and Zheng in this book) but ultimately we
need to retain a concept of capitalism that has system regularities, such
as the drive for capital accumulation, the reproduction of waged labour,
and the structured antagonism between capital and labour. Sometimes
societal effects have systemic features. For example, the focus on labour
mobility is essential for understanding the labour process in China, as
industrialization has been driven by the movement of millions of workers across China, and mobility and the split between locals and migrants
is significant not only for the for life chances of individuals, but critically, to our purposes, for the organization of the labour process. But
there is also a systemic (capitalist) character to labour mobility as part of
what constitutes waged labour and hence China is not unique here. The
chapter by Andrijasevic and Sacchetto in this book excellently plots the
overlaps between labour processes organized around internal-migrant
labour in the Foxconn factories in China, with the strong use of intra-
European migration to segment the workforce in Foxconn's European
factories. This highlights an important point that we stress throughout

the book, the importance of separating country, system, and emerging dominant templates to work organization, while also seeing these forces as fluid and coalescing.

Alongside some sense of country manifestations (including local and regional differences) of capitalist forces we need to see how these are enacted, localized and embodied by actors on the ground. Through a workplace-based approach, which the labour process perspective offers and many chapters in this book exemplify, we are able to see in microcosm the acting out of systemic and local practices, and judge how agential action penetrates structures in dynamic and emerging ways. Institutionalized approaches, such as the VoC, generally tend to see social structure as relatively fixed; a labour process perspective makes such structure active and fluid, through exploring the daily enacting and testing of the robustness of social structures inside the production process.

Finally, as well as holding onto the idea of capitalism as a system, and the boundary, heritage and institutional properties that come through the idea of society, we also need to capture some sense of the direction of travel that an economy and labour processes within it might be taking, especially where home models are internationalizing and challenging existing dominant templates of work organization, be these American or Japanese in recent times. Asking where China is going is a legitimate question, and we can see, in the labour process, managers as directors of labour process organization, looking towards Japan (Aoki, 2008; Chan, 1995b) or towards the US (Zheng, 2013; Liu et al., 2015) for country trends. In other words, country-models are assumed of other dominant societies in pragmatic acts of management action. But we cannot assume either China or the US or Japan are static in this scenario – when all are under pressures to change caused in no small part by the scale and significance of China's growing presence in the world economy.

We need to understand these interactions at the firm level – as it is at this level where dynamism can be seen. So for example, Zheng's chapter in this book has Chinese managers inside Japanese MNCs in China rejecting the Japanese recipe of work organization and employment relations because it's too much like the prescriptions of former Chinese SOEs which the same managers (and the society) have ideologically and institutionally abandoned. Her chapter underscores how these Chinese managers advocate instead embracing extreme employment flexibility, which they associate (wrongly in many cases) with the success of American capitalism and American MNCs. In microcosm we see being played out here the stresses and contradictions of old, new, and alternative recipes for work and employment in this one workplace which speaks to wider societal choices and trends. This is the strength of a labour process approach. Institutions are animated by the agents of capital and labour within real workplaces.

Thompson (2003: 359) critically summarised general patterns of the shifts in work and employment across capitalist societies:

> Since the early 1980s the big picture franchise has passed to and through a variety of paradigm break theories. We have moved from and through flexible specialization, new production concepts, lean production, post-Fordism, post-modernization, and lately the knowledge economy. While there have, of course, been variations in these perspectives, we can also observe a number of common themes.
>
> - The disappearance of the 'old economy' characterized by large firms, mass production and standardized work; supplanted by flexible, creative, knowledge-based labour in a largely service context.
> - A shift from technical, financial or bureaucratic controls to cultural coordination, internalized commitment and self-discipline among employees.
> - The substitution of hierarchy by networks, boundaryless or decentralized units in a globalized world in which private capital is the only significant actor, with the state and labour marginalized.

On a global scale, and especially when we look at China, this summary of new developments in the workplace is largely wrong. In China factories have got much bigger, with hundreds of thousands of workers locked in an extended integration of reproduction and production of labour power within spaces which operate like closed communities or industrial cities. Mass standardized work has been extended to new levels and applied to the most sophisticated, powerful, aesthetic and valuable products (such as iPads and smart phones) which are produced within mass production principles of extreme standardization and divisions of labour (see Andrijasevic et al., 2016 on Foxconn).

Controls remain diverse, with repressive, technical, and cultural controls combining with personal controls by supervisors and managers of an extreme nature. Finally agreeing on the importance of the disintegration of organizations (through outsourcing etc.) does not eliminate the importance of hierarchy, and controls through lead firms in value chains. But private capital is not as marginalized as labour and the state is only weakened in some contexts. Thompson might be accused of summarizing these trends in the case of neoliberal economies (like the UK and US) where units of production are becoming less powerful and less integrated (hence disconnected) and managers within them are increasingly subalterns, in subordinate roles in more marginalized and intra-competitive subsidiaries, with real strategic power elsewhere (whether in other countries or places or sections of capital, such as finance). But the state is not marginal in countries like China, where in both the country and overseas, it remains a central actor.

While outlining these trends as *systemic* in the first part of his paper, Thompson (2003: 368) later notes that: 'much of the research referred to in this section is drawn from the recent experience of liberal market economies'. With the specificity of country and regions in mind, Thompson (ibid, 368) says that it is 'better to talk of disconnected capitalisms, in a manner that would be more consistent with the comparative political economy literature (Coates, 2000; Hall and Soskice, 2001; Whitley, 1999)'. He notes systemic features of capitalism are increasingly uniform: 'however, trends in product and capital markets are making the world a smaller place and the extent of institutional distinctiveness is diminishing' (ibid, 368). As noted above, this book, aims to retain this stress on specificity which comes through a focus on society, but without abandoning these systemic trends, and at the same time seeking to understand the direction of travel of work in different Chinese workplaces.

Labour Process Theory in China

This book shines light on employment and work relations in China from inside the workplace – where on a daily basis the reproduction of commodity production is made. The theories used to discuss these trends are drawn from a labour process intellectual heritage which in its modern form is over 40 years old and largely built on the work of non-Chinese scholars working in different times and different capitalisms. This has consequences for the understanding of work in China today.

Harry Braverman's *Labor and Monopoly Capital* (LMC), published in 1974, has been central to the development of the labour process approach, perspective, and theory (Thompson, 1997; Thompson and Smith, 2000; 2009; 2010). The book gave sociology of work more breadth and scope. Braverman argued that (American) capitalism in the twentieth century had systemized the destruction of craft or skilled work. In its place we saw the rise of managerial, technical, and white collar workers who grew through management alignment of control of a largely unskilled or semi-skilled manual workforce, working within labour processes in which judgement and knowledge were diminished, as management and its agents monopolized the conceptual side of work. Control over workers was cemented for Braverman by the systematic removal of craft apprenticeship systems, and the expansion of technology and bureaucracy in which professionalized managers controlled the planning, scheduling and organization of the labour process, leaving workers with limited autonomy and discretion to execute skill-depleted, fragmented, and routinized tasks.

The labour process is a transformation process, converting raw materials with labour power and technology for the purpose or drive of profitability to produce commodities for sale through markets. While the idea of the 'labour process' is taken from Marx *Capital Vol 1* ([1867] 1976), and European Marxist activists and writers explored capitalism through the idea of the labour process, Taylorism, Fordism, and production types and systems prior to *LMC* (Thompson, 1989; Smith and Thompson, 1998), this book remains a central reference for the contemporary debate.

LMC was translated into Chinese four years after it appeared in 1978, but given the US-centric heart of *LMC*, its want of a comparative approach or understanding of capitalism, it is not therefore surprising that indigenous Chinese scholars did not utilize the book when seeking to understand transformations in work and employment in their country over the last three decades. Its story did not fit their reality.

The craft or guild apprenticeship systems were marginal not mainstream in China – existing in Southern pre-revolutionary China (Frazier, 2002: 6–12; Perry, 1993: 32–45) but fragile or absent in the North (see Hershatter (1986) on Tianjin workers, for example). These systems were transformed post-1949, as the Chinese working class became layered, with workers in SOEs with urban household registration in a cradle-to-grave *danwei* welfare system – permanent job tenure, housing provision, life-long medical and pension benefits, and superior wages – at the apex of the Chinese working class and constituting 42 per cent of the industrial labour force (Lee, 2005:1). These elite workers existed in a predominantly peasant society; the industrial working class a relatively privileged urban elite, with peasant workers locked in the countryside with internal passport controls preventing movement, and hence competition with industrial workers – something that has dramatically changed in the last four decades. The highly institutionalized character to the production of skilled labour, and the strong internal labour market in the pre-reform period, contrasted to the voluntarism and mobility in the US. Therefore a book with craft at its centre had limited traction in China.

Additionally, in terms of chronology, the theoretical basis of Braverman's work – his determinism in judging Scientific Management the 'one best way' of capitalist practice and his historical chronology in judging capitalism to have evolved from contracting relations to employment relations and Taylorism (see Clawson, 1980; Littler, 1982; Burawoy, 1985) – looked out of place in China, where changes to employment contracts have been a major driver of labour process transformation (Kuruvilla et al., 2011).

We have also seen in the US since the 1980s an unbundling of workers, firms, and employment relations; and the returns to earlier forms of contracting, and new forms of casual or temporary employment, with trends towards labour market spot contracting as in zero-hours contracts (Kalleberg, 2000, 2009; Brinkley, 2013). This neoliberal rupture affects America and Europe, but also China, which has also seen workers, careers, and firms becoming unbundled and disassociated, rather than tightly integrated as in the old *danwei* model. Braverman is not theoretically helpful here. Writers that have looked at levels, separated labour process, and employment relations, are more useful – the work of Michael Burawoy especially.

Labour process theory is mainly an import into China from overseas Chinese and non-Chinese academics and activists in the US, UK, Hong Kong, Australia, and Europe, as we discuss below. This parallels the importing of new or other models of the labour process practice into China with foreign investment, and the definite transfer role of managers in foreign MNCs (Gamble, 2000, 2010; Zheng, 2013; Zhang, 2015; Lüthje, 2015). Chapters in this book by Yu Zheng on Japanese firms and Jaesok Kim on South Korean firms bring out these practical concerns of transfer and mediation. But it is not only private Chinese firms that can act as receptors for the importation of new management methods. Partnerships between private firms and Chinese SOEs can also be a conduit for transfer and change. Thus Wenjuan Jia's chapter on the emergence of dualism between directly employed workers and contractors' workers in an SOE notes that it was 'after 2001, when China entered the WTO that South Factory [his case study] began to cooperate with a German Company, Heinrich, to produce a new product, the shield machine. This cooperation turned out to be an opportunity for the South Factory to change its production methods'. It was 'during the initial cooperation of the South Factory with Heinrich that managers implemented the 'modern enterprise management system' in the workshop – although 'formal workers fought against the enforcement of the modern enterprise management system by slowdowns and disobedience'.

Labour process ideas are therefore heavily mediated though discourse within different societies and hence the influence of Braverman has to be measured through these dialogues – and ongoing labour process debates (Thompson and Smith, 2010) that this book is an active part of.

Dominant Labour Process Theories in China

Workplace-based research remains minor, but is developing in China, and this book contributes to this growing literature. Labour process research draws from two sources – academics (sometime academic-activists), within ethnographic traditions, but who have also sought to link micro and macro elements of the social structure, and borrow extensively from the work of Michael Burawoy – CK Lee (a student of Burawoy) and Pun Ngai, for example. These academics often utilize post-structuralist writers, such as Foucault, to write about power, surveillance, and control inside closed communities of many Chinese mass-factories (see especially Pun Ngai, *Made in China* (2005) and Jaesok Kim, *Chinese Labour in a Korean Factory* (2013)). Secondly, academics with strong NGO links – Anita Chan, Pun Ngai, Jenny Chan, and Chris Chan, for example – focus on labour action and protest, and orientate their writing to the possibility of more democratic change in China, and hence often look at the importance of agency and transformation in the Chinese experience. This strand of writing is also captured in this book, which examines the role of different change agents in China – whether workers from new and declining industrial sectors, fractions of the Chinese central union, or labour activists within NGOs in China.

There is a generational divide amongst China labour researchers. Historians of labour – Perry (1993), Honig (1986), and Hershatter, (1986) for example – did not explore the labour process directly or ethnographically, but instead relied on accounts of factory life in Tianjin (Hershatter, 1986) or Shanghai (Honig and Perry) for their work. This work has inspired and been built upon by anthropologists and sociologists of labour in the current period, who either worked in or reported on factories (Lee, 2009; Pun) or entered dormitories to gather ethnographies of workers in dorms and in leisure areas (Jenny Chan, 2014) or interviewed workers away from the workplace (Lee in *Against the Law*, 2007). Many were also allied with ongoing activist work, unlike the historians. These academics, in the US, CK Lee (1998), Liu (2010; 2014), Zhang (2015); in Australia – Anita Chan – *Workers Under Assault* (2001), *Walmart in China* (2011) and *Chinese Workers in Comparative Perspective* (2015) – have also supervised PhD students – Kevin Lin, Kaxton Siu, for example – who have gone on to produce contemporary ethnographies of employment and work in China. In Hong Kong and the UK, Ngai Pun, Chris Chan, and Jenny Chan, are a new generation of young scholars. Many in this book (see chapters by Lulu Fan, Yunxue Deng and Chris Chan and Elaine Hui) have been important contributors to contemporary debates on work in China. Finally, in Europe, German researchers, especially the work of Boy Lüthje (2013) and Florian Butollo (2014) have developed important accounts of recent changes in the labour process in China. British-trained researchers, such as Gamble (2000, 2010) and most importantly Pun Ngai – engaged in Marxist and Foucauldian work for her award-winning and highly cited *Made in China* and her early papers. Chris Smith introduced a more Marxist orientation, and through the development of the concept of the 'dormitory labour regime' helped construct a frame of analysis around the new Chinese working class and link labour process writing to the spatial literature on work into understanding Chinese workplaces (Smith, 2003; Smith and Pun, 2006; Pun and Smith, 2007). Pun Ngai has inspired a generation of young activist academics and their work is currently appearing in papers and through PhDs. Several of this generation are in this book. Chris Chan, for example – a Warwick PhD who worked under the Marxist and theorist of socialist transitions, Simon Clarke, has focused on trade unions and activism within a Marxist tradition, comparative focus, building on a Warwick-University industrial relations tradition.

Burawoy, Dualism, and the Labour Process in China

Writers on the labour process post-Braverman – Edwards, Clawson, Friedman, Thompson, Littler, Rubery, (see Smith, 2015 for a review) hardly feature in Chinese discourse on labour process theory and empirical research. But one writer stands out. Michael Burawoy has been most influential in labour process studies in China. Burawoy's work has been translated into Chinese, one of the few labour process theorists to have this honour. Several chapters in this book explicitly utilize the work of Burawoy to theorize changes in 'factory regimes' in China. His *Manufacturing Consent* appeared in 1979, *The Politics of Production* in 1985, but only the latter has been translated and published in 2005 (in Hong Kong and Taiwan). *Manufacturing Consent* has more references to Donald Roy and Marx, than it does to Braverman, but it comes out of a Marxist sociology of work in the 1970s.

Burawoys' students (especially CK Lee – *Gender and the South China Miracle* (1998 – over 600 GS citations) have been influential in diffusing Burawoy's work to Chinese researchers. In the US Burawoy commands a strong position both for ethnographic work and creatively writing about the labour process, and his two main books are part of the same intellectual projects – *Politics*, was flagged as forthcoming in *Manufacturing Consent*, despite appearing six years later. Burawoy was innovative in separating the micro element of the labour process (social organization of work, tasks and technical division of labour) from wider production structures (the institutions that regulate the workplace and shape workplace politics) – the class politics of industrial relations and wider sources of legitimation or ideology for class structures and class compromises that permit exiting capitalist social relations to be reproduced.

Two generic types of factory controls are suggested by Burawoy. In *Manufacturing Consent* the 'factory regime' (a sort of total management control system) is *hegemonic* – the workplace is regulated by institutions of state welfare capitalism, trade unions, and workers collective power which, following the Italian Marxist Antonio Gramsci, produces 'hegemonic' control. This is where workers buy-in to the material returns and values of high wages, high production, and high consumption compromises of monopoly capitalism. Workers give *consent* to being 'controlled', rather than being dominated or oppressed by dictatorial managers within the factory or by the whip of labour market discipline from outside the factory. Later labour process writers wrote about *compliance* rather than consent, to emphasize some reluctance on the part of workers to accepting management control (Littler and Salaman, 1982). But for Burawoy consent is given to managers to rule because workers support the system through economic benefits and the pleasures of shop-floor games that make time pass quicker. The discipline of the market is mediated and contained through the strength of state and worker organizations. So against, the 'despotic factory regimes' of pre-welfare capitalism, coercive controls (the monopoly voice of capital, iron discipline of the labour market, and non-interventions of the state) are not as dominant.

In *Politics*, the two generic types of factory regime (despotic and hegemonic) are multiplied through ethnographic accounts and macro-theorizing about Hungarian state socialism and the Zambian colonialist state. There is chronology of the labour process in the writing of Burawoy – despotic to hegemonic; coercive to more cultural, ideological and bureaucratic forms of control – but his work is more dynamic than the simplistic linear evolutionary approach to management control evident in the work of Edwards (1979). But in China, this chronology has been questioned, and writers such as Anita Chan (2001), Lee (1999), and O'Leary (1998), who have suggested that factory despotism has been reinforced with the privatizations of SOEs and the weakening of labour contracts within the firm as well as the open door to foreign capital and clamp down of workers' rights to unionize, collectivize, and strike. But as discussed in separate chapters by Lefeng Lin and Wenjuan Jia in this book, the idea of hegemonic factory regimes remains an important reference to research on SOEs in China.

CK Lee (1999) characterizes the shift from SOEs to private capital as a move 'from organized dependence to disorganized despotism' – which she discusses in the growth of the so called Guangdong model in China, a production regime reliant upon migrant labour, deskilled work, foreign firms, large scale contract manufacturing, authoritarianism in the workplace, and largely unchecked management domination. State reform of SOEs is described as chaotic as well, and chapters by Lefeng Lin and Wenjuan Jia on SOE reforms in this book utilize Burawoy to discuss the lack of clear direction to the development of labour process regimes in China.

The idea of different 'factory regimes' introduced in *Politics* has enjoyed widespread application, even where workplaces are not explored ethnographically (which Burawoy certainly advocates) but through outputs (strike activity, labour disputes, labour turnover) or inputs (numbers of skilled and unskilled workers, education levels, employment contracts of workers, or whether they are locals or migrants), or simply through interviews with workers and managers removed from micro observations and reflections that can be obtained from direct workplace experience. Lu Zhang (2015) in an excellent book on auto companies in China (*Inside China's Automobile Factories*) did visit, observe, and interview workers and managers in the auto plants she studied (working as an office/liaison worker in two companies, for different blocks of time – typically one month) and her work presents a very rich picture of work inside SOE and JV auto companies in China. But she did not work on the line as Burawoy would advocate, and therefore direct experience and reflection on working is absent, while being in the factories for extended periods did allow a building of trust with workers and the production of very rich interviews, comparative statistics, and observational materials, which have comparative breadth (and a lot of depth) – breadth is something direct ethnographies usually sacrifice for the minutia of working in often static situations. Nevertheless, her work is typical of what can be called the *Burawoy in China* approach.

There is an analytical fit between Burawoy and China. The appeal of Burawoy's work in China is in his totalizing approach – attempting to characterize the whole labour process within factories, sectors, and even at the country level – through different 'production regimes'. Burawoy is good at seeking to connect dynamics inside and outside the immediate labour process. He gives attention to levels. Critically he has a lot to say about the state – and the state is most obviously a significant actor in Chinese society. It is also big picture stuff, and from the simple production models of 'despotic' and 'hegemonic' (repressive and ideological regimes) one can play around with hybrids, and makes up new typologies. Lee's (1998) concept of 'localistic despotism', would be such an example.

This approach tries to generalize from production politics to whole sectors. So Lu Zhang's study of the auto industry in China – which looks at Chinese, German, and Japanese car firms – uses the metaphor of lean production, to say two things. Firstly, that firms are adopting lean production, but also creating segmentation between core workers with secure working conditions and temporary workers in more marginal positions – which some say is typical of the Japanese model (Elger and Smith, 2005). But she also suggests that the lean model is distinct in China as the split is between local regular and migrant, non-local workers – a unique citizenship or political split in the workforce. Secondly, and in contradistinction, this split is seen as systemic and not something 'with Chinese characteristics'. Hence: 'notably, similar to the Toyotist lean-and-dual model, the job security of formal employees in China's auto assembly plants is buffered by a large number of insecure and lower-paid temporary workers. In fact, *it seems an industry trend for automakers worldwide to move toward the lean-and-dual model.* Cost-cutting measures associated with 'lean production' proliferated' (Zhang, 2015: 167, *emphasis added*).

But this way of looking at the labour process has been criticized. Lee (1998) is critical of Burawoy's neglect of gender but nevertheless uses the schema to create typologies with which to characterize a whole set of industries – 'disorganized dependency'. Typologies might be useful within the China context, where labour-market segmentation between industries (private, SOEs etc.) and social and historical segmentation between worker types are highly institutionalized. Migrants and locals, for example exhibit deep structural, prescribed differences with regard to their claims on society and firms and both have been used to build different accounts of what it is to be a worker in China with and without local hukou, settlement, local claims, and so on.

Zhang (2015: 167) notes 'labor force dualism became widespread as firms sought to increase flexibility through the hiring of peripheral, temporary workers, while retaining the loyalty of a more permanent, core labor force'. The structural differentiation of the Chinese working class means it makes a lot of sense to think in categories and typologies (often top-down, not bottom-up), rather than, as in more liberal capitalist societies, to build accounts of the labour process from the workplace, and stress the relative autonomy of the labour process or workplace level (as advocated by labour process writers such as Paul Edwards, Paul Thompson, and Craig Littler – see Smith, 2015 for a review). But the dangers of what we are calling *Burawoy in China* remain, especially as the application of his approach can underplay agency and contingency and create rather neat and totalizing views of factory regimes, disregarding the tensions and contradictions that exist in all labour processes. As noted by Zhang 'the management-constructed divisions among workers have become a continuing source of irritation and an impetus for the temporary workers to demand equal treatment. Thus the lean-and-dual model has its contradictions and limits, and it has not provided a stable solution to the labor control problem under lean production' (Zhang, 2015: 167).

Criticisms of Burawoy's approach made by early reactions to his work in the UK have yet to surface in China. Labour process writers noted that his theory moves between levels of analysis in regard to these concepts – from dealing with management control techniques, to descriptions of labour process regimes, to intermediate categories between micro politics within the factory and macro politics in production at the societal level. (Littler, 1990: 62-4) makes this criticism about shifting levels in the analysis. A second criticism is what Littler and Salaman (1982) refer to as the 'panacea fallacy' – the idea that one regime solves management's problems, rather than simply creating new ones. John Storey (1985) called this 'monism' – the functionalist idea that capital finds solutions to its problems when needed. The idea of a production regime – a top-down management system that leaves workers relatively passive – is also a problem that has been widely criticized by labour process theorists. The third criticism is that idea of fixed alternative forms of control – big types such as Burawoy's despotic and hegemonic forms; or Andy Friedman's (1977) direct control and responsible autonomy (Edwards and Scullion, 1982; Littler, 1990). Recent thinking (see Thompson and Van den Broek, 2010) argues for multiple forms of control often coexisting; the lack of one over-arching 'regime' or control type; and the importance of contestation and resistance at many levels of capital-labour interaction.

Nevertheless, Burawoy is popular because his work makes connections between levels of the social structures, especially between the shop floor and the industry or economy, and this has special reference for economies in transition. So, despite the above criticisms, there is much to recommend in his work. This book stresses the importance of inductive research, and building up a picture of the labour process from within the workplace.

'Subjugation Thesis' in Labour Process Studies in China

The accumulation of workplace research has proposed some general propositions about work and workers in China. In addition to dualism, mentioned above and expanded in many chapters in this book, other empirical work by researchers, activists, and NGOs has largely operated with what can be called a 'subjugation thesis' of Chinese labour. This is especially relevant to the new Chinese working class of migrant, rural workers working in export-oriented factories where there is a close integration of the reproduction of labour on a daily basis and utilization of labour power production within mass factory complexes (Pun, 2005; Pun and Smith, 2007; Pun and Chan, 2012). Workers are spatially separated from families; they live apart from hometown, local cultures, and sources of socialization and solidarity within family and community. Labour control is tight and labour contracts are used to segment workers. The migrant status and citizenship divide due to the hukou system, typically means second-class conditions for migrant workers (Solinger, 1999; Peng, 2011). There is also restrained mobility, and the retention of documents essential for mobility and withholding of wages to reduce the chances of exit. The 'subjugation thesis' fuses political controls within employment relations at the micro-level of factories together with employers use of state control (around citizenship) – to restrain quitting which under this level of 'subjugation' was the principle method of labour resistance.

More recent workplace-based studies have suggested modification to this ideal type of labour subordination in China. Siu (2014, 2015) in chapters, papers, and his thesis has suggested a developmental disruption. There is a developmental logic running through his narrative on garment workers, which basically argues that due to shifts in the composition of the garment workforce created through an emergent regional division of labour, the workforce has changed in terms of gender hierarchies, firm segmentation, and the way the reproduction and production of labour power is integrated. What Siu terms the dominant 'subjugation thesis' on Chinese labour is in a state of transition empirically (although most writers in the field remain attached to this thesis, see recent work by Pun and Chan, 2012). Siu argues quite convincingly that workers are no longer dominated by employers within what is termed the 'dormitory labour regime' (Smith, 2003) rather independent living has expanded and replaced employer-dependent living, freeing workers from employers, and creating space and greater freedom (with a growing orientation towards individualism and consumerism) as workers are no longer 'living at work' with the coercive control of the employer overseeing eating, communication, and lived lives. This is a critical development, and forms the centre of his thesis which suggests that shifts in lifestyles and 'family life' of the worker put constraints on the employer. In other words 'workers private and family lives' (Siu, 2014: 231) constrain capital – a reversal of Marx's idea that capital penetrates into family life and converts family members into different categories of the collective labourer. Others suggest that even with independent living, the conditions are so poor for migrant workers that this does not represent a major developmental step from the subordination experienced in the factory dormitories. The access to housing benefits are a feature of the divide between SOE workers and migrants, as chapters by Lefeng Lin and Wenjuan Jia in the book make clear. While the chapter by Lulu Fan highlights the importance, especially for female workers, in gaining more control over living and working conditions.

Labour Process Studies of Agency in China

Structural analysis has been the dominant approach in the field of labour studies particularly in the US, which has also been reflected in the studies of Chinese labour such as Chan A. (1993; 1995); Chen (2003; 2009; 2010; 2015), Chen and Xu (2012); Clarke et al. (2004), Friedman (2014a), Gallagher (2005; 2016), Howell (2008; 2015), Kuruvilla et al. (2011), Elfstrom and Kuruvilla (2014), Liu et al. (2011), Liu (2014), Unger and Chan (1995), and Zhuang and Chen (2015). However, recent research in employment relations and labour and social movements suggests an emerging paradigm shift of the theoretical focus from structure to agency, with strategic capacity (e.g. Ganz, 2000, 2009), strategic agency (e.g. Jasper, 1997, 2004, 2010), or strategic choices (e.g. Kochan et al., 1986) being increasingly emphasized.

In contrast to the relative stability of labour institutions in the West, China is a story of institutional change which further calls on an agency perspective to study the changing labour and employment issues in China. Indeed a few scholars have taken on this issue: Friedman (2014b), Liu (2010), and Pringle (2011) examine the agency role of regional union federations in China's labour reform; Liu and Li (2014), Choi and Peng (2015), and Hui and Chan (2015) look into the responses of employers or employer associations to unionization or changes in labour market or labour policy that play a critical role in shaping labour-relations outcomes; and Chan (2009, 2010, 2014) and Chan and Pun (2009) investigate the agency role of workers in improving working conditions and changing workplace relations as well as labour policy. With different disciplinary backgrounds, these researchers take various approaches to study agency including the sociological, industrial relations, and labour process perspectives. While the other approaches are valuable, the labour process perspective has a unique advantage in capturing dynamic and nuanced interactions among employment relations actors. Several chapters in this book further contribute to the labour process perspective to agency in the Chinese context.

Three chapters in this book examine the role of workers, workplace unions, regional union federations, the local state, labour activists, labour NGOs, and employers, as well as their interactions, in shaping the Chinese labour movement or labour regime. Chan and Hui's chapter, based on case studies of direct union elections in two factories in Guangdong after the 2010 wave of strikes, finds that workers, through their industrial actions, have become a key change agent for union reform or more specifically direct union elections in Guangdong. However, their cases show that the union elections were not genuinely democratic or direct, as workers' participation in elections stopped at the union branch level while management and local union federations controlled or manipulated the process of electing union committee members and union chairs. As such, the quasi-democratic unions could not well represent workers' interests and were challenged by workers through strikes. Without freedom of association, Chan and Hui argue that direct union elections are just a new strategy of the state and management in controlling workers.

Drawing on her ethnography work and intensive interviews in the auto parts factories in Guangzhou, Yunxue Deng studies the agency role of workers in the newly established system of collective bargaining between directly elected unions and management in those factories. Similar to Chan and Hui, she also finds that the directly elected workplace unions after 2010 were quasi-democratic and not able to achieve significant gains for workers during collective bargaining. However, the auto parts workers challenged the unions and management through strikes and won significant gains in the following negotiations. Different from Chan and Hui, Deng suggests that the direct union elections did improve the autonomy and representativeness of workplace unions. Deng also challenges Chan and Hui's (2014) view of the newly established collective bargaining system as party-state-led collective bargaining. For her, the improved effectiveness of collective bargaining is largely due to the auto workers' bargaining power, particularly their strike capacity rather than the authority of the state or regional union federations. Given these, Deng concludes that direct union elections and the newly established collective bargaining systems are 'not merely a means for the state to control worker activism, but also a mechanism manufacturing new workplace militancy'.

Deng's view is largely echoed by Li and Liu who study a rare, workplace union-led protest against Walmart in Changde, Hunan Province. Based on participant observation of this protest, they find that workplace unions may possibly transform into genuine representatives of workers when employer policies greatly affect all of the employees including the union leaders. As such, Li and Liu argue for a new pathway to a vital labour movement in China, that is, integrating actions of transformed workplace unions with society-level activism for justice. The development of this pathway, however, is still not certain due to the possible suppression of transformed unions and civil society groups by the Party-state and ACFTU.

Rather than focusing on strike-driven collective bargaining in Guangdong, Wang and Liu's chapter examines the agency role of management in the dominant pattern of collective bargaining or collective consultation in China. Based on intensive interviews with managers, union staff, and workers, as well a survey of workers and managers in two auto companies, they find significant differences in collective consultation in terms of the degree of worker involvement, procedures, and outcomes of collective consultation. They argue that the more authentic collective consultation in the joint venture is largely an outcome of organizational politics resulting from the 'fight for control' between the two equal equity partners: a Chinese SOE parent and a Japanese company. More specially, the Chinese side, including the Party, management, and union, uses collective consultation as a leverage to negotiate with the Japanese side on issues related with both labour and business operation. In addition, given the Chinese nationalism against Japan, the Chinese management is more cautious and responsive to worker demands.

In addition, the chapters of Liu and Ouyang, and Zhang examine employer strategies and their antecedents and impacts. While their approach is largely structural, these authors do to some extent show the role of employers' choices in shaping workplace outcomes such as employment relationships, work organization, and working conditions. Liu and Ouyang look into employment and working conditions in the Chinese call-centre sector, a rapidly growing service industry in China which has not been studied in the literature. They find an important employer strategy in managing labour in the Chinese call centres, i.e., is the wide use of dispatched labour or agency workers. They also find that the labour dualism strategy of employers has had mixed effects on contingent workers – low pay, job insecurity, and unpleasant working conditions on the one hand and opportunities to improve skills through employer-provided training on the other hand. As such, this work contributes to our better understanding of work and employment in the Chinese service industries.

Hao Zhang's chapter investigates employer responses to labour shortage, a striking change in the Chinese labour market in the past decade. Through intensive fieldwork and interviews with workers and employers in the knitwear industry in Dalang town, Guangdong and Wenling, Zhejiang, he finds two prominent employer strategies to labour shortage, namely, labour substitution (including industrial upgrading and production relocation to areas with lower labour and other costs) and labour upgrading or more specifically in his study, industry-level wage coordination or collective bargaining. He argues that work organization and labour process, the local state, and employer characteristics all play a role in shaping these employer strategies. In particular he finds that work organization and production process characterized by a low level of automation, a high degree of reliance on skilled manual labour, and the use of piece-rate wage system are likely to result in employers' uptake of the labour upgrading strategy. Zhang also finds that the labour substitution strategy, once implemented, may change work organization and production processes in a way that discourages employers to take labour upgrading at a later stage.

Chinese Practices Beyond China

The chapters in the book reject the idea of a single national model of work and employment relations, given patterns of structural and geographical diversity that persist in China. But the prospect of honing and distilling a body of identifiable national practices (at least for MNCs) through the process of internationalization is proposed in the two concluding chapters, which explore the nature of labour process and employment practices in Chinese-based companies operating outside of China.

The chapter by Andrijasevic and Sacchetto focuses upon the world's largest electronics contract manufacturer, the Taiwanese giant Foxconn, which from its giant plants in China, has become an international player, with factories across many countries, including the Czech Republic and Turkey, which are two country cases the authors examine. The authors pay special attention to the character of the workforce in the two countries 'in order to show how the specificity of workforce composition shapes the firm's labour management practices'. They note the export of dependency in the form, in the Czech case, of migrant workers drawn from several countries, thus reproducing patterns of labour segmentation found in Foxconn's Chinese factories. But in an analysis of the agency of such migrant workers, the authors stress their mobility capacity has been enhanced through movement, which creates a paradoxical power over local managers. The chapter looks beyond capital-labour dynamics at the level of the labour process and 'investigates the ways in which the role of labour, the state, and the trade unions co-constitute the firm's behaviour and its production politics'. While structural forces are important in building 'work and employment practices that Foxconn establishes in its European subsidiaries' this chapter aims to 'capture the overlapping influences of actors, sites, and institutions, as well as the power relations between them that inform the workings of transnational firms across borders'.

The final chapter of the book by Smith and Zheng reviews what we know from the scant research on the labour process and employment relations in Chinese firms operating outside of China. They reveal the growth of outward foreign direct investment from China, its state-centred composition (by value), and initial orientation towards developing countries and resource or extractive industries. But they also note the emergence of Chinese MNCs in developed economies and the expansion of manufacturing and service firms from China. With regard to common messages from the practices of Chinese employers in these firms, the stand out feature is the high usage of Chinese expats, and the distribution of these at all levels of the subsidiary – a feature unique to Chinese MNCs and reflective of two attributes: firstly, the availability of trained and inexpensive workers in China willing to work overseas, and secondly, the productiveness and control inherent in the labour management system in the local context and its ability to be internationalized through the Chinese firm. 'Expats are there because they follow Chinese firm tenets, they are more focused on work, and as migrants usually living in company-based industrial dormitories, they are tightly controlled, and more likely to focus on work during the contract period and submit to compulsory overtime, which is resisted by local workers, and work flexibly with less voice, which locals shun'.

Talk of Sino or Chinese capitalism perhaps overvalues nationality, when the fundamentals of capitalism are more universal, and stable national variants limited, as countries interact more than ever within a more globalized world. Hence, while we need to know as much as possible about Chinese capital-labour relations at home and abroad, we need to be cautious about 'reading any *new* capitalism through myopic (and blurred) national lenses, when we need to always separate out systemic practices of capitalism, alongside societal differences and dominant lead-country trends in work and employment (Smith & Meiksins, 1995; Smith, 2008).'

Note

1 There are two types of firefighters in China. The major body is military firefighters who are soldiers rather than employees. So there is no bonus system for them. Another type is enterprise firefighters such as those in Tianjin Port. Most enterprise firefighters in Tianjin Port are agency workers.

REFERENCES

Andrijasevic, R., Drahokoupil, J. and Sacchetto, D. (2016) (eds.) *The Rise of Newcomer MNCs in Electronics as a Challenge to the European Social Model? The Case of Foxconn* (provisional title) (forthcoming) ETUI, Brussels.

Aoki, K. (2008) Transferring Japanese kaizen activities to overseas plants in China. *International Journal of Operations & Production Management*, 28(6), 518–539.

Braverman, H. (1974) *Labor and Monopoly Capital: the Degradation of Work in the Twentieth Century*. New York: Monthly Review Press.

Brinkley, I. (2013) Flexibility or insecurity? Exploring the rise in zero hours contracts. *The Work Foundation, London*.

Burawoy, M. (1979) *Manufacturing Consent*. Chicago: University of Chicago Press.

Burawoy, M. (1985) *The Politics of Production: Factory Regimes under Capitalism and Socialism*. London: Verso.

Butollo, F. (2014) *The End of Cheap Labour? Industrial Transformation and 'Social Upgrading' in China*. Frankfurt-on-Main: Campus Verlag.

Chan, A. (1993) Revolution or Corporatism? Workers and Trade Unions in Post-Mao China. *Australian Journal of Chinese Affairs*, 29, 31–61.

Chan, A. (1995a) The Emergence Patterns of Industrial Relations in China and the Rise of Two New Labour Movements. *China Information*, 9 (5), 36–59.

Chan, A. (1995b) Chinese enterprise reforms: convergence with the Japanese model? *Industrial and Corporate Change*, 4(2), 449–470.

Chan, A. (2015) (ed.) *Chinese Workers in Comparative Perspective*, Ithaca & London: Cornell University Press.

Chan, C. K. C. (2009) Strike and workplace relations in a Chinese global factory. *Industrial Relations Journal*. 40(1). 60–77.

Chan, C. K. C. (2010) *The Challenge of Labour in China – Strikes and the Changing Labour Regime in Global Factories*. London: Routledge.

Chan, C. K. C. (2014) Constrained Labour Agency and the Changing Regulatory Regime in China. *Development and Change*, 45(4), 685–709.

▶

Chan, C. K. C., & Hui, E. S. I. (2014) The development of collective bargaining in China: from 'collective bargaining by riot' to 'party state-led wage bargaining'. *The China Quarterly*, *217*, 221–242.

Chan, C.K.C. & Pun, N. (2009) The making of a new working class? A study of collective actions of migrant workers in South China. *The China Quarterly*. 198 (June). 287–303.

Chan, J., & Selden, M. (2014) China's Rural Migrant Workers, the State, and Labor Politics. *Critical Asian Studies*, 46(4), 599–620.

Chen, F. (2003) Between the State and Labour: The Conflict of Chinese Trade Unions' Dual Institutional Identity. *The China Quarterly*, 176 (December), 1006–1028.

Chen, F. (2009) Union Power in China: Source, operation, and constraints. *Modern China*, 35(6), 662–89.

Chen, F. (2010) Trade Unions and the Quadripartite Interactions in Strike Settlement in China. *The China Quarterly*, 201 (March), 104–24.

Chen, F. (2015) China's Road to the Construction of Labour Rights. *Journal of Sociology*, forthcoming.

Chen, F., & Xu, X. (2012) 'Active Judiciary': Judicial Dismantling Of Workers' Collective Action in China. *The China Journal*, 67 (January), 87–108.

Choi, S. Y.-P., & Peng, Y. (2015) Humanized management? Capital and migrant labour in a time of labour shortage in South China. *Human Relations*, 68(2), 287–304.

Clarke, S., Lee, C.H., & Li, Q. (2004) Collective Consultation and Industrial Relations in China. *British Journal of Industrial Relations*, 42(2), 235–54.

Clawson, D. (1980) *Bureaucracy and the Labor Process*. New York: Monthly Review

Coates, D. (2000) *Models of Capitalism*. Oxford: Oxford University Press.

Edwards, R. C. (1979) *Contested terrain: The Transformation of the Workplace in America*. New York: Basic Books.

Edwards, P. K., & Scullion, H. (1982) *The Social Organization of Industrial Conflict: Control and Resistance in the Workplace*. Oxford: Blackwell.

Elfstrom, M., & Kuruvilla, S. (2014) The Changing Nature of Labor Unrest in China. *Industrial and Labor Relations Review*, 67(2), 453–80.

Elger, T. and Smith, C. (2005) *Assembling Work: Remaking Factory Regimes in Japanese Multinationals in Britain* Oxford: Oxford University Press.

Frazier, M. W. (2002) *The Making of the Chinese Industrial Workplace: State, Revolution, and Labor Management*. Cambridge: Cambridge University Press.

Friedman, A. (1977) Responsible autonomy versus direct control over the labour process. *Capital & Class*, 1(1), 43–57.

Friedman, E. (2014a) Economic Development and Sectoral Unions in China. *Industrial and Labor Relations Review*, 67(2), 481–503,

Friedman, E. (2014b) *Insurgency trap: Labor politics in Postsocialist China*. Ithaca, NY: Cornell University Press.

Gallagher, M. (2005) *Contagious Capitalism: Globalization and the Politics of Labor in China*. Princeton and Oxford: Princeton University Press.

Gallagher, M. (2016) *Authoritarian Legality: Law, Workers, and the State in Contemporary China*. Cambridge University Press, forthcoming.

Gamble, J. (2000) Localizing management in foreign-invested enterprises in China: practical, cultural, and strategic perspectives. *International journal of human resource management*, 11(5), 883–903.

Gamble, J. (2010) Transferring organizational practices and the dynamics of hybridization: Japanese retail multinationals in China. *Journal of Management Studies*, 47(4), 705–732.

Ganz, M. (2000) Resources and Resourcefulness: Strategic Capacity in the Unionization of California Agriculture, 1959–1966. *American Journal of Sociology*, 105(4), 1003–62.

Ganz, M. (2009) *Why David Sometimes Wins: Leadership, Organization, and Strategy in the California Farm Worker Movement.* New York: Oxford University Press.

Hall, P.A. and Soskice, D. (2001) 'An introduction to varieties of capitalism' in Hall, P.A. and Soskice, D., editors, *Varieties of capitalism: the institutional foundations of comparative advantage.* Oxford: Oxford University Press, 1–68.

Hershatter, G. (1986) *The Workers of Tianjin, 1900–1949.* Stanford: Stanford University Press.

Honig, E. (1986) *Sisters and Strangers: Women in the Shanghai Cotton Mills, 1919–1949,* Stanford: Stanford University Press.

Howell, J. (2008) All-China Federation of Trades Unions beyond Reform? The Slow March of Direct Elections. *The China Quarterly,* 196 (December), 845–63.

Howell, J. (2015) Shall We Dance? Welfarist Incorporation and the Politics of State–Labour NGO Relations. *The China Quarterly,* forthcoming.

Hui, E. S. I., & Chan, C. K. C. (2015) The Associational Power of Overseas Business in China —A Case Study of the Shenzhen Collective Consultation Ordinance and the Guangdong Regulations on Democratic Management of Enterprises. *The China Quarterly,* forthcoming.

Jasper, J.M. (1997) *The Art of Moral Protest.* Chicago: University of Chicago Press.

Jasper, J.M. (2004) A Strategic Approach to Collective Action: Looking for Agency in Social Movement Choices. *Mobilization,* 9(1), 1–16.

Jasper, J.M. (2010) Social Movement Theory Today: Toward a Theory of Action? *Sociology Compass,* 10, 965–976.

Kalleberg, A. L. (2000) Nonstandard employment relations: Part-time, temporary and contract work. *Annual Review of Sociology,* 341–365.

Kalleberg, A. L. (2009) 'Precarious work, insecure workers: Employment relations in transition'. *American Sociological Review,* 74(1), 1–22.

Kim, J. (2013) *Chinese Labor in a Korean factory: Class, Ethnicity, and Productivity on the Shop Floor in Globalizing China.* Stanford: Stanford University Press.

Kochan, T., Katz, H., & McKersie, R. (1986) *The Transformation of American Industrial Relations.* New York: Basic Books.

Kuruvilla, S., Lee, C.K., & Gallagher, M. (2011) *From Iron Rice Bowl to Informalization: Markets, Workers, and the State in a Changing China.* Ithaca and London: Cornell University Press.

Lee, C. K. (1998) *Gender and the South China Miracle: Two worlds of factory Women.* Berkeley: University of California Press.

Lee, C. K. (1999) From organized dependence to disorganized despotism: Changing labour regimes in Chinese factories. *The China Quarterly,* 157, 44–71.

Lee, C. K., & United Nations Research Institute for Social Development. (2005) *Livelihood struggles and market reform: Unmaking Chinese labour after State socialism*. UNRISD.

Lee, C. K. (2007) *Against the Law: Labor Protests in China's Rustbelt and Sunbelt*, Berkeley: University of California Press.

Lee, C. K. (2009) 'Raw encounters: Chinese managers, African workers and the politics of casualization in Africa's Chinese enclaves', *The China Quarterly*, 99: 647–666.

Littler, C. R. (1982) *The Development of the Labour Process in Capitalist Societies*. London: Heinemann.

Littler, C. R. (1990) 'The labour process debate: a theoretical review 1974–1988' in David Knights and Hugh Willmott (eds.) *Labour Process Theory*, pp. 46–94.

Littler, C. R., & Salaman, G. (1982) Bravermania and Beyond: Recent Theories of the Labour Process. *Sociology*, 16(2), 251–269.

Liu, M. (2010) Union Organizing in China: Still a Monolithic Labor Movement? *Industrial & Labor Relations Review*, 64(1): 30–52.

Liu, M. (2014) Conflict Resolution in China. In W. K. Roche, P. Teague, & Colvin, A. (Eds). *Oxford Handbook of Conflict Management in Organizations* (pp. 494–519). Oxford, UK: Oxford University Press.

Liu, M., & Li, C. (2014) Environment Pressures, Managerial Industrial Relations Ideologies and Unionization in Chinese Enterprises. *British Journal of Industrial Relations*, 52 (1), 82–111.

Liu, M., Bentley, F. S., Evans, M. H. T., and Schurman, S. J. (2015) 'Globalization and Labor in China and the United States: Convergence and Divergence' in Anita Chan (2015) (ed.) *Chinese Workers in Comparative Perspective*, Ithaca & London: Cornell University Press.

Liu, M., Kim, S., & Li, C. (2011) 'Chinese Trade Unions in Transition : A Three-Level Analysis' in P. Shelton, Kim, S., Li, Y., & Warner, M. (Eds.). *China's Changing Workplace : Dynamism, Diversity and Disparity* (pp. 277–300). London and New York: Routledge.

Lüthje, B., Luo, S., & Zhang, H. (2013) *Beyond the iron rice bowl: regimes of production and industrial relations in China*.

Lüthje, B. (2015) 'Exporting Corporatism? German and Japanese Transnationals' Regimes of Production in China' in Anita Chan (2015) (ed.) *Chinese Workers in Comparative Perspective*, Ithaca & London: Cornell University Press.

Marx, K. ([1867] 1976) *Capital Volume 1*, Harmondsworth: Penguin.

O'Leary, G. (Ed.) (1998) *Adjusting to Capitalism: Chinese Workers and the State*. London: Routledge.

Peck, J., & Theodore, N. (2007) Variegated capitalism. *Progress in human geography*, 31(6), 731–772.

Peck, J., & Zhang, J. (2013) A variety of capitalism... with Chinese characteristics? *Journal of Economic Geography*, 13(3), 357–396.

Peng, T. (2011) The impact of citizenship on labour process: State, capital and labour control in South China. *Work, Employment & Society*, 25(4), 726–741.

Perry, E. J. (1993) *Shanghai on Strike: the Politics of Chinese Labor*. Stanford: Stanford University Press.

Pringle, T. (2011) *Trade Unions in China: The Challenge of Labour Unrest*. London: Routledge.

Pun, N. (2005) *Made in China: Women Factory Workers in a Global Workplace*. Durham, NC: Duke University Press.

Pun, N. and Chan, J. (2012) Global Capital, the State, and Chinese Workers The Foxconn Experience. *Modern China*, 38(4), 383–410.

Pun, N. and Smith, C. (2007) 'Putting transnational labour process in its place the dormitory labour regime in post-socialist China'. *Work, Employment & Society*, 21(1), 27–45.

Siu, K. (2015) Continuity and Change in the Everyday Lives of Chinese Migrant Factory Workers. *China Journal*, (74), 43–65.

Siu, Yu-Kwan (2014) The Work, Lifestyles and Domination of Chinese Migrant Garment Workers in Comparative Perspective. *PhD Thesis*, The Australian National University.

Smith, C. and Meiksins, P. (1995) 'System, Society and Dominance Effects in Cross-National Organisational Analysis'. *Work, Employment & Society*, 9(2), 241–267.

Smith, C. and Pun, N. (2006) 'The dormitory labour regime in China as a site for control and resistance', *The International Journal of Human Resource Management*, 17(8): 1456–1470.

Smith, C. and Thompson, P. (1998) 'Re-evaluating the labour process debate. *Economic and Industrial democracy'*, 19(4), 551–577.

Smith, C. (2003) 'Living at work: Management control and the dormitory labour system in China'. *Asia Pacific Journal of Management*, 20(3), 333–358.

Smith, C. (2005) 'Beyond convergence and divergence: explaining variations in organizational practices and forms'. In Stephen Ackroyd, Rosemary Batt, Paul Thompson and Pamela Tolbert (eds.) *The Oxford Handbook of Work and Organisation*, Oxford: Oxford University Press pp. 602–625.

Smith, C. (2015) Rediscovery of the Labour Process. Edgell, S., Gottfried, H. and Granter, E. (eds.) *Sage Handbook of the Sociology of Work and Employment*. London: Sage (forthcoming)

Solinger, D. J. (1999) Citizenship issues in China's internal migration: comparisons with Germany and Japan. *Political Science Quarterly*, 455–478.

Storey, J. (1985) The means of management control. *Sociology*, 19(2), 193–211.

Thompson, P. (1989) *The Nature of Work: An Introduction to Debates on the Labour Process* (2nd Edition), London: Macmillan.

Thompson, P. (1997) *The Nature of Work: an Introduction to Debates on the Labour Process*. London: Macmillan.

Thompson, P. (2003) 'Disconnected capitalism: or why employers can't keep their side of the bargain', *Work, Employment and Society*, 17(2): 359–378.

Thompson, P., & Van den Broek, D. (2010) Managerial control and workplace regimes: an introduction. *Work, Employment & Society*, 24(3), 1–12.

Thompson, P. and Smith, C. (2000) Follow the Redbrick road: Reflections on Pathways in and Out of the Labor Process Debate. *International Studies of Management & Organization*, 40–67.

Thompson, P. and Smith, C. (2009) Labour power and labour process: Contesting the marginality of the sociology of work. *Sociology*, 43(5), 913–930.

▶

Thompson, P. and Smith, C., (eds.) (2010) *Working Life: Renewing Labour Process Analysis*. Houndmills, Basingstoke: Palgrave Macmillan

Unger, J. & Chan, A. (1995) China, Corporatism, and the East Asian Model. *The Australian Journal of Chinese Affairs*, 33, 29–53.

Whitley, R. (1999) *Divergent Capitalisms: The Social Structuring and Change of Business Systems*. Oxford: Oxford University Press.

Zhang, L. (2015) *Inside China's Automobile Factories: the Politics of Labor and Worker Resistance*. Cambridge: Cambridge University Press.

Zhang, J., & Peck, J. (2014) Variegated capitalism, Chinese style: Regional models, multi-scalar constructions. *Regional Studies*, (ahead-of-print), 1–27.

Zheng, Y. (2013) *Managing Human Resources in China: The View from Inside Multinationals*. Cambridge: Cambridge University Press.

Zhuang, W. & Chen, F. (2015) 'Mediation First!' The Revival of Mediation in Labour Disputes in China. *The China Quarterly*, 222 (June), 380–402.

Work and Employment by Sector and Firm

Control and Consent in the Process of Employee Participation in a Chinese State-Owned Enterprise: The Case of BZ Iron and Steel Company

Mengjie Lu

Introduction

The practice of employee participation has been widely advocated in capitalist countries for its potential to bring industrial peace, high performance, and social integration (Ramsay, 1977; Li, 2008: 244). Methods of employee participation change significantly over time, and new patterns replace or coexist with the traditional ones (Wilkinson et al., 2010). Environmental and political factors like fiercer competition in the product market and workers' struggles in the labour market have been identified as factors in the development of employee participation (Wilkinson et al., 2010; Ramsay, 1977). Unlike researchers who regard the development of employee participation as an evolutionary process, Ramsay found participation schemes appeared cyclically from the 1860s to the 1960s as managerial strategies to secure labour's compliance following one of the four patterns including 'success', 'triviality', 'instability', and 'change of committee status' (Ramsay, 1977). Since the 1980s, management began to remould participation into a less collectivist and less independent pattern, bringing individual participation regimes like quality circles into industrial practice (Lucio, 2010). In this cyclically developing process, there coexist two main participation methods: representative participation, which consists of trade unions and collective bargaining, and direct participation regimes introduced by employers (Hyman and Mason, 1995).

Since direct non-union participation mechanisms have been widely used in workplace management practice (either coexisting with or replacing unions and other representative participation methods), a lot of research has been conducted to discuss this transformation of employee participation to explore the logic behind this trend and to evaluate its effects. As indicated by existing studies, workers' demand for voice can be viewed as universal, constantly sensitive to workplace problems (Bryson and Freeman, 2006; Gomez et al., 2010). Meanwhile, employers pick and choose among direct and representative participation regimes according to their own organizational characteristics, strategies, and institutional environment (Huang et al., 2005; Bryson et al., 2007; Busck et al., 2010). Government, as the third actor in labour relations, also plays an important role in promoting employee participation in many countries and regions, such as the European Union's promotion of the European Works Councils Directive, the European Company Statute, and the Directive on the Information and Consultation of Employees (Gold, 2010). Thus, although the influence of representative participation systems has diminished in countries such as Britain in recent years, this has been offset by the appearance of various non-union participation mechanisms (Gomez et al., 2010).

Based on Hirschman's (1970) 'exit, voice, and loyalty' model, Freeman and Medoff (1980, 1984) concluded that unions could be beneficial to both employees and employers as a voice and response channel. Kochan et al. (1984) found that only some participation schemes were able to help improve employees' real influence on work, and the most successful schemes required higher union participation, higher employment security, and improved economic performance of the firm. In other words, such schemes are weak without trade union support. In recent years, more methods and data have been used in research about what influence workplace participation regimes exert on organizational performance, staff welfare and attitudes, and workplace labour relations (Cooke, 1992; Cox et al., 2006; Guest, 2011), but the results are mixed.

In China, representative employee participation has a long history. The primary goal is to enable worker ownership of enterprises, and its main modes are employee representative congress and democratic participation led by a labour union. Most research about unions in China focuses on the relationships between the union and the state, union and employers, and union and workers, trying to compare unions in China with those in the industrialized countries (Taylor and Li, 2007). 'Transmission belt' and 'state corporatism' theories are often used to emphasize the close relationship between unions in China and the state, and the estrangement between unions and workers (Chen, 2009). Since the reform period, the increasing level of market competition and the introduction of human-resources-management (HRM) strategies have promoted the implementation of direct employee participation mechanisms, including quality cycles, information sharing, employee complaint channels, and so on, in Chinese enterprises, especially the state-owned enterprises (SOEs).

Although SOEs have a complete employee participation system, there are still voices and actions which occur outside the participation system, particularly during periods of organizational reform. Sometimes spontaneous and fierce collective actions occur. From 2009 to 2010, cases of labour conflicts in Tongzhou Steel, Lingzhou Steel, and Pingdingshan Textile highlighted the unstable quality of labour relations in SOEs. Many researchers studied and discussed the change of labour relations and labour disputes occurring during the transformation of SOEs, paying attention to workers' consciousness and behaviour choice (Lee, 1999; Liu, 2003; Chen, 2004; Tong, 2006; Wu, 2007; Xie, 2009). To some extent, these studies all pointed out that, when disputes occurred, the existing employee participation system did not represent employees' voice effectively. Thus, the 'three parties; four actors' frame,[1] which implies a separation between labour unions and workers (Taylor et al., 2003: 121), became a tacit assumption in Chinese-labour-relations research, leaving the effects of representative participation methods in the margins.

This chapter aims to re-examine this assumption of an implicit gap between workers and the existing participation regimes with a case study of BZ Steel company focusing on the following four questions:

(1) What changes occur in the participation mechanisms of Chinese SOEs during their transformation?
(2) How does enterprise management apply control in the operation of participation mechanisms?
(3) How do the employees evaluate and react to both the traditional and the newly introduced mechanisms of participation?
(4) Is it possible for different participation mechanisms to satisfy workers' demand to participate in decision-making processes and express themselves, and then to adjust labour relations in the workplace?

To answer these questions, this chapter discusses the interaction between management and employees in the process of employee participation, focusing on managerial control and employees' attitudes based on interviews and a questionnaire survey in BZ. Participation mechanisms, both traditional democratic and newly introduced, are widely used in BZ's workplace. But the underlying management control beneath the participation process limits employees' voices. Survey results show that employees prefer direct participation channels at the workshop and group levels and the formal information-sharing system through which they could monitor and influence the production and management process. Besides, there is an overall high-level consent to the existing participation mechanisms, which is supported by the paternalistic welfare tradition and influenced by market competition and state intervention. During organizational reforming, it is difficult for existing participation systems to satisfy employees' demand for voice. When excessive welfare reduction or internal labour-market change occurs, employees tend to take action outside the formal participation framework.

Conceptual and Theoretical Issues

Concept Definition

Although the concept of employee participation has a long history in industrial relations, it remains diverse in different disciplines and research areas (Heller, 1998). Employee participation, employee involvement, industrial democracy, co-determination, or the simple word 'voice', each of these notions has their own features and subtle differences (Wilkinson et al., 2010). For example, employee participation may emphasize workers' role and initiatives in the participation process, while involvement may stress empowerment from a management perspective, and industrial democracy focuses more on workers' collective power.

The Webbs' book *Industrial Democracy*, published in the 1890s, is typically considered the basis of employee participation. It stresses that employees should have their own interest representation and their own voice through collective bargaining and unions. What's more, in workplaces, employees should enjoy basic rights, as citizens do in society. Employee participation could be depicted as an institution through which employees interact with the management to influence decisions. Salamon (1992) defined employee participation as an idea and a means of organization management which acknowledges the needs and rights of individual employees and involves them in the processes of decision making and problem solving besides unions' collective bargaining power. According to Li (2008: 224–226), employee participation exists in order for employees to share power with the management. Employee participation could cause a management revolution and enjoy support from the three parties of labour relations: the labour union movement and its pursuit of industrial democracy, government and its vision of social integration, and employers and their quest for high efficiency.

This chapter focuses on different participation types, which fall into two classes: direct participation and indirect participation. Direct participation mainly refers to low-level decisions such as quality circles, work groups, and group/shift meetings, while indirect participation belongs to the representative participation model and generally involves high-level decisions like collective bargaining and workers' congress (see Li, 2008: 224). This study will analyse two types of employee participation in BZ Company: representative participation set by formal institutions and direct participation which is mainly driven by management. Representative participation mainly consists of democratic union management and workers' congress. Direct participation can be further classified into two categories: direct participation in production processes and direct participation in decision-making processes.

Inspiration from Labour-Process Theory – Control and Consent in the Workplace

In China, existing studies on employee participation mainly focus on three issues: comparative theories and the introduction of different participation mechanisms; factors determining employee participation; and the effects of participation on employee satisfaction, loyalty, and company performance. A combination of qualitative and quantitative methods is used to examine the causal relations between different factors and the extent of participation and employees' attitudes towards participation. However, existing research has seldom examined the real context and participation processes, or the relationship between different actors at the shop-floor system of labour relations.

The process of employee participation is an interaction between individual or collective workers and employers (or management). Labour-process theory mainly focuses on the conflictual interaction between labour and capital around issues of control, resistance, and consent. One writer in this literature is Michael Burawoy, and his control-consent theory framework will be applied here when analysing the interaction between management and employees.

In his book *Manufacturing Consent*, Burawoy developed a control-resistance-consent model, showing that consent is manufactured within the autonomous set of production relations (Thompson and Newsome, 2004: 141). Based on what he learned through participant observation,

Burawoy raises a question in a different manner to the traditional discussion about 'control-resistance', namely, why do workers work so hard (Burawoy, 1979: 34)? In Burawoy's opinion, Marxist theories of the labour process, from Marx to Braverman, had not addressed this question, but instead focused on the use of managerial force or labour market compulsion to explain the work effort by workers. However, in strongly unionized workplaces at the time of Burawoy's fieldwork, a welfare system provided workers' with some protection, and when the production was delayed by some flaws of management, workers frequently came up with various new ideas to achieve the management's goal, rather than being reconciled to the existing situation.

The 'control-consent' theory attributes the formation of employee consent to the management rules and programmes in the internal labour market as well as the economic compromise in employee benefits and wages made by the 'internal state'. By paying attention to workers' behaviours and consciousness, this theory also equips us with a theoretical tool which provides an interactive perspective on the labour process. In addition, this theory emphasizes the analysis of the production system from the perspective of workers' action, and also places emphasis on the influence of the 'context' on labour relations. The importance of 'context' is stressed by Smith (2016) linking the high-level consent in firms like Geer/Allied to the context that these firms all have unionized workers, strong internal labour markets, collective bargaining, and an 'internal state' of consent and compromise between labour and capital in a wider economy dominated by monopoly capital.

By utilizing Burawoy's perspective from *Manufacturing Consent*, this study will first introduce the employee participation mechanisms in BZ Company, and then gradually deconstruct the underlying labour-capital interactions. After that, we will discuss the consent of employees towards the mechanisms, and then try to identify the reasons behind the current participation practices and worker's attitudes through analysing the changing context of BZ in recent years.

Reform of Labour Relations in SOEs and the Development of Participation in China's Workplaces

During the three decades since the late 1970s, China has reformed from a planned to a market economy and from an agricultural to a modern industrialized society. During these two transformational processes, labour relations in the context of an emerging market economy also changed, as the four actors, that is, employers, workers, unions, and government, all experienced transformation. As the basic step of economic reform, whose slogan was 'liberate and develop productivity', SOEs witnessed 'decentralization of power and profits' (*Fang quan rang li*) from 1978 to 1984; 'separation of government functions from enterprise management' (*Zheng qi fen kai*) and 'separation of management from ownership' (*Liang quan fen li*) from 1985 to 1992; establishment of a modern enterprise system and strategic reorganization through retaining large and releasing small enterprises (*Zhua da fang xiao*) from 1993 to 2002; and promotion of joint-stock system reform from 2003 till the present.

During the reform period, the state has gradually relaxed its management control, acting more as the third party to adjust labour relations through labour market institutions and surveillance. The enterprise itself has become an independent actor while management plays the role of employer as the labour user; and workers have become wage labourers rather than 'masters' of their '*danwei*' after steps like 'downsizing for efficiency' (*Jian yuan zeng xiao*), 'laying off workers' (*xiagang*), and workers' identity replacement (*Shen fen zhi huan*) (Chang, 2013). In 2008, the implementation of Labour Contract Law further regulated the relation between employers and individual employees, propelling the transformation of SOE labour relations towards a new phase in collective labour relations (Chang, 2009: 152–180; Chang and Brown, 2013).

However, this latest reform does not mean that actors in labour relations have finished their formation, especially in state-owned workplaces. Change of industrial policies and fiercer competition further deepen the reform of SOEs and labour relations. Within this transforming labour-relations environment, employee participation has been widely used as a method to maintain harmonious industrial and social relations. In terms of context, one can say that all Chinese citizens are endowed with the right to participate in democratic management. In a broad sense, this right means citizens could take part in social, economic, and political affairs in both the workplace and living areas, while in the narrow sense it refers to the participation rights of workers in the workplace (Li, 2008). Different from the first goal of participation in industrial societies: to adjust labour relations, participation in China was first used in publically operated mining firms in the agrarian revolutionary period promoted by the communist party (Liu, 2004). In the opening and reform era since the late 1970s, the representative employee participation system in SOEs has been formally established through a series of policies and laws.

In the ninth national employee representative conference of ACFTU in 1978, Xiaoping Deng stressed that the appointment or change of a management leader such as the shop head and section manager should be discussed in workers' congress, and the union should transform from a dispensable organization to an operating mechanism of workers' congress. Then the State Council issued the Provisional Regulations for Workers' Congress in SOEs in 1981, and in 1986, the formal regulation was published, giving workers' congress the rights to review the firm's developing policies, rules, compensation, and welfare plans and to evaluate leaders in different levels. In 1988, the Law of SOEs was published stressing that workers' congress was 'the basic form of workers' democratic management'. Until then, workers' congress was established through a top-down promotion by state policies and laws as the main body of representative participation, with the union taking care of its daily routine. In the context of modern enterprise institution establishment since the 1990s, representative participation and some supporting direct participation methods like information disclosure (*Chang wu gong kai*) have been reinforced through Labour Union Law in 1992, Corporation Law in 1993, Labour Law in 1994, also through Labour Contract Law and Law of Labour Disputes Mediation and Arbitration in recent years. All of these formal institutions regulating employment participation promote and insure the foundation and the development of participation regimes in the workplaces, especially workplaces in SOEs. But researchers in areas of labour studies seldom choose this topic to assess the effects of these institutions or effects of the formal participation regime itself due to lack of data or because some researchers think formal regimes are all controlled by the state and hence have no real meaningful participation.

Unlike top-down, formal representative participation, the development of direct participation is triggered more by enterprise management. Enterprise reform changes SOEs from socialist '*danweis*', with sufficient resource allocation from the state, to individual actors in a competitive market. Fierce industrial competition pushes management to utilize modern HRM theories and systems to enhance productivity and efficiency, within which direct participation plays an important part in encouraging communication and commitment. For instance, in Baosteel Group, employee communication and evaluation mechanisms were put into place together with employee development channels and incentive systems aiming at 'taking individual employees as the basic experiencer and evaluator to make sure management policies and practices could be assessed by employees and hearing workers' voice'.[2] Through these mechanisms, the HRM department tries to link the development of individual employees to that of the enterprise, to ensure a harmonious relationship between workers and management, and to assist enterprise's strategic planning in the new round.[3] At the same time, more enterprises add participation into their organizational culture and vision, supporting an ideology of being 'people oriented'. But central to these participation methods and ideas is the intention to encourage organizational loyalty, like the slogan of State Grid, 'loyal to firm and contributing to society'.[4]

Methods Used in this Study

In order to get access to the participation process in the real context of workplaces at SOEs in China, I chose the BZ Iron and Steel Company as my case study. There were two reasons for choosing BZ: first, the mode of labour relations in the steel industry, which is mainly owned by the state, is typical and emblematic of China's state-owned workplaces since the country started to develop its secondary industries; second, since its early foundation in the 1960s, BZ has experienced the complete reform of SOEs.

In-depth interviews and questionnaire surveys were used in this study, and historical documents about managerial policies and workers' congress meetings were provided by the BZ union. The in-depth interviews and the observation during the interviews helped to uncover the structure and the process of BZ's participation regime, to outline its changes during the transformation period, and to capture the workers' real feelings about participation. Data collected through the survey was used to quantify employees' attitudes towards the existing participation regime. A stratified sampling method was used in the survey to make sure the collected data was representative: firstly two plants were chosen randomly from seven production plants at BZ, and then operators, technicians, and management staff were selected according to the proportions of the two plants. The design of the questionnaire used here was based on the questionnaire of the Workplace Employment Relations Study (2004) from the UK with additional questions about participation.

Employee Participation in Workplaces at BZ Company

BZ Iron and Steel Company was founded in the early 1960s, and it has experienced the whole process of SOE reform. In the 1990s, it became an experimental unit of state-owned limited share enterprise in the first group of transitional enterprises and became a listed company. In recent years, with changing market conditions and industrial policies, BZ Steel Group has tried to adjust its structure and production mode through new equipment, modern techniques, and cost reduction to improve its profitability and performance.

The process of iron and steel production in BZ Company includes coking, sintering, iron smelting, steel making, and steel rolling. The company consists of seven production plants, four assisting plants, like the oxygen-making and distribution plant, and three sub-company organizations focused on sales. Nearly 20 departments, including management promotion, human resources, and quality management were built in the company headquarters to compose a matrix organization. The production zone is located just next to the headquarters, around which BZ Avenue, BZ Hospital, BZ Kindergarten, BZ First and Second Primary School, BZ Middle School, BZ Park, Workers' Palace, and BZ TV Station form a complete living zone for all the workers and their families.

Basic-level operators, technicians, and management staff constitute the whole employee group, accounting for 75 per cent, 21 per cent, and 4 per cent respectively. Most employees graduate from high school and vocational schools, occupying 60 per cent of the total. Based on skill levels and seniority, there are five kinds of professional titles from primary workers, middle-level workers, high-level workers to technicians and high-level technicians, within which the high-level worker is the largest proportion at about 40 per cent. Employees aged between 35 and 55 account for 60 per cent of the total due to low mobility and the long company history.

Influenced by the economic crisis and the changing situation of supply and demand in the steel industry, BZ Company readjusts its development strategy via three methods: introducing new technology, reducing production costs, and simplifying the organizational structure. During the founding of the modern enterprise system, employee participation mechanisms were also changed structurally, which meant that former mechanisms such as workers' congress and labour-union democratic systems were combined with new mechanisms like quality-control circles, work-group meetings, employee forums, and employee-satisfaction surveys.

Representative participation practice and limited workers' voice

BZ Company has a complete representative participation system including workers' congress and democratic union management. The annual workers' congress meeting is held at the beginning of each year, and the labour union of BZ takes charge of the general affairs of workers' congress and contract signing, and takes care of the workers' voice in their daily working life.

Through reading historical documents and interviews, we learn that the workers' congress meetings have a similar routine: representatives of the workers are elected every three years directly from every workshop, and that meetings contain three basic parts: annual work report, proposal discussion and selection, and votes for important decisions like financial budget and organizational change in the next working year. There are also two standing bodies – the economic and technological committee, and the committee for the protection of workers' rights and benefits – supervising the implementation of proposals. The routine work of the union includes organizing congress meetings every year and arranging employee participation channels like employee representative inspections (*Zhi gong dai biao xun shi*), information disclosure (*Chang wu gong kai*), and democratic communication (*Min zhu dui hua*), the means of selecting employee representatives to communicate with high-level management. In addition, the enterprise's union also represents all the workers that sign the collective contract with the management. The collective contract, while I was researching, was signed in December 2009, for a three-year term, and included four parts: (1) labour contract, (2) compensations, work hours, breaks, and vacations, (3) labour protection, occupational safety and health, and environmental protection, and (4) labour insurances and benefits.

In spite of the complete system and programme, 75.7 per cent of the survey sample considered the function of the workers' congress to acquaint employees with the company's conditions, and less than 20 per cent of them agreed that they were able to express their opinions through their representatives. This kind of attitude may come from the functions of workers' congress in giving legitimacy to management decisions and its one way transmission of decisions – in other words, controlling workers' responses, rather than to providing workers with control of the enterprise.

Legitimacy could be seen in political science as the public recognition and acceptance of authority derived from legal and institutional procedures, social customs and traditions, or just from the personal charisma of the leader. Votes and supervision by employee representatives in workers' congress could also be seen as the process to legitimize management policies' authority. This authority of workers' congress is granted by law and the voting results reflect the level of representatives' acceptance, but whether one decision is truly legitimized can be directly influenced by how far the voting results represent workers' real attitudes. As a result, questions about workers' real feelings about newly set policies were asked during the interviews. However, the best way to get workers' real voice may still be through an independent labour organization which is not easily influenced by other actors in the labour-relations system.

Due to a changing business strategy, terms like 'economic responsibility', 'performance assessment', and 'fixing number of employees with positions' which were proposed by the high-level management became key ideas of policy votes in workers' congress. When asked about the voting results, a union officer in BZ said that 'policies proposed by management are seldom voted down by the workers' congress, although some worker representatives may show their different opinions by abstaining in the vote'.[5] For newly elected representatives, the BZ union will 'provide centralized training to acquaint them with representatives' obligations and how to be a qualified representative to protect fellow worker's rights and benefits; thus after training, most of the representatives could understand the problems BZ faces and make the rational choice'.[6] With this kind of 'training', most worker representatives might be led to think that these policies promoted by management are beneficial to both the enterprise and workers in the long run, although it may hurt some workers' benefits in the short term. In this way, the representatives would more likely agree with the managerial strategy.

Besides voting, there were around 150 proposals by representatives each year, most of which focused on living benefits, production and operations, and only 10–15 per cent of the proposals were related to enterprise management and reform. When talking about making proposals, Sun, the superintendent of a machine maintenance shop in the smelting and rolling plant, said they would first evaluate the possibilities of having proposals established and any problems solved.

> Generally it is very hard to have proposals about significant enterprise decisions accepted, and therefore we would select issues in production processes, such as machines, safety protection, or living facility supply as proposal themes. These proposals have a higher chance to get established and related problems are more likely to get solved.[7]

With mechanisms like representative training and traditions of proposal choosing, representative participation functions were more like a unilateral channel in which management maintains its control on the whole participation process. It may be a good opportunity for workers to get the latest information about the operating conditions of the enterprise through reports given by CEOs and other managers. But it is still difficult to have their voice heard or seriously considered if they aim to influence decisions which are already made by management. And it is also difficult for workers to really take part in the decision-making process with the help of their representatives even if the union president has already become one of the board members and has a chance to convey workers' voice to the management.

Direct Employee Participation in Production Processes and Improvement of Enterprise Profits

As a way of ensuring workers' influence and a sense of responsibility to the enterprise, participation in production processes is a significant and traditional part of the employee participation regime in state-owned workplaces in China. Participation in the production process has endured the transforming period in stated-owned workplaces. Most participation methods in the production process are direct participation, and this section will focus on two major components of them: shift meetings and quality circles.

Workplace production processes in BZ Company consist of four hierarchies: factory, shop, work section, and group. A group is the basic organization in the frontline production processes, and the size of a group varies from less than ten to dozens according to work types. BZ Company applies '4–3 rotation shift' system, which has been widely adopted in the metallurgy industry since the 1950s. During each shift, meetings are held to assign or summarize tasks and to stress demands about safety and quality. Since 2008 this method was enhanced by BZ management from the one-way control and supervision to internal communication with workers' participation. In the new meeting mode, each individual worker is encouraged to talk about his task and problems in production. 'Important suggestions such as machine adjustment and temperature control from workers could be directly accepted and put into practice, and the proposer will also be rewarded by getting a higher performance score which could bring him/her more performance pay. Thus although the new meeting takes more time, most workers are paying more attention to meetings positively' (Qiao, group leader, steel rolling shop of smelting and rolling plant).[8]

Quality circles, on the other hand, were introduced to BZ in production decision making in the 1980s, and have been recently promoted by management with the aim of cost reduction, lean production, and technology innovation through exploring the intelligence of frontline workers, especially experienced operators and technicians. Employees could form groups according to the production problems they encountered, and regularly hold meetings to seek the optimal strategy to solve them. In order to encourage QC groups, BZ holds competitions annually to select valuable reports and groups, and the selected groups could get generous bonuses and be chosen for industrial, provincial, and national competitions.

Different from the management emphasis of quality circles, two leaders in shops and groups point out that the effect of quality circles was closely related to work contents, and most of the participants were highly skilled and experienced workers rather than regular operators. At the same time, they placed more emphasis on the effects of shift meetings because 'they could reveal production problems through employees' participation and communication and smooth the production process serving as the first link in production information flow'.[9] Interviewees also admitted that 'rather than QC, shift meetings have fewer demands and are easier to participate in, and it's good to see reported problems being considered and to get a higher performance score'.[10]

Although managers and workers held different opinions about participation in production processes, these methods did bring benefits for BZ's production performance. With the promotion of quality circles, the number of QC groups increased from 132 in 2008 to more than 200 between 2009 and 2011 (see Figure 2.1), and technology innovations achieved in quality circles also increased enterprise profits (see Figure 2.2), while, with reformed shift meetings, BZ completed the production process adjustment and reduced the production cycle by about 15 days on average.[11]

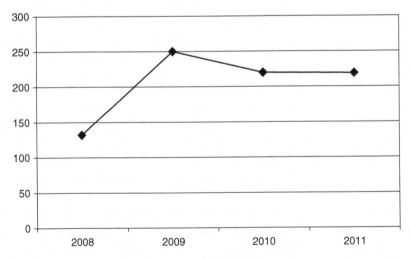

Figure 2.1 Number of QC groups in BZ from 2008 to 2011

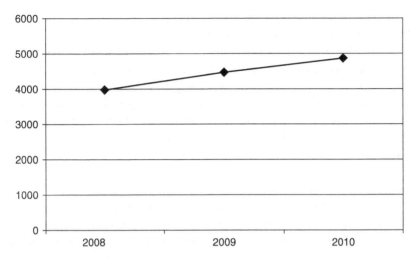

Figure 2.2 Profit enhanced through technique improvement by QC from 2008 to 2010[1] (unit: 10,000 Chinese yuan)

---

[1] Calculated and provided by the QC office which belongs to the Department of Quality Management.

Direct Employee Participation in Management Implementation Processes and Grassroots Democratic Management

Besides production processes, direct participation could also be seen in the implementation process of management decisions. On the one hand, it functions as an information sharing and communication exercise initiated by the functional management department,[12] such as employee satisfaction surveys and employee forums in BZ which started in 2008. On the other hand, direct participation also plays a role in the implementation process of certain managerial decisions at frontline workplaces as a method of workshop-level democratic management to collect workers' opinions and evaluations of the new decision. There is no formal regulation for this participation method, but when important decisions are being implemented downwards to the shop-level, especially during the organizational transformation period, this participation channel is always opened by shop and plant-level managers to keep the implementation process going smoothly.

Employee satisfaction surveys were held annually by BZ's HR office and management promotion office in order to observe workers' attitudes and to avoid disputes during the organizational changing period.

The survey is operated independently by the management promotion office to reduce influence from managers at the lower levels. The most mentioned issue in surveys over the past three years is compensation, where many frontline workers demanded salary increases and complained about the high internal wage gap.[13] Responding to these findings, the HR office did research and described 'too many levels of bonus and performance pay forming large wage gaps between workers and management'.[14] But when addressing this concern, the management increased workers' allowance standards for night shift and high temperature to enhance frontline wages rather than amending the compensation system. This incremental drift in wage adjustments is 'dysfunctional' considering it adds to levels of complexity and internal differentiation which workers were complaining about as well. Thus, although surveys and grievance channels convey workers' voices to the management, workers have little power to influence the decision-making process.

Different from surveys and grievance channels, workshop-level democratic management usually occurs when a new managerial decision or policy is implemented in the shop level, and this kind of participation could result in minor modifications on how to practice the new policies in the workshop-level workplaces. Here an example of the practice of a performance maintenance policy in one of BZ's machine maintenance shops will be used to illustrate the participation process of shop-level democratic management.[15]

In 2011, the method of performance management was put into practice in BZ, and workshops became the basic unit to assess workers' performance. Besides calculating workload performance, employees in one workshop were asked to grade each other's performance, and the weighted score was considered when allocating workshop bonuses. During the first three months of the performance management, leaders of the machine-maintenance workshop collected workers' views and suggestions regularly and found this method was too subjective to get a fair assessment – 'workers who had got along well with other operators in the workshop were always given higher scores by their fellows, while some workers always gave all his workfellows the same low score'.[16] When addressing this problem, every worker was invited to participate in the design process of new assessment methods and finally a committee composed of production workers in charge of assessment was formed through direct vote. When this committee was put into practice, the superintendent of the shop found the scores given by the committee to each worker were very close unless some workers made big mistakes during the production process. Considering this phenomenon, scores graded by the committee were given a smaller weight when calculating the total performance score, and were used as an adjustment to control the internal wage gap.

Through surveys, grievance channels, and workshop-level democratic management, employees could have their voices heard, but it remained difficult to change the direction of management decisions. The space of participation varied according to types of managerial decision and the leadership style of different managers. For example, policies such as 'simplification of the organizational structure' and 'rearrangements of personnel and positions'[17] are pushed down without any space left for frontline workers to give their opinions, although these policies were directly related to the their jobs and some of them may have been assigned to other positions with lower wages and benefits.

Employees' Consent in Their Workplace Participation in SOEs

In order to estimate employees' participation and consent level in different participation types, we gave out 250 questionnaires, and 214 usable ones were collected.[18] Most of the employees surveyed were technicians and operators (87.3 per cent), of whom 57.94 per cent signed open-ended labour contracts, and 41.27 per cent signed 3–5-year fixed-term labour contracts. And different from SOEs like China Post and Sinopec, the percentage of agency workers in BZ was less than 1 per cent. Most of the sample had worked in BZ for more than ten years and 12.7 per cent of them had worked there for five to nine years.

In the questionnaire, we presented the following statement to informants: 'The participation regime is able to help me to express my opinion in management and production, and I would like to take part in it'. And informants were asked to score different participation regimes along a continuum ranging from 5 (very helpful) to 1 (not helpful at all). The participation regimes can be divided into five levels according to the corresponding evaluation levels in descending order:

(1) Shift meetings, workshop/group-level information share;
(2) The enterprise TV station and newspaper, workshop-level democratic management, proposal system, workers' congress;
(3) Company-level information sharing, advanced-operation contests, internal network;
(4) Information boards, quality circles, employee-satisfaction surveys;
(5) Employee-representative inspection, employee forums, collective bargaining, worker directors, and manager hotline.

Table 2.1 Employees' evaluation of participation types in BZ Company (per cent)

	5	4	3	2	1
Bulletin board	39.68	38.89	15.08	3.17	3.17
Enterprise TV/newspaper	47.62	42.06	8.73	1.59	0.00
Intranet	46.83	34.92	11.90	5.56	0.79
Shift meetings	52.38	38.89	6.35	1.59	0.79
Employee satisfaction surveys	30.16	42.86	19.84	3.17	3.97
Manager hotline	19.05	23.81	36.51	8.73	11.90
Company-level information share	43.65	39.68	9.52	3.97	3.17
Workshop/group-level information share	49.21	43.65	5.56	0.00	1.59
Workshop-level democratic management	42.06	46.83	7.14	1.59	2.38
Proposal system	38.10	48.41	11.11	1.59	0.79
Employee representative inspection	28.57	36.51	26.19	5.56	3.17
Advanced-operation contest	38.89	44.44	13.49	2.38	0.79
Quality circles	27.78	46.83	16.67	5.56	3.17
Employee forums	38.89	26.19	23.81	5.56	5.56
Workers' congress	44.44	41.27	9.52	3.17	1.59
Collective bargaining	30.16	27.78	35.71	2.38	3.97
Worker director	26.98	26.19	35.71	3.17	7.94

According to the survey data (see Table 2.1), all participation types except manager hotline, collective bargaining, and worker directors received high consent levels with more than 60 per cent. Direct participation mechanisms in shop and group levels are considered most helpful, followed by new methods like intranet, but quality cycles and employee satisfaction surveys are not rated very highly. Although some of the interviewees showed their distrust of workers' congress, among the representative participation methods, workers' congress and the proposal system still obtained an overall positive acceptance, while collective bargaining and 'worker directors' mechanisms are considered least helpful. And this may be because there are obvious participation processes in mechanisms like workers' congress and the proposal system even if workers cannot exert influence on important managerial decisions through them, but there is still no real collective bargaining procedure in the existing 'collective bargaining' mechanism, and only a few worker representatives could be chosen as the 'worker director', thus most workers have no chance to take part in the regime.

Around 62.7 per cent of the sample reported that management would consider employees' opinions sincerely and properly, and 48.3 per cent

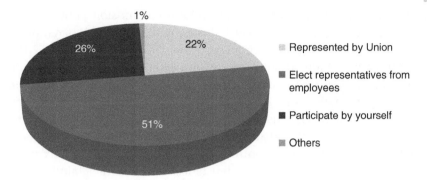

Figure 2.3 Workers' choices in methods of participation

of them think their working conditions could be influenced by their participation, but only 30.2 per cent agreed that their voices are influential during the company decision-making processes. When replying to questions related to representative participation, 55.6 per cent of the respondents consider the union a reliable organization when they encounter difficulties, but when asked about participation in management and disputes, only 22 per cent want to be represented by the union when they wish to convey their voice, and 26 per cent want to participate by themselves, while 51 per cent of them hope that they could elect their own representatives (see Figure 2.3).

Discussion – Choice between Consent, Voice, and Quitting

While the interview results highlight workers' doubts, the survey data shows a relatively high consent level towards most forms of participation. This discrepancy may come from the methodological difference, that is, interviews are more effective in reaching the true feelings of workers compared to questionnaire surveys. Also, it may come from the different sample choices of the two methods, that is, the interview sample represents more frontline workers. Here I will use three factors, including market competition, the paternalism legacy, and the role of state intervention, to help explain workers' choice between consent and resistance. While the participation in the production process where workers could really exert influences may contribute a lot to their consent, the three factors above have a great influence on their choices.

In the first place, the changing context in the iron and steel industry required companies to adapt quickly to fiercer market competition. In

2005, the national development and reform commission published the development policy for the steel industry, demanding consolidation of the industrial structure through mergers and combination. Then in 2011, the Ministry of Industry and Information published the 12th five-year development plan for the steel industry calling for deeper mergers. When one company fails to maintain demand or to change its production according to the newly-emerging demand, it would be hard to retain the high levels of consent and silence in the workforce. On the one hand, stricter output and quality control plus downgrading welfare may result in rising worker complaints and resistance. On the other hand, attractive welfare plans provided by private or foreign-invested companies may push the employees to leave their homeland and to accept a new job even if it were not relevant to their basic skills in steelmaking.[19]

The legacy of company paternalism could be seen in almost every corner of BZ, especially in the living areas. The company continued to provide public infrastructure and welfare to support the extended (not just daily) reproduction of labour power, including children's education, convenient transportation, and shopping facilities. This maintained the reputation of the company as a good employer. Many interviewees mentioned the feeling when they first stepped into the BZ zone of being impressed by the great variety of welfare provisions which they saw as indicating that the company was considerate of its employees and created a feeling of safety. Their working lives and leisure time happened in the same place, their children were born and grew up in the company yard, and this is why they used to call the company 'homeland'. This feeling of safety and welfare cultivated by the company's practice of deep paternalism underpinned workers' confidence and consent towards the plans and practice of the management. Although in the atmosphere of the market economy these paternalistic practices were challenged by newly introduced management methods, their legacy had the power to attract workers and to enhance the degree of consent, especially with what we will discuss next, state intervention.

State intervention in the industry was another important factor that helped influence employees' attitudes towards the company. It could change the disadvantaged situation of the enterprise through governmental advertisement and promotion. State support would protect the company in fierce market competition and provide the ability to maintain paternalistic practices and welfare provision. Additionally, the state had the final say over the direction of reform. Although small companies may not be assisted by the city or county where ownership lies, the government would usually intervene in labour disputes and conflicts by compelling a wage increase or even compensating with local revenue.

Both kinds of intervention may reduce workers' resistance and make the underlying structure of management– employee relations more obscure.

Although a relatively high level of consent towards participation mechanisms was revealed in the survey, employees also expressed high demands for participation, especially regarding income distribution policies during the interviews. For example, many employees wanted to know 'how is one's wage determined; especially the compensation policy during difficult times'.[20] Meanwhile, informal participation channels like the BZ company intranet community emerged as a new platform where employees could express themselves. Posts with titles like 'Call for suggestions to lower costs', 'Ways to re-prosperity for BZ in the eye of an ordinary production worker',[21] and 'How to determine the minimum wage for BZ Company' attracted intensive attention and discussion. Even without formal mechanisms for feedback from management, this new channel could be viewed as a symbol of SOE workers' voice in the new era, rather than keeping silent until fierce disputes occurred.

Besides the high demand for voice, workers' choice of 'exit' in Hirschman's 'exit, voice, and loyalty' model could also be found in BZ. During interviews, several employees who had joined the company after graduating college in 2001 said that their trust in enterprise management came from the atmosphere in factories and living quarters, the welfare in housing, health services, and the education of their children provided by the enterprise which made them feel that BZ company was a place they could stay for life, and that the company would not neglect their interests in favour of profits.[22] But this impression was gradually damaged by the 'reduction of employee benefits', 'limited wage growth and career prospects', 'bureaucratic management', and 'ignorance of workers' opinions'. Thus, Yang, who had worked in BZ for ten years, decided to accept a job offer from a private steel-making company with annual pay of about 100,000 yuan, much higher than the basic monthly wage of 1,200 yuan in BZ. Yang used the word 'hopeless' to depict his work life in BZ, and he said there were several more workfellows like him who had already quit from BZ and started their work in larger cities like Wuhan. But he also admitted that courage was necessary to make the decision, especially when one had his/her family settled down in BZ.

The traditional welfare in SOEs reflects the company's 'paternalist' care of employees. In this situation, the company is the authorized representative of employees' voice and interests, and employees have accumulated deep trust in the management as well as low demand in participation, thus tending to consent to the participation mechanism with low participation levels based on their consent to traditional welfarism. However, the coexistence of traditional welfarism which treats workers as equal and the pursuit of efficiency could be easily broken by the changes of context and the labour process.

The external competitive market environment and internal transformation of management and production processes constitute the changing context of BZ, under which traditional welfare decreases dramatically and the pursuit of profit becomes the primary goal of the company. Decreasing compensation and safety may lead to a change in levels of consent and raise the demand for workers' direct participation. Workers' discussions within the intranet community and the fact that some experienced operators quit the company both reflect that other choices like voice and exit have already been considered by workers in BZ underneath the manufactured consent and silence in the firm.

Notes

1 Different from the typical framework of labour relations systems which involve three actors (workers and their trade unions, employers and their agencies, and the state), in contemporary China, the structure of labour relations is formed by four actors, because unions are responsible to the government, enterprises, and workers at the same time rather than just acting as the representative of workers.
2 See http://www.baosteel.com/group/contents/1719/30120.html
3 See http://www.baosteel.com/group/contents/1719/30120.html.
4 See http://www.sgcc.com.cn/qywh070813/zonglan/hxjzg/default.shtml.
5 Quoted from the interview of BZ Company's union democratic office manager L on February 20, 2012.
6 Quoted from the interview of BZ Company's union democratic office manager L on February 20, 2012.
7 Quoted from the interview of the superintendent of the machine maintenance shop in BZ's smelting and rolling plant on February 15, 2012.
8 Quoted from the interview of Qiao, the group leader in steel rolling shop in BZ's smelting and rolling plant on February 15, 2012.
9 Quoted from interviews of superintendents of the continuous casting shop and the machine maintenance shop H and S, as well as group leaders Q and W in BZ Company on February 15 and 16, 2012.
10 Quoted from the interview of BZ Company continuous casting shop workers C, L, and X on February 16, 2012.
11 Calculated with data provided by the management of BZ Company.

12 Information sharing has a relatively low participation level, and it is widely implemented in China's enterprises. Communication mechanism mainly focuses on the collection and feedback of employee voices.

13 Quoted from results of BZ's satisfaction survey in 2010.

14 Quoted from the interview of BZ's HR office manager D on February 20, 2012.

15 Quoted from interviews of workers in the machine-maintenance shop.

16 Quoted from the interview of Sun, the superintendent of the machine-maintenance shop in BZ's smelting and rolling plant on February 15, 2012.

17 With this policy, technical and operational posts will be reduced by 10 per cent and 7 per cent respectively.

18 The questionnaire design referred to the UK workplace questionnaire, and questions about employees' participation were added.

19 Quoted from the interview of L who would left BZ and went to Guangzhou for a new job on February 22, 2012.

20 Quoted from the interviews of L and X from the continuous casting shop, and F and M from the coking shop on February 16 and 17, 2012.

21 This is the title of a post in the intranet community about suggestions to reproduce the prosperity of BZ in the good old days written by a production worker.

22 Quoted from interviews of Y and his three fellow workers with the same entry time at the living zone on February 22, 2012.

REFERENCES

Bryson, A., & Freeman, R. (2006) Worker needs and voice in the US and the UK. NBER Working Paper, no. 12310, National Bureau of Economic Research.

Burawoy, M. (1979) *Manufacturing Consent.* Chicago: University of Chicago Press.

Burawoy, M. (2008) *Manufacturing Consent: Changes in the Labor Process under Monopoly Capitalism.* Beijing: The Commercial Press.

Busck, O., Knudsen, H., & Lind, J. (2010) The transformation of employee participation: consequences for the work environment. *Economic and Industrial Democracy,* 31(3): 285–305.

Chang, K. & Brown, W. (2013) The transition from individual to collective labour relations in China. *Industrial Relations Journal,* 44:2, 102–121.

Chang, K. (2013) From individual labor relations to collective labor relations—the transformation towards collective labor relations and the improvement of labor policies in China. *Journal of Chinese Social Science,* 06: 91–108.

▶

▶

Chang, K. (2009) *Report of labor relations in China—features and development directions of labor relations in contemporary China*. Beijing: Labor and Social Security Press of China.

Chen, F. (2004) Legal mobilization by trade unions: the case of Shanghai. *China Journal* 52: 27–49.

Chen, F. (2009) Union Power in China: Source, operation, and constraints. *Modern China*, 35 (6), 662–89.

Cooke, W. N. (1992) Product quality improvement through employee participation: the effects of unionization and joint union management administration. *Industrial and Labor Relations Review*, 46(1): 119–134.

Cox, A., Zagelmeyer, S., & Marchington, M. (2006) Embedding employee involvement and participation at work. *Human Resource Management Journal*, 16(3): 250–267.

Freeman, R. B. (1980) The exit-voice tradeoff in the labor market: Unionism, job tenure, quits, and separations. *Quarterly Journal of Economics*, XCIV(4): 643–673.

Gomez, R., Bryson, A., & Willman, P. (2010) 'Voice in the wilderness? The shift from union to non-union voice in Britain' in: Wilkinson, A., Gollan, P., and Marchington, M. (Ed.), *The Oxford Handbook of Participation in Organizations*: 382–397. New York: Oxford University Press.

Guest, D. E. (2011) Human resource management and performance: still searching for some answers. *Human Resource Management Journal*, 21(1): 3–13.

Heller, F. (1998) 'Playing the devil's advocate' In: Heller, F., Pusić, E., Strauss, G., Wilpert, B. (Ed.), *Organizational Participation: Myth and Reality*: 144–148. New York: Oxford University Press.

Hirschman, A. O. (1970) *Exit, voice, and loyalty: responses to decline in firms, organisations, and states*. Cambridge: Harvard University Press.

Huang, X., Vliert, E., & Vegt, G. (2005) Breaking the silence culture: stimulation of participation and employee opinion withholding cross-nationally. *Management and Organization Review*, 1(3): 459–482.

Hyman, J. & Mason, B. (1995) *Managing employee improvement and participation*. London: Sage.

Kochan, T., Katz, H. C., & Mower, N. (1984) *Worker participation and American unions: threat or opportunity?* MI: Upjohn Institute for Employment Research, Kalamazoo

Lee, C. K. (1999) From organized dependence to disorganized despotism: changing labor regimes in Chinese factories. *The China Quarterly*, 157:44–71.

Li, Q. (2008) *Introduction of industrial relations*. Beijing: Labor and Social Security Press of China.

Liu, A. (2003) Workers' choice of action in the institutional reforming process of SOE—an empirical research of no collective action. *Chinese Journal of Sociology Research*, (06):1–12.

Liu, W. (2004) *Consistency and inconsistency—research of China's employee democratic participation*. Beijing: Labor and Social Security Press of China.

Lucio, M.M. (2010) Labour Process and Marxist Perspectives on Employee Representation. In *The Oxford Handbook of Participation in Organizations*, ed. Adrian Wilkinson, Paul J. Gollan, Mick Marchington, and David Lewin, 105-131. Oxford: Oxford University Press.

▶

▶

Ramsay, H. (1977) Cycles of Control: Worker participation in sociological and historical perspective. *Sociology.* 11 (3): 481–506.

Salamon, M. (1992). *Industrial Relations: Theory and Practice* (2nd Edition). New York: Prentice Hall.

Smith, C. (2016) (forthcoming). Rediscovery of the Labour Process. In Edgell, S., Gottfried, H., & Granter, E. (Eds.), *Sage Handbook of the Sociology of Work and Employment.* London: Sage.

Taylor B., Li Q (2007) Is the ACFTU a Union and Does it Matter? Journal of Industrial Relations 49(5), 701–715.

Taylor, B., Chang, K., & Li, Q. (2003) *Industrial Relations in China.* Cheltenham, United Kingdom: Edward Elgar Publishing Limited.

Thompson, P., & Newsome, K. (2004) Labor process theory, work and the employment relation. In Kaufman, B. E. (Ed.), *Theoretical perspectives on work and the employment relationship*: 133–162. Industrial Relations Research Association.

Tong, X. (2006) The continued socialist cultural tradition—a case study of workers' collective action in SOE. *Chinese Journal of Sociology Research*, (01):59–76.

Webb, S. & Webb, B. (1897) *Industrial Democracy.* Longmans, Green, and Co.: 39 Paternoster Row, London: New York and Bombay.

Wilkinson, A., Gollan, P., Marchington, M., & Lewin, D. (2010) Conceptualizing employee participation in organizations. In Gollan, P., Lewin, D., and Marchington, M., & Wilkinson, A. *The Oxford Handbook of Participation in Organizations*: 3–27. New York: Oxford University Press.

Wu, Q. (2007) *Reform of state-owned enterprises and transition of old industrial workers.* Beijing: Social Science Literature Press.

Xie, Y. (2009) Institution and function of China's industrial democracy and employee participation: comparison of state-owned enterprise, foreign invested enterprise and private enterprise. *Chinese Journal of Social Economic System Comparison*, (01):129–135.

Workers under Disorganized Despotism: A Case from the State-Owned Shipbuilding Industry

Lefeng Lin

Introduction

Over the last decade, studies on Chinese labour politics have mainly focused on migrant workers in the private sector. We still know little about the workers in state sectors. State workers who had contracts with state-owned enterprises (SOEs), in face of layoffs, management corruption, and factory bankruptcy, seemed to become the vanguard of anti-neoliberal reform from the late 1990s to the early 2000s. However, later reform showed they did not sustain resistance in ways that we might have expected and therefore there is a question about why Chinese state-sector workers did not become the furnace of labour unrest in the late reform period. Recent reform has raised the question of why state workers have not launched any effective challenges to reform schemes, especially when they are considered to possess powerful socialist legacies, with significant ideological power and organizational resources.

In this chapter, I enter the micro-foundations of labour relations in a state-owned shipbuilding factory and examine workers' politics on the shop floor. I argue that the uncoordinated state intervention and SOE restructuring created a 'disorganized despotic factory regime'. However, this regime did not trigger state workers' unrest because both macro uncoordinated state intervention and micro labour-control strategies in the factory undermined the resources that workers could use to produce collective action.

In the next section, I introduce the October Shipbuilding Industry Corporation (OSIC), and the workshop where I did my research. In the third section, the institutional arrangements, the restructuring of the factory organization, and the practices of managerial despotism are examined as contributors to the formation of the disorganized despotic factory regime. In the fourth section, I examine everyday lives on the shop floor where we can see the reorganization of shop-floor management, strategies for labour control, labour resistance, and the demoralization and degradation of workers. The final section summarizes my findings and provides a conclusion.

OSIC

OSIC grew out of the Liberation Shipbuilding Factory (LSF), which was built by Russia in 1898 and then expanded by Japan. After the Soviet Army defeated the Japanese Kwantung Army near the end of World War II, the factory was taken over by the Soviet government, and then joint-operated by China and the Soviets. In 1955, the Chinese government established the right to operate the factory independently, and gave it the name 'Liberation Shipbuilding Factory' in 1957.

With central government support, LSF expanded rapidly. In the 1960s, it built a new subdivision in the same city whose businesses mainly involved ship-repair and small shipbuilding. By the 1980s, the subdivision had been able to build large ships. In 1984, three workshops in the subdivision each set up new independent firms – Marine Diesel Works, Marine Valve Manufactory, and Marine Propeller Corporation – and today they are still located inside the factory. After the mid-1980s, the subdivision's scale and productivity had caught up with that of the mother factory. One important difference between them was that LSF held the military orders from the Chinese navy, while the subdivision built commercial ships that generated significant foreign currency for the central government. In 1990, the subdivision finally became an independent shipbuilding factory named 'October Shipbuilding Factory' (OSF). This is where the fieldwork for this chapter was undertaken.

During the 1990s, when drastic SOE reform led to massive unemployment and public protests, the two shipbuilding factories felt little resonance. Contrary to the bleak image of SOEs in the 1990s, OSF was relatively prosperous. When facing a layoff policy from the central government, it established a new firm named October Shipbuilding Labour Service Company where the so-called laid-off workers acquired new jobs. In 2002 a lack of orders threatened workers with layoff for the first time. However, with central government's approval, OSF accepted the business of building four VLCC (very large crude container) ships for Iran, who paid in crude oil instead of US dollars, and this helped OSF overcome its immediate problems. LSF's business was not as good as OSF's after 1990, but it fared well. The real crisis for LSF came in 2005 when a corruption scandal involving top managers paralysed the factory operation. Ironically, the previous subdivision – OSF – incorporated LSF under central governmental arrangements. So, a new shipbuilding dinosaur named 'October Shipbuilding Industry Corporation' (OSIC) was founded which included two subdivisions. Before the 2009 downturn, OSIC's production showed a 20 per cent growth rate per year, and the number of orders received ranked fourth in the global shipbuilding market.

From autumn 2008 to spring 2009, I did my participant observation as an assistant in a manual cutting team in the steel processing workshop, which processed all steel boards before they were sent to other shops for shipbuilding. There were six steps (shot-blasting, lofting, digital cutting, manual cutting, bending, apportioning) and six lines. After my arrival in September, a new nearby workshop named New Steel Company opened, and this was a joint investment of Steel Company (51 per cent stock) and OSIC (49 per cent stock) and was due to eventually replace the current steel processing workshop.

At first sight, production in the workshop looks busy and orderly. Iron dust, fire, light, and noise created an atmosphere of work intensity, as overhead cranes ceaselessly went back and forth with steel boards. Workers crouched to cut the boards with torches, or bended to draw the lines on the boards under dim lights, or sat operating the digital lathes according to the drawings, or shout and direct the crane drivers. Occasionally, the foreman looked around to say something to a worker. Everything went smoothly. And in fact, based on the output, we could further attest to its efficiency. With increased business orders and more retired workers (but no replacements), its processing quota per year had grown tremendously from 80,000 to 400,000 tons from 2003 to 2008. Disregarding the media praise for the production model and the production data, what was going on behind the scenes?

Disorganized Despotism under Bureaucratic Legacies

Lee, using the archetypes developed by Michael Burawoy (1985), suggested the factory regime of 'disorganized despotism' as an ideal type of industrial firm under Chinese market reform. The lack of effective coordination and implementation among diverse reform measures created a 'disorganized' institutional context which allowed for the managerial despotism inside the enterprise, but state workers were unable to resist due to the threat of layoff and their inability to compete in the private sector (Lee 1999; 2002). In this section, I show how a disorganized despotic regime evolved by looking at the effect of recent institutional reforms and the observed characteristics of the workplace.

State Intervention: Ideal and Reality

Burawoy's studies (1983; 1985) showed that social insurance and state regulation of work and employment were key factors that affected factory regimes. In China, SOEs have widely participated in distributing pensions, medical care, maternity benefits, unemployment benefits, and industrial injury compensation funds. Besides the social security scheme for the employee, three major national labour-related laws were passed in 2007, all intending to regulate work and employment in China. For instance, the Labour Law required collective consultation between managers and workers when significant changes were made in work and employment conditions, and it also clarified that workers had the right to form a union. The Labour Contract Law seriously constrained employers' power to dismiss workers who might confront managers or expressed labour grievances to officials. The Labour Dispute Mediation and Arbitration Law made it easier for workers to make a case against their employers. Given that SOE managers comply with state laws and the reformed economy provides employment opportunities outside the state sector, a hegemonic or a paternalistic factory regime should emerge, but this did not happen.

Though all the workers in OSIC had social insurance, it was very hard to use the state regulation against managers and employers. The uncoordinated implementation restricted workers' mobility, thus restricting their ability to exercise labour power by 'exit' (Smith 2006). In OSIC, social insurance resources did not reduce workers' dependence on the factory for their livelihood, but in fact became an obstacle to workers who wanted to leave. In order to keep social security benefits, dissatisfied workers often chose not to leave the state sector, because many private employers did not pay (or underpaid) social insurance. In 2014 a National Peasant Workers Survey showed the coverage of social insurance for peasant workers who worked in the private sector was very modest: injury insurance had only 26.2 per cent coverage; medical insurance, 17.6 per cent; unemployment insurance, 10.5 per cent; pension provisions, 16.7 per cent; maternity insurance, 7.8 per cent; and housing benefit, a mere 5.5 per cent coverage. Moreover, in the private sector, factory management was no less despotic than in SOEs (Lee 1998; Pun 2005). This socio-economic context increases state-sector workers' dependence on their current jobs.

Although the state passed three new laws to regulate increasingly unstable labour relations, law enforcement remains a problem in China. Current labour-related laws only provide some legitimacy and rationality for labour protest, but are far from creating a framework for bargaining with capital or government. More importantly, the laws individualize workers' resistance. The court usually breaks the collective case into many individual cases, and most workers do not have time and money to back up legal cases themselves, especially as the whole legal process often takes years from petition to mediation to arbitration to litigation. Therefore, the protection of individual labour rights does little to help workers to avoid managerial despotism. Social security packages, labour market opportunities, and labour laws are insufficient to create an organized institutional context to limit managerial power, even though they have ostensibly been designed to protect labour rights.

Market Reform: Transformation of Bureaucratic Legacies

While property rights and managerial powers have undergone some changes, the bureaucratic and hierarchical organization inherited from state socialism remains in SOEs, albeit transformed under market reform. Managerial autonomy has been operating in Chinese SOEs for a long time, which has led to widespread illicit asset stripping or spontaneous privatizations, but now the 'central enterprise' asset is controlled by the central government.

Workers recalled that before SOE restructuring they could protest about unequal bonuses through the use of strikes or collective absenteeism, which usually forced management to make compromises. Also, it was reasonable for workers to reject extra quotas that came without additional pay. Managers and workers had relatively equal status and the income gap between them was small. The general director, who had been gradually promoted through the ranks from being a skilled worker, was familiar with production and came to the shop floor every day to check work in progress, product quality, and workers' difficulties, and he also maximized bonus and housing welfare for workers. As a senior worker remembered in 1992, when his leg was broken and he was sent to the hospital, the general director, workshop director, union chair, and team leader all came to see him on that day, but such visits from management were no longer the norm. The senior worker thought that at that time workers' self-discipline, morale, and efficiency were higher than now. Senior workers said in the past they felt they worked for their factory and themselves. Perhaps this recollection was coloured by workers' recent experiences of changes. However, it showed, at least for workers, workplace relations in the past were not despotic.

Though the organizational structure was still similar, the contemporary situation became different. Managers used 'insider contracting' and the so-called 'collective contract' to reshape the factory regime. 'Contractors' were workshop directors and outsourcing companies. For workshops, workshop directors contracted production quotas with a certain amount of money (including bonuses). As workers increased productivity, their bonuses remained unchanged, but the management takes higher salaries and bonuses. This insider contracting was an old way to organize production in an early period of industrialization (Clawson 1980), but in OSIC it is the different workshops, rather than the skilled worker or craftsman, that contract the production quota. This modern form of insider contracting goes beyond the individual level – between the skilled worker and his followers – and evolves to the organizational level – between the workshop director and his workers – making the antagonistic class relations much more transparent in the workshops.

Through insider contracting, the workshop looked like an independent factory and the director acted like a capitalist with autonomy to deal with profit distribution, work time arrangements, personnel policy, welfare items, and production processes. In the past, the manager–worker relationship was relatively harmonious and cooperative, and the workshop director showed more interest in workers. The director, like the workers, earned wages and the income gap with workers was small. Now, the manager–worker relationship became an antagonistic class division. The director and other managers tried to maximize their own interest – the profit – that came from squeezing workers' effort. There was increasing conflict between workers and workshop managers. On one occasion, workers informed the media of their long working hours and reduced overtime pay, but managers, trying to legitimize their position, said that workers had a 'collective contract', though the workers were never informed about such a contract with the factory. The slogan 'return our money' appeared on the workshop gate, although it was repeatedly erased and replaced. Through insider contracting, state workers, who are employed by the SOE and enjoy employment privileges to some degree, actually have experienced a structural change in their workshop – the relationship between manager and workers has become a class division. The situation makes sense when we look at the outsourcing companies.

Usually, workshop or department managers controlled outsourcing companies through quota assignment. A department included several workshops. To make money, outsourcing companies gave money to the managers in exchange for more quota or more production materials. Most of them, if they wanted to survive in OSIC, must have an insider who had personal connections to certain factory managers. Another function of outsourcing companies was as a weapon against state workers. Because the wages in the outsourcing company were very low, managers would like to replace state workers at some time, if they could. Managers under the reform structure could always threaten state workers with the slogan 'if you don't like it, you can go! There are many peasant workers waiting outside'.

We can see workshop managers and outsourcing companies transformed through insider contracting. On the one hand, the employment relations, once relatively democratic and harmonious between managers and workers in the SOE, turned into antagonistic class relationships between contractors and workers in workshops; on the other hand, managers used a dual labour force to keep state workers in check, in which the peasant workers from outsourcing companies had worse conditions and lower wages and benefits compared to state workers. In OSIC, managers used to be technological bureaucrats in the socialist-industrial system; but now they had become entrepreneurs and took more profit generated by workers' increased productivity. The relatively democratic factory in the early reform era became a despotic factory where managers dictate to production workers on the shop floor.

Managerial Despotism: Bureaucratic Organization of Production

In the office building, the 'scientific management movement' received unprecedented attention. Office work was divided into new positions and filled with people who were recruited due to their special connections with particular factory or workshop managers. In the workshop archive office, for example, according to one of my worker informants, the work that previously only took two people was now done by six people, and since the room was small, some people had to sit on the desk if all the six are on duty. In the OSIC administration building, a worker

Lao Liu told me at least 60 per cent of the staff in the Shipbuilding Research Institute was superfluous. Xiao Sun also said:

> Once, I went there to get the blueprint. Curiously, there were only a few staff members in the office (because there should be many). One staff said others had other things to do (so they are not here), and then he just turned on the computer and printed the blueprint. That's done! They had nothing to do. Fuck their research. Even the blueprints were bought from South Korea! I can also do the job! But, do you have the 'people' (inside connection with the factory managers)?

A nepotistic and bureaucratic administrative organization weakened the industrial authority and reduced managerial skills. In order to obtain profit and maintain a redundant bureaucratic organization, it was necessary to extract labour from workers' efforts and earn as much as possible, hence a despotic factory regime ensured.

Here, the familiar measures were overtime work, labour intensification, and income control. Working hours were continuously extended since 2003. To start with, workers were required to begin work earlier, at 7 am, and occasionally work later than 5 pm. In addition, they must work six hours on Saturday and Sunday. Later, in the three Golden Weeks (Chinese statutory holidays) on four out of seven days workers had to work six hours. By 2009, workers' rest consisted of just three holidays and they were required to work eight hours at weekends. From 2003 to 2009, the production quota soared from 80,000 tons to 400,000 tons. Just as significantly, every year, workers who retired were not replaced, thus putting pressure on the remaining workers and increasing the intensification of work. But despite this labour intensification and longer working hours, workers' income rarely increased, while the income gap between managers and workers grew quickly. A department director's year-end bonus was 500,000 RMB, a workshop director's 100,000 RMB, but a worker only received 3,000 RMB. The bonus for the celebration of the 110th anniversary of the company was 150,000 RMB for a workshop director but only 1,100 RMB for a worker. Moreover, worker's income did not increase in the most profitable years. When state wage regulation in 2007 prescribed a worker's wage increase, workshop managers reduced bonuses in order to prevent total income increasing. Meanwhile, office staff enjoyed real income increases. Xiao Qiang told me:

> My wage (including bonus) is 1,600 RMB – the same as in 2002. Sometimes, I even got less than that! Fuck! Leaders took the money we made.

Actually, workers' income was mysteriously reduced from their stated salaries. This was referred to as 'taking money' (an illegal tax by managers), and it meant workshop officers would dock some money (200–1000 RMB) from a worker's total income when the money was dispensed to the workshop by the factory. No matter how angry workers became – sometimes slogans were written on the door to show their rage – managers were never forced to explain why they took the money.

Besides intensified production, longer hours, lower wages, and irregular wage reductions, managers also exerted control over workers by limiting their mobility, and thus increasing their dependence on their jobs. Generally, skilled workers with more than ten years' experience were more likely to resign because they were more likely to be able to find a better job. But interviewees reported that managers used tactics, such as failing to provide the certificate of seniority, or withholding personal archives, or demanding arbitrary fees, in order to prevent workers from leaving. After all, it was in the managers' interest to block skilled workers from going to competitor factories. Such measures frustrated workers, but kept them on the shop floor. I heard Xiao Sun several times curse the factory and Lao Lin told me:

> Do you know why Xiao Sun hopes for bankruptcy? If OSIC is really bankrupt, he will be free! He wants to leave but is locked [into remaining] by managers' foolish policies.

Workers had no outlet to express their grievances. Factory managers did not care as long as shop directors achieved their production goals, and they sided with shop-floor managers against the workers. As a central enterprise, it had such a high degree of autonomy that its top managers' political status and bureaucratic level were not lower than the local governor, which was why the phrase 'enterprise bureaucrats' is a useful description of their status. The factory functioned like an inner state, and its bureaucrats brandished their despotic whip and harnessed market principles to rule and dominate workers.

In this section, I have described the formation of a disorganized despotic factory regime. Although the social-security scheme and labour-related laws have been passed to protect workers, these measures did not constrain the despotism in a bureaucratic SOE. OSIC utilized its autonomy, central enterprise status, uncoordinated institutional context, and market success to transform itself into a bureaucratic capitalist organization. The top managers took the positions accompanied by political rank, and the mid-level managers became entrepreneurs who were employed by them. They together developed an inner system by exchanging power and money. The outsourced companies acquired subcontracts through networking and exchange with factory managers. Power, production, and money exchange were well organized in OSIC, and the old democratic values and practices of OSF became but a distant memory. However, such an organization could not maintain itself by power and money alone. Why would workers tolerate such a regime today when they would have undoubtedly resisted it in the 1980s and 1990s? Why didn't workers take any action? We have revealed the institutional and organizational aspects that contribute to this despotism, but additionally, managers needed to adopt more control strategies to frustrate workers' resistance while maintaining minimum cooperation to meet production quota. This requires us to look more closely at shop-floor politics.

Labour Politics on the Shop Floor

On the shop floor I observed that there were two kinds of managerial control. One was practised by workshop managers who work in the office building, and the other by shop-floor managers, such as section chiefs, team leaders, and foremen. Workshop managers must ensure shop-floor managers remained loyal to them and helped them extract more effort from workers' labour power, and the shop-floor managers had to use strategies to get workers' cooperation. Through various arrangements of labour control, we can see how the potential of workers to bond or form associations was dismantled and degraded and thus served to inhibit expressions of their collective interests.

Shop-Floor Manager: 'Betraying His Workers'

In my fieldwork, I found shop-floor managers played a significant role in labour control. Compared to the workshop managers, they shared work experiences and identity with, and were closer to, workers. Because the labour process can only be controlled through shop-floor managers' support, a 'new' method of human resource management had been adopted.

Firstly, the managerial structure on the shop floor changed. In the past, there had been the section chief, team leader, and foreman comprising a three-level managerial structure, but during the reform years the section chief was eliminated. Today, the real managers on the shop floor were team leaders, while foremen played an auxiliary role. Through this measure, workshop managers nullified the resistance of workers led by section chiefs. On the one hand, section chiefs were promoted in the 1990s based on their performance, so they gained seniority and high prestige on the shop floor, which meant they possessed the capacity to mobilize workers. On the other hand, the skilled section chiefs were members of an older generation compared with workshop managers, and they never bent to those office 'youngsters' who did not possess the status of the older guys. Lao Lin (a senior worker) explained the impact that the age and experience of the workers had on the effort bargain on the shop floor:

> When Big Lao Wang was section chief, the workshop director demanded us to operate two manual cutting machines simultaneously, but Big Lao Wang stared at him and said: 'With two machines? No problem! How much do you pay? Do you pay workers double wage or bonus?' The workshop director said nothing and had to maintain the situation. Afterwards, they removed the section chiefs but still gave him a sinecure with the same income and benefits. In less than two years, Big Lao Wang retired.

According to the workers, there were only a few section chiefs because as section chiefs gradually retired there were no new appointments. Following the change of managerial structure on the shop floor, shop-floor managers were replaced by young, skilled team leaders (aged between 30 and 40 years) whose seniority was lower than workshop managers, and in comparison with old section chiefs, they shared the value of the market reform rather than the early socialist experience. However, it was still problematic to ensure these young team leaders aligned with the workshop managers; after all, they shared much of the workers' experiences. Consequently, an additional change was implemented regarding the pattern of bonus distribution on the shop floor. In the past, wages and bonuses would be distributed within a team and everyone knew one another's income. This included team leaders who also received their wages within the team plus the bonuses shared with workers. A worker told me that in the past if they were underpaid for their work, the team leader would lead them into strike or absences until a satisfactory outcome was achieved. But, today team leaders had their wages and bonuses listed with staff in the workshop offices, while workers' wages were listed separately. That meant team leaders were absorbed into the workshop management as one stratum of the new bureaucratic organization. This encouraged team leaders to share managers' interests and endeavour to improve output, thus eliminating the possibility of team leaders steering workers' resistance. Workshop directors promised them certain bonuses if they could meet the production quota. This added pressure on team leaders to impose those oppressive methods on workers that would improve output. Unconsciously, the new generation of shop-floor managers – team leaders – turned their interests into labour control rather than bargaining with superior managers. They moved their interests away from those of the worker and were no longer potential leaders for collective resistance, which made an insurgency less feasible.

Labour Control on the Shop Floor

Because workers were very hostile to management and have low morale in production, team leaders had to use certain methods to get workers' minimum cooperation in order to finish the quota.

First, team leaders controlled the distribution of bonuses. That helped them to divide workers' solidarity and built a paternalistic tie both with core workers as well as so-called 'trouble makers'. Generally, the team leaders appointed foremen who were highly skilled workers with seniority or prestige – core workers – and these core workers were given a 'foreman's bonus'. Within my team (in manual cutting) the team contained 52 workers; a typical case was Lao Liang. As the foreman of the No. 3 line he had worked in the steel processing workshop for the longest time. He was also a team leader in the early 2000s, but he was removed for what were deemed 'overly selfish behaviours'. Lao Liang, as a senior skilled worker, had many apprentices, so he had the capacity to mobilize and organize workers. To eliminate this potential danger, Xiao Xu (the manual cutting team leader) not only gave him a 'foreman's bonus', but also awarded him a 'team leader subsidy' which was strictly reserved for team leaders. After a workshop manager forbade the subsidy, Xiao Xu took money from the team bonus and paid Lao Liang.

Lao Lin, a senior skilled foreman, gave up his position after some disagreement with Xiao Xu, but Xiao Xu still gave him the 'foreman's bonus' in order to pacify his discontent. The team leader also used bonuses to pacify workers considered to be troublesome. For example, Xiao Nan Zi often created trouble within the team, and Xiao Xu gave him the 'red card' (the monthly excellent worker bonus of 300 RMB) in exchange for peace. By using bonuses to bribe core and troublesome workers, the team leader was able to maintain peaceful production on the shop floor.

Secondly, social networking also served an important means for facilitating workers' cooperation. On the one hand, the master–apprentice relationship was a useful means of labour control. If a team leader was relatively younger, his master and other brothers would support his leadership, and of course they would expect to get benefits such as bonuses or special vacations. If the team leader was relatively older, he had many apprentices who generally supported him. I have observed a team on the shop floor whose leader, Xiao Wei, was very domineering. He often threatened his workers or abused them with swear words. Lao Liu told me that all foremen in that team were the leader's apprentices and received good bonuses. On the other hand, an important part of Chinese culture – eating and drinking – strengthened labour control indirectly. Apparently, the team leader and workers occasionally went out to have a big meal and sing karaoke. In this informal environment and personal interaction, they all poured out their dissatisfaction and difficulties. The leader modestly apologized for his superior's bossiness and asked for workers' understanding and support; workers unleashed their grievances and asked for the leader's guardianship. At such moments, the team leader once again identified himself with the workers. Through such social networking and interaction, some workers returned cooperation in the production.

The third measure of labour control was the internal labour market. If a worker could not easily resign to find a new job and was disgruntled with his current position and leaders, a team leader could arrange another position in order to avoid the potential of him causing production disruption. This task needed coordination among managers across different workshops. A worker who was extremely dissatisfied with his leader and job could apply for transfer, and usually this problem would be resolved within the workshop. Managers hoped this would pacify a worker's discontent, and, indeed, this strategy worked. But, ironically, the transferred worker might end up in his original position. Xiao Nan Zi, a well-known troublesome worker, had several different job positions until, finally, he ended up where he started! Perhaps this occurred because most shops were similarly tyrannical and their control nets had been knitted together, so the transferred worker would be viewed as an outsider and therefore alienated in the new team. The team leader did not pay much attention to him since he knew the reason why the worker had come to the new team, and most other workers would also ignore him. Some workers may prefer this anonymity, while others may find the silence oppressive and, needing more social interaction, decide to go back to their old position. Whether internal mobility succeeds or not, it could act to pacify the individual worker's anger and kept him working.

The final labour-control strategy I observed was de-politicization. In the workshop office, the role of the Party, the Youth League, and the Labour Union had diminished significantly. On the third floor of the workshop building, I saw an office named Party, League, and Union Associated Office, which meant the three organizations had become one. Except for the entertainment room, where some managers and workers played table tennis or billiards at noon, the associated office looked abandoned. Workers' grievances never reached this office. The restructuring reduced the political resources that could mobilize workers' militant action, thus increasing the effect of de-politicization on the shop floor. Though the materials for political studies were placed in the team room, workers never studied them: political studies could have nurtured workers' critical consciousness and legitimized their militancy – a potential labour resistance. In the workshop office, the photo of managers in political studies was seen as just a facade, and the ideological power was no longer a weapon for workers. Indeed, political ideology was excluded as much as possible. The same important measure of de-politicization was seen in the development of Party members. The Party membership was once seen as a sign of high status among workers, but I observed that workers no longer wanted to join the Party. More importantly, the Party did not seek to recruit new members among workers. No matter how workers perceived Party recruitment, managers made sure that the Party no longer instilled class-consciousness and ideas of mobilization among workers. In the manual-cutting team, there was only one worker, Lao Yan, who was a Party member, and he was re-employed after he retired. Therefore, the Communist Party was no longer the champion of shop-floor workers. De-politicization had, to some extent, nullified the source of workers' critical consciousness and organizational capacity.

Through these managerial methods, workers as a group were disassembled and reduced to individuals and unable to take collective action to prevent managerial despotism. The workshop managers had deprived workers of the resources, including leadership, ideological legitimacy, and organization, and had further utilized bonuses, social networks, and an internal labour market to diminish workers' dissatisfaction. Workers without insurgent capacity seemed only to passively accept fringe benefits and give lukewarm cooperation or compliance to production demands. However, given the structural nature of workers' and managers' antagonism, workers' discontent could never be eliminated. But what I experienced was that the disintegration of workers' collective consciousness forced discontent to be expressed along individual lines in the labour process.

In the Labour Process: Resistance or Despair?

We have seen a disorganized despotic factory regime and sophisticated control strategies dominated workers on the shop floor, and that these workers were disassembled into individuals and deprived of possibilities for collective resistance. All the managers had done, ultimately, was to control the labour process in order to improve output, but workers found ways to resist. Unfortunately, although these methods of resistance were effective, they reveal a kind of despair.

The most frequent method of resistance was slacking-off at work – reducing effort in a classic effort-bargain manner (Baldamus, 1961). In the manual-cutting team, workers controlled the semi-automatic machines' speed, cutting angle, and gas blending. Lao Lin, being the No. 2 line foreman, after being told by Xiao Xu (the team leader) to turn on four machines simultaneously, just turned on two and lowered their speed. He asked Xiao Xu who would receive the penalty if the machine cut the board out of trajectory while he was watching another machine? Xiao Xu just went away silently. I thought one man could deal with four machines and asked Lao Lin, and he told me:

> Damn! How much money will he pay me if I set four of them? Yes, I can deal with four machines, but it needs much effort! I don't think my income is worth such effort.

Perhaps because I assisted him, he finally turned on the third machine and let me take care of it. The digital lathe was automatic and just required a button to be pressed according to the blueprint. The lathe was fast but the operators could waste time by delaying moving the boards. Unlike the description in *Manufacturing Consent* given by Burawoy (1979), where he tried his best to secure the cooperation of the crib attendant and truck drivers for 'making out', here the operators (including the manual-cutting workers) were happy to see non-cooperation from the crane drivers and apportioning workers because they could have a rest and chat. Generally, the crane driver and apportioning workers must watch the cutting progress by themselves. Similar slack ways were so numerous that team leaders had to constantly walk around to check workers and it was cat-and-mouse between workers and team leaders.

A serious problem on the shop floor was the bad quality. This may have been the fault of the managers, who continuously increased quotas and demanded speed-ups. However, workers also ignored their responsibilities for procuring quality. There were quality controllers who were in charge of production quality, but I rarely saw them on the shop floor. Lao Liu told me that they knew nothing and lived an idle life. In other workshops making sub-hulls, Lao Liu said, quality controllers could be seen but were bribed by the outsourcing companies. It was hard to describe how terrible the production quality was. In the shipyard, the hulls made in workshops could not be assembled as a whole ship because they did not fit together properly and needed to be modified.

That problem had its origins in the workshop in which I did my participant observation – steel processing. It was not hard to imagine what would happen if a worker was forced to improve output under despotic management, low pay, and minimum coordination. In the lofting stop, a worker would mistake the type of steel board because he did not have the time to find it from the stacks of steel boards. The bevelling cutting would not be accurate and smooth because the worker was rushing to process so many boards. When I asked workers whether work could be done with a higher quality if the manager did not press so hard, a typical answer was:

> If you get such low bonuses no matter how good your work is, if you get the same bonus with the lazy egg, if the lazy egg gets more than you, will you pay much attention to your job? Stupid! Well, fuck this money.

This attitude was common among workers. They lost their sense of responsibility for quality control, so for example, if they saw that the blueprint was wrong or not suitable for cutting, they would not report it so that it could be revised. They did not care if the next shop could not easily process their products and just let the problematic board move on. In the sub-hull manufacturing shop, workers had to modify inaccuracies by heating and bending. Even if the workers' skills were up to the task, the steel's physical nature would be altered in this process. I didn't know the details of what happened in other shops, but the assembling problem in the shipyard highlighted the failure of quality control. OSIC published an internal magazine called *Quality Quarterly* hoping to improve quality. The writers of this magazine were workshop staff, not from workers who knew most about quality. In an OSIC newspaper an article contained this passage:

> ... But, (we) must recognize in the process of shipbuilding, the phenomena that violates procedure and standard ... led to internal and external quality problems. Recently, some ships were sent back for repair which damaged OSIC's image and reputation.

Closely linked to production quality, the workers' skill was also another problem. To express discontent, workers lowered production quality. If this was occasional before, it had become generic on the shop floor during my fieldwork. The apprentices could no longer get the best guidance from the masters who had acquired bad working habits. As there were no incentives for good quality work, workers did not care how skilful they were. In the skill test, there were young workers who cheated on the exam or bribed the chief examiner to get the certificates for their skill level. Surprisingly, in one test held by a US client who wanted to make sure there were an adequate number of high-skilled workers for his project, 60 per cent of the welders in the hull assembling workshop (who represent the highest-skilled workers in OSIC) did not pass the test. But workers felt no shame because they had no reason to assume that high skill made a difference to their work or wages. Without adequate rewards and time to do quality work, the situation I experienced constituted a degradation of workers' skills and could be seen as revenge for the despotic production regime.

Therefore, through slacking-off, bad quality control, and degradation of skill, workers aimed to partially control their individual labour process in a negative manner. They did what they could do, using individual strategies, to disrupt the labour process at the cost of their reputation and skill. But I judge this more as a kind of despair than resistance. So the state workers were not only de-collectivized into individual actors, but they were also degraded to what they themselves referred to as a category of 'stink workers'.

In this section, I have described how workshop managers reorganized the managerial structure on the shop floor, how shop-floor managers used the strategies of labour control to get cooperation and disorganize workers into isolated individual actors, and how state workers resisted managers by degrading their skills and lowering product quality. Managers have created a disorganized despotic factory regime. Though workers were tightly dominated by managers and had to provide minimal cooperation in production, their discontent in their hearts and minds never disappeared. They resisted, or expressed despair, in various ways. But managers appeared not to care about workers' resistance as long as production quotas were fulfilled. Workers' individual approaches to resistance degraded themselves. It therefore appeared that workers could not organize themselves to resist the despotic factory regime collectively.

Conclusion

Based on my participant observation, I suggest that a disorganized despotic factory regime was constructed in OSIF. For the state workers, state intervention, like the social-security schemes and labour codes, did not protect them from despotism. The social-security reforms had the indirect effect of blocking the mobility of skilled workers and forcing them to remain in their current position, while the enterprise bureaucrats violated the labour-related laws at will. The ability of the workers to form independent organizations, which is the most powerful way for workers to defend their interests, was lacking. Though the institutional arrangements had changed compared to that in the 1990s and early 2000s, these rules still formed an uncoordinated institutional context that indulged managerial despotism in the SOE. In OSIC, though supervised by central government, enterprise bureaucrats legally profited through insider contracting, which encouraged mid-managers to become independent entrepreneurs and imposed despotism and coercion on the shop floor. In order to maximize their interests, managers also made deals with outsourcing companies. This kind of inner economic system, however, needed sophisticated controls to assure the minimum cooperation of workers and adequate output in order to maintain itself.

On the shop floor, the struggle occurred between workshop managers, shop-floor managers, and workers. We should remember that at an earlier period, shop-floor managers shared interests and identity with workers, including bonus distribution and working experience. As such they identified themselves more with workers than workshop managers. Thus, although there was an adverse institutional context and factory organization, workers still controlled the shop floor, and were effectively led by shop-floor managers. However, the changes in managerial and distributional structures altered that situation. Shop-floor managers were absorbed into a bureaucratic management layer, sharing interests with officers and higher-ups instead of workers. Workers not only lost their leadership, but under the new team leaders' strategies, they also lost their solidarity, critical consciousness, and resistant morale. They were confined in a fictitious social network they never trusted. However, workers never ceased to show their discontent. Deprived of all possibilities of collective action, workers were forced to defend their position in the only way left to them: slacking-off, bad quality control, bad skill practice, theft, and so on, through which they disrupted the labour process instead of controlling it. In such a factory regime, workers not only fragmented into individual actors who could not challenge the power and oppression any more, but they also became degraded into a cynical, sluggish, and skill-declined set of individuals.

Beyond the examination of the factory regime and fragmented workers, my analysis can be extended to discuss the politics of production and class relations in a Chinese central SOE. According to Burawoy's (1985) analytic framework, a paternalistic factory regime will emerge when there are five factors: external state intervention, complete separation from the means of subsistence, real subsumption of labour, surplus labour supply, and limited inter-firm competition. However, in my field, there was no such paternalistic factory regime. I therefore question why a disorganized despotic factory regime exists even though the five variables mentioned by Burawoy were present. Though further inquiry is needed, I believe that the relationship among state, enterprise, and market might be the avenue to further explore the determinants of despotism in the SOE sector. Specifically, it is political power that connects the three parts and creates a model of market economy. Top managers in central SOEs, whom I call 'enterprise bureaucrats', have a double status – entrepreneurs and high bureaucratic officials. Externally, they used the advanced industrial power, which essentially came from the support of state power, to seize the market, and internally, they used the bureaucratic power to practice autonomy – reorganizing management and operations – through which they could grab profits. In addition, state intervention in the market was uncoordinated. The state enacted laws to protect workers, but blocked the approach that could best utilize the law – an independent labour union. And the low wage level in the labour market was also shaped by the state. We can see not only the pure economic relations between market and production, but also grasp the political relations between them. The unique model of connection among state, enterprise, and market created a background where the five variables mentioned above could form a very different factory regime. Therefore, to understand production politics, we must consider the relationship among state, enterprise, and market in each concrete instance.

REFERENCES

Baldamus, W. (1961) *Efficiency and Effort: An Analysis of Industrial Administration*, London: Tavistock Press.

Burawoy, M. (1979) *Manufacturing Consent: Changes in the Labour Process Under Monopoly Capitalism*, Chicago: University of Chicago Press.

Burawoy, M. (1983) 'Between the Labour Process and the State: the Changing Face of Factory Regimes under Advanced Capitalism', *American Sociological Review*, 48(5): 587–605.

Burawoy, M. (1985) *The Politics of Production: Factory Regimes under Capitalism and Socialism*, London: Verso.

Clawson, D. (1980) *Bureaucracy and the Labour Process: The Transformation of United States Industry, 1860 – 1920*, New York: Monthly Review Press.

Lee, C. K. (1998) *Gender and the South China Miracle: Two Worlds of Factory Women*, Berkeley and Los Angeles: University of California Press.

Lee, C. K. (1999) 'From Organized Dependence to Disorganized Despotism: Changing Labour Regimes in Chinese Factories', *The China Quarterly*, 157: 44–71.
▶

▶

Lee, C. K. (2002) 'From the Specter of Mao to the Spirit of the Law: Labour Insurgency in China', *Theory and Society*, 31(2): 189–228.

Lee, C. K. (2007) *Against the Law: Labour Protests in China's Rustbelt and Sunbelt*, Berkeley and Los Angeles: University of California Press.

Lee, C. K. and Shen, Y. (2009) 'The Paradox and Possibility for a Public Sociology of Labour in China', *Work and Occupations*, 36(2): 110–125.

Pun, N. (2005) *Made in China: Women Factory Workers in a Global Workplace*, Durham and London: Duke University Press.

Smith, C. (2006) 'The Double Indeterminacy of Labour Power: Labour Effort and Labour Mobility', *Work, Employment and Society*, 20(2): 389–402.

The Making of a Dualistic Labour Regime: Changing Labour Process and Power Relations in a Chinese State-Owned Enterprise under Globalization

4

Wenjuan Jia

Andrew Walder's influential formulation of "neo-traditionalism" provides a theoretical starting point for summarizing the character of the labour regime in China's factories during the Maoist era. Workers were a minority within a largely peasant society. The factory was not only an economic organization but also a fundamental unit for political integration and social control in state-socialist China. Under the *danwei*, or work unit, system, which was an institutional apparatus of social control and resource distribution, workers got their social identity, chances for development, welfare, and all living resources from the factory. 'Organized dependency' – whereby workers were socially and economically dependent on the enterprises, politically dependent on the party, and personally dependent on superiors – constituted the basis for management domination in the workplace during the Maoist era (Walder, 1988; Lee, 1999). Burawoy believed that the bureaucratic despotic regime that he witnessed corresponds to the one described by Walder. Under the bureaucratic despotic regime, 'management uses its monopoly over consumer goods to reward a leading cadre of activists ... who become involved in directing production, set norms to be emulated, or surveil rank-and-file workers' (Burawoy, 1992: 33).

However, the 'organized dependency' did not necessarily lead to the 'bureaucratic despotic' character of labour control for three reasons. Firstly, the 'Angang constitution', the guiding principle of state-owned enterprise (SOE) management which was issued by Mao Zedong, demanded that 'cadres should participate in production; workers should participate in management; unreasonable rules should be abandoned; workers, cadres and the technicians should cooperate with each other'. So the workers had formal authority to criticize managers. Secondly, under state socialism, supply constraints generate continual reorganization of the labour process.[1] Workers were granted autonomy during the labour process to deal with the continually changing production requirements (Burawoy, 1985: 163). Finally, migration from rural areas to cities was forbidden under the regulation of the 'household registration system', which protected the SOE workers from market competition posed by the mass of peasants who were effectively locked in the countryside. The *danwei* provided SOE workers with permanent membership and sufficient social welfare, which also granted them considerable power.

In the 1990s, the labour regime in SOEs dramatically changed. Many scholars found that the role of the Party in overseeing enterprise declined, and the managerial autonomy had enhanced, and many new methods of labour control were used. For example, in their research conducted in three state cotton mills located in Henan province, Zhao and Nichols reported that enterprises had created a strict labour-control system including quota increases and speed-ups, longer working hours, new draconian controls over labour attendance, and monetary sanctions and penalties (Zhao & Nichols, 1996). A similar situation was noted by Ching-Kwan Lee. She found a regime of 'disorganized despotism' had been established in China's SOEs, which was characterized by a coercive mode of labour control, with the application of economic penalties, proliferation of shop-floor conflict, and the demise of patron-clientalism (Lee, 1999). Under the situation of uneven implementation of social insurance, welfare commodification, and the declining influence of the party and trade unions, workers in SOEs faced unilateral reliance on the enterprises, which forced them to accept this despotic labour regime.

After the establishment of the State-owned Assets Supervision and Administration Commission (SASAC) in 2003, the labour regime in China's state sector departed from 'organized dependency', and became increasingly similar to other sectors. Through comparing two reformed SOEs in Anhui province, Zhao Wei found that the SOE adopted equally strict labour controls over workers, as in private enterprise (Zhao, 2010). Gallagher (2005) has also argued that labour control and production management in China's SOEs became increasingly similar to that of foreign capital invested enterprises.

In 2008, the People's Republic of China (PRC) Labour Contract Law was implemented, which made enterprises face a stricter legal environment. The PRC Social Insurance Law, which was issued in 2010, detailed the payment and expenditure of endowment insurance, employment injury insurance, unemployment insurance, health insurance, and maternity insurance. With the labour contract law, management could not dismiss a worker without a reasonable cause. And with the support of the social insurance system, the SOE workers were not afraid of losing their jobs. What, therefore, is the character of the labour regime in China's SOEs under these changed social and institutional conditions?

In this chapter I will discuss a newly emerging labour regime based on my investigation in a state-owned heavy machinery factory from 2010 to 2013, located in Guangzhou city. This labour regime is based on the concept of 'working dualism', which was formed when the managers invited the subcontractors' teams into the workplace to directly supplement employed workers. The use of the so-called 'internal subcontract system', which means that contractors' teams are invited into the workplace and do the same work as the formal workers, has changed the power relations in the workplace dramatically, and put all the directly employed workers in a relatively peripheral position. Zhang Lu has found a hybrid factory regime operating in some of China's automobile firms. This hybrid regime was called a 'lean-and-dual' regime, which combines both hegemonic and despotic elements. Under this regime, 'hegemonic relations have been established between management and formal workers', while despotic labour control characterizes the condition for temporary agency workers (Zhang, 2008: 24). The main finding of this chapter is that with the rise of the 'internal subcontract system' a dualistic labour regime was also adopted by the South Factory where I did my investigation. However, in contrast to the situation in the automobile industry, in South Factory different worker groups were under diverse systems of labour control, with both formal workers and informal workers in a peripheral position relative to the core role of emerging subcontractors' labour teams in the workplace.

South Factory and the Rise of the 'Internal Subcontract System'

A Brief History of the South Factory and the PV Branch

The South Factory is a state-owned heavy machinery enterprise in Guangzhou city. Using industrial ethnography, I did field research in the pressure vessel (PV) branch of this factory from November 2010 to July 2011 and re-visited the factory in 2013. The South Factory was established in 1953 and was one of the six heavy machinery enterprises that the 'First Industrial Bureau of PRC First Ministry of Machinery Industry' set up across the country to develop Chinese machinery industry. It was the largest general machinery enterprise in Southern China during the whole Maoist era, with more than 6,000 employees at its peak. Similar to the development path of many SOEs in the Maoist era, the South Factory had gone through an extremely 'glorious period'. In the 1990s, the South Factory began to develop diversified businesses and established 43 subsidiaries, most of which entered serious economic difficulty around 2000. In order to lighten the economic burden, the South Factory laid off more than 3,000 workers between 2002 and 2003, and at the time of my research the number of employees in the whole factory was less than 1,000.

After 2001, the year when China entered the WTO, the South Factory began to cooperate with a German Company, Heinrich, to produce a new product: the shield machine. This cooperation turned out to be an invaluable opportunity for the South Factory to change its production methods. Heinrich is one of the largest tunnelling machine manufacturers in the world, with more than 5,000 employees internationally and controlling more than 70 per cent of the European market before it entered China.[2] After China's entrance into the WTO, Heinrich began to capture the Chinese tunnelling-machine market by cooperating with the local SOEs in Sichuan, Beijing, and elsewhere to establish an original equipment manufacturer (OEM) base and an assembly base. The South Factory had been a partner with Heinrich in South China since 2001, manufacturing machine bodies, cutter heads and large structural components of the shield machine for Heinrich. Up until 2005, 16 sets of shield tunnelling machines had been manufactured under the cooperation of the two enterprises, of which half were used in the subway tunnel construction in Guangzhou City while the other half were sold to Beijing, Tianjin, and Singapore.[3] After 2012, Heinrich occupied more than 70 per cent of China's shield machine market.[4]

The cooperation with Heinrich had totally changed the product structure and technologies of the PV branch of the South Factory. Before 2001, the PV branch was mainly engaged in independently designing and manufacturing anti-acid pumps and PVs of various metals with large numbers of professional engineers and technical workers. After cooperating with Heinrich, the main job of the PV branch was the manufacture of larger structural components, whose production, based on conventional welding, was relatively simple with lower technical-skill requirements. This was different from the more technically complex rivet and weld processes that dominated earlier production. During the following period, the shield machine OEM business suppressed the design and manufacturing business of the PV branch. After 2013, the South Factory abandoned PV manufacture, and became exclusively an OEM workshop of Heinrich.

During this period, the production process of the PV branch also went through a transformation. During the initial cooperation of the South Factory with Heinrich, managers implemented the 'modern enterprise management system' – epitomized by the TQC (Total Quality Control) and 5S system – (Sustain, Sort, Set, Shine and Standardize) in the workshop. A few tasks in the PV branch began to be outsourced to contractors' teams in 2001, and by 2008, a great deal of work had been outsourced. During fieldwork in the South Factory (from 2010 to 2011), there were eight contractors' teams in the workshop of the PV branch – covering painting, shelf-making, cleaning, production, and four teams for plug welding, which together occupied a relatively important position in the workshop. After 2013, the number of rivet-welding contractors' teams increased to six, higher than the rivet welding teams of the PV branch.

The Internal Subcontract System and the Contractors' Teams in the Workplace

The subcontract system is a mode of work organization based on in-sourcing production and a piecework wage system. Contractors, the middlemen between the capitalist and the worker, don't own the means of production, but some of them own the tools for production, and control the production process. The rewards that contractors sought came from the difference between the price which the capitalist pays, and the part of that which actually reaches the worker. During my field work, I found that the management of the South Factory had invited four contractor's teams into the workplace, and provided them with production space, the means of production, including tools. The contractors were responsible for the recruitment of their own workers, and undertook certain production tasks. As the subcontractors worked in the enterprise workplace, rather than in the contractor's workshop, it was named 'internal subcontracting'.[5]

In 2013, the contractors' teams assumed a quarter of the total manufacturing tasks of the PV branch, and undertook two-thirds of the rivet welding tasks. During normal production time, there were around 80 to 100 informal workers from contractors' teams involved in production, and during the rush or crush time, the population of informal workers increased to around 200. However, the population of the formal rivet welding workers of the PV branch was fewer than 55. Why did the PV branch of the South Factory introduce the contractors' teams in such high numbers after 2008?

Firstly, the PV Branch needed more flexible workers under the tightening of the time available to produce orders in the changing global economy. In the globalization era, the Western enterprises had taken the strategy of "spatial fix"and moved their manufacturing sites to the Global South, in order to escape from the trade unions and high cost labour in their own country (Silver, 2003). David Harvey used the concept of the "flexible accumulation" to summarize the character of the capital accumulation under postmodernity (Harvey, 1991). When the South Factory started international shield machine production in 2001, it also got involved in the process of flexible accumulation. The production process of the PV branch had changed in two ways under flexible accumulation. On one hand, the time to produce orders was tightened, and the PV branch would be punished by Heinrich with an overdue fine, or even by the revocation of the order, if it failed to be fulfilled on time. The vice director of the South Factory told me: 'The delivery period was not enough, and it will definitely be continually shortened in the future! Only if we speed up the production will we survive in this market.'[6] On the other hand, a few sections – especially the rivet welding section – became extremely important relative to the past when all sections were equally important. Whether the tasks could be fulfilled on time highly depended on the production speed of the rivet welding section, rather than how well different sections coordinated with each other.

After the global financial crisis in 2008, Chinese central government had invested 2.9 trillion yuan into the construction of infrastructure (Ren & Jia, 2009), which promoted the development of the subway system in cities and high-speed railway, and the market for the shield machine was significantly expanded. A big part of this market was controlled by Heinrich, which meant its OEM workshop, the PV branch, received overwhelming orders. The challenge for the management was to recruit a large number of workers when needed, and to dismiss them when the market became tight. And it so happened that there were numbers of rivet welding subcontractors in the Pearl River Delta, which supplied informal and flexible workers to the heavy machinery enterprises in this area. Actually, the PV branch started to introduce the subcontractors into the workplace in 2001, and after 2008, both the scale and the numbers of the subcontractors' teams were dramatically expanded. The participation in the international production process, and the changing environment of the global economy around 2008 became one of the strengths which made the PV branch speed up production, and introduce more internal subcontractors into the workplace.

Secondly, the South Factory introduced more contractors' teams into the workplace in order to take advantage of the cheaper informal labourers following the enforcement of the Labour Contract Law after 2008. This law had detailed and rigorous provisions about employment relationships, working conditions, social insurance, labour protection, length of the working day, and so on. Since the labour contract law also clearly stipulated penalty provisions for behaviours breaching regulations, there were very limited grey areas available for enterprises to deviate from the law (Huang, 2013). The labour contract law increased the cost of employing large numbers of formal or directly recruited workers, and it introduced rigidity into labour usage so that employers began to move towards more flexible deployment of labour. The vice director of the South Factory told me:

> After the implementation of the Labour Contract Law, you cannot hire too many formal workers. You know, our tasks are not easy to anticipate, sometimes we have too much, but sometimes we don't have enough tasks to do. If you hire too many formal workers, you know, according to the Labour Contract Law, you will need to pay them money, buy social insurance for them, and what's more, if you want to dismiss them, you will have to pay a lot of compensation for them. If you don't follow the law, you will be definitely punished once you are reported. The fine is too much! (Interview: HKJ, 2011-06-30)

However, because only the formal labour market is under strict supervision of the law, the informal labour market in China became more attractive to employers. The informal employment system revived and flourished as a centrepiece rather than as an appendage of the production system (Harvey, 1991:152). Research by Lee and Kofman (Lee & Kofman, 2012) found that informally employed workers accounted for 46–68 per cent of the labour force in China's cities, and the percentage is presently rising. Many enterprises in China profited from the use of informal workers, and according to my interview with the vice director of the South Factory, there were two benefits:

> The contractors' teams have helped us with many problems. Firstly, we can easily adjust the amount of teams, and also the amount of labourers simultaneously, according to our orders during a given period. Secondly, we don't have any labour contracts with informal workers; they are the responsibility of the contractors. That means the contractors are responsible for their wage, social insurance, training, work-related injury, and all the other things. Under these conditions, our labour costs can be decreased significantly.
>
> (Interview: HKJ, 2011-06-30)

In practice, the informal workers have not signed any contracts with either of their bosses, the South Factory or the individual contractors. Informal employment cheapened the costs of hiring and firing, and allowed the firms to flexibly adjust labour supply to demand without pushing up labour costs.

Thirdly, management invited the contractors' teams into the workplace in order to replace the more rebellious formally employed SOE workers. More than 3,000 employees were dismissed between 2001 and 2003 in the South Factory, and the modern-enterprise-management system was implemented in the workplace. From 2003 to 2006, lean production, the 5S system, the TQC, and the 'codes of conduct' were implemented in the workplace. The formal workers found out that not only had all the former welfare been cancelled and wages frozen at the original level without any increments, but also the management system became increasingly strict. Many formal workers were born in the 1950s, started to work in the South Factory in the 1970s, were in their fifties, had gone through the Maoist era, and were influenced by the anti-officialdom tradition. These SOE workers were very dissatisfied with both their low wages and the new system of management control. One female worker told me:

> Our workers are neither stupid nor dull; we just had lower education status than them (the management). To speak bluntly, they (the management) had a little more fortune than us, and they became leaders. However, they shouldn't ignore workers' feeling and situation; our wages haven't changed for many years, and they even want us to work harder now! (Interview: ZJ, 2011-07-03)

The formal workers in the South Factory have been taking various opportunities to express their dissatisfaction with the new 'interference management' by strategically disobeying, slowing down, shutting down, arguing, even threatening management, and by other methods since 2006. Influenced by this workplace culture, a new generation of newly-employed migrant workers and young workers from technical school also gradually participated in the conflicts with the management. An Qi, a young worker who had been working at the PV branch for one year, complained about the wage system, just like his master. He told me:

> This system should be OK, but the situation now is unfair. They (the management) will cut your quota if you overfulfill the tasks. I don't know why they do this; this is too weird and also stupid. Anyway, I'm not very worried, because my master will bargain with them. He is very authoritative here, and I will operate the machine for him. (Interview: AQ, 2011-02-28)

Managers were troubled by the growing solidarity among different generations of workers. The chief of the personnel department said: 'You know, even the young men learned how to goldbrick from their masters, and many of them leave the South Factory in one year'. The quality assurance manager was worried by workers' disobedience; he told me:

> The long-term education of 'master of the house' in China has been too much! Everyone is a master, so who will follow your management? No one! A worker said his kid got sick, and then refused to work overtime. Some workers shouted at me in public: 'Fire me! I will treat you for dinner tomorrow if you fire me today!' They don't work seriously, they feel they are formal workers and we dare not do anything to them. (Interview: FXF, 2013-11-30)

The conflict between formal workers and the management grew worse after 2008. As the slowdown from the world recession affected the workplace, the required delivery period of the shield machine became shorter. It was difficult for management to dismiss the rebellious workers for two reasons. Firstly, it's impossible to fire all the workers and secondly, the formal workers signed a 'non-fixed-term contract' with the South Factory after the implementation of the labour contract law, so they could not be dismissed without good reason. This situation made management more disposed to increase the numbers of contractors' teams. The chief of the production department told me:

> You know, when our workers feel dissatisfied, they will either quarrel with you or just slow down. [I say to them] it's OK if you don't want to do this work, I can invite the informal workers to do it, but you should stand aside, you cannot occupy the machine. We have many contractors' teams, so I would say to the formal workers: If you don't want to work, I will let other people to do your work, and let them to earn your money. (Interview: MQT, 2013-11-30)

Braverman, following Marx, suggested that in capitalist societies, there was always a 'pool of unused labour', an 'industrial reserve army', which could be used to keep the value of labour power at the level of subsistence for the individual or below the level of subsistence for the family (Braverman, 1998: 323). The informal workers used through the subcontracting practices at South Factory were members of this 'reserve army of labour', and they were used by the management not only as flexible labour, but also as a threat to the conditions of work, security and pay of formal workers, their engagement making formal workers acutely aware that they were themselves replaceable.

The Dualistic Labour Regime Under the 'Internal Subcontract System'

In the development of the Marxist labour theory of value, Braverman believed that 'labour, like the life process and bodily functions, is an inalienable property of the human individual' (Braverman, 1998: 37). What the worker sells, and what the capitalist buys, is not an agreed amount of labour, but the power to labour over an agreed period of time. So what the capitalist purchased is an uncertain quality and quantity of labour power, which is variable in potential rather than in reality. So, 'the labour process has become the responsibility of the capitalist', and during which the capitalist will try to get full usefulness of the labour power he has bought (Braverman, 1998: 39). However, the labour process is not only economical and technical, it is also political. The notion of 'labour regime' refers to the overall political form of production, including the political effects of the labour process and the political apparatuses of production (Burawoy, 1985: 87). The question of the character of the labour regime of the South Factory, as an SOE and part of China's market reform and integration into global capitalism is central to this chapter.

Before 2008, when the South Factory introduced the contractors' teams on a large scale, formal workers were the subjects of management control. A despotic regime, with a set of self-regulating practices, had been set up in the workshop to restrict the behaviour of workers. This regime encountered serious difficulties when workers started to resist management within the wider formation of more positive labour laws and a social insurance system. Based on his experience of a machinery factory in Chicago, Burawoy postulated that under monopoly capitalism it was state provision of welfare that proves the undoing of despotic regimes (Burawoy, 1985). However, in South Factory, an SOE, the transition to 'market hegemony' was stalled. Instead, the uneven implementation of the Labour Contract Law and widespread informal labour market combined to produce a new kind of labour regime, what I call a 'dualistic labour regime'. Dualism was formed when the managers invited contractors' teams into the workplace on an extended basis. Although full-time workers and outsourced workers work at the same production site, there are great differences in their employment status, skill level, payment method, social security and welfare, and labour control. These can be outlined in more detail.

Contractors' teams: patriarchal control and the contractor's kingdom

The organizational mode for contractors' teams is the 'labour contracting system' which is a special organizational form for labour employment, use, and management. Marx argued that there are two basic forms of a 'hierarchically organized system of exploitation and oppression': the first form is the 'subletting of labour', and that 'the gain of the middlemen comes entirely from the difference between the labour-price which the capitalist pays, and the part of the price which they actually allow to reach the labourer'. And under the second form is the 'internal subcontract', where 'piece-wage allows the capitalist to make a contract for so much per piece with the head labourer – in manufactures with the chief of some group ... at a price for which the head labourer himself undertakes the enlisting and payment of his assistant work people' (Marx, 1992: 341). The outsourced team of the South Factory looked similar to the second form of the hierarchically organized system. Under this form of employment, the individual contractor recruited their own labourers and undertook a certain amount of work. The contractors neither sign any contract with their workers, nor purchase social insurance for them, which makes the employment and use of this labour force quite flexible and cheap – a form of 'social dumping' whereby informal workers fall outside the net of security provided to formal workers.

Apart from the modern outsourcing system, 'pre-modernity' and 'abnormality' are the important features of the subcontractor's system. Most of the informal workers in the contractors' teams were under 20 or over 50 years old. They either lacked work experience or found difficulty finding formal work as discharged workers. Similar to construction workers, the informal workers in the South Factory could not find work through formal markets, and therefore they were dependent on contractors to bring them into the workplace. Workers in a contractor's team always came from the same township, even the same village, and they were relatives, friends, or classmates. Sharing common language, eating habits, and dress that was different from the formal workers in the South Factory, the contractors' teams congregated into separate 'contractors' kingdoms' within the workplace. Most of the informal workers in contractors' teams found work after they left junior middle school; most of them had not been to high school. They had learned simple hand-soldering skills and oxygen-welding skills from more experienced workers in their teams. Most of the contractors' teams worked on two shifts with more than ten hours per shift.

The informal workers in the contractors' teams were strongly influenced by the patriarchal culture of traditional community, and the management mode of labour contracting caters to this culture. Take, for example, one of the rivet-welding teams which came from Hubei province; all the informal workers were managed by a foreman, Mr Huang, who was 38 years old, and under the authorization of the contractor. Mr Huang received RMB 6,000 per month, and the labour contractor not only purchased five kinds of social insurance and housing funds for him, but allocated him a car. Just like a patriarch of a big family, the foreman was strict, energetic and aggressive, dominating younger workers, which naturalized his overall authority. This is simple patriarchal or personal control – arbitrary or random control executed by contractors and variable according to the personality of the contractor (Edwards, 1979).

There were three aspects to the implementation of this regime. Firstly, wage-effort was structured by contractors to motivate informal workers. They were not paid by piece work, but fixed wages, according to their skill levels and working performance. In the rivet-welding team which came from Hubei province, the maximum monthly wage was RMB 6,000, the minimum wage was RMB 2,500, and the average monthly wage was between RMB 3,500 and RMB 4,000. As South Factory paid contractors at the end of a project, the contractor team was not delayed in payment. In 2011, the minimum monthly wage of a worker in Guangzhou city was RMB 1,300, the average wage of all the employees in Guangdong Province was RMB 3,763, and the average in Guangzhou city was RMB 4,789, so the wage of the informal workers was high enough to motivate them to work hard. When I asked a young informal worker why he worked so hard, he answered: 'To make money! Our wage is twice the formal worker's wage; it's really high!'

The insecurity and uncertainty was also a reason for driving informal workers' productivity. Although the level of wage was reasonable, the informal workers had no idea about their exact payment, which was determined by the foreman or the contractor. Without social insurance and social welfare, the wage was the only thing on which the informal workers' could rely, and thus the informal workers needed to obey the contractor in order to survive.

Secondly, informal workers worked harder than formal workers in the South Factory, due to tighter monitoring by foremen. Mr Huang, the foreman of the Hubei team, came to the workplace very early in the morning in order to check informal workers' attendance; if the workers were late for work, they were berated and fined. Mr Huang watched informal workers all the time, except when he was away discussing issues with managers. Once, when I was talking with a welding worker, Qing, two more workers were coming near in order to join us, Mr Huang walked to us cautiously and doubtfully, asking one of the formal workers what we were talking about. Qing was very scared and equivocated with Mr Huang, which made him angry. He said to me: 'Don't talk with them now! You will have enough time to talk after work! Go to work!' Qing curled his lip for a little bit and then lowered his head to weld a huge steel sheet. Several days later, I asked Qing:' 'You're not on a piece-rate wage system, so why do you still work so hard?' Qing took a glance at Mr Huang who was in the distance, and told me: 'Huang has been watching us...', and then lowered his head again. (Interview, Qing, 2011–03–02)

Thirdly, there is the very real threat of dismissal for informal workers. As stated above, if an informal worker does not work hard enough, he will be exhorted or berated; if this worker does not learn a lesson and continues to be sluggish at work, his wages would be reduced, and if monetary punishment has no effect, the worker would be fired. More seriously, if an informal worker makes trouble, such as starting a slowdown, fighting with the foreman, and showing disobedience towards the foreman, he would be blacklisted. There was a tight-community in the industry and contractors all know each other well, so blacklisting could be enforced. And if this worker returned to his hometown, his reputation in the 'rural community' would be damaged and other contractors would not be willing to hire him. Young informal workers who took urban jobs and possessed low technical skills were greatly restrained by these threats. Faced with such threats, workers were willing to work hard to make money.

Indulgent labour control and the peripheral position of the formal workers

Most formal, directly employed workers in the South Factory were locals, with an average age of 45.6 years; the average age of the machine operation section of PV branch was even higher – among the 78 workers, there were only 11 who were under 30. Some workers were directly assigned to the factory after their graduation from the technician school of the South Factory, some entered the factory by replacing a parent, some were migrant workers, and some were recruited by the factory from other technical schools. Most of the formal workers were skilled and some of them had obtained a technician certificate. Unlike the informal workers, all of the formal workers had signed a labour contract with the

South Factory, and also benefitted from the five kinds of social insurances and the housing fund. Under the Labour Contract Law regulation, the South Factory could not force workers to work overtime, punish them with fines, or fire them without reasonable grounds.

As mentioned above, the formal workers had fought against the enforcement of the modern enterprise management system by slowdowns and disobedience. After the development of the protective legal system, management found it even more difficult to control the workers' labour process. As trying to change the behaviour of formal workers was judged impractical, a common strategy adopted by production management was what could be called 'indulgent control' (Gouldner, 1954).[7] However, the purpose of 'indulgent control' was not to stimulate an agreement of workers on labour output, but to reduce the rights of formal workers in the working process, and decrease the workers' destruction of production caused by their resistance. The permissive management of South Factory involved the following two methods:

First, the *low-basic-wage strategy*. In 2010, the average wage of the employees in Guangzhou city was RMB 4,541, but the average monthly wage of workers of the PV branch of the South Factory was only RMB 2,100. After 2011, the PV branch of the South Factory implemented a piece-rate wage system, and a worker's wages included two parts: the basic wage and the bonus. The basic wage was between 1,300 and 2,200 RMB according to differences of positions and technical levels. The mechanical operator would get the basic wage if his/her working hours exceeded 174 a month, otherwise the worker would only receive the minimum wage of the Guangzhou city, which was 1,300 RMB in 2011. The bonus was calculated according to the unit price of a working hour, quantity of the extra working hours, and the 'weight',[8] and the amount of bonus totally depended upon the workload and the production efficiency of workers.

Although formal workers enjoyed both social insurance and the policy benefits, their wage was not enough to sustain the reproduction of their labour power: their subsistence. The management established the piece-rate system to stimulate labour productivity, decrease workers' slowdown, and make workers work harder, despite them having access to social insurance. The vice director of the South Factory told me:

It will be fine if the worker doesn't want to work hard. Of course, he can get the five kinds of social insurance and also the housing fund. I can only afford to pay him RMB 1,300 monthly. However, the wage is too limited to raise his family. But if you work hard enough, you can earn more than four thousand yuan! (Interview: HKJ, 2011-06-30)

Second, the *indulgent labour discipline*. Slack labour discipline was the other aspect of indulgent labour control. The chief of the production department told me: 'I don't care how they finish their work. If you finish more work, you will make more money, and if you finish less work, you will lose your own money'. (Interview: MQT, 2013-11-30)

Under the 'indulgent labour discipline', managers no longer needed to pay attention to the production process of the formal workers, what they needed to do was to pay the workers money according to their working hours; the most important work of a working section leader was neither to assign the work to workers nor urge the workers to finish their jobs, but to fill various types of outsourcing forms, and coordinate with contractors' teams. Such management methods were difficult to accept for the formal workers. Workers used to adopt the method of slowdown and slovenliness to show their dissatisfaction; however, after the implementation of 'indulgent labour control', the 'collective inaction' would not help workers gain the attention of management, but rather it would lead to a decrease in their wages.

Workers' Interest Cognition under the Dualistic Labour Regime

The informal workers and the formal workers were not only in different culture systems (different languages, uniforms, living habits, and behaviours), but also in different labour regimes, so the two worker groups were mutually isolated from each other, despite being in the same workplace. Under such conditions, the manager can use divide and rule, using one group to threaten the other. The formal workers were protected by the existing laws and social welfare system, but they had gradually been pushed into the margins of the production system; and the informal workers had emerged as the main labour force in the flexible production system, although they were neither protected by the laws nor social insurance. Both the formal and informal workers were in peripheral positions, but with seemingly separate interests. We need to look in more detail at their relative interests.

Outsourced workers: 'bottom-line benefit' and the internalization of labour–capital conflict

Cai divided workers' benefits into 'bottom-line benefits' and 'incremental benefits'. Bottom-line benefits referred to the basic benefits which were under the protection of laws and regulations within well-defined criteria, and individuals who sought these benefits could find solutions through arbitration or litigation (Cai, 2010). Informal workers' interest recognition was established on the basis of the 'bottom-line benefit', and they would feel deprived only when they lost these basic interests. When I asked Ning, a welder, whether the 'five insurances and housing fund' was important to him, he answered dismissively: 'Who cares! My wage is two times more than them (formal worker)!' Although the outsourced workers suffered from poorer working conditions, high-intensity working and insufficient labour protection, they did not complain due to the higher wages, and provision of meals and accommodation. (Interview: Ning, 2011-03-02)

The informal workers didn't suffer wage delays, but they were under the threat of job-related injury. The former director of South Factory told me that the contractor was responsible for informal workers' welfare and job security. The headman used private settlements for occupational injuries. For example, A. Xiang, an informal welder, cut his instep due to carelessness during work. The contractor terminated his employment after paying his medical costs, the current month's wage, and several thousand yuan in compensation.

Along with the outsourcing of products, conflict between labour and capital was also internalized in the contractor team. The conditions and sentiments of outsourced workers did not bring trouble to the South Factory, such as disturbing production schedule, government investigations, increases in labour costs, and damaged reputation. Like a subcontractors' team on a construction site, the contractors' teams function as the 'isolation belt' and 'pressure relief valve' between outsourced workers and the South Factory, which hid the actual employment relationship between the informal workers and the factory.

Formal workers: the 'incremental benefit' and the continuous conflict between labour and capital

Unlike the informal workers, many formal workers had been through the Maoist era, and had criticized capitalism at that time. Under the influence of *danwei* culture, the formal workers believed that the value of labour should be respected, and their living conditions should be improved together with national economic development and company profitability. Their demands were focused on 'incremental benefits', which could only be expressed through collective action.

Actually, before the contractors' team were introduced, formal workers were dissatisfied with the slow increase in wages and the degradation of their social position. Under such conditions, they rebelled if they did not get a high temperature subsidy on time, or their 'red envelopes' after the Spring Festival.

The introduction of informal workers affected formal workers significantly. On one hand, as urgent and large deliveries were assigned to the contractors' teams, the production task of formal workers was greatly reduced. On the other hand, when producing the same products, the price for the outsourcing team was greater than for the formal workers' team. This naturally created a strong sense of relative deprivation among formal workers and their enhanced conflict with management. Before 2011 formal workers expressed their dissatisfaction through go-slows, quarrels, and complaints, but after 2011, small-scale stoppages occurred in the workshops of the PV branch.

In April 2011, a week-long stoppage occurred in the No. 2 rivet-welding group of PV branch as the tonnage unit price was less than that of the outsourced group, and the group leader was deposed, and this led to the manager reaching an agreement with workers that the tonnage unit would be increased by RMB 150 and the assignment of a deputy leader. In May 2011, a four-day stoppage occurred in the blanking section as the fluctuation of tonnage units was high, and again the manager had to negotiate an increased tonnage unit price with the workers. Again, in July 2011, some of the machine operators started a two-day stoppage to show their discontent with their wages. However, the management did not respond to the workers, which pushed workers into a slowdown protest.

But overall the protests of formal workers were limited. To prevent being fired due to 'personal faults' and to avoid the political risk, formal workers in different work sections and work groups would neither get together nor participate in activities outside the workshop boundary. The goal of their protest was economical, rather than political. For them, retirement was always the final success.

The Role of the Party Branch and the Workplace Trade Union in the workplace

Many scholars have observed that the declining significance of the party branch and the trade union in SOEs led to unchecked management supremacy and increased workers' powerlessness. Actually, the essential roles of both the union and the party branch in the workplace did not change; however, the methods to enact their roles changed a lot after China's marketization and SOE reform. Although the factory was also a unit of social integration and political control, its main job was still the development of production in the Maoist era, even in the Cultural Revolution, especially for a heavy machinery factory. An important difference in production in the Maoist era from the situation today was the use of mass campaigns and political motivation adopted in Maoist times to inspire workers' enthusiasm. The practices of emotional pressures developed during the revolutionary era were systematized and standardized and used in production after the political victory in 1949 (Perry, 2002: 116). The party branch was responsible for the organization of the production movement, and the trade union was an assistant to the party.

In the market-led development period, the production tasks assigned by the state were replaced by the orders from the global market, the political motivation and emotional work had been replaced by the dualistic management control to increase the workers' productivity, and the core role of the party branch in production was replaced by the professional managers. However, these changes did not equate to the disintegration of the cooperation of the party branch, the union, and the management. The party branch and the union in the workplace remained a substantial asset to the management in achieving profit.

Today, the party branch assists with management control through two channels: firstly, there is the common practice of merging party secretary and managerial personnel via a system of cross-appointment. In the PV branch of the South Factory, the director is the same person as the party secretary, which means the party branch will always support the management. It was this secretary who invited contractors' teams into the workplace. Secondly, one of the secretary's jobs was to cope with workers' challenges. The stoppages of the welding workers and the blanking workers in the PV branch were ended after the workers had 'heart to heart' talks with the party secretary separately. A worker told me that many workers were threatened during the talks. As the production apparatus in the workplace, the party branch became a monitor which always kept an eye on the workers.

The concrete work of the trade union in the workplace had also changed since the market reform. The work of the union chairman in the South Factory was to issue honour certificates to outstanding employees and to organize the one-day 'staff and workers' congress' each year. The union chairman of the South Factory, also the ex-director of the financial department, was an arrogant woman, who was exposed as the lover of the party secretary, and together embezzled factory funds to start their own business. Almost all the workers in the South Factory complained about the uselessness of the union and they said the chairman never talked with them. The union chairman's disregard for the workers' situation made them feel quite helpless. During the machine operators' two-day stoppage, a mill machine operator told me:

> We cannot make any progress without the help of the trade union. If this happened in the western country, the trade union would organize workers to strike. But we don't have a union, and our solidarity is easy to be destroyed. (Interview: LSF, 2011-07-11)

Actually, the uselessness of the union was very useful for destroying workers' confidence, and making them realize their helplessness.

Conclusion

After 2008, the production regime in many Chinese SOEs changed dramatically. On one hand, many SOEs started to adopt the strategy of flexible accumulation to survive the fierce market competition under the conditions of the global economic recession. On the other hand, the enforcement of the Labour Contract Law in 2008 and the Social Welfare Law in 2010 encouraged managers to introduce new methods of managerial control to deal with formal workers' resistance. However, the production regime of Chinese SOEs did not become increasingly similar to other types of enterprises as many scholars had anticipated. Rather, new production regimes emerged in Chinese SOEs, shaping new types of exploitation and resistance.

Based on my case-study research, it is possible to speculate that a new model of labour control may have emerged in Chinese SOEs – a dualistic production regime. The working dualism was formed when managers invited the subcontractors' teams into the workplace. The strategy of indulgent labour control was established for the formal workers based on more relaxed working conditions, basic benefits, secure employment, but also a harsh piece-rate system with a low basic wage. Patriarchal controls were imposed on the contractors' teams together with harsh working conditions, insecure employment, but noticeably higher wages. With increasingly outdated skills and relatively older, the formal SOE workers were threatened by their vulnerable position in the labour market, while temporary workers were threatened by their lack of legal contracts and their second-class position in the internal labour market.

The uneven distribution of power between management and workers was essential for the emergence of the dualistic labour regime in China's SOEs. The presence of the state apparatus – the party branch and the trade union – in the workplace, made the formal workers fearful of collectively challenging the management's authority. On the other hand, the union leader's disregard for the workers' situation undermined the workers' confidence when they tried to pursue their interests against management. The result was that management was able to recruit contractors' teams to replace formal workers, while the workers lacked any effective strategy to protect their interests.

While labour NGOs and social activists play an important role in organizing workers to pursue their interest in the Pearl River Delta, the SOE workplace is still a forbidden zone. So, until labour legislation can enforce collective bargaining as well as more genuine union autonomy, the transition to any form of hegemonic factory control may be stalled in China's machinery SOEs. It can be anticipated that the dualistic labour regime in China's SOEs will last for a long time, no matter how advanced the social welfare system becomes.

Notes

1 Under state socialism, soft budget constraints and pressure to expand led to an insatiable investment hunger, and this investment hunger led to the supply constraints in the whole society. For details, please see: Kornai (1980).
2 DunGouJi: Gang Chu Lu De DanGao ('Shield Machines: An oven-fresh cake?') http://www.mei.net.cn/news/2012/01/409307.html (Accessed December 10, 2015)
3 ZhongGuo JiDian GongYe (China's electro-mechanics industry): http://www.mei.net.cn/news/2012/01/409307.html (Accessed December 10, 2015)
4 DunGouJi ZhengZai LingXian ZhuYan ChengShi 'DiDaoZhan' (The Shield machine acts the leading role in the 'tunnel warfare'), http://www.mei.net.cn/news/2012/01/409307.html (Accessed December 10, 2015)
5 The system of the internal contract was first analysed by John Buttrick in 1952. He described the operation of the insider contracting system and the labour relations under this system with the case of the Winchester Repeating Arms Company. Harry Braverman also made a brief mention of the insider contracting system in *Labor and Monopoly Capital*, and argued that workers who exchange their labour were a commodity (labour result) rather than labour power. Dan Clawson made an important supplement to Braverman's account of the evolution of labour process organization in the US in the nineteenth and twentieth centuries, particularly for its extended treatment of the

function and decay of insider contracting prior to the development of Taylorism. For more detailed information about the insider contracting system and its change, please refer to the following resources: Buttrick (1952); Englander (1987); Jones (1982); Braverman (1998); Clawson (1980); Marglin (1974); Montgomery (1979).

6 Interview with HKJ, 2011-06-30.

7 Gouldner once described the administrative system of a gypsum mine in the US as an 'indulgency pattern', which was characterized by low surveillance and high autonomy.

8 For a mill machine operator, a piece of steel plate = 0.5 working hours a piece of plastic plate = 0.17 working hours

monthly wage = basic wage + bonus

basic wage = worker's position value = finished products which includes 174 working hours in total

bonus = the unit price of a working hour (RMB 12.37) × personal 'weight' × quantity of the extra working hours (total working hours – 174 working hours)

REFERENCES

Braverman, H. (1998 [1974]) *Labor and Monopoly Capital: The Degradation of Work in the Twentieth Century.* New York: Monthly Review Press.

Buttrick, J. (1952) 'The Inside Contract System'. *The Journal of Economic History* (12): pp. 205–221.

Burawoy, M. (1985) *The Politics of Production: Factory Regimes under Capitalism and Socialism.* London: Verso.

Burawoy, M. (1992) *The Radiant Past: Ideology and Reality in Hungary's Road to Capitalism.* Chicago: University of Chicago Press.

Cai, H. (2010) 'From the 'Bottom-line' Benefit to the 'Incremental' Benefit'. *Open times.* 219(9): pp. 37–45.

Clawson, D. (1980) *Bureaucracy and Labor Process.* NY: Monthly Review Press.

Edwards, R. (1979) *Contested Terrain: The Transformation of the Workplace in the Twentieth Century.* New York: Basic Books, Inc.

Englander, E. (1987) 'The Inside Contract System of Production and Organization: A neglected Aspect of the History of the Firm'. *Labor History* (28): pp. 429–446.

Gallagher, M. (2005) *Contagious Capitalism: Globalization and the Politics of Labor in China.* New Jersey: Princeton University Press.

Gouldner, A. W. (1954) *Patterns of Industrial Bureaucracy,* Illinois: Free Press.

Harvey, D. (1991) *The Condition of Postmodernity: An Enquiry into the Origins of Cultural Change.* Wiley: Blackwell Press.

Huang, D. (2013) 'Da Zao He Xie She Hui De Lao Dong Guan Xi: Hou Gai Ge Shi Dai Zhong Guo Lao Dong Guan Xi Zhi Yan Jiu', Unpublished Article.

Jones, S. R. H. (1982) 'The Organization of Work: A Historical Dimension''. *Journal of Economic Behavior and Organization* (3): pp. 117–137.

▶

▶

Kornai, J. (1980) *Economics of Shortage Vols. A,* New York and Oxford: North-Holland.

Lee, C. K. (1999) 'From Organized Dependence to Disorganized Despotism: Changing Labour Regimes in Chinese Factories', *The China Quarterly.* 157(3): pp. 44–71.

Lee, C. K. & Kofman, Y. (2012) 'The Politics of Precarity: Views Beyond the United States.' *Work and Occupations,* 39(4): pp. 388–408.

Marglin, S. (1974) 'What do Bosses Do? The Origins and Functions of Hierarchy in Capitalist Production'. *Review of Radical Political Economy* 6, no. 2 (n.d.): pp. 60–112.

Marx, K. (1992) *Capital: Volume 1: A Critique of Political Economy.* Melbourne: Penguin Classics.

Montgomery, D. (1979) *Workers' Control in America: Studies in the History of Work, Technology, and Labour Struggles.* Cambridge, MA: Cambridge University Press.

Perry, E. (2002) 'Moving the Masses: Emotion Work in the Chinese Revolution'. *Mobilization: An International Journal,* 7(2): pp. 111–128.

Ren, Y. & Jia, W. (2010) 'Subcontract System in Construction Industry: The Institutional Logic of the Usage of Rural Labor and the Production of Urban Space'. *Open Times.* No. 12: pp 5–23.

Silver, B. (2003) *Forces of Labor.* New Work: Cambridge University Press.

Walder, A. (1988) *Communist Neo-Traditionalism.* London: University of California Press.

Zhang, L. (2008) 'Lean Production and Labor Control in the Chinese Automobile Industry in an Age of Globalization'. *International Labor and Working-Class History,* 73: pp. 24–44.

Zhao, M. & Nichols, T. (1996). 'Management Control of Labour in State-Owned Enterprises: Cases from the Textile Industry'. *The China Journal,* 36(7): 1–21.

Zhao, W. (2010) *The Change of Factory Regime in China and Its Impact on Workers.* China: Social Science Academic Press.

Prolonged Selection or Extended Flexibility? A Case Study of Japanese Subsidiaries in China

5

Yu Zheng

Introduction

The employment practices adopted by multinational corporations (MNCs) is a key research area. While researchers endeavour to conceptualize 'country differences' from culturalist, institutional, and socio-political perspectives, there has been a long-standing tendency to play down the role of agency in making sense of country differences and employment practices, especially at the subsidiary level. To assume the MNC is an integrated actor misses the importance of MNC strategy and locality management which can choose or be pushed through internal politics to do different things in different contexts. This chapter takes the view that employment practices are subject to socio-political construction through interactions between subsidiary dynamics, headquarters, and local environments (Almond et al., 2006; Edwards et al., 2007; Edwards et al., 2010; Ferner et al., 2012; Quintanilla & Ferner, 2003).

The intended contribution of this chapter is threefold: first of all, the study responds to the call to explore research frameworks that go beyond the 'global integration/local responsiveness' orthodoxy in understanding employment practices in MNCs (Rosenzweig, 2006). The research extends our knowledge of the emergent and developmental nature of employment practices exercised at subsidiary level. The author has chosen to study Japanese MNCs in China in order to examine the implications of relocating from an established labour market to an emerging labour market. Unlike existing research that focuses on possibilities and barriers of transferring established employment practices from mature economies to emerging economies, the author asks if country differences make the idea of transfer unachievable or undesirable. The key issue here is how companies embedded in a relatively homogenous and stable labour market (Japan) develop employment policies and practice to manage their workforce in a relatively diverse and mobile labour market (China). The chapter shows contrasting patterns of employment practices to manage the boundary between the internal (core) and external (periphery) labour forces. The findings shed light on the meaning and functions of employment practices in the subsidiary context. Different patterns of duality emerged as a result of social construction, in which 'extended actors' (Cooke, 2011) such as subsidiary mangers, workers, officials of labour bureaus, employment agents, and universities, all played important roles in shaping the employment practices in the workplace.

The chapter is organized into five parts. The first part offers a review of existing literature on segmented labour-market theory with an emphasis on implications to MNCs, followed by discussions on the research methodology. The third part of this chapter introduces the context of our study by showing the transitional nature of China's labour market. The fourth part shows the development, function, and institutionalization of different patterns of employment practices used by subsidiaries. Particular attention is given to the analysis on employment practices applied to manage the boundary of the internal and external labour markets. The final section concludes the chapter by summarizing the key research findings and offering suggestions for future research directions.

Literature Review: Labour Market Segmentation, the International Division of Labour, and Human Resource Management Transfer

Labour-market-segmentation theory identifies the distinctive nature of jobs in different labour-market segments and that these segments are isolated from each other (Atkinson, 1984; Doeringer and Piore, 1971). In opposition to the neo-classical assumptions of a unified and perfectly competitive labour market, labour market segmentation theorists argue that labour markets are composed of fundamentally different sectors and that movement between sectors is highly constrained. Labour markets can be broadly divided into primary and secondary sectors, each of which can be further stratified into different tiers. Jobs in primary and secondary sectors show distinct characteristics. Primary jobs offer generous wage and welfare packages, job security, as well as training and career advancement opportunities whereas secondary jobs are often paid at the minimum wage level, are insecure, and provide limited opportunities for career development. The level of job complexity and the degree of autonomy also differ between jobs in the primary and secondary labour markets.

In the context of MNCs, labour market segmentation theorists posit that the unit labour cost varies in different national business systems, which in turn leads to the division of labour on a global scale. The development of telecommunication and transportation technology enables firms to mobilize operations beyond national borders. MNCs are therefore capable of dividing production (or services) process into functional segments, allocating different segments across countries and thereby creating a spatial division of labour on a global scale, a phenomenon known as the 'new international division of labour' (Frobel et al., 1980). As cross-country differences in labour-market institutions persist, MNCs continuously stratify production and service processes into functional units and relocate these units to the countries that offer the best possible cost and efficiency return to the consortium. In particular, the labour intensive segments, which are characterized by standardized production/service processes and low-skill requirements, should be allocated to countries where there is sufficient supply of disciplined and low-waged local labour force.

The new international division of labour thesis is challenged by studies examining how MNCs make use of international labour markets by analysing the organization of global commodity chains (Gereffi, 1999), global value chains (Kaplinsky, 2000), or global production networks (Ernst and Kim, 2002). These researchers move attention from the segmentation of production functions to the coordination of different functional units across countries. They argue that MNCs run a chain or a network of functional units in order to effectively develop, manufacture, and deliver products and services to the consumers worldwide. The ways MNCs coordinate these functional units vary in different types of commonality chains or production networks. These researchers also mapped out a hierarchy of various functional units according to the technological complexity and labour intensity required for performing the specific functions. They further contend that firms performing the lower end functions need to develop the capability to move up the hierarchy (or 'upgrade') by accumulating necessary capital, knowledge, and human resource (HR).

MNCs' division of functional segments in the international labour markets and its impact on subsidiary employment practices deserve further investigation (Edwards and Kuruvilla, 2005). Observing that MNCs tend to keep the core functions in the home country and relocate the peripheral functions overseas, some scholars suggest the relationship between the parent plants and the overseas subsidiaries reflects a core–periphery division of labour at the international level. Empirical evidence gathered so far seems to indicate that MNCs are less likely to systematically transfer established employment practices to subsidiaries that are engaged in standardized and low-cost production functions. Dedoussis and Littler (1994) documented employment practices of eight Japanese manufacturing plants in Australia and argued that observed employment practices that enhance the functional flexibility of the workforce (such as job rotation and internal training) were adopted, whereas the 'high-cost' employment practices such as seniority pay and employment tenure were absent from the subsidiaries. They explained the selective transfer of employment practices by the footloose nature of MNCs in host countries. Wilkinson's et al. (2001) study of Japanese manufacturing plants in Malaysia also suggested distinctive contrasts between jobs in the Japanese and Malaysian plants. Jobs in the Japanese parent plants were characterized by security, some degree of autonomy, and personal development opportunities. Jobs in the Malaysian plants, on the other hand, were relatively insecure, tightly controlled, and offered little room for personal development. They argued that there was a clear division of production functions between the Japanese parent plants and Malaysian subsidiaries. The subsidiaries' role as 'reproduction plants' were identified to be the underlying rationale for the absence of the parent practices that would encourage long-term employee commitment. Another study that has reached similar conclusions was conducted by Taylor (2001), who focused on the Japanese invested companies in China. While Taylor found some similarities in terms of employment practices adopted in the local plants and the Japanese parent, he found these employment practices were given different interpretations and played different functions at the subsidiary level. He therefore argued that such practices as seniority pay are more a legacy of the local (or Chinese) practices of labour control rather than the transferred practices of the parent MNCs. More recent research conducted by Morris et al. (2009) included an extended sample of MNCs from different home countries. Their findings supported the previous research and suggested that companies seeking to compete by cost minimization would rarely transfer established home country employment practices to subsidiaries. These empirical findings suggest that the functional division of production creates a spatial division of labour within MNCs. However, before we accept the idea that the global workforce has been interwoven into segments of MNCs' internal chains of production functions, some critical questions need to be addressed.

One question is, how will local labour-market dynamics shape the division of labour within MNCs? The notion of the new international division of labour tends to overstate the homogeneity of national labour markets and plays down the dynamics and diversity of local labour markets within countries. In reality, population density, unemployment rates, unionization, and immigration can vary significantly, which all affect the mobility chances of local workers. Variation in the educational infrastructure in the host country affects the skill profiles and employability of the local workforce. In geographically large and politically diverse societies (such as China, India, and the US) labour laws and implementation can vary significantly as provincial governments are designated legislative and administrative power over employment issues. More importantly, being an international economic and political agent, MNCs are often found to be engaged in the co-production or construction of local labour-market institutions. In their study of Japanese manufacturing plants in Telford, Elger and Smith (2005) showed how clusters of Japanese MNCs coordinated their labour-market policies to maintain the supply of a flexible workforce to fill in the routine and low-wage jobs. In countries where skill shortage instigates mobility among the local workforce, sourcing and maintaining a stable workforce can restrain MNCs' ability to consolidate a labour-market segment favourable to them. Li and Sheldon's (2010) study of the foreign-invested companies in Suzhou, China reported the poaching of skilled workers as challenging the firms' efforts to adopt employment practices to build a high-commitment workforce. More interestingly, their study found that foreign companies started to build alliances with the local vocation schools to maintain a steady supply of low-waged and flexible workers. In other words, MNCs were *co-producers* of labour-market institutions in local settings. The shaping of subsidiary employment practices therefore has to be understood in the context of the dynamic nature of MNCs' internal division of labour and the local labour-market institutions.

The related question is: can headquarters of MNCs strategically decide which subsidiary functions and subsequently employment practices are to be adopted? The new international division of labour approach and the global commodity chain analysis introduced above give MNC headquarters strategic vision as creators of labour markets. But such static models ignore organizational or workplace dynamics. Establishment of employment practices are often an outcome of struggles between agents of institutions within and outside MNCs. The common ground for many studies of managing the workforce in MNCs is their research focus on the corporate headquarters, studying MNCs' rationales of internationalization, the effectiveness of different organizational structures, and the complexity in managing overseas subsidiaries. Such a headquarter-centred approach plays down the developmental nature of subsidiary human resource management (HRM) and the initiatives of subsidiary managers in the institutionalization of employment practices at the local level. These local initiatives are also the outcome of local manager's struggles with local workers and local labour markets. In their seminar work on why independent companies chose to join MNC production networks, Kristensen and Zeitlin (2005) show that parent company's HR policies are often implemented in a way to advance subsidiary managers' interests rather than to serve the intended strategic objective designated by the headquarters. They show that subsidiary managers are at the centre of interpreting corporate policies and developing detailed action plans for policy implementation. By deploying various actors that possess the power to influence decision-making at headquarters, subsidiary managers can also influence the direction of corporate policies that concern subsidiary HR management (Edwards et al., 2007). Since subsidiary managers' actions are purposeful, their view on the competitive advantage of existing employment practices made institutionalization of such practices in subsidiaries a selective, political, and emergent process (Gamble, 2010). Following such a 'bottom-up' view of MNCs, the research focus of this chapter is the action and choice of subsidiary managers in managing the division of labour. In particular, subsidiary managers' perspective and interests in 'upgrading' subsidiaries' function within MNCs will have a strong influence on their choice of subsidiary employment practices.

Research Design and Research Methodology

I took a case-study approach with a mixture of qualitative research methods to conduct my research. I followed a 'theoretical' sampling strategy (Buck, 2011; Eisenhardt, 1991). Case selection was projected against Morris et al.'s (2009) research on Japanese 'reproduction plants' in Malaysia. Two Japanese white-goods manufacturers in Shanghai (referred to as WG1 and WG2) were selected. Both can be categorized as *reproduction* plants: product model design was centralized at the headquarters in Japan; the subsidiaries manufactured standardized models for the local consumer market; and the plants were in the low-cost segment of their parent companies' global production networks. The subsidiaries shared a range of standard criteria: location, company size, age, level of parent companies' international experiences, product range, and production model. At the time the companies were visited, both were in the middle of undertaking major business reorientations in the Chinese market. Concurrently, the local labour market was experiencing major changes – details of which are discussed below. Such settings allowed an investigation of the scope of employment practices being constructed at the subsidiaries.

Data were collected in two stages. At the first stage, I spent one month at each plant, doing detached observation, interviews, and archival research at two Sino-Japanese joint-venture plants in Shanghai, China. Detailed notes were made to record my observations and reflections on the employment practices exercised at each plant. Semi-structured interviews were conducted with the subsidiary managers, who were the key informants on the development of subsidiary employment practices. A number of informal discussions (Briggs, 1986) with the managers and the workers were held at various venues (such as canteens, dormitories, and dinner parties). This approach helped to develop a holistic picture of the multiple realities in the field by triangulating 'insiders' views' (Cooke, 2011), as well as allowing new research questions to emerge during the research process (Moore, 2011). At the second stage, the author revisited the plants a year later to conduct follow-up interviews. Because 'the role of institutional agency outside the subsidiaries in shaping subsidiary employment practice' has emerged as a new research theme after the author analysed the data collected from the first stage, semi-structured interviews were also conducted with the local government officials and employment agents to further probe the role of these 'outsiders'.

The Chinese Context: The Dynamics of a Transitional Labour Market

China's labour market has been in drastic transition since the Chinese government deepened the market-oriented reform in the early 1990s (Knight and Song, 2005). On one hand, the state has retreated the dominant *danwei* (or work unit) system, which used to offer employees lifetime employment and social welfare. Companies have been strongly encouraged to adopt employment contracts to specify the rights and responsibilities of employers and employees. The government monitors the labour market through legislation and the administration of employment laws. A social insurance system, whilst as yet under-developed, is expected to provide employees with social benefits that used to be covered by the *danwei*. The Chinese state no longer employs the majority of the working population. However, the state's control over labour movement through the *hukou* (residence registration) system – a system that divides the rural and the urban household by the way in which social welfare, healthcare, housing assistance and education are provided – remains strong (Chan and Buckingham, 2008; Liu, 2005). *Hukou*-based labour-movement control has in turn led to structural imbalance in the local labour market and segmentation between employee groups (Knight and Song, 2005; Zhang et al., 2010).

Structural imbalance is an important characteristic of China's transitional labour market. On the one hand, there is a huge surplus, unemployed population in China: according to the National Statistics Bureau, the total unemployed urban population was 71.9 million and total unemployed rural population was 297.3 million by the end of 2009 (NBSC, 2010). This means that 26.3% of the urban populations and 61.3% of the rural populations remain unemployed. On the other hand, many companies in China have reported difficulty in sourcing and retaining skilled workers, engineers, and managers (Howard et al., 2008). High turnover among local employees, especially migrants and those with scarce skills – technical workers, engineers and experienced managers – are believed to be the cause (Ross, 2007). China's largest head-hunter company conducted a survey of 26 Chinese cities in 2007. The results indicate that annual labour turnover is highest among shopfloor workers (31.5%), followed by that of line managers (27.6%) and office clerks (25%) (51JOBS, 2007). While the expansion of higher education, the development of vocational schools, and the introduction of management development programmes are expected to attenuate the shortage of skilled workers (Cooke, 2012), it is likely that structural imbalance in the local labour market will continue to shape MNCs employment policies towards the 'under-skilled'/'inexperienced' workers and the 'skilled'/'experienced' works.

Geographical inequality in terms of the demand and supply of labour also characterizes China's transitional labour market. Since China's economic reform and open-door policy was implemented unevenly, the majority of employers are clustered in the coastal regions, whereas the unemployed population mostly resides in the less developed regions such as central and west China. This has instigated the movement of labour from less developed regions to the more developed regions, as the reform of *hukou* system lifted the bar on intra-country relocation.

The *hukou* system has important implications to the segmentation of employment groups in the local labour markets. Downsizing of the

Table 5.1 Average age and average tenure of employees in MNCs of Japanese subsidiaries

	Average age		Tenure (years)	
	2003	2005	2003	2005
Asia	32.1	32.1	6.9	6.7
China	29.1	29.9	4.4	5.0
Other Asian Countries	33.1	33.3	7.8	7.7
Middle and Near East	36.8	40.3	8.0	11.3
Europe	37.4	37.0	8.2	8.9
North America	38.9	39.4	8.2	7.7
Central and South America	36.0	36.4	7.7	8.0
Africa	37.0	41.4	11.5	13.0
Oceania	38.5	39.0	6.3	7.4

4th Survey of Human Resource Management in Japanese MNCs conducted by The Japan Institute for Labour Policy and Training, 2006

SOEs created the '40/50' group, who were laid off in their forties or fifties with some redundancy compensation. The total numbers of industrial workers employed by the SOEs went down from 149.08 million (59%) in 1995 to in 64.20 million (21%) in 2009 (NBSC, 2010). This group of employees were trained, disciplined, and keen on finding work again in the rising urban sectors. Their urban *hukou* status means that they enjoy some unemployment compensation and reemployment assistance offered by the state. The state policy prioritizes relocating the '40/50' group to urban employment by restraining rural migration into cities (Knight and Song, 2005). However, this group often found themselves in an unfavourable position because non-state owned employers preferred younger workers, who were more adaptive and cost-effective (Lee, 2007). Long years of employment in the SOEs meant that employers had difficulty training these employees to gain new skills or to fit into a different company culture.

The second employee group are 'peasant-workers'. Thirty per cent of the peasant-workers work in the township and village enterprises and the majority of them moved to the urban areas for jobs (Chan and Pun, 2010). While peasant-workers were often referred to as 'migrant workers', to many of them, especially the young generation, moving back was not an option because farms allocated to their rural home could not support the whole family. They move between jobs, expecting to eventually settle in cities (Chang, 2008). With few qualifications, these migrant 'peasant-workers' often take up those marginal jobs with low skill requirements in the manufacturing, service, and construction sectors, which were often characterized by job instability and high labour turn-over (Chan and Pun, 2010). Once a job is secured, migrant workers can apply for a temporary urban *hukou* sponsored by their employers. However, their permanent *hukou* remains non-urban, which means they are not entitled to the social welfare benefits and employment assistance available to the urban *hukou* holders.

The last group of employees that forms the urban workforce are the young graduates. The legacy of the *hukou* system under a planned econ-omy is still evident in the *hukou* arrangement of the university students. When registered as a full-time student, he/she is supposed to transfer the household *hukou* to collective *hukou* at the university. Having col-lective *hukou* means students do not need a temporary urban *hukou* to take on internships or temporary employment in cities. After gradua-tion, the collective *hukou* can also be transferred to the employers, who are allocated annual *hukou* quotas by the states (normally public sectors or SOEs). Otherwise, graduates have to move their *hukou* back to their household. Since the expansion of universities has outpaced the demand for graduates in urban areas, some graduates find it hard to secure a job that matches their qualifications and have to take on low-grade jobs, let alone finding jobs in the shrinking public sectors and SOEs. Some uni-versity graduates, originally from rural areas, choose to dwell in cities, take on low-end jobs, and try to advance their careers by accumulating work experience. This threefold segmentation, therefore, is a key feature of the Chinese labour markets.

Contrasting Patterns of Employment Practices at the Subsidiary Level

The two Japanese MNCs selected for this study are highly successful white-goods manufacturers and have built up extensive global produc-tion networks since the early 1980s. The Chinese subsidiary plants: WG1 and WG2 are semi-automated assembly lines set up in the mid-1990s to explore the growing Chinese consumer market. Throughout the 2000s, both subsidiaries were facing major price competition in the local white-goods markets. They were pressed to both reduce production costs and upgrade their product profiles. Price competition also forced the compa-nies to reconsolidate their 'compete by quality' strategy to cater for the rising middle class and upper class in China. Faced with the imbalanced, mobile, and segmented local labour market, the subsidiary managers' main HR concerns were how to maintain workforce flexibility, lower production costs, and control labour turnover at a 'reasonable' level.

In terms of job design, shop-floor work was, overall, highly routinized with rather limited formal skill requirements from the workers. This was reflected in the detailed division of labour, precise positioning of workers on the assembly line, precise calculation of the standard task completion time at each position and the standard unit production time, as well as specified and written working procedures in manufacturing manuals. From mere observations on the work in the two plants, the argument that both subsidiaries were playing a low-cost standardized production function was confirmed, which meant they were less likely to adopt high-cost employment practices. However, 'commitment-based' employment practices were not completely absent. Only a core group of employees (including repatriates, senior local managers, technical engineers, and workers with sophisticated and multiple skills) were offered above-market-average pay, mid- and end-of-year appraisal, job security, and career development support. The rest of the employees were recruited on a short-term contract basis. The contract length ranged from three months to one year. Wage level is slightly above the local average and monthly bonus was tied with individual productivity. Training was preliminary and had no clear career-advancement implications. These results correspond with Silver's (1997) definition of a 'lean-and-dual' model of labour control. Further scrutiny of employment practices applied to different employee groups suggests distinctive patterns of divide between core and periphery employee groups at subsidiary level. Figure 5.1 illustrates the contrast.

WG1 maintains relatively fluid boundaries between most employee groups. WG1's recruitment and selection policies favour the younger

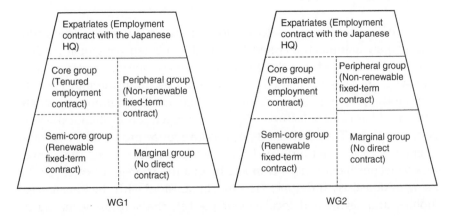

Figure 5.1 Employee groups in WG1 and WG2

Zheng, 2015

workforce. The average age of the employees was 25. The employees were mainly recruited directly after they finished vocational schools or graduated from universities. Vocational school students formed the peripheral group of labour and performed semi-skilled jobs. Recruitment of the group, however, was by no means done randomly or by recommendation from existing workers as some foreign-invested factories normally do (Smith, 2003). Most employees were channelled through the 'Youth Training Centre', which was set up in alliance with the local vocational schools for internship training. These trainees work side by side with contractual workers. Upon completion of the internship, those who performed well would be offered a fixed-term contract (normally a year) in WG1. Such an internship system hence played both sourcing and selection functions. Alongside the technical school students, university graduates were brought in under the 'managerial candidate' programme to mainly fill in the shop floor team leader and junior manager positions. Based on their performance at work, these managerial candidates could be promoted to mid-level positions after working in the company for two to three years. Pay-for-the-job-scale was adopted to specify the connection between positions, although reported promotion opportunities were rare. Performance-based pay, tenure benefits, and family allowance were offered to all employees apart from the student interns, which indicates the subsidiary's inclination to encourage employees to stay on with the company. A core–periphery divide functioned as a prolonged selection process from which the competent and loyal employees were retained.

In sharp contrast, movement across employee groups is much less common in WG2. Such a core–periphery divide served more of a cost-control function, with employment policies clearly favouring experience. The core employee group was formed by workers, managers, and engineers who were layoffs from a state-owned company, which used to be the WG2's parent company. This group of employees were on permanent contracts and offered relatively generous salary and bonuses linked to the financial performance of WG2. The shop-floor workers group was mainly made of migrants, who were given three-month renewable contracts and would not build tenure in the company. During the peak season, more than 80 per cent of the shop-floor workers were short-term migrants, who were recruited through a number of local employment agents. They worked in WG2 on a temporary basis and performed detailed tasks: welding, assembling, painting, and packing. Very limited training was given to these workers and the pay was largely based on their daily output. As the short-term migrant workers would return to the agent after short-term services at WG2, the company was not entitled to pay any social insurance benefits for this group of workers, which normally made up 37 per cent of the employers' salary bill. At the same time, WG2 chose to recruit experienced group leaders, line managers and supervisors, who formed a core group to lead the migrant workers in the workshop. No HR policies were available to clarify internal promotion policies or to support the migrant workers to gain a permanent position. Salary for more experienced employees was not significantly higher than the migrants, but job security was guaranteed for those with experience.

The abundant supply of the 'under-skilled' segment of labour and the institution of labour mobility control were important for subsidiary managers to organize their workforce in distinctive patterns. Neither subsidiary reported difficulty in sourcing and recruiting employees. According to the local HR managers, whenever jobs were advertised, applications always outnumbered vacancies. This indicates that the local labour market was in favour of employers offering routinized jobs. Equally important is that in order to control labour mobility local institutions allowed employers to source the 'under-skilled' segment of the workforce in bulk quantity. As explained earlier, the Chinese state retained strong control over labour mobility through the *hukou* system in order to redirect movement of labour and improve the quality of the local labour force. Control over labour mobility was executed by a number of local agencies such as employment agents (job centres), vocational schools, and universities. The amount of labour dispatch handled through employment agents and job centres had gone up substantially over the past decade (Cooke, 2011). By 2009, a total of 28.4 million employees were dispatched through employment agents, tripling the number of 9.75 million in 2001 (NBSC, 2001, 2010). Also, vocational schools and universities' role in channelling migrants to work in cities had become more significant as well (Li and Sheldon, 2010). By building alliances with these local agencies, WG1 and WG2 were able to develop preferred employment practices to source a group of flexible and low-waged workers.

Targeting the segment of 'literate but inexperienced' workers, WG1 collaborated with the local vocational schools and universities, who were keen on finding students practical training opportunities to enhance their employability. Upon completion of the internship, students were awarded a certificate of training, which was ratified by the local government as elementary skill recognition. With such official validation, certificates of training issued by WG1 were useful to these student workers in job hunting. For WG1, an alliance with vocational schools and universities helped connect the firm with an extended pool of candidates, who were under-skilled but systematically trained by both the vocational schools/universities and the plant. Such an alliance allowed WG1 to pre-select those 'competent' ones to be integrated into the firm's internal labour market.

In WG2's case, it was the local employment agents that played a key role in securing abundant, flexible, and low-waged labour. Sourcing migrant workers and controlling turnover among this group has been reported as a challenge to foreign invested companies in China (Howard et al., 2008). The local employment agents are normally connected to the regional labour bureaus and collect information about the migrants. They also offered discipline training, covering basic insurance and worker grievance handling, which allowed WG2 to externalize these employment functions. When the demand for agency workers increased over the past few years, WG2 signed up long-term contracts with a number of job centres in order to maintain numerical flexibility in the firm. As explained by the local managers, using different employment agents expanded the source of workers and avoided migrants forming alliances based on their hometown. In the Chinese context, hometown alliances are common and a key source of solidarity and integration for workers (Smith, 2003). Here, an alliance with the employment agents enabled the exclusion of migrant workers from WG2's internal labour market.

In terms of managing the 'core' group of employees, the two subsidiaries showed more similarity in terms of employment policies and practices. Corresponding to Li and Sheldon's (2010) observation that enduring the skill shortage instigates 'poaching' of skilled workers, both companies reported concerns over losing competent employees and managers to their major competitors.

> There seems to be a routine among the employees. They will join us after working for a Korean or a Taiwanese company for several years. Staying here for a while, then they move on to European companies. (Management and Accounting Department, WG2, female, Chinese, 33)

> There are some engineers we really want to keep. But they seem to believe that they could realize better developments in the European or American companies ... Maybe this will be counted as our contribution to Chinese society? (HR Department, WG1, male, Chinese, 35)

As a short-term resolution, WG1 increased the number of expatriates after a trial of promoting local managers. They assigned several expatriates to subordinate roles to 'support' the local managers. WG2 introduced an 'inpatriation–repatriation' programme aimed at developing a cadre of 'systematically trained' local managers.

Knowing the high mobility among the managerial and engineering employees, subsidiary managers made use of some retention measures, which were used to generate long-term commitment, in order to exert direct control over the local employees. For example, WG2 provided apartments to managers before they purchased their own property. This differs from the old SOE company accommodation in the sense that company housing was supposed to be a short-term, contract-based lease and the company was not under an obligation to provide accommodation to all the employees. Neither was this practice consistent with the parent company practice where company accommodation was considered a form of compensation for *young* employees on low wages. Instead, dormitories not only helped to retain the *experienced* managers but also to extend their working hours as they were generally expected to work voluntary (unpaid) overtime. The workers would leave the premises when the eight-hour work shift was over. The managers, by contrast, would normally stay longer and might be called back when there was something that needed urgent attention. In fact, WG2 did not enforce any policy to persuade staff who had purchased their own apartment to move out of the company accommodation. This shows that company accommodation served the purpose of providing convenience to managers with additional after-work duties rather than compensation to the young low-paid employees. One manager's comments confirmed the different meaning of company accommodation between the parent company and the subsidiary:

'We might be the only [Japanese] company in China having a company housing system like an old state owned company... Our company dorms in Japan are for single employees and they are very small and they are 1 hour away by train. The employees will normally move out of the dorm after 2-3 years. But here, I don't think anyone would move unless they are forced to do so. (Manager in Accounting and general management department, WG2, female, Chinese, 33)

Besides accommodation, some parent company management practices were also applied to control mobility and absenteeism of the managers. WG2 used company mobile phones to keep a record of the movement of local managers:

The company will retain the list of calls of all the company mobile numbers. We sometimes detect that someone applied for sick leave and he/she used the mobile in other regions. The 'sick leave' then won't be verified and the person will get a deduction. (Clerk in administrative department, WG1, Chinese, female, 36)

Subsidiary managers explained that these employment practices took the same form as those of the parent companies but were given a different interpretation by subsidiary managers. In view of the difficulty in cultivating commitment in the local labour market with much higher mobility, direct control was presumed to be a viable alternative to indirect control through forming social relationships between employees and the company.

Distinctive patterns of the core–peripheral divide were also reflected in the route by which local managers were promoted. WG1 displayed a strong intention to build an internally trained and selected local management team. There was a clear statement in the corporate policy to increase the number of local managers in the subsidiary management team. There were a few Chinese managers promoted to senior positions. At the same time, WG1 centralized training of local technical engineers and local managers to the China centre in Beijing. A liaison with several Beijing-based universities ensured the supply of 'high-quality graduates' to join the company management trainee programme, which aimed to build a cadre of competent and locally trained managers. However, a significant proportion of managerial candidates (roughly 50 per cent according to the HR manager) chose to leave WG1 after finishing the first one-year contract due to not being able to cope with the intensive work pressures on the shop floor, difficulty in fitting in with the work teams, or finding better employment opportunities. While some adjustment has been made, such as involving subsidiary HR managers into the selection of candidates into the management trainee programme, the general principle of hiring fresh graduates and promoting internally trained managers remained at the heart of WG1's promotion policy. As explained by the general manager, WG1 was 'determined to build a workforce that shares the value of the company'. Here, again, an alliance with higher education institutions was used to extend the pool of selection employees into the firm's internal labour market.

WG2 had so far relied heavily on experienced workers and mid-career managers to form the core employee group. More than 70 per cent of the new recruits are in mid-career, either from the Chinese parent company or the external labour market. The local managers explained the rationale of the HR policy as a reaction to the mobility associated with different groups of workers.

We understand that it is faster for the fresh graduates to learn and adapt to our company. And we do have some wonderful young graduates working here. But they leave soon for better personal development. I think the average length young graduates worked for our company is about 2 or 2.5 years. This is not good enough for the company. We need our employees to be more responsible and be willing to connect their personal development with that of the company, people who believe in the company at its prosperity and its setbacks. I think my Japanese colleagues agree with me at this point. (Deputy general manager, Chinese, 49, male)

The local senior managers argued that a stable and loyal mid-management team had been the key to WG2's past success. They tended to recruit directly from the local labour market and experienced team leaders, salesmen, and managers, who were perceived to be more mature and serious employees. Many of them had a background working in SOEs and shared some views on work with the senior Chinese managers. Fresh graduates were more likely to start with clerical jobs, which were described as 'repetitive' yet 'stressful'. In WG2's case, a state-directed policy to set up joint-ventures in China had influenced the forming of the local management teams, and hence, the direction of employment practices. WG2 was jointly owned by a Japanese and a Chinese white-good manufacturer. At the time the joint venture was set up, the Chinese side faced serious financial difficulties and were at the risk of going bankrupt. As part of the joint-venture agreements, a group of managers, engineers, and skilled workers were relocated to WG1. This group, who would otherwise be laid-off should the Chinese side have gone bankrupt, had formed strong solidarity and sympathy with the urban layoffs. Such solidarity was reflected in WG2's employment policies in favour of *experienced* employees. However, the employment policies also created a divide between the *experienced* urban workers and *young and inexperienced* migrants, with the latter being excluded from the firm's internal labour market.

In summary, employment practices observed at subsidiary level reflect different patterns of linking the firm's internal segmentation of labour to the local labour market. The comparison between WG1 and WG2 suggested that distinctive HR policies and practices were subsidiary specific and highly contextual to the management team. Subsidiary employment policy and practices were advanced in the way to reflect subsidiary managerial initiatives of labour control. Segmented local labour markets, supply and mobility opportunities of different labour market segments and the way subsidiary managers interact with the local agencies of labour mobility control were found to have enabled such distinctive patterns in dividing (and linking) the core–peripheral groups of labour at subsidiary level.

Conclusion

In this chapter, the author has set out to apply a segmented labour-market analysis to the development of employment practices at subsidiaries of MNCs. The chapter explored how the international division of production functions within MNCs has shaped the way subsidiaries manage the boundary between the internal and external labour market. Both cases of this study engaged in the labour intensive end of production and were highly cost conscious. Both divided the employees into core and periphery groups as a measure of production cost control. However, the core and periphery employee groups were managed differently. In WG1, the peripheral group (student interns and management trainees) were used as an extended pool of candidates, from which the core group (regular employees) was selected. In WG2, however, a divide was drawn between the employees and agency workers. Agency workers (migrants) were marginalized and excluded from the firm's internal employment system. The young graduates (mostly migrants) were also marginalized, if not completely excluded from the firm's internal labour market. Querying why subsidiaries developed such significantly different patterns of core–peripheral division of labour, the author compared the composition of employee groups in the subsidiaries and the relationship between subsidiaries and local labour supply and development institutions. A supply of diverse groups of workers in the segmented local labour market was found relevant to the development of such different subsidiary employment practices. Local labour-market institutions also played a central role in channelizing the firm's internal labour market and the local labour-market segments.

What, then, are the implications of these results to studying the selection and management of workers in MNCs?

First of all, the research findings offer a critique of the existing international HRM literature by considering the implications of global division of production functions to managing employees at the subsidiary level. The findings lend some support to the view that subsidiaries performing standard production will employ low-cost employment practices. However, this chapter also revealed more complexity to employment practices developed at the subsidiary level. There was no evidence that subsidiary employment practices were converging to a standardized low-cost model. Rather, subsidiaries employed distinctive policies and practices to manage different groups of workers. At the same time, some new employment policies and practices emerged to accommodate the local labour-market conditions. While being in low-end production has pressed subsidiaries to extend the use of the peripheral employee groups, the boundary between the core (internal) and peripheral (external) labour markets was managed to ensure flexibility of the workforce and to retain skills to some extent.

Secondly, the results also offer some critique to the contingency approach, which suggests that subsidiary management practices should reflect multiple pressures faced by MNCs in the internationalization process. Analysis along a contingency approach focuses on the forces within and outside MNCs to shape or direct subsidiary management practices. However, the findings of this chapter suggest that the subsidiary can develop distinctive patterns of employment practices under similar external contingent constraints. For example, contrary to the idea that the *hukou* system will 'automatically' create a core and peripheral division of labour in the workplace (Knight and Song, 2005; Lu 2006; Zhang et al., 2010), the findings of this chapter suggest that segmentation in the local labour market was by and large enacted by actors from within and outside the workplace. In the two cases both played 'reproductive factory' roles, but subsidiary managers ended up targeting different segments of the local labour markets, developing varied recruitment policies to maintain a relatively stable source of labour, employing contrasting reward packages. And adopting different measures to control the mobility of the local workforce. More importantly, by building alliances with the agencies of local labour-market institutions, subsidiary managers were able to extend the resources to secure a sustainable supply of labour and to control the mobility of labour. In other words, different patterns of employment practices were co-produced by the agencies of MNCs and local institutions. Employment practices within the subsidiary were seldom the direct manifestation of institutional, industry sector or organizational pressures faced by the subsidiary. Rather differences in subsidiary employment policies and practices were locally constructed and reflected strong subsidiary initiatives.

Finally, the results of this chapter are significant because they suggest that local labour markets can be linked to MNCs' production functions in many *different* ways. While exploring the impact of MNCs' global strategy on the different patterns of dividing the local labour force is beyond the scope of this chapter, the findings here seem to lend some support to the argument that firm's local competitive strategies strongly influence subsidiary employment practices (Takeuchi et al., 2009; Yao and Wang, 2006). Further research is recommended to consider how upgrading of product models may affect the contrasting patterns of subsidiary HR policies and practices reported in this chapter. In particular, researchers need to consider the implication of China's transition from an export-led economy to a consumption-led economy for MNCs' stratification of production functions into the country and management of employment practices at MNC subsidiaries.

The author is aware that the findings cannot be overgeneralized as the study is based on two companies from a country with relatively homogenous and distinctive employment relations (Japan) located in the same employment and work relations context of China, where external institutional patterns remain fluid and not settled. Due to resource constraints, the author was not able to visit the companies' Japanese headquarters to further investigate the parent–subsidiary dynamics in shaping subsidiary employment practices. Instead, the chapter revealed the continued subsidiary initiatives, thus highlighting the real need for more workplace-based case studies to understand the social reality and diversity of employment relations in contemporary China.

REFERENCES

51JOBS (2007) *A Survey on Salary in China*, http://www.docin.com/p-42322538. html. (Accessed 2 February, 2012).

Almond, P., Ferner, A., Colling, T., and Edwards, T. (2006) 'Conclusions', in *American Multinationals in Europe: Managing Employment Relations Across National Borders* pp. 341–352.

Atkinson, J. (1984) 'Manpower Strategies for Flexible Organisations', *Personnel Management,* August, pp. 28–31.

Bartlett, C. A. and Ghoshal, S., (1992) Managing Across Borders: The Transnational Solution. Boston, Mass.: Harvard Business School Press.

Björkman, I. and Lu, Y. (1999) 'The management of human resources in Chinese-Western joint ventures'. *Journal of World Business.* 34: 3, pp. 306–324.

Björkman, I., Smale, A., Sumelius, J., Suutari, V. and Lu, Y. (2008) 'Changes in Institutional Context and MNC Operations in China: Subsidiary HRM Practices in 1996 versus 2006'. *International Business Review.* 17:2 pp 146–158.

Boisot, M. and Child, J. (1999) 'Organizations as Adaptive Systems in Complex Environments: The Case of China' in *Organization Science* 10; 3, pp. 237–252.

Brewster, C., Carey, L., Dowling, P., Grobler, P., Holland, P. and Warnich, S. (2003) *Contemporary Issues in Human Resource Management: Gaining a Competitive Advantage,* (2nd edition) Cape Town: Oxford University Press.

Briggs, C. L. (1986) *Learning How to Ask: A Sociolinguistic Appraisal of the Role of the Interview in Social Science Research.* Cambridge: Cambridge University Press.

Brooks, R. and Tao, R. (2003) *China's Labour Market Performance and Challenges* IMF Working Paper, Asia and Pacific Department, Authorized for distribution by Eswar Prasad.

Brown E. (2006) *Chinese Labor Law Reform: Guaranteeing Worker Rights in the Age of Globalism,* (WorldPress), http://www.worldpress.org/Asia/2574.cfm (Accessed 22 November, 2007).

▶

Buck, T. (2011) 'Case selection informed by theory' in Piekkari, R. and Welch, C. (eds.) *Rethinking the Case Study in International Business and Management Research*. Cheltenham: Edward Elgar. pp 192–209.

BusinessWeek (27 March 2006) *How Rising Wages are Changing the Game of China*, http://www.businessweek.com/magazine/content/06_13/b3977049.htm (Accessed 19 January, 2008)

Carver, A. (1996) 'Open and Secret Regulations and Their Implication for Foreign Investment', in Child, J. and Yuan, L. (eds.) *Management Issues in China* Vol. 2, London and New York: Routledge, pp. 11–29.

Castells, M. (2000) 'The rise of the network society', *The Information Age* 1:2 Oxford: Blackwell.

Chan, K. W and Buckingham, W (2008) 'Is China abolishing the Hukou system?' The China Quarterly. 195: pp 482–606.

Chan, J and Pun, N. (2010) 'Suicide as Protest for the New Generation of Chinese Migrant Workers: Foxconn, Global Capital, and the State' *The Asia-Pacific Journal: Japan Focus*, http://japanfocus.org/-Ngai-Pun/3408 (Accessed 20 January, 2011).

Chang, L. T. (2008) Factory Girls: From Village to City in a Changing China. New York: Spiegel & Grau.

Child, J. (1991) 'A foreign perspective on the management of people in China' in *The international Journal of Human Resource Management*. 2:1, pp. 93–107

Child, J. (1994) *Management in China during the age of reform*. Cambridge: Cambridge University Press.

Chinanews.com, (7th Mar 2005) *FIEs in Chinese legislation*, http://www.chinanews-week.com.cn/2005-03-10/1/5339.html (Accessed 19 January 2008)

Cooke, F. L. (2011) 'The role of the state and emergent actors in the development of human resource management in China'. *The International Journal of Human Resource Management*. 22 (18), pp. 3830–3848.

Cooke, F. L. (2012) *Human Resource Management in China: New Trends and Practices*. London: Routledge.

De Cieri, H., Cox, J. W. and Fenwick M (2007) 'A review of international human resource management: integration, interrogation, imitation'. *International Journal of Management Reviews*, 9:4, pp. 281–302.

Dedoussis, V. and Littler, C. R. (1994) 'Understanding the Transfer of Japanese Management Practices. The Australian Case', in Tony Elger and Chris Smith, eds, *Global Japanization? The Transnational Transformation of the Labour Process*, New York: Routledge, pp. 175–195.

Doeringer, P. and Piore, M. (1971) *Internal Labor Markets and Manpower Analysis*, Mass.: Lexington.

Dunning, J. H. (1993) *The globalisation of Business: The Challenges of the 1990s*. London: Routledge.

Edwards, T., Colling, T., and Ferner, A. (2007) 'Conceptual approaches to the transfer of employment practices in multinational companies: an integrated approach', *Human Resource Management Journal*, 17: 3, pp. 201–217.

Edwards, T., Edwards, P. K., Ferner, A., Marginson, P., and Tregaskis, O. (2010) 'Multinational Companies and the Diffusion of Employment Practices: Explaining Variation Across Firms' *Management International Review*, 50(5), pp. 613–634.

Edwards, T. and Kuruvilla, S. (2005) 'International HRM: National business systems, organisational politics and the international division of labour in global value chains.' *International Journal of Human Resource Management*, 16: 1, pp 1–21.

Eisenhardt, K. M. (1991) 'Better stories and better constructs: the case for rigor and comparative logic' *Academy of Management Review*. 16: 3, pp. 620–627.

Elger, T. and Smith, C. (2005) *Assembling Work: Remaking Factory Regimes in Japanese Multinationals in Britain*, Oxford: Oxford University Press.

Ernst, D. and Kim, L (2002) 'Global production networks, knowledge diffusion and local capability formation'. *Research Policy*, 31: 8–9, pp. 1417–1429.

Ferner, A, Edwards, T. and Tempel, A. (2012) 'Power, institutions and the cross-national transfer of employment practices in multinationals'. *Human Relations* 65: 1, pp 1–25.

Fletcher, M. and Plakoyiannaki, E. (2011) 'Case selection in international business: key issues and common misconceptions' in Piekkari, R. and Welch, C. (eds.) *Rethinking the Case Study in International Business and Management Research*. Cheltenham: Edward Elgar, pp. 171–191.

Frost, T. S., Birkinshaw, J. W., Ensign, P. C., (2002) 'Centre of Excellence in Multinational Corporations', *Strategic Management Journal*, 23: 11, pp. 997–1018.

Forsgren, M. (1990) 'Managing the International Multi-Centre Firm'. *European Management Journal*, 8: 2, pp. 261–267.

Forsgren, M. and Pederson, T., (1998) 'Centers of Excellence in Multinational Companies: The Case of Denmark' in Brikinshaw J. and Hood N. (eds.), *Multinational Corporate Evolution and Subsidiary Development*, New York: St. Martin's Press, pp. 141–161.

Frobel, F., Heinrichs, J. and Kreye, O. (1980) *The New International Division of Labour: Structural Unemployment in Industrialised Countries and Industrialisation in Developing Countries*, Cambridge: Cambridge University Press.

Gereffi, G. (1999) 'International trade and industrial upgrading in the apparel commodity chain' *Journal of International Economics* 48: 1, pp. 48–70.

Global Labour Strategy, (2007), *Undue Influence: Corporations Gain Grounds in Battle Over China's Labour Law date*, http://laborstrategies.blogs.com (accessed 18 November, 2007)

Harzing, A. K., (1999) *Managing the Multinationals: An International Study of Control Mechanism*, Cheltenham, UK. Northampton, MA, USA: Edward Elgar

Heery E. and Frege, C. (2006) 'New Actors in Industrial Relations'. *British Journal of Industrial Relations* 44: 4, pp. 601–604.

Hoopes, D.G., Madsen, T.L. and Walker, G. (2003) Guest Editors' Introduction to the Special Issue: Why is There a Resource-Based View? Toward a Theory of Competitive Heterogeneity. *Strategic Management Journal* 24, pp. 889–902.

Howard, A., Liu, L. Wellins, R. S. and Williams, S. (2008) *The flight of human talent: employee retention in China*. Society for Human Resource Management, http://www.ddiworld.com/pdf/employeeretentioninchina2007_es_ddi.pdf (Accessed 14 November 2009).

Huselid, M.A., Jackson, S.E. and Schuler, R.S., (1997) Technical and strategic human resource management effectiveness as determinants of firm performance. *The Academy of Management Journal*, 40: 1, pp. 171–188.

Japan-China Trade Promotion Organization (JCTPO), (2005) *Summary of Japan-China Trade Promotion Organization in the past decade* [in Japanese] JCTPO

Japan External Trade Organization (JETRO), (2002) *JETRO White Paper on Foreign Direct Investment 2002.* http://www.jetro.go.jp/en/stats/white_paper/invest2002.pdf (Accessed 20 November, 2007).

Japan External Trade Organization (JETRO), (7th Apr 2006) *Survey on Activities of the Japanese Invested Companies Overseas*, JETRO, (in Japanese) http://www.jetro.go.jp/jpn/reports/05001120, (Accessed 21 November 2007).

Japan Institute for Labour Policy and Training (JILPT), (2006) 4th *Survey on Human Resource Management of Japanese Multinational Corporations* Tokyo: JILPT.

Kaiser S., Kirby, D. A., and Fan, Y. (1996) 'Foreign Direct Investment in China: An Examination of the Literature' in Rowley C. and Lewis, M. (eds.), *Greater China: Political Economy, Inward Investment and Business Culture*. London: Frank Cass

Kaplinsky, R. (2000) Globalisation and Unequalisation: What Can Be Learned from Value Chain Analysis? *Journal of Development Studies*, 37(2): 117–146.

Kristensen P.H and Zeitlin, J. (2005) *Local Players in Global Games. The Strategic Constitution of a Multinational Corporation*, Oxford: Oxford University Press.

Knight, J.B. and Song, L. (2005) *Towards a Labour Market in China*. New York: Oxford University Press.

Lee, C. K. (2007) *Against the Law: Labor Protests in China's Rustbelt and Sunbelt.* Berkeley: University of California Press.

Li, J. (2003) 'Strategic human resource management and MNEs' performance in China' in *International Journal of Human Resource Management.* 14: 2, pp. 157–173.

Li, Y. and Sheldon, P. (2010) 'HRM lives inside and outside the firm: employers, skill shortages and the local labour market in China' *The International Journal of Human Resource Management.* 21: 2 pp. 2173–2193.

Liu. Z. (2005) 'Institution and inequality: the hukou system in China' *Journal of Comparative Economics* 33: pp. 133–157.

Lu, X. Y., (2006) 'Paying attention to research and resolve the problems related to mingong'. In Research Office of China State Council, (ed.) *Survey Report on the Problems of Rural Migrant Workers in China*. Beijing: China Yanshi Press, pp. 487–492.

Milliken, F. J., (1987) 'Three Types of Perceived Uncertainty about the Environment: State, Effect and Response uncertainty', *Academy of Management Review* 12: 1, pp. 133–143.

Moore, F., (2011) 'Holistic ethnography: studying the impact of multiple national identities on post-acquisition organisations'. *Journal of International Business Studies*. 42: pp. 645–671.

Morgan, G., Kristensen, P. H. and Whitley, R. (2003) *The Multinational Firm.* Oxford: Oxford University Press.

Morris, J., Wilkinson, B. and Gamble, J. (2009) 'Strategic international human resource management or the 'bottom line'? The cases of electronics and garments commodity chains in China'. *The International Journal of Human Resource Management.* 20: 2, pp. 348–371.

National Bureau of Statistics of China (2001) *China Statistics Year Book 2001*, http://www.stats.gov.cn/english/statisticaldata/yearlydata/YB2001e/ml/indexE. htm (Accessed 2 February, 2012).

National Bureau of Statistics of China (2010) China Statistics Year Book 2010. http://www.stats.gov.cn/tjsj/ndsj/2010/indexeh.htm (Accessed 2 February, 2012).

Porter M. E. (1986) *Competition in Global Industries: A Conceptual Framework* Boston, Mass.: Harvard Business School.

Prahalad C. K. and Doz Y. L., (1987) *The Multinational Mission: Balancing Local Demands and Global Vision.* New York, Collier Macmillan, London: Free Press.

Pudeloko, M. and Harzing, A., (2007) Country-of-origin, localization, or dominance effect? An empirical investigation of HRM in foreign subsidiaries. *Human Resource Management,* 46: 4, pp. 535–559.

Quintanilla, J. and Ferner, A., (2003) 'Multinationals and human resource management: between global convergence and national identity' *International Journal of Human Resource Management* 14: 3, pp. 363–368.

Reutersward, A. (2005) 'Labour Protection in China: Challenges facing Labour Offices and Social Insurance' OECD Social, Employment and Migration Working Papers, http://www.oecd.org/dataoecd/48/18/35621263.pdf (Accessed 19 January 2008)

Ross, A. (2007) 'Outsourcing as a way of life? Knowledge Transfer in the Yangze Delta' in Lee C. K. (ed.) *Working in China: Ethnographies of Labour and Workplace Transformation* New York: Routledge, pp. 118–208.

Rosenzweig, P. M (2006) 'The dual logic behind international human resource management: pressures for global integration and local responsiveness' in Stahl, G. K. and Bjorkman, I. (eds.) *Handbook of Research in International Human Resource Management.* Cheltenham: Edward Elgar, pp. 36–48.

Silver, B. (1997) Turning Points in Workers' Militancy in the World Automobile Industry, 1930s-1990s. *Research in the Sociology of Work,* 7, 43–71.

Silver, B. (2003) *Forces of Labor: Workers' Movements and Globalization since 1870.* Cambridge: Cambridge University Press.

Smith, C., Child, J. and Rowlinson, M. (1990) *Reshaping Work: the Cadbury experience* Cambridge: Cambridge University Press.

Smith, C. and Meiksins, P., (1995) 'System, Societal and Dominance Effects in Cross-national Organisational analysis', *Work, Employment and Society,* 9: 2, pp 241–368.

Smith, C. (2003) 'Living at Work: Management Control and the Dormitory Labour System in China' *Asia Pacific Journal of Management* 20: 3, pp. 333–358.

Smith, C. (2005) 'Beyond Convergence and Divergence: Explaining Variations in Organisational Practices and Forms' in Stephen Ackroyd, Rosemary Batt, Paul Thompson and Pamela Tolbert (eds.) *The Oxford Handbook of Work and Organisation,* Oxford: Oxford University Press.

Smith, C. (2008) 'Work organization within a dynamic globalising context: a critique of national institutional analysis of the international firm and an alternative perspective' in Smith, C, McSweeney B. and Fitzgerald R. (eds.) *Remaking Management: Between Global and Local,* Cambridge: Cambridge University Press.

▶

Stopford and Wells (1972) *Managing the Multinational Enterprise: Organization of the Firm and Ownership of the Subsidiaries*, New York: Basic Books.

Surlemont, B. (1998) 'A Typology of Centres within Multinational Corporations: An Empirical Investigation' in Birkinshaw, J and Hood N. (eds.) *Multinational Corporate Evolution and Subsidiary Development*, London: Macmillan, pp. 178–230.

Takeuchi, N., Chen, Z. and Lam, W. (2009) 'Coping with an emerging market competition through strategy-human resource alignment: case study evidence from five leading Japanese manufacturers in the People's Republic of China' *International Journal of Human Resource Management* 20: 12, pp. 2454–2470.

Taylor, B., (1999) 'Patterns of control within Japanese manufacturing plants in China: doubts about Japanization in Asia'. *Journal of Management Studies*, 36: 6, pp 853–873.

Taylor, B. (2001) 'The management of labour in Japanese manufacturing plants in China' *The International Journal of Human Resource Management*. 12: 4, pp. 601–620.

Warner, M. (2000) 'Introduction: the Asia-pacific HRM model revisited' in *International Journal of Human Resource Management* 11:2, pp. 171–182.

Wilkinson, B., Gamble, J., Humphrey, J., Morris, J. and Anthony, D. (2001) 'The New International Division of Labour in Asian Electronics: Work Organization and Human Resources in Japan and Malaysia' *Journal of Management Studies*. 38: 5, pp. 675–695.

Woo, M. (1993) 'Exportation promotion in the new global division of labour: The case of South Korean automobile industry', *Sociological Perspectives*, 36:4, pp. 335–357

Yao, X. and Wang, L. (2006) 'The predictability of normative organizational commitment for turnover in Chinese companies: a cultural perspective' in *International Journal of Human Resource Management*. 17: 6, pp. 1058–1075.

Zhang, M., Nyland, C. and Zhu, C. J. (2010) 'Hukou-based HRM in contemporary China: the case of Jiangsu and Shanghai' *Asia Pacific Business Review*, 16: 3, pp. 377–393.

Zhu, H., Moe, T., Eoyang, C., Wang, H and Bei, B. (2011) 'Hukou reform: a mid to long term goal, picking up pace'. *Equality Research* Goldman Sachs Global Investment Research Series.

The Self-organization of Women Workers in the Informal Sector of the Garment Industry: A Study of Female-led Cooperative Production Teams in the Yangtze River Delta Region of China

6

Lulu Fan

Introduction

Research into Chinese women workers in the reform era concentrates on migrant workers in south China (Lee, 1998; Pun, 2005). The manufacturing industry regards single women between 18 and 25 as first choice workers since they are dexterous, allegedly 'docile', and have few household burdens. These workers are called *Da Gong Mei* (migrant maiden workers). The reproduction mode of migrant maiden workers is split. They live in dormitories to reduce costs and therefore the wages that the capitalists have to pay them are also reduced (Pun and Smith, 2007). With the development of the capitalist mode of production in China and the implementation of the one-child policy, labour shortages have become more severe. These shortages have affected the female-dominated industries. Liu (2011) found that an increasing number of married women work in the garment industry and Deng (2014) noted how male workers now dominate the electronics industry. Another significant factor is the accelerated process of proletarianization in China. Capital flow to the countryside has expanded and peasants' land (owned by the state but occupied for years by peasants) is being expropriated, which results in increasing numbers of landless peasants entering the proletariat (Chen and Tang, 2013; Leung, 2013). Moreover, the new generation of migrant workers lack experience in rural production and do not view returning to the country as a future goal (Pun and Lu, 2010). Hence, a new class formation exists within China as a new working class (at least a class-in-itself) emerges. These social, structural, and demographic changes affect management control and labour resistance (Liu, 2011; Chen and Tang, 2013; Leung, 2013; Deng, 2014). This chapter will explore the influence of local married women workers on the organization of production. Work–life conflicts exist widely in China, especially for local married-women workers since they have the additional duties of pregnancy and child rearing as well as unpaid domestic work. The gender differentiation in unpaid domestic work is clear.

Female Workers in the Informal Sector

Informal employment in the era of globalization

The notion of an 'informal sector' was developed in the early 1970s for the purpose of analysis and policy-making. The 15th International Conference of Labour Statisticians stated that:

> The informal sector may be broadly characterized as consisting of units engaged in the production of goods or services with the primary objective of generating employment and incomes to the persons concerned. These units typically operate at a low level of organization, with little or no division between labour and capital as factors of production and on a small scale. Labour relations—where they exist—are based mostly on casual employment, kinship or personal and social relations rather than contractual arrangements with formal guarantees. (ILO, 2013: 14)

Linked to the informal sector is the term 'informal employment': employees without labour contracts, social insurance, paid annual leave, or sick leave (ILO, 2013: 41). Informal employment exists in both the formal and informal sectors. Informal employment has been a clear trend in capitalist and post-socialist countries since the late 1970s. Since the advent of neoliberalism, there has been a tendency for a race to the bottom to develop. Looking at the global picture, informal employment as a percentage of overall employment in South Asia is 82 per cent and in India this figure was 84 per cent from 2004 to 2010. In sub-Saharan Africa, East and Southeast Asia, Latin America, the Middle East, and North Africa, informal employment makes up 66 per cent, 65 per cent, 51 per cent, and 45 per cent of overall employment, respectively

(WIEGO, 2014). Informal employment is also commonplace in China. Informal employment[1] made up 63.19 per cent of non-agricultural employment in China in 2010 (Yan and Liu, 2013).

Since the government policies and labour laws are the outcomes of class struggle and the expressions of class forces, to explore the possibilities of enhancing labour's power to deal with the problems of 'informal employment' we should go back to class structure and the agency or subjectivity of workers rather than hope the state can act as a neutral party to discipline the misconduct of capitalists.

Informal employment and female workers

Studies of developing countries indicate that women are more likely to be informal workers (ILO and WIEGO, 2013). In urban China, 36 per cent of female labourers were informal workers compared to 30 per cent of men.[2] Informal workers are a heterogeneous group of people with different reasons to work in the informal sector. The schools of dualists (ILO, 1972), legalists (De Soto, 1988), structuralists (Portes, Castells and Benton, 1989), and voluntarists (Maloney, 2004) have different explanations for informal employment. It is possible to express the condition of being informal through the 4Es Model: exclusion (mismatch between demand for and supply of labour); entry barriers (unreasonable regulations and a hostile legal environment); exploitation (subordination of informal units and workers to capitalist firms); and exit (calculated decision by informal entrepreneurs to exit).[3]

WIEGO summarized seven types of employment status in the informal sector and sorted six of them according to risk of poverty, average earnings, and gender segmentation. They discovered that women are predominant in low-wage and high-risk work in the informal sector.[4]

Many reasons account for the segmentation of job opportunities and wage level by sex, such as the sex stereotypes in the social division of labour[5] (Hartmann, 1976), the predominant position of male workers in unions (Colgan and Ledwith, 2002), gendered educational levels, and gendered social divisions in technical jobs (Tan and Li, 2003).

However, according to the study of the garment industry in the Yangtze River Delta (YRD), the author of this chapter found that local skilled women workers who possess strong marketing bargaining power preferred to work as informal workers. Moreover, some skilled workers are not isolated as they organize cooperative production teams to enhance their 'associational power' (Wright, 2000; Silver, 2003). They initiate collective bargaining[6] with agents who send them production orders and achieve much higher wages than the regular (formal) workers in factories. This study may provide some insights to the following questions:

a) Why some workers with higher marketing bargaining power voluntarily become informal labour?
b) Under what conditions wages for informal workers can be higher when compared to their formal counterparts?
c) How female workers in the informal sector protect their rights and benefits?

Research Methodology

Industry selection

Widespread informal employment in the garment industry

The main features of the garment industry, such as labour-intensity, proneness to relocation, and low levels of capital investment constitute 'buyer-driven' governance, which can indicate that labour is in a disadvantageous position (Mezzadri, 2014). Subcontracting and outsourcing production has been a feature throughout the history of the international garment industry. A research report, published in 2005, indicated that garment productions in nine countries[7] were dominated by small-scale factories and workshops. These production units frequently employ workers on short-term contracts or without contracts (WWW, 2005).

The garment industry is female-dominated in China

Female workers make up a significant proportion of labour in the garment industry (see Table 6.1).

Because of the female-labour shortage in the garment industry, many factories have to accept males as sewing workers (Siu, 2015). Although the percentage of male workers has increased in the past ten years, garment manufacture remains a female-dominated industry.

Research sites and research method

According to the *China Garment Industry Development Report 2013–2014* (China National Garment Association, 2014), there are 50 garment clusters in China. Among them, ten are located in Guangdong Province while eight are located each in Jiangsu Province and Zhejiang Province.

Table 6.1 Gender segmentation of the labour force in the garment industry

Year	Female	Male
2003	72%	28%
2004	72.2%	27.8%
2005	71.7%	28.3%
2006	71.2%	28.8%
2007	70.2%	29.8%
2008	69.1%	30.9%
2009	68.2%	31.8%
2010	68.7%	31.3%
2011	65.6%	34.4%
2012	66.5%	33.5%

The data are extracted from the China Labour Statistical Yearbook (2004–2013)

However, existing research into the Chinese garment industry has mainly focused on the Pearl River Delta (PRD) (Pun, 1994; Gao, 2006; Pun and Smith, 2007; Chan and Siu, 2009; Liu, 2011; Huang, 2012). There has been comparatively little research into the situation in the YRD.

Pilot study: six cities of YRD

The UK Economic and Social Research Council (ESRC) funded research, the Working Poor Project,[8] and the China research team chose six cities in the YRD for a pilot study carried out between December 2011 and July 2012. Trading companies and big factories in Shanghai, export-oriented apparel manufacturing factories in Jiaxing, garment factories produced for online retailing in Hangzhou, textile factories in Ningbo, children's clothing factories in Huzhou, sock factories in Shaoxing, and non-factory production units in these areas were explored in the first round of fieldwork. A total of 34 textile and garment factories and ten non-factory production units were investigated[9] during this period.

From an initial pilot study, we categorized six types of workers in production organizations, listed in Table 6.2.

Jiaxing includes all the six types of workers found in the textile and garment industry in the YRD region. Therefore we chose to carry out further research in Jiaxing to better understand the predicament of garment workers in different positions in production organizations.

Investigation in Jiaxing and Shanghai

In January 2013, an investigation was undertaken in Jiaxing and Shanghai[10] to explore the situation of factory workers in these cities.

Table 6.2 Six categories of workers in production organizations in YRD

Types of workers	Regular workers[1]	Workers of contractor team[2]	Workers in cooperative production teams[3]	Individual outsourced workers[4]	Wage earners in workshops[5]	Home workers[6]
Area of Distribution	Jiaxing, Hangzhou, Shanghai, Ningbo, Shaoxing, Huzhou	Jiaxing, Hangzhou, Shanghai, Huzhou	Jiaxing	Jiaxing, Hangzhou	Jiaxing, Hangzhou, Shanghai, Ningbo, Shaoxing, Huzhou	Jiaxing, Hangzhou, Shanghai, Ningbo, Shaoxing, Huzhou

From research in six cities

[1] These workers come to the factory individually and are without any dependent relations with the contractor or workers' organizations. Generally, the employers forbid them to transform the employment status into members of contractor teams or cooperative production teams in current the workplace since it may change the wage level and payment method. However, the workers can join the contractor teams or cooperative production teams when these teams quit the factory and transfer to other production units.

[2] Some contractors recruit workers from their hometown and introduce them to factories. These workers are under a dual management system, from both the contractor and the factory. Contractors receive referral fees and management fees from the factory employers. At the same time, contractors have responsibilities of putting workers under their protection in urgent moments like when they confront wage arrears or are abused by other workers.

[3] In Jiaxing, some skilled workers organize teams to produce clothing in home-based workplaces for nearby garment factories. If these workshops lacked sufficient subcontracting orders, the workers collectively work in factories or larger workshops to undertake production tasks. Once a production order is completed, the profit is shared equally among members. As these cooperative production teams are autonomous associations of garment workers who voluntarily cooperate for mutual economic benefits and treat each other fairly, we can thereby regard them as sharing some characteristics of producers' cooperatives. However, this kind of team lacked explicit membership or a formal structure according to a written constitution. It also had no connections with other cooperatives or cooperative associations. So the author coined the term cooperative production team to describe this type of production unit.

[4] They are skilled workers who would like to become casual workers rather than regular workers. The payment is based on daily wages instead of piece rates. Normally, their daily wage is higher than the wage standard of regular workers. Unlike members of cooperative production teams, individual outsourced workers have no organization in the workplace. They can quit the job whenever they want since there is no deposit grasped by the employers like that of regular workers.

[5] This kind of labour works in non-factory production units and they have no kinship with workshop owners.

[6] Homeworkers refer to those who work in a home-based workplace and collaborate with family members to deal with production orders.

We collected questionnaires from 121 garment workers in Shanghai and Jiaxing. Most of the respondents worked in medium-sized and large factories (see Table 6.3).

Information regarding the social profile, migration pattern, labour process, reproduction mode, association, and collective actions were gleaned using the questionnaires.[11] The information was then used to compare these workers' situations with their counterparts in the informal sector. Some home workers in Shanghai were also interviewed in this period.

Table 6.3 Employee size (N=121)

		Frequency	Per Cent
Valid	Below 50	4	3.3
	50~99	8	6.6
	100~499	37	30.6
	500~999	30	24.8
	1000~4999	21	17.4
	Above 5000	1	.8
	Total	101	83.5
Missing		20	16.5
Total		121	100.0

Fieldwork study in Jiaxing, Huzhou, and Hangzhou

From March to August of 2013, I worked in a medium-sized garment factory as an auxiliary worker for two and a half months as well as one and half months in a small factory to carry out participant observation. Another two months were spent interviewing workers in nearby workshops and home workers fulfilling factory orders as well as workshops in Huzhou and Hangzhou. About 18 production units and 870 workers were involved in my fieldwork during this period.

Overview of the research object in informal sector

Data from workers in non-factory production units in four cities[12] are used in a comparison with factory workers (see Table 6.4). The four cities refer to Shanghai Municipality and three cities of Zhejiang Province. The three cities in Zhejiang Province are Hangzhou, Jiaxing, and Huzhou. The clothes produced in Hangzhou, Jiaxing, and Huzhou have some distinctive regional features. The non-factory workshops in Hangzhou are mainly produced for domestic online retailing. At the same time, Hangzhou is well-known for ladies' wear brand enterprises. Some such enterprises subcontract a few orders to workshops. Huzhou workshops supply the domestic children's clothing market. The workshops in Jiaxing Pinghu prefer to receive orders of down coats for relatively high processing fees. These three cities are close to Shanghai and are in the YRD. The non-factory units investigated in this study are located in the outskirts or towns of these cities. A total of 70 workers in non-factory units and 14 production units are examined in this study. There are four types of non-factory production units (see Table 6.5). The cooperative production team could only be found in Jiaxing but this is an important

Table 6.4 The regional distribution of the research object

Production units / Region Distribution	Contractor workshops		Workshops involving family members and wage earners		Cooperative production teams		Home workers		Total	
	Units	Workers	Units	Workers	Units	Workers	Units	Workers	Units	Workers
Shanghai	0	0	0	0	0	0	2	2+1	2	3
Hangzhou	0	0	1	6	0	0	2	2+1	3	9
Jiaxing	2	14+10	1	9	2	6+6	3	1+1+1	8	48
Huzhou	0	0	1	10	0	0	0	0	1	10
Total	2	24	3	25	2	12	7	9	14	70

Table 6.5 Four types of non-factory units in the garment industry in YRD (China)

	Contractors workshops	Workshops involving family members and wage earners	Cooperative production team	Home worker
Number of workers	Normally, between ten and 20 workers are employed.	Normally, fewer than ten workers are employed.	Normally, the number of workers is between six and eight.	Only one or two workers.
Production activities	Sewing whole clothes.	Sewing whole clothes/ sewing parts of clothes.	Sewing whole clothes.	Sewing whole clothes/ sewing parts of clothes/ knitting sweaters with machines/ attaching beads on clothes/ cutting thread.
The space for production and living	The living space and production space is different. Contractors and workers live in different houses.	The living space and production space normally is in the same building. Contractors and migrant workers also live in the same buildings or houses (some may choose to live outside).	Most workers are locals living in their own homes. The workplace may be a worker's home.	Workers produce at home or the place they rent. The production and living space are the same.
Personal relationships in the organization	There is a hierarchy between contractors and ordinary workers.	There is a hierarchy between workshop owners and wage earners.	Equal partnership between members. There is no contractor and all members use collective bargaining with the employers together. The team members are skilled workers and they share the processing fees equally.	Workers are individuals or family members.

Summarized from investigation in the Yangtze River Delta Region (China) (Both the ESRC Working Poor Project and the PhD thesis fieldwork study of the author) aspect of this study and we will explore its characteristics by comparing it with three other types of production units.

Both contractor workshops and workshops involving family members and wage earners can be categorized as enterprises of informal employers according to the ILO (2013) definition, since they employ at least one worker on a continuous basis. These are distinct from own-account enterprises that only employ workers on an occasional basis. Home worker workshops are a kind of own-account enterprise. Contractor workshop and workshops involving family members and wage earners are separate here mainly because of their differing production activities. Workshops involving family members and wage earners sometimes focus on producing parts of garments while contractor workshops always process whole clothes. There can sometimes be more than 20 workers employed in contractor workshops. Although these workshops can be larger scale than other enterprises in the informal sector in other parts of the world,[13] they remain unregistered and do not pay tax and therefore are still categorized within the informal sector.

Research Findings

Do workers have choice?

The demographic bonus of surplus labour is supposed to be one of the comparative advantages of China, which bolsters rapid economic growth. However, labour shortages have occurred in Chinese coastal regions since 2003 (Research Group of Ministry of Labour and Social Security of the People's Republic, 2004). Since 2010, at a national level, the demand/supply ratio in the labour market continues to exceed 1 (Cai, 2013). In the first quarter of 2014, the demand/supply ratio was 1.11 in China. This means, on average, when there are 111 vacancies, only 100 jobseekers apply for them. Meanwhile, 97.5 per cent of demand is concentrated in enterprises.[14]

With regard to garment workers, labour shortages in coastal areas of China are severe. We can take garment workers in Jiaxing as an example. According to the Jiaxing labour market report, in 2007, there was demand for 34,657 cutting and stitching workers. However, only 10,156 workers applied for these kinds of jobs. The demand/supply ratio was 3.41.[15] The demand/supply ratio was 2.45 in 2013. Men made up 53.18 per cent of applicants.[16] These figures indicate a clear labour shortage, which boosts the bargaining power of labour, particularly the bargaining power of skilled women workers.

The informal sector has been seen as absorbing many unskilled and semi-skilled workers. However, recent research into labour-intensive manufacturing industry in the PRD region of China has revealed that many skilled workers now choose to be informal workers in order to extract higher wages and greater freedom (Liu, 2011; Huang, 2012). Based on the study of garment workers in YRD, I also found some skilled workers, such as the all-round skilled workers (Quan Neng Shu Liang Gong)[17] who have a rich experience in the garment industry, autonomously choosing to work in non-factory units rather than factories. Table 6.6 illustrates the working experience of all-round skilled workers who choose to work in the informal sector in Jiaxing Pinghu.

These all-round skilled workers hope to earn higher wages and have more control in the labour process. Moreover, taking care of households (domestic tasks) is another concern for them. All-round skilled workers and auxiliary workers have different routes into the informal sector. This will be explored in the following sections.

Reasons for working in the informal sector

Higher wages

According to data from the 121 factory garment workers in Shanghai and Jiaxing we surveyed, the mean average monthly wage in 2013 was 2,684.59 RMB. When dividing the average monthly wage by the 12.5 hours a day and 26 days a month (a common working time arrangement in garment factories of YRD), the average hourly wage is 8.26 RMB, lower than the sewing workers in the informal sector (see Table 6.7).

Table 6.6 Work experience of all-round skilled workers in the informal sector

Place of work	Average years of experience in garment industry (factory and non-factory units) (Units: Year)
Contractor workshops in Jiaxing (14 workers)	6.2
Workshops involving family members and wage earners in Huzhou (10 workers)	8.6
Cooperative production team A in Jiaxing (6 workers)	22.3
Cooperative production team B in Jiaxing (6 workers)	25.2

Fieldwork data

Table 6.7 Average hourly wage of workers in the informal sector

Work activity	Production organizations	Average hourly wage (RMB)
Knitting sweaters with machines	Jiaxing home worker	29
Sewing whole items of clothing	Huzhou workshops involving family members and wage earners	17.1–21.4
Sewing whole items of clothing	Jiaxing cooperative production team	14.5–18.6
Sewing whole items of clothing	Hangzhou workshops involving family members and wage earners	14.2–17.9
Sewing whole items of clothing	Hangzhou home worker	12.3
Sewing whole items of clothing	Jiaxing contractor workshops	10.8–11.5
Sewing whole items of clothing	Shanghai home worker	11
Sewing parts of clothing	Jiaxing home worker	10
Sewing parts of clothing	Jiaxing workshops involving family members and wage earners	8.5–10.3
Thread cutting	Jiaxing home worker	7
Thread cutting and attaching beads	Hangzhou home worker	6
Thread cutting	Shanghai home worker	4.5

Summarized from fieldwork data

Autonomy and dignity of work

Regulations and discipline in garment factories are very strict: being late or leaving early by more than five minutes results in a 1 RMB deduction from wages for each minute. A factory (in which the author carried out participant observation) enforced the following code of conduct:

- Absenteeism for one day resulted in a fine of 100 RMB.
- Using a cell-phone and surfing on the internet was forbidden during working time. Listening to MP3 and MP4 players was also prohibited, and resulted in a 1 RMB fine for the first occurrence, 2 RMB for the second occurrence, and so on.
- Eating was forbidden in the workshop. Any occurrence results in a 1 RMB fine.

Workers were not allowed to eat or talk during work. The labour process is strictly controlled by the employer and manager. Many factories use cameras to monitor workers. Workers experience a strong sense of alienation during work and they feel humiliated if they are scolded. Therefore, many workers would like to work in workshops without strict discipline or choose to become home workers so that they can totally control the labour process.

Taking care of household duties

The *danwei* system used to exist in Chinese state-owned enterprises. Workers enjoyed free access to child-care centres, schools, hospitals, and housing, which helped workers deal with reproduction issues and achieve a work–life balance. However, since marketization and privatization, discipline is increasingly pro-capital, and labour (especially women workers) is more vulnerable. The pressure of work–life conflict is especially borne by women workers (Fan, 2014).

Regarding the garment industry, work–life conflicts become more severe as working time is very lengthy in this industry. Table 6.8 illustrates the arrangement of a working day in a regular garment factory in YRD.

Generally, Sundays were time off and there was no overtime work on Wednesday.

In factories, workers are required to focus on their own working procedures. If a worker is absent, the output of an assembly line will be affected significantly since co-workers are not familiar with other workers' procedures. Hence, employers do their utmost to prevent absenteeism.

Although migrant workers leave their hometowns to pursue employment, they still have family responsibilities. Generally, women workers have more emotional attachment to the family compared with male workers. For example, a female migrant worker with two children at home mentioned her anxiety when her children were ill. She said: 'I really hope to go back home to look after my children, but I am afraid that the boss may not give me permission to leave.' She also mentioned

Table 6.8 Timetable of a working day in a garment factory in YRD

Time period	The issues related to production in factory
Before 7:30	The time before going to work
7:30–11:00	Working time in the morning
11:00–11:30	Lunch time
11:30–17:00	Working time in the afternoon
17:00–17:30	Dinner time
17:30–21:30	Working time in the evening
After 21:30	Off work

Fieldwork data

that she envied her husband because, as a construction worker, he could return home from time to time so he had a closer relationship with the children.

Female workers' responses to work–life conflicts include quitting their jobs and becoming full-time housewives – although economically difficult – as well as moving into other sectors such as the informal sector.

One female worker who knitted woollen sweaters with machines at home and sold them as a source of income told me that seven years previously her mother had passed away and this meant there was no one to help her care for her two children. She had to give up her job in a large woollen sweater enterprise and started to work at home. She used the garage basement as the workshop. The machinery was worth several thousand RMB, and the cost of electricity was about 3 RMB per day. Colleagues of her husband, family friends, and new contacts buy the sweaters she produced. The margin for a woollen sweater is 50 RMB to 100 RMB. She normally knitted five sweaters a day. Her working schedule was flexible to accommodate household duties (see Table 6.9).

Another home worker was a local elderly woman whose land was expropriated. She had to take care of her grandson and could not work the whole day in the factory. So she cut garment threads at home. The fee for cutting the thread of a pair of short pants is 0.1 RMB.

Women make up 70 per cent of labour in the informal sector in this research. Moreover, 77.1 per cent of workers in the informal sector have mastered the skill of sewing whole clothes and most of them are female workers. For all-round skilled workers, working in non-factory workplaces guarantees them higher wages than working in garment factories as assembly line workers. The operating costs of a non-factory unit are much lower than a factory since they do not pay taxes and the cost of electricity is lower.[18] A small volume of high-qualified orders are subcontracted to the non-factory units. This may be the reason that the workers can share more value.

Table 6.9 The schedule of a home-based worker

6:30–9:00	Prepares the breakfast, sends children to school, and cleans the house
9:00–16:00	Works in the basement or receives the client[7]
16:00–18:00	Prepares for the dinner, supervises children with their homework
18:00–22:00	Works in the basement or receives the client

Fieldwork data

[7] Measure the customer's size, create the design, and knit the sweater and press.

Self-organizing workers in the informal sector

It seems that the cooperative production team is very significant since this is an effective form of workers' self-organization, boosting bargaining power under the authoritarian regime. The political context which frames Chinese workers' associational power has distinctive indicators. Since the reform and opening up policy was put into effect in the late 1970s, the Chinese Communist Party has dramatically changed its relationship with workers and has begun to promote capital accumulation (Lee, 2007). The characteristics of authoritarian government mean multiple political parties have not yet emerged in current China and hence, a party that represents workers' interests does not exist. Moreover, trade unions are obliged to play a role in the state apparatus, especially at central and local government levels. The enterprise trade union has to adhere to the interest of employers, which is totally different from the functions of unions in Hong Kong (Choi, 2008), Taiwan (Qiu, 2011), and other countries and regions (Koo, 2001).

Pursuing the coverage and growth rate of unions, many enterprise unions become the puppets of employers and the state. To complete the index formulated by upper-level government, collective consultation has transformed into bargaining between government, trade unions, and capital. This results in collective contracts without bargaining and implementation effects (Wu, 2012). Some effective collective consultations unify wage levels and constrain workers' mobility. In Zhejiang Wenling, a noted woollen sweater-producing area, collective wage bargaining has been in effect since 2003. The garment union and employer association together determine the minimum wage for each working procedure. This is called the Wenling Mode (Zheng, 2011). This mode of collective bargaining is thought to ensure annual wage increases for workers and help employers reduce turnover and strikes (Xu, 2005).

Most garment enterprise unions studied in the research project failed to protect workers' rights and interests because, firstly, union leaders are managers or are selected by the management; and secondly because union membership rates among migrant workers is very low. The majority of the respondents (about 61.8 per cent) indicated that they were not members of a trade union. Only 19.2 per cent of workers surveyed stated that their workplace trade unions have monitored and defended labour rights. In contrast, about 18.2 per cent and 25.3 per cent of interviewees characterized the role of trade unions as 'no use' and 'delivering holiday welfare and entertainment' respectively. This survey was conducted mostly in mid-to-large-scale enterprises, and the situation is likely to be worse in small-scale production units and non-factory units.

Without effective assistance from the Chinese trade union system, the workers have no choice but to rely on their own pre-existing localistic networks to build cultures of solidarity, but once the workers' solidarity is built, they can articulate their aggregate interests along the line of class (Chan and Pun, 2009: 290). Except for the cooperative production team, the team under the contractor management system in the factory was another typical form of workers' self-organizing association. These teams are generally connected with the original place-based gangs out of the workplace. The book *Shanghai on Strike: the Politics of Chinese Labour* discusses the contractor manager system from 1839 to 1949 in China. Some industries in Shanghai used contractors to recruit semi-skilled or unskilled workers from rural areas and supervise performance. Contractors also controlled the job opportunities of non-industry sectors, such as nightmen and dock workers. These workers had strong personal attachments with contractors. Workers needed to obey contractors' rules both in the workplace and in gangs since the contractors were usually their gang superiors (Perry, 1993). These contractor management systems and local gangs still exist in China today according to our study of the garment industry.

In Table 6.10 the author summarizes the differences between the contractor management system and the cooperative production team in terms of the four levels of class formation theory of Katznelson and Zolberg (1986).

Table 6.10 Two types of worker self-organization

	Contractor management system/Gang	Cooperative production team
Class structure	Semi-proletariat	Proletariat
Social organization	The organization is mainly based on native place and kinship network.	This kind of association is mainly based on networks that form in workplace.
	Hierarchical relationships between contractor and general workers, elders and the younger generation as well as skilled workers and novices.	Equal partnership between members.
The faith of the organization (class disposition)	Hard work pays.	There has to be a reasonable piece rate.
The reason that initiates collective actions	Defensive reasons like their wages not being cleared at the end of the year or workers being abused by managers or workers from other provinces.	Aggressive appeal such as dissatisfaction with the piece rate. Contradiction between labour and capital.

Summarized from fieldwork data

Workers under the contractor management system are normally migrant workers who 'own' land and identify themselves as rural migrant workers rather than industry workers. The production and reproduction is separated in different regions. This kind of organization is mainly based on native places and kinship networks. There are hierarchical relationships between contractors and general workers, the elderly and the younger generation, as well as skilled workers and novices. The contractor has a superior position since he or she is a skilled worker and normally in the elderly generation of a family network. Contractors have a dual character in the relationship between capital and labour. Their incomes rely on workers' obedience and productivity. Normally, only when workers stay in a factory more than six months do contractors receive referral fees from the factories. So contractors persuade workers to work hard and endure poor working conditions. At the same time, to ensure workers accept contractors' supervision, sometimes contractors represent the workers in bargaining with the employers over the wage and conditions. Collective action is primarily motivated by defensive purposes, such as workers' wages not being cleared at the end of the year or abuse by managers or workers from other provinces. In the workplace, working pressure sometimes results in conflicts between workers from different regions and under different contractors' supervision. The working quotas are usually very high and stressful for workers, who are then easily irritated by other workers' errors. This kind of problem may lead to contradictions between workers of different contractors' teams. Resistance from contractors or gangs indicates a propensity to violence. Male workers play a central role in violent actions.

Initially, cooperative production teams are constituted by local Jiaxing middle-aged women workers. These local workers' land has been taken away gradually, and hence they identify themselves as workers rather than peasants. They have a rich working experience in the garment industry and possess skills that are in high demand by employers. Since 2006, with labour shortages becoming increasing serious in YRD, these skilled workers organized cooperative production teams to evade the constraints of factory discipline, to earn more, and to better balance domestic and paid work spheres. This organization is mainly based on the network formed in the workplace. Recruitment by the cooperative production team takes working experiences seriously, so job performance is much more crucial than kinship or friendship connections. They either work collectively in home-based workplaces or go to factories together to complete orders over a certain period. There is no contractor in the cooperative production team blurring the contradiction between labour and capital, so the workers know their common interests are against capital or the agents of capital.

The principle in the cooperative production team is reciprocity. They help each other with the production and competitiveness among team members was not observed. Normally team members share the processing fees equally. In this type of team, workers can collectively bargain around the piece rate issue with factory owners or other agents who subcontract the order. Workers' bargaining powers is enhanced through this type of production organization, relative to individual workers. They do not accept the vague calculating wage system, but insist on a reasonable piece rate according to production time. Most of them have verbal contracts rather than written contracts. These workers could build trust with agents they have collaborated with for a long time and were willing to wait for the processing fees. However, for those where trust relations had not yet been embedded, workers only delivered products when they received 100 per cent cash payment. If the day wage produced by the piece rate price is below a standard normal daily wage (generally 170 RMB a day in slack season and 220 RMB a day in peak season), they will hold back the products and raw materials to ask for a reasonable piece rate price, which is usually a very effective bargaining ploy, especially during peak seasons.

Discussion and Conclusion

Gendered structural power

The shortage of labour in China is typically judged to be about a shortage of female workers. Labour intensive industries, such as garment manufacture, textiles, shoemaking, toys, and electronics, have a strong preference for female migrant workers since they are believed to be patient, meticulous, docile, and able to handle repetitive and boring work (Lee, 1998; Pun, 2005). According to the study of Cai and Tan (2006), the demand/supply ratio of Hangzhou in the fourth quarter of 2004 was 1.32 for male worker and 3.0 for female workers. In a county of Shaoxing, there was a 50,000 shortfall of female workers. Young female workers are in high demand by employers: in 2004, 78 per cent of job postings of Guangdong factories mentioned they hoped to recruit female workers aged 18 to 25 years old (Cai and Tan, 2006). According to 101 cities' labour supply report, the demand/supply ratio for men was 1.09 and 1.11 for women in the first quarter of 2013[19] and 1.06 for men and 1.09 for women in the third quarter of 2013.[20]

Two factors may lie behind the female labour shortage. Firstly, the male preference at birth results in an unbalanced sex ratio. According to the 2011 National Sample Survey on Population Changes, the total sex ratio of China had reached 105.17 (female = 100). This will affect the Chinese labour force in the long term. Secondly, the female labour shortage represents the lack of support for women workers' simple reproduction and social reproduction. The highly intensive work, industry injuries, and occupational diseases are detrimental to women workers' health and other rights, which can result in women workers quitting. A lack of living wages, social insurance (Cai, 2013: 13), and support for social reproduction (such as pregnancy and giving birth) means women cannot work in a certain period. Moreover, 74.3 per cent of migrant women returned to their hometown for marriage and children while only 30 per cent of migrant men returned home for these reasons. The employment rate for mothers with children under six years old is lower than for those without (Tan, 2013).

Class, gender, localism, and workers' associational power

In the literature on Chinese labour politics, the politics of place is usually crucial (Perry, 1993; Honig, 1986, 1992). Perry studied the strikes in Shanghai and discovered that workers from different areas of China were diverse in terms of languages, culture, organization, habits, and customs derived from preindustrial society, leading to differences in industry, types of work, and skill levels. Worker segmentation in native areas also gave rise to protest politics, both divisively and in solidarity. The politics of place influenced workers so deeply that the Nationalist Party and the Communist Party needed to integrate the politics of place to organize workers in the labour movement in 1930–1940s China (Perry, 1993). Research into workers in the reform and opening-policy era also discusses how native places can impact worker solidarity and division (Pun, 1994; Lee, 1998; Gao, 2006; Shen and Zhou, 2007; Wen, 2008; Chan, 2009). These researchers stress the dialectical interplay between locality or ethnic group and control and resistance in workplaces. In a different context, Fantasia (1988) tried to connect solidarity based on native place and living community with class consciousness. Here, I wish to explore the implications of native place on the extent of proletarianization and workers' protest patterns.

Place is not alone as a structural marker in the Chinese context. It is widely reported that skill levels also affect worker struggles (Perry, 1993; Honig, 1986, 1992; Pun, 1994; Lee, 1998; Chan, 2009). For example, skilled workers from southern China organize democratically and launch aggressive collective actions against capitalists. While, at the same time, semi-skilled or unskilled workers from northern China join hierarchical gangs and obey gang masters' orders to strike (Perry, 1995). These observations underline the fact that the situation of labour market and workers' skill levels will influence their bargaining power and the forms of organization. Chan (2009) has also shown that when workers' bargaining power increases, gang leaders were inclined to protect worker interests rather than help managers to pacify workers.

It seems that different workers constitute varying organizations with diverse internal power structures and various collective actions (see Table 6.11). This chapter discusses class formation to interpret relationships among class, localism, gender, skill level, and worker's struggles.[21]

The characteristics of the workers' place of origin are related to the proletarianization process. Not all local residents will become industrial workers. Most local rural residents in the PRD become landlords or entrepreneurs in the process of urbanization and they do not need to live on wages. Therefore, research into garment workers or informal workers in PRD does not often involve local workers (Liu, 2011; Huang, 2012). Even in other cities in YRD, like the Hangzhou Jiubao community, local rural residents also have spare houses for rent. Therefore, there are relatively few people working in the garment industry in our study from the Hangzhou Jiubao community. However, the Two for Two Policy[22] in Jiaxing means most local rural residents have lost their means of production and have become part of the proletariat. The long experience of working in the garment industry bolsters their understanding of the conflicts between capital and labour. Moreover, social networks are built based on the workplace. These are the important foundations of cooperative production team.

Another crucial factor refers to gender. Most members in the cooperative production team are women. This is due to social gender divisions. Local men are encouraged to start their own businesses or pursue technical positions in the garment industry like mechanics or cutting masters. However, women are encouraged to seek stability and give up development opportunities for household duties. Women face barriers to entering some technical positions such as mechanics and cutting masters in the garment industry, so they tend to accumulate skills only in sewing procedures. With increasing bargaining power and the accumulated experience of struggles against capitalists, Chinese women workers' resistance moves from individual defensive struggles towards more organized interest-oriented actions. The cooperative production team organized by skilled women workers is a manifestation of class formation. This association also includes some gendered features, like the

Table 6.11 Different workers constitute different organizations

Native place	Skill level	Proletarianization	Organization	Gender characteristics	Internal power structure	Features of collective action
Local residents	All-round skilled workers	Complete proletarianization: they consider themselves as industry workers	Cooperative production team	Initiated by women	Equal and reciprocal	Class-oriented for aggressive goals
Outside province residents	Skilled, semi-skilled, and unskilled	Semi-proletarianization: they view themselves as migrant rural worker	Contractor team or gang	Males play a pivotal role in violent collective action.	Hierarchical	Control by contractor or gang leader for defensive reasons

Summarized by the author[8]

[8] This table is a generalization of workers' characteristics and their association types. Some skilled male and female workers from outside provinces also organize or join cooperative production teams inside and out of the factories. They also collectively bargain with employers around piece rates and receive higher wages than regular workers.

spirit of equal and mutual help based on the emotional resonance of women's life courses.

At the same time, there are still some limitations. Usually, cooperative production teams are autonomous or isolated and they cannot be used to rally together when they operate in a factory. Members of different teams will keep the piece rates they have bargained with employers secret from workers in other cooperative production teams even when they process the same product. Some larger cooperative production teams may unite more workers, but the solidarity is still confined to a certain workplace. There is no association of cooperative production teams to deal with problems of informal employment, such as industrial injuries and occupational diseases.

Notes

1 Including employment without labour contract or social insurance in both the formal and informal sectors.
2 Informal worker refers to workers in informal employment. The data are extracted from the website of Women in Informal Employment: Globalizing and Organizing. http://WIEGO.org/informal-economy/statistical-picture
3 The website of Women in Informal Employment: Globalizing and Organizing   http://WIEGO.org/informal-economy/WIEGO-network-holistic-framework
4 The website of Women in Informal Employment: Globalizing and Organizing   http://WIEGO.org/informal-economy/WIEGO-network-holistic-framework
5 Hartmann noted that 'Women's subordinate position in the labour market reinforced their subordinate position in the family, and that in turn reinforced their labor-market position' (Hartmann, 1976: 153).
6 This kind of collective bargaining is based on workers' self-organization such as cooperative production teams rather than the formal trade union–management negotiations. At the same time, the bargaining issues are around wage level and standard labour problems.
7 Including the UK, Bangladesh, Bulgaria, India, Pakistan, Sri Lanka, Philippines, Thailand, and Hong Kong/China.
8 The ESRC Project: 'Labour Conditions and the Working Poor in China and India', supported by the ESRC-DFID Joint Fund for Poverty Alleviation Research (grant number ES/I033599/1) (hereafter referred to as ESRC Working Poor Project).

9 The research team conducted in-depth interviews with frontline workers, factory owners, and managers to obtain a deeper understanding of labor process, employment practices, spatial, and social organization of production in this region. These textile and apparel enterprises were approached through team members' personal networks and the assistance of local scholars in Shanghai.

10 Shanghai was the major area for the ESRC Working Poor Project in comparative study with the New Delhi area in India.

11 Prof. Pun Ngai, Prof. Liu Aiyu, Dr Lu Huilin, Dr Xue Hong, Chen Wei, Fan Lulu, Tian Zhipeng, Fu Wei, A La Tan, Tu Zhen and Feng Xiaojun all contributed to this survey in Shanghai and Hangzhou.

12 The production units in Ningbo and Shaoxing produce for the textile industry. The labour process in the textile industry is different from that of the garment industry, for example workers in the textile industry do not need to collaborate with each other to complete a product. So the data of Ningbo and Shaoxing are not used in this chapter.

13 According to definitions in 12 countries, the characteristics of 'informal sector enterprises' normally include household unincorporated enterprises with fewer than six employees, without a formal account and paying no tax (ILO, 2013: 23).

14 The analysis of market supply and demand of public employment service agencies in some cities of the first quarter of 2014, retrieved from the website of China's Employment. http://www.chinajob.gov.cn/DataAnalysis/content/2014-04/25/content_919027.htm

15 Jiaxing labour market report of 2007. Retrieved from website of Texindex.com http://www.texindex.com.cn/Articles/2008-3-26/136358_1.html

16 The supply and demand analysis report of Jiaxing enterprise employment and human resources market in the first half of 2013, retrieved from http://www.jxjiuye.com/Article/display.asp?ID=3259

17 All-round worker refers to workers who are familiar with all the working procedures of apparel production.

18 Many places in China use a multi-tier step tariff system, which means the more you buy electricity in a calendar month, the more you will pay per unit.

19 The analysis of market supply and demand of public employment service agencies in some cities of the first quarter of 2013, retrieved from China's employment website: http://www.chinajob.gov.cn/DataAnalysis/content/2013-04/12/content_803270.html/

20 The analysis of market supply and demand of public employment service agencies in some cities of the third quarter of 2013, retrieved

from China's employment website: http://www.chinajob.gov.cn/
DataAnalysis/content/2013-10/16/content_851988.htm

21 This table is a generalization of workers' characteristics and their
association types. Skilled male and female workers from outside
provinces also organize or join cooperative production teams. They
also collectively bargain with employers around piece rates and
receive higher wages than regular workers.

22 Two for Two Policy, called *Liang Fen Liang Huan* in Chinese. This
is a policy of developing rural lands in Jiaxing City of Zhejiang
Provinces. Each town government registers a development company
to receive investment. The rural residents are asked to exchange their
homesteads in the country for commodity houses provided by the
government and give up the right to use farmland for the endowment insurance of being in a town. The peasants' lands are used for
building industrial districts or other development projects. The policy should in theory abide by law and rely on peasants voluntary
agreement. However, in reality peasants were not able to refuse the
execution of this policy.

REFERENCES

Cai, D. G. and Tan, L. (2006) 'A Study of the Reason of Female Migrant Workers
Shortage in Coastal Area and Its Countermeasure', Population Research, 30
(2):56–60.

Cai, F. (2013) *Reports on China's Population and Labor (No.14), From Demographic
Dividend to Institutional Dividend*, Beijing: Social Sciences Academic Press.

Chan, A. and Siu, K. (2009) Wal-Mart's CSR and Labor Standards in China.
BDS Working Paper series no. 4. Retrieved from http://bdsnetwork.cbs.dk/
publications/Working%20Papers/bsd_working_paper_(paper4).pdf. (accessed 9
December 2015).

Chan, C. K. C. (2009) 'Strike and workplace relations in a Chinese global factory',
Industrial Relations Journal, 40 (1): 60–77.

Chen, F. and Tang, M. X. (2013) 'Labor Conflicts in China: Typologies and their
Implications', *Asian Survey*, 53(3): 559–583.

China National Garment Association. (2014) *China Garment Industry Development
Report 2013-2014*, Beijing: China Textile & Apparel Press.

Choi, P. K. (2008) *Thousands of Needles and Threads: The Oral History of Hong Kong
Garment Workers*, Hong Kong: Step Forward Multimedia.

Colgan, F. and Ledwith, S. (2002) *Gender, Diversity and Trade Unions: International
Perspectives*, London and New York: Routledge.

De Soto, H. (1988) 'Constraints on People: The Origins of Underground
Economies and Limits to Their Growth'. In Jerry, J (ed). *Beyond the Informal
Sector: Including the Excluded in Developing Countries*. ICS Press, pp. 15–47.

▶

▶

Deng, Y. X. (2014) *Gendered Global Factory: Male Workers, Labor Market and Masculinized Labor Process in Foxconn*. 32nd International Labour Process Conference. King's College, University of London, 7 to 9 April.

Division of population and employment statistics of the National Bureau of Statistics of the People's Republic of China. (2004–2014) *The China Labour Statistical Yearbook*, Beijing: China Statistics Press.

Fan L. L. (2014) 'The Time Management of Factory in Gender Perspective: A Chinese Case', in Ngok K. L. Kuhnle, S. and Yan, X. Y. (Eds) *Work-life Balance: Theoretical Implications and Chinese Reality*, Sanghai: Truth & Wisdom Press, pp. 177–189.

Fantasia, R. (1988) Cultures of Solidarity: Consciousness, Action, and Contemporary American Workers, Berkeley: University of California Press.

Gao, C. (2006) 'The Making of Migrant Entrepreneurs in Contemporary China: an Ethnographic Study of Garment Producers in Suburban Guangzhou', The PhD Thesis of University of Hong Kong.

Hartmann, H. (1976) 'Capitalism, Patriarchy, and Job Segregation by Sex', *Signs*, 1 (3): 137–169.

Huang, Y. (2012) 'The 'Making Out' Game outside the Factory: A Case Study of 'Making Out' Production in Pearl River Delta Area', *The Sociological Study*, (4): 187–203.

Honig, E. (1986) *Sisters and Strangers: Women in the Shanghai Cotton Mills*. 1919– 1949, California: Stanford University Press.

——(1992) *Creating Chinese Ethnicity: Subei People in Shanghai*, 1850–1980, New Haven: Yale University Press.

ILO (International Labour Organization) (2013) *Measuring Informality: A Statistical Manual on the Informal Sector and Informal Employment*, Geneva: ILO.

——(1972) *Employment, Income and Equality: A Strategy for increasing productivity in Kenya*, Geneva: ILO.

ILO (International Labour Organization) and WIEGO (Women in Informal Employment: Globalizing and Organizing) (2013) Women and Men in the Informal Sector: A Statistical Picture, 2nd Edition.

Katznelson, I. and Zolberg, A. (1986) *Working Class Formation: The Nineteenth Century Patterns in Western Europe and United States*, Princeton: Princeton University Press.

Koo, H. (2001) *Korean Workers: The Culture and Politics of Class Formation*, Ithaca: Cornell University Press.

Lee, C. K. (1998) *Gender and the South China Miracle: Two Worlds of Factory Women*, Berkeley: University of California Press.

Lee, C. K. (2007) *Against the Law: Labor Protests in China's Rustbelt and Sunbelt*, Berkeley: University of California Press.

Leung, P. N. (2013) Leading Strike in the Workshop of the World: Labour Activists and Struggles of the New Working Class in the Pearl River Delta (Doctoral Dissertation). Hong Kong: Hong Kong University of Science and Technology.

Liu, Y. Z. (2011) 'Women in Migration: An Examination of Married Women's Migration Experiences in South China's Garment Industry'. Toronto: The PhD Thesis of York University.

▶

Maloney, W. F. (2004) 'Informality Revisited', *World Development*, (7): 1159–1178.

Mezzadri, A. (2014) 'Indian Garment Clusters and CSR Norms: Incompatible Agendas at the Bottom of the Garment Commodity Chain', *Oxford Development Studies*, 42(2): 217–237.

Perry, E. J. (1993) *Shanghai on Strike: The Politics of Chinese Labor*, California: Stanford University Press.

Portes, A., Castells, M. and Benton, L. A. (1989) *The Informal Economy: Studies in Advanced and Less Developed Countries*, Baltimore: The Johns Hopkins University Press.

Pun, N. (1994) Shenzhen Factory Girls: Family and Work in the Making of Chinese Women's Lives, The master thesis of Hong Kong University.

Pun, N. (2005) *Made in China: Women Factory Workers in a Global Workplace*, Durham & London: Duke University Press.

Pun, N. and Lu, H. L. (2010) 'Unfinished proletarianization: self, anger, and class action among the second generation of peasant-workers in present-day China', Modern China, 36(5): 493-519.

Pun, N. and Smith, C. (2007) 'Putting transnational labour process in its place: the dormitory labour regime in post-socialist China', *Work, Employment and Society*, 21(1): 27–46.

Qiu, Y. B. (2011) 'The Historic Limitations of Independent Labour Movement's Strategies: an Analysis to the Leaderships of Unions' in He, M. X. and Lin, X. X. (Eds) *The Age of Social Movement*, Taipei: Socio Publishing Co. Ltd.

Research Group of Ministry of Labour and Social Security of the People's Republic (2004) Investigation Report on shortage of migrant workers. Retrieved from: http://news.xinhuanet.com/zhengfu/2004-09/14/content_1979817.htm. (accessed 9 December 2015).

Shen, Y. and Zhou, X. (2007) 'The Related Hegemony: A Study of Construction Workers' Labour Process' in Shen, Y. (Ed), *Market, Class and Society*, Beijing: Social Sciences Academic Press.

Silver, B. J. (2003) *Forces of Labor: Workers' Movements and Globalization Since 1870*, Cambridge: Cambridge University Press.

Siu, K. (2015) 'Continuity and change in the everyday lives of Chinese migrant factory workers', *The China Journal*, (74): 43-65.

Tan, L. and Li, J. F. (2003) 'An analysis of gender characteristics of informal employment in China', *Population Research*, 27(5): 11–18.

Tan, L. (2013) *Green Book of Women: Annual Report on Gender Equality and Women's Development in China (2008–2012)*, Beijing: Social Sciences Academic Press (China).

WIEGO (2014) Working Paper No. 2, Statistics on the Informal Economy: Definitions, Regional Estimates and Challenges. Retrieved from: http://wiego.org/sites/wiego.org/files/publications/files/Vanek-Statistics-WIEGO-WP2.pdf. (accessed 9 December 2015).

Wright, E. O. (2000) 'Working-class power, capitalist-class interests, and class compromise', *American Journal of Sociology*, 105(4): 957–1002.

▶

Wen, X. (2008) 'The Ethnicity in Luggage Factory: Revisit the Household Workers in Bei Town' in Zheng, Y. F., Shen, Y and Pan, S. M. (Eds), *Selected Works of Peking University, Tsinghua University and Renmin University Sociology Master Thesis*, Jinan: Shan Dong People's Publishing House, pp. 46–50.

Wu, Q. J. (2012) 'Collective consultation and the governance of labor relations under state dominance: the strategies and practice of index management', *Sociological Research*, (3): 66–89.

WWW (Women Working Worldwide) (2005) The Report of 'The Rights of Workers in Garment Industry Subcontracting Chains: A Research, Education and Action Project with Workers Organization in Asia and Eastern Europe'. Retrieved from: http://www.google.com.hk/url?sa=t&rct=j&q=&esrc=s&source=web&cd=1&ved=0CBsQFjAA&url=http%3A%2F%2Fwww.cleanclothes.org%2Fresources%2Fnational-cccs%2Fgarment-report-www.pdf%2Fat_download%2Ffile&ei=oBZoVaiPPNOA8gWYnoPYAQ&usg=AFQjCNFreXYPFJVjifoo1z rDn2dizCyDKQ&sig2=nIyDFnFeJoDt9JYOUSKYlg&bvm=bv.93990622,d.dGY. (accessed 9 December 2015).

Xu, X. H. (2005) 'Collective and discussion on the wages under the natural condition', *Journal of Tianjin Trade Union Administrators College*, 13(3): 29–32.

Yan X. F. and Liu J. L. (2013) 'The new characteristics of increasing informal employment and the countermeasure', *Economic Review*, (1): 57–60.

Zheng, Q. (2011) 'An Important Method to Promote the Collective Bargaining: Collective Barraging at Industrial Level' in Zhao, M. H. Zhao, W. and Fan, L. L. (ed), *Chinese Trade Union and Labour Law: a Critical Review and Reflection*, Social Sciences Academic Press, pp. 396–405.

Contingent Work in the Chinese Call Centre Sector

Xiangmin Liu and Can Ouyang

Introduction

While accelerated technological innovation, intensified global competition, and macroeconomic volatility continue to act as powerful drivers for the new trends of work and employment, many countries are experiencing a deepening segmentation between traditional long-term employment relationships and contingent jobs based on temporary, fixed-term work contracts (Polivka, 1996; Kalleberg, 2000). In the United States, the contingent workforce has grown by 29 per cent from 2009 to 2012, while regular employment grew by less than 1 per cent during the same time period (Puglia and Tikiwala, 2013). This increased reliance on contingent workers in large corporations such as WalMart, Amazon, and PepsiCo has received widespread media attention, which highlighted the persistent standing of temporary jobs (USA Today, 2013). A similar pattern is occurring in China where more than 60 million urban workers, roughly one-fifth of the total workforce, held contingent jobs (Bloomberg, 2012). This growth in temporary jobs poses a fundamental challenge to the evolving employment relationships in China and beyond, because contingent work is generally associated with low wages, no benefits, negligible job security, and limited opportunities for career advancement (Ashford, George, and Blatt, 2007; Kalleberg, Reskin, and Hudson, 2000). In its recent report of Global Employment Trends (2014a), the International Labour Organization underscored that the unprecedented growth in contingent work constituted a worldwide challenge for economic recovery and social development in the next decade.

The present chapter focuses on China's call-centre sector, where the use of contingent work arrangements that do not provide an implicit or explicit guarantee of continued employment has become more common than many other industries. Specifically, we operationalize contingent workers as those who are hired through employment agencies (i.e., dispatched labour and outsourced labour) and who hold non-renewable fixed-term contracts lasting no longer than three years. Exploring the drivers and characteristics of contingent work provides a useful lens for examining the changing nature of employment relations in China, and more importantly, it advances our understanding of the rise of contingent work as a contemporary global phenomenon. On one hand, China has been an attractive destination for multinational corporations (MNCs) due to its low labour costs and weak employment protections over the past three decades. However, in the face of widespread labour unrest caused by precarious jobs and poor work conditions, some companies have started to restructure their relationships with Chinese suppliers, while some even relocated their operations to Bangladesh, Cambodia, Indonesia, Vietnam, and other cheaper countries (Wall Street Journal, 2013). An in-depth analysis of contingent work in China therefore helps us to probe the shifting geography of global value chains and foreign direct investment. On the other hand, in contrast to patterns in other countries such as Germany and the Netherlands where deregulation policies to liberalize short-term contracts spurred the proliferation of temporary jobs (Houseman, Kalleberg, and Erickcek, 2003; Peck and Ward, 2005), contingent work in China has grown amidst a series of major regulatory efforts to strengthen employment protection. China's recent experience thus provides a fascinating case study on the complex interaction between the government, business, and labour.

This chapter begins with an overview of employment in the call-centre sector in China. We then analyse the spread of contingent work in this sector and the driving forces behind its growth. Next we examine the link between contingent work and job quality by comparing length of employment, employer-provided training, rewards, and turnover among workers in three types of companies, including those hiring only regular workers, those hiring only contingent workers, and those hiring both types. This chapter concludes with a brief summary and a discussion of future trends in this area.

Characteristics of the Call-Centre Sector in China

Call centres provide technology-based centralized operations of customer services, marketing, and sales, which therefore constitute a major connection between companies and their customers (Russell, 2008). In China, call centres' first function was primarily to deliver hotline services and technical support in large corporations such as China Telecom and Legend (later Lenovo) in the mid-1990s. In only two decades, the call-centre sector has experienced a rapid growth not only indicated by its overall employment size but also by the full range of business functions that it enables. For example, the State Information Center reported that Chinese call centres housed 580,000 agent seats and employed over 1.2 million workers at the end of 2012 (Zhang, 2014). While most of these jobs are in major cities such as Beijing, Shanghai, Guangzhou, and Shenzhen in the coastal regions, recent years have witnessed an increasing number of new call centres in the central and southwest regions such as Luoyang, Chengdu, and Guiyang. Furthermore, more and more Chinese call centres have sought to expand their service functions, focusing on cost and quality to incorporate sales operations that drive profits and revenues.

To understand organizational characteristics and employment in this sector, we conducted national surveys of over 300 Chinese call centres in 2008 (118 centres) and 2012 (218 centres). Based upon previous studies (Batt, Doellgast, and Kwon, 2006), we chose establishments as the unit of analysis and general managers as the target respondents in the surveys. In addition, we conducted in-depth interviews with senior managers, supervisors, and frontline employees to acquire further information. As reported in Table 7.1, call centres in our surveys on average housed 319 frontline service workers in 2008 and 581 workers in 2012, while the median size housed 100 workers in 2008 and 150 workers in 2012. These numbers were comparable to those of US call centres with an average organizational size of 289 workers and a median size of 120 workers (Batt, Doellgast, and Kwon, 2006). That means Chinese call centres have not only increased in number but also in the numbers of workers in each establishment. In other words, Chinese companies (especially those in the telecommunications and banking industries) have sought to consolidate call centre operations from smaller, dispersed locations into larger, centralized units, a trend also observed in many Western countries (Holman, Batt, and Holtgrewe, 2007).

The majority of call-centre workers were female, with 78 per cent in 2008 and 75 per cent in 2012. Most of these workers have completed

Table 7.1 Overview of the call-centre sector in China

	2008	2012
Employment		
Employment size (median)	100	150
Employment size (mean)	319	581
Proportion of female workers	0.78	0.75
Education levels of typical workers		
High school degrees	21.79	22.58
Vocational/Associate degrees	58.97	61.83
Bachelor degrees and above	19.23	15.59
Primary business functions		
Services only	0.42	0.41
Sales only	0.13	0.13
Both services and sales	0.45	0.46
Customer segmentation models		
Universal	0.56	0.43
Specialized	0.44	0.57
Scope of service		
Local	0.10	0.06
Regional/Provincial	0.23	0.16
National	0.58	0.63
International	–	0.15
Number of companies	118	218

Establishment surveys conducted by the authors

13 to 15 years of formal education. An increasing number of call centres have started to adopt customer segmentation strategies. Specifically, 57 per cent of call centres in our study focused on a particular customer segment (e.g., large businesses, small businesses, or individual consumers) when handling customer inquiries and delivering services, which has increased from 44 per cent in 2008. Other call centres chose a universal offerings model of serving multiple segments through the same channel. Among the range of different types of business functions, 41 per cent of call centres provided service activities alone without handling sales, while 46 per cent of centres combined service and sales functions. The latter type of call centre has considerably high skill requirements (Jasmand, Blazevic, and de Ruyter, 2012). Workers not only need good communication and problem-solving abilities, but also substantial knowledge about the variety of products offered and the skills

to identify sales opportunities and close deals. A majority of call centres in our survey served the national market, instead of a local or regional one. Such a trend has become even more obvious in 2012 than in 2008. Finally, more and more call centres started to capitalize on cloud-based computing and other advanced information technologies to complement traditional voice-based communications with non-voice contact including text messaging, web chat, email, and social media channels such as Weibo and WeChat.

Labour Law Reforms and the Expanded Contingent Workforce

China's industrial labour regulation[1] prior to 1980 was essentially a bureaucratic device to support centrally planned economic activities and urban welfare (Warner, 2004; Zhao and Du, 2012). By the early 1980s, a majority of the state workforce consisted of permanent workers with lifetime employment (Whyte and Bian, 1995). Since China embarked on massive economic reforms and the private sector began to grow rapidly, the state began to transform the centralized employment system toward a more decentralized and flexible labour market (Frenkel and Kuruvilla, 2002). The 1995 Labour Law requires a written employment contract between an employer and a worker in one of three forms: open-ended, fixed-term, or assignment-based. Open-ended contracts, or contracts without a fixed term, specify an employment relationship with an indefinite term between the employer and the employee. By law, firms are not required to use open-ended contracts unless both parties decide to renew the contract after a consecutive service of ten years. Fixed-term contracts establish a legally binding employment relationship that lasts for a predetermined definite period of time. Under a fixed-term contract, the employer or the employee can terminate the employment relationship unilaterally upon expiration of the contract, for good cause, bad cause, or no cause at all. Otherwise, the employer has to make severance payments to discharge an employee before the ending date of the contract. The third type, assignment-based contracts, refers to an employment contract that expires upon the completion of a certain job. These contracts are far less common than the first two types, usually found among seasonal, low-skilled jobs in the agriculture and construction sectors. In this way, the Labour Law provides a unified regulatory framework for all types of employment relationships and eliminates previous distinctions based on ownership arrangements (Lee, 1998).

Since the enactment of the Labour Law, the use of fixed-term contracts has become a major form of employment. Before the mid-1990s, over 80 per cent of the urban workforce had job security through open-ended and renewable fixed-term contracts (Hu and Zhao, 2006). This proportion dropped drastically to less than 40 per cent in 2009 (Zhou, 2013). Moreover, the use of repeated short-term contracts to cover enduring personnel needs has become widespread. For example, in 2004, 38 per cent of all urban workers in Beijing were employed on fixed-term contracts that did not exceed 12 months, 32 per cent were on contracts that lasted between one to three years, 17 per cent were on fixed-term contracts that lasted three to ten years, and 13 per cent were on open-ended contracts (Beijing Bureau of Labour and Social Security, 2007). Nevertheless, it is important to note that before 2007 fixed-term contracts were generally renewable, while temporary agency employment was limited to state-controlled Foreign Enterprise Human Resources Service Companies (FESCO) who supplied local staff to foreign companies.

Amid rising labour disputes and social unrest from 2003 to 2005, the Chinese government was under mounting political pressure to restore long-term employment relationships (Lee and Tierney, 2008; Ngok, 2008; Elfstrom and Kuruvilla, 2014). Therefore, the government has since begun to establish more restrictive employment protection legislation including the Labour Contract Law, Labour Dispute Mediation and Arbitration Law, Social Security Law, and a number of administrative rules and policies at various levels of local governments. A particularly major legislative reform was the enactment of the Labour Contract Law in 2008 (including its amendments in 2013 and 2014), which contained new provisions on labour dispatching and other forms of contingent work (Chen and Funke, 2009; Wang, Appelbaum, Degiuli, and Lichtenstein, 2009). First, the Labour Contract Law restricts the use of consecutive, fixed-term contracts. An open-ended contract is concluded when a fixed-term labour contract is extended twice. Second, the law significantly raises the minimum registered capital requirement for intermediary employment agencies (i.e., labour dispatching companies or employment subcontracting agencies) from RMB 500,000 to RMB 2,000,000. The maximum fine on employers who violate rules regarding labour dispatching is further raised from RMB 5,000 to RMB 10,000 per worker. Third, labour dispatching is suitable only for temporary, ancillary, or replaceable positions. In other words, companies should hire dispatched workers only in short-term positions, to perform duties that are not part of the user company's core business, and to fill positions vacated by regular workers on leave. Recent amendments of the law further state that companies shall strictly control the number of dispatched employees to a certain ratio of its total staff (e.g., 10 per cent), subject to specific administrative regulations issued by the Ministry of Human Resources and Social Security (MOHRSS) and local governments. Lastly, the law emphasizes the rule of 'equal pay for equal work'. In other words, regular and dispatched workers in the same positions shall receive the same compensation, including basic salary, bonuses, subsidies, and allowances.

Table 7.2 describes major features of employment protection legislation in 11 countries, including rules on the use of fixed-term contracts, individual dismissals, and severance pay (International Labour Organization, 2014b). Table 7.3 compares the regulation of temporary agency work reported by the Organization for Economic Cooperation and Development (2014). These indicators suggest that China imposes stringent protection for regular workers while regulation on contingent employment is moderate.

It was against this legislative background that the contingent workforce has expanded dramatically and contract lengths have decreased significantly (e.g., Park and Cai, 2011; Liu, 2015). For example, the MOHRSS reported that the number of dispatched workers has increased from 20 million at the end of 2007 to 27 million in 2009. The All-China Federation of Trade Unions (ACFTU) reported even more striking statistics: more than 60 million urban workers in China were dispatched workers, representing one-fifth of the urban workforce (Bloomberg, 2012).

Two cases from our field research provide rich details and interesting insights into the use of contingent work in call centres. The first case came from the customer contact centre operated by LIE (a pseudonym), a foreign home appliance manufacturer. Employees in this call centre handled three types of calls. First, they answered customer service inquiries and provided technical support over the phone. Second, the centre received repair requests and distributed the requests to over 2,500 local service stations. Finally, employees made outbound 'Happy Calls', which asked existing customers to complete a customer satisfaction survey in order to improve products and services. The general manager of LIE's call centre explained how the mixed use of regular and contingent workers came into place:

> We set up this call centre with about 30 agent seats. As a foreign subsidiary [sic], we had an existing business relationship with FESCO. Therefore, it was a no-brainer decision for us to hire FESCO as a recruitment tool and use its knowledge of the local labour market. All recruited agents became regular LIE employees after a three-month probationary period.

Table 7.2 An international comparison of employment protection regulation

	Australia	Canada	China	France	Germany	Japan	Korea	Spain	United Kingdom	United States	Vietnam
Rules on the use of fixed-term contracts (FTC) Valid reasons	No limitation	No limitation	**No limitation**	Objective and material reasons	Objective and material reasons	No limitation	No limitation	Objective and material reasons	No limitation	No limitation	Objective and material reasons
Maximum use of successive FTCs	No limitation	No limitation	**2**	2	4	No limitation	No limitation	2	No limitation	No limitation	2
Maximum cumulative duration of successive FTCs	No limitation	No limitation	**10 years**	24 months	24 months	No limitation	24 months	24 months	4 years	No limitation	6 years

(Continued)

157

Table 7.2 (*Continued*)

	Australia	Canada	China	France	Germany	Japan	Korea	Spain	United Kingdom	United States	Vietnam
Rules on individual dismissals											
Valid grounds	Any fair reasons	Any fair reasons	**Economic reasons; worker's capacity; worker's conduct;**	Any fair reasons	Any fair reasons	Any fair reasons	Any fair reasons	Economic reasons; worker's capacity; worker's conduct;	Any fair reasons	None	Economic reasons; worker's capacity; worker's conduct;
Notification requirements	Written	Written	**Written**	Written	Written	Not specified	Written	Written	Written	Not specified	Not specified
Notice period	1–5 weeks depending on tenure	2 weeks	**30 days**	1–2 months depending on tenure	1–7 months depending on tenure	30 days	30 days	15 days	1–12 weeks depending on tenure	Not specified	45 days
Severance pay											
Tenure = 2 years	6 weeks	5 days	**2 months**	0.4 months	1 month	None	None	40 days	Depends on the age of employee, the length of service	None	1 month
Tenure = 5 years	10 weeks	10 days	**5 months**	1 month	2.5 months	None	None	100 days	Same as above	None	2.5 months
Tenure = 10 years	12 weeks	20 days	**10 months**	2 months	5 months	None	None	200 days	Same as above	None	5 months

International Labour Organization. Employment Protection Legislation Database (EPLex). www.ilo.org/dyn/eplex/termmain.home

Table 7.3 An international comparison of the regulation of contingent work arrangements

	Australia	Canada	China	France	Germany	Japan	Korea	Spain	United Kingdom	United States
Limits on the use of temporary work	Generally none	Generally none	**Temporary, ancillary, or replaceable positions only**	Only for temporary replacement and seasonal employment	Generally none, unless specified in collective agreements	Prohibited in some industries	Prohibited in some industries	Only for temporary replacement and seasonal employment	Generally none	Generally none
Maximum duration of agency employment	No	No	**6 months**	18 months with some exceptions	No	3 years	3 months to 2 years	6 months to 4 years	No	No
Licensing and registration	No	No, except in some provinces	**Yes**	Yes	Yes	Yes	Yes	Yes	No	No, except in some states
Equal pay and benefits to agency workers	No	No	**Yes**	Yes	Yes	No	Yes	Yes	Yes, after a 12 week qualifying period	No

Organization for Economic Cooperation and Development. Indicators of Employment Protection. http://www.oecd.org/employment/emp/oecdindicatorsofemployment
protection.htm

As our business grew rapidly, we needed more people to handle calls. A debate raged in the corporate office concerning whether to keep the call centre in house or entirely outsource its operations. Upper-level management eventually decided to ask FESCO not only to recruit but also carry the payroll of new employees. Since then, we have recruited forty agents on labour dispatching contracts. That was why we have both regular and agency employees.

While FESCO dispenses monthly pay cheques as the employer of record, LIE sets the wage rates and benefits of agency workers to make sure that they get the same as permanent employees. In addition, all employees have the same access to the employee lounge and recreational activities available in the larger corporate community. Obviously, these benefits are not required by FESCO or explicitly covered in the work contract. Not all our competitors are so generous to their employees, not to mention agency employees. We voluntarily do so because we are committed to providing a fair and favorable working environment for all employees. (Interview, May 2008)

The second case involves CNT (a pseudonym), a large state-owned telecommunications company providing a wide range of landline and wireless services to residential and business clients. We visited one of CNT's call centres in a major southern city, which not only provided customer contact and support, but also ran sales and marketing operations. The human resource manager of this large call centre described the use of different work arrangements:

This call centre has four types of workers who hold customer service representative jobs. The first type includes about 200 employees whose positions were pre-approved by the corporate budget planning and therefore shown as headcount (Zheng Shi Bian Zhi). The second type consists of 700 dispatched workers hired and assigned by temporary help agencies. Third, we have a group of 2 to 20 on-call workers who come only during peak business periods that typically last for days or weeks. Finally, ten workers are assigned and paid by the local government's Employment Assistance Program. They work here as career re-training in preparation for new jobs in other companies.

Prior to 2008, the company equally treated these first two types of workers in assigning and scheduling jobs, evaluating performance, and even setting starting salaries, although dispatched workers receive far fewer benefits. Indeed, at that time a major objective of human resource management was to increase employee identification with the company, including both regular and agency workers. The new

Labour Contract Law, however, requires firms to clearly distinguish between permanent and contingent workers. Firms are not allowed to use contingent labor to perform the same type of jobs that regular workers take. Agency workers should only be assigned work tasks that are 'temporary, complementary, and substitutable'. Consequently, we had to differently treat regular workers and agency workers in all internal administrative processes. This created two new challenges for us managers. On the one hand, we have to regularly remind agency workers that they are not 'our people', even if they work side by side with regular workers. An example was a dispatched worker who was injured in a car accident on her way home after work. Whereas in the past we might provide some assistance through CNT's employee assistance program, now the only thing we do is to ask this injured worker to seek help from her temporary agency employer who does not have any assistance programs at all. On the other hand, our dispatched workers came from four temporary services agencies with various cultures and existing practices on their own. Therefore, it is difficult for us to call for the same standards for all of them. For example, regular employees received a gift box of moon cakes at the Mid-Autumn Festival. While three agencies agreed to follow the same practice for temporary agency workers, the last agency refused to do so because it did not deliver such gifts to other agency workers working at other user organizations. (Interview, October 2011)

These case studies indicate that contingent work has not only grown rapidly within a relatively short period of time, but also it is increasingly integrated into a firm's core operations. In contrast to earlier studies reporting that contingent work was most typical in seasonable and cyclical jobs characterized by fluctuating and unpredictable labour demand (Gramm and Schnell, 2001; Houseman, 2001), our surveys indicated that a large number of companies hired contingent workers in jobs with relatively stable personnel needs. That was why the popular press described the rise of temporary jobs as a long-standing pattern of work and employment.

Driving Forces for the Growth of Contingent Work: Employers' Perspectives

What has caused this drastic shift toward contingent employment? Below we discuss three key catalysts for the growth of contingent work based on extensive fieldwork. We argue that the development and structure of employment practices must be understood in terms of a firm's cost-benefit calculations, concordance with organizational decision-making and politics, and responses to uncertainties arising from the external environment. First, employers may use agency workers to reduce labour costs and save administrative resources in order to achieve economic efficiency. Second, even when hiring temporary workers via agencies is not economically justifiable, managers choose to do so in order to increase power and cope with organizational politics. Finally, firms shift risks to temporary employees and shirk social obligations in order to limit their exposure to future uncertainties.

Economic Considerations

Contingent employees are generally associated with lower wages and benefits. In our survey, 40 out of 75 call centres that used some or all contingent workers reported 'agree' or 'strongly agree' that lower salaries and benefits was an important reason to use contingent workers. As a manager in a supporting centre of an IT manufacturer said: '*We are operating in a highly competitive environment. Cutting costs is always a priority*'. The use of contingent work thus provides call centres with a convenient way to create a differentiated pay structure. Employers have incentives to offer above-market wages only to a small cadre of workers who are critical to business performance, who have a high level of firm-specific human capital, and whose performance is difficult to monitor. Meanwhile, the creation of a joint employment relationship (i.e., a temporary staffing company as the employer of record) allows for differential treatment in wage and benefits in the same organization, unlimited by labour laws and regulations.

In the case of temporary agency employment, call centres may save administrative resources with the aid of specialized staffing agencies. In small companies or branches without independent HR departments, general managers who are responsible for revenue generation have to supervise many HR activities such as hiring and firing. Staffing agencies provide an efficient alternative to reduce this extra workload for general managers. Staffing agencies are often rooted in the local labour market and continuously collect information from both the employer and the employees. Over time, they accumulate extensive knowledge about particular occupational groups and develop networks to sort job seekers into matched positions (Benner, 2003). When certain types of skill are in high demand, the agencies may channel this information to job seekers and even provide basic training (see Autor (2001) for similar practices in the US). This considerably lowers the costs of searching and hiring for client firms. As a manager in the customer support centre of a manufacturing MNC explained:

> Many job applicants don't have a realistic picture of what customer service representatives do at work. That is why a large proportion of new hires quit within two weeks after the completion of initial training. It is a big waste of our time and money. Hiring a temporary help agency can save money because the agency brings in workers who have skills and who know the working conditions well. (Interview, May 2008)

In addition to face-to-face interviews, we obtained samples of service contracts from staffing agencies. These contracts clearly specified the agency's joint responsibilities in maintaining a qualified, stable pool of employees: if an agency worker quits, the agency must refill this opening within 20 days. Moreover, if more than one-third of total agency workers leave within a quarter, the agency has to pay a penalty fee. These provisions are especially beneficial to call centres as turnover rates are typically 30–35 per cent per year. Consistent with these findings, 26 out of 56 companies hiring contingent workers in our study reported that lower recruitment and training costs were a major reason for contingent work arrangements.

Intra-organizational Politics and Managerial Power

Line managers have incentives to hire contingent workers because they have more control over these workers than over regular workers. Prior research has suggested that organizations established structured employment practices, such as the development of internal market rules, to curb the power of line managers on personnel activities such as hiring, rewarding, and dismissing workers (Cappelli, 2000; Jacoby, 1985). A component of formal employment structures entails the measure of 'headcount', or the number of employees that a company carries on its payroll. It is an essential part of corporate-wide resource planning. Companies that use headcount for this purpose typically allot divisional and line managers a fixed headcount, or number of employees, to accomplish the work of their departments. Because the number of contingent workers is not included in headcount restrictions, line managers may expand their authority by expanding the proportion of temporary employees in the workplace. A line manager in a call centre owned by an IT manufacturer said: '*My boss is very open-minded to the idea of hiring temporary workers because he doesn't need to report such matters to his boss. My boss makes it very clear: If you can stick to the profit-loss goals that you've set, you've got my support'*.

Head count is more than a mere tracking of numbers (i.e., workforce size and labour costs); it sometimes implies an organization's decision to make a change. For example, in order to increase labour efficiency, a company may push line managers to increase overall output while diminishing headcount. The expectation is that line managers will substantially change the way that work is organized and may even redefine what that work is. This is why headcount restrictions are often the result of restructuring efforts such as increasing automation, eliminating redundant functions, merging units, using self-managing teams, expanding the span of supervisory control, and flattening hierarchical levels. When bringing additional workers on board on a temporary basis, however, line managers may disguise the fact that they did not or did not intend to implement structural changes. In these cases, managers consciously obey formal, visible requirements of headcount limits in order to disguise the fact that they have not made substantial changes that were anticipated by or imposed from the top.

Finally, state-owned enterprises (SOEs) may use temporary employment to evade the pay limits imposed on corporate managers by the government. This is consistent with the prior finding that managerial compensation schemes lead to political actions that may bear little relationship with economic performance (Hoskisson, Hitt, Turk, and Tyler, 1989). Corporate executives in SOEs have considerably increased their earnings since the adoption of performance-based compensation in the 1990s. The supervision commissions of SOEs at national and provincial levels used several measures in command and control fashion to curb the widening salary gap within organizations. For example, the commission in Beijing requires that total annual income of the CEO not exceed 12 times the average income in the company. Also, the commission will send out a warning if labour costs of managerial employees exceed a reasonable proportion of total payroll expenses. Among SOEs in Shanghai, the average pay rise among managerial employees was 23.9 per cent between 2002 and 2006, while frontline employees only received an increase of 6.5 per cent during the same period. As a result, in 2008, the supervising agency decided to include annual pay rises of frontline employees as a key item in the performance reviews of SOEs in Shanghai. For these reasons, top management in corporate offices has a strong incentive to externalize some relatively low-paid positions while keeping the high-paid workforce on the books. This effectively reduces the ratio of management to worker pay within the organization while the actual rate of all employees working at the organization is higher.

Clearly, managers make use of contingent work for personal gains and political legitimacy, despite the fact that such practices impose costs that are unaccounted for when companies rely on headcount to control labour costs. Specifically, line managers use temporary employees to increase their authority and control in the workplace. Finance managers seek to boost labour productivity and enhance a firm's financial performance for the evaluation of investors. Finally, corporate managers in SOEs embrace or even induce temporary employment in order to raise their own pay beyond what is legally allowed. In short, managers at different hierarchical levels revealed how conflicts of interests arise as different organizational sub-units pursue their own goals, which in turn influences the use of contingent work.

Uncertainties of the External Environment

Although human assets are valuable resources to achieve competitive advantage, they entail inherent risks and uncertainties (Bhattacharya & Wright, 2005). Furthermore, the radical and sometimes disruptive changes during the massive transformation in China gave rise to significant market and institutional uncertainties. Therefore, the use of contingent work has allowed firms to strategically redistribute risks between the employer and the employees, and hedge against unfavourable uncertainties in the future.

Drawing upon real options theory, Bhattacharya and Wright (2005) explained that uncertainties associated with human resources arose from uncertainties in returns, volume and combination, and costs. Uncertainty in returns arose from the unpredictability of the future value of human resources or the cash flow they generated. Uncertainties in volume and combination included varying labour demand that might fluctuate with market conditions and unexpected demand for skills that employees did not possess. Finally, uncertainty in costs referred to the resources that a firm had to invest in order to acquire and develop qualified employees. Foote and Folta (2002) emphasized the irreversibility of investment decisions on human resources, as a result of labour-market rigidities, implicit contracts between the employer and the employees, and social norms. The authors also argued that companies hired temporary employees in order to minimize uncertainties and maximize flexibility.

Discussions of the uncertainties of human resources are particularly relevant to the Chinese context. Some scholars and business practitioners whom we interviewed were sceptical of China's sustainable economic development. They were concerned about economic and social problems ranging from bad loans in the banking system to an under-funded pension insurance scheme, the lack of a rural health-care system, and bankrupt local governments. The uncertainty and instability that characterizes a firm's external environment has reduced the effectiveness of traditional investment decisions that are inadequate to anticipate and deal with such changes with requisite accuracy. Under such conditions, management's ability to operate with flexibility in its investment decisions brings more value to the firm. From a real options perspective, investments with built-in flexibility provide more than one option for future courses of action to the firm (McGrath, Ferrier, and Mendelow, 2004). As future conditions unfold, managers can choose the most appropriate course of action in order to adapt to emergent new circumstances. Some of the managers that we interviewed worked in extremely profitable companies because of their monopoly market power. For them, hiring people on a temporary basis provides a way to acquire human resources with built-in flexibility to accommodate market and institutional uncertainties, such as changes of regulatory structures and the deregulation of state industries. As a manager from a mobile telecommunications said:

> We did not use temporary workers to save money. Low cost is a by-product. What we care about are the long-term prospects of the company. Employees start working here in their early twenties with knowledge and skills up to date. But who knows what radical changes will happen to our company in ten years? It is possible that these workers' skills become so obsolete that they are not needed any more. We don't know exactly what will happen but the company cannot take a risk of keeping these workers forever or firing a tenured regular worker. The company must retain an exit strategy. (Interview, May 2008)

Another type of uncertainty comes from the inadequacy of the current labour legislation framework, or the liability associated with dismissals in particular. The influences of political institutions, including pressure from the government and laws, are highly complex in a transitional economy like China. As policy makers were experimenting with alternative regulatory approaches in order to construct effective labour protection and enforcement strategies, managers worried that the government would institute a more sophisticated and rigid labour regulatory system in the near future. Hence, some employers have withdrawn their commitment to workers by hiring them on a limited-term basis or placing them under the payroll of a different business unit.

To summarize, our field research suggests that managers adopt contingent work arrangements in response to pressures from market competition, political contests within the organization, and uncertainties in the political and economic environment. First, employers use temporary workers to reduce labour costs and achieve economic efficiency. This finding is consistent with most discussions of temporary work in industrial economies (e.g., Houseman, 2001; Masters and Miles, 2002). To reduce costs, management has a strong incentive to decrease the number of in-house, permanent employees. How far one can go along these lines may rest upon the supply of willing temporary employees and the possible adverse cost impacts. For firms that face a heightened level of market competition, cost considerations are imperative.

Even when the use of contingent work is not economically justifiable, managers may choose to do so to advance their own personal interests. We found that headcount limits within companies drove the widespread use of labour employed on a temporary basis. Line managers used temporary employees to increase their authority and control in the workplace. Finance managers sought to boost the company's financial performance to the expectations of investors. In addition, corporate managers in SOEs favoured temporary employment in order to raise their wages.

Finally, Chinese managers are increasingly concerned with long-term security and strategic outlook for their companies (Nee, 1992). This study suggests managers feel a high level of uncertainty due to market competition and institutional transformations. Hence, companies shift some employers' obligations to temporary help agencies, so that they are better able to hedge against future uncertainties that may arise from markets or institutional changes.

The Effect of Contingent Work on Job Quality and Worker Outcomes

Prior literature suggests that the structural shift toward tenuous employment relationships in the economy has a profound impact on both regular and contingent workers (Kalleberg, Reskin, and Hudson, 2000; Broschak and Davis-Blake, 2006). In order to analyse the influences of work arrangements on job quality as measured by contract length, training, incentives and rewards, electronic monitoring, and worker mobility, we drew upon the survey conducted in 2012 and differentiated companies into three groups, including ones hiring regular employees only, hiring both regular and contingent workers, and hiring contingent workers only.

Contract length. A typical contractual appointment for contingent workers reported in our survey was 2 to 2.5 years (as shown in Table 7.4), whereas contingent workers are hired on contracts for a few days or weeks, or sometimes months in most European countries. Interestingly, this important observation is consistent with recent reports on new hiring strategies in some companies in the United States. For example, a Reuters survey (2013) of 52 Walmart stores showed that 27 were hiring only temporary workers, 20 were hiring a combination of regular full, part-time, and temporary jobs, and five were not hiring at all. Most of these contingent workers were hired on 180-day contracts. Reuters reported that this was the first time that the world's largest retailer disproportionally hired temporary workers outside of the holiday shopping season. Second, our study asked managers whether their companies would maintain or increase the current workforce size in the next three to five years; 72.8 per cent of companies hiring regular workers reported 'Sure' and 'Very sure', while 69.4 per cent of companies reported using a combination of regular and contingent workers and 81 per cent of companies hiring contingent workers had the same reports. These differences

Table 7.4 Duration of contingent jobs in call centres

	Companies using regular employees only	Companies using both regular and contingent employees	Companies using contingent employees only
Typical contract length (in years)			
non-renewable, fixed term appointment	–	2.0	2.0
Temporary agency appointment	–	2.3	2.5
Are you going to maintain or increase your staffing needs in the future? (sure/very sure=1, otherwise=0)			
In the next 12 months	76.0	70.8	85.7
In the next 1–3 years	72.8	69.4	81.0
In the next 3.1–5 years	52.8	59.7	61.9
In the next 5.1–10 years	44.8	50.0	42.9
After 10 years from now	40.8	45.8	38.1
Number of companies	125	72	21

Establishment surveys conducted by the author. Data collected in 2012 before the restrictions on the length of agency employment enacted in 2013 in Table 7.4 were not statistically significant. This finding suggests that for many companies, hiring contingent workers was a deliberate staffing practice, rather than a passive, buffering measure in response to external market volatility.

Training. We compared the amount of company-provided formal training and the purposes of training among these three types of companies in Table 7.5. Call centres hiring only regular workers provided an average of 21.13 days of training for new hires, whereas initial training required over 30 days in companies hiring contingent workers only. Furthermore, while workers in companies hiring regular workers only needed 14.12 weeks to be fully competent on the job, it took 18.3 weeks for workers in companies hiring contingent workers only. Even when working in the same company, contingent workers required more initial training (28.2 days) and time to reach job competence (18.07 weeks) than those of regular workers (27.31 days and 15.27 weeks). This suggests that although companies may increase flexibility and save costs by offering temporary jobs, workers who fill these positions tend to be less skilled and thus need more training before they can effectively perform their jobs.

Company-provided ongoing training provides an important opportunity for experienced workers to develop new job-related skills. According

Table 7.5 Company-provided training in call centres

	Companies using regular employees only	Companies using both regular and contingent employees		Companies using contingent employees only
		Regular	Contingent	
Days of initial training	21.13	27.31	28.20	30.75
Weeks to become proficient on the job	14.12	15.27	18.07	18.3
Days of ongoing training	13.45	18.07	17.75	16.45
Content of Training				
Product updates	3.91	4.05	3.95	4.15
Operation systems	3.11	3.41	3.24	3.3
Team building	2.84	2.95	2.76	2.45
Stress management	2.82	2.88	2.76	2.7
Number of companies	125	72		21

Establishment surveys conducted by the authors in 2012

to our survey, companies hiring both regular and contingent workers provided slightly more ongoing training to regular workers (18.07 days) than contingent workers (17.75 days). However, we found that workers in companies hiring regular workers only received less ongoing training than those in companies hiring contingent workers only. A possible explanation is that workers with stable jobs have more opportunities to accumulate human capital in informal ways such as peer interaction and social learning, which then reduces the need for formal training. We also asked managers to report the types of ongoing training provided on a Likert scale (1=little training provided, 5=a substantial amount of training provided). Interestingly, contingent workers receive significantly less training in areas that promote personal well-being (i.e., team building and stress management) than those that enhance skills to perform tasks (i.e., product updates and operational systems).

Pay levels and incentives. Managers in this study reported the median annual earnings of front-line call-centre workers including base pay, individual commissions, group bonuses, and other pay for performance. That means half the employees were paid more and half were paid less. We found that levels of annual earnings varied considerably by work status and types of call centres. As indicated in Table 7.6, median annual earnings were highest for workers in companies hiring regular workers only (40,841 RMB), followed by regular workers in companies with mixed uses of work arrangements (39,561 RMB) and workers in companies hiring only contingent workers (36,806 RMB). Median annual earnings were lowest for contingent workers in companies hiring both regular and contingent workers (31,404 RMB), which was over 20 per cent less than that of regular workers in the same companies. While such a pattern is consistent with prior research reporting lower pay levels for contingent workers, the observed earning gap in our study survey may be partly related to tenure profiles of these workers. On average, managers reported that the median tenure was 1.38 years for contingent workers and 3.69 years for regular workers in call centres with a combination of regular and contingent workers. It suggests that when the effect of job tenure is accounted for, wage differentials caused by work status might be lower. Furthermore, we found companies hiring contingent workers were most likely to use variable pay practices based on individual performance. While managers in companies hiring only contingent workers reported that over 30 per cent of annual earnings was performance-based, the comparable figure was 24 per cent in companies with some regular workers. This finding suggests that contingent workers not only received lower pay, but were exposed to greater levels of pay variability.

Table 7.6 Incentive practices in call centres

	Companies using regular employees only	Companies using both regular and contingent employees		Companies using contingent employees only
		Regular	Contingent	
Median annual earnings (RMB)	40,841	39,561	31,404	36,806
Percentage of earnings based on individual performance	26.84	26.67	23.91	30.05
Number of companies	125	72		21

Establishment surveys conducted by the authors in 2012

Contrary to what we found in companies that use only regular or contingent workers, the results of the survey indicate that the percentage of earnings based on individual performance is actually lower for contingent workers in companies that use a mixture of employee groups. One possible explanation lies in the differences of work tasks that the two groups of employees are responsible for. Regular workers deal with high-valued customers and bear the dual responsibilities of service and sales. Sometimes they even need to transfer customer enquiries into potential sales. The jobs that regular workers perform yield a greater need to boost employee motivation. In response, call centres tend to increase the ratio of performance-based pay. Contingent workers, in contrast, are assigned routine and repetitive work tasks that are less significant to the companies. These work tasks correspond to a payment structure that is less related to individual performance.

Electronic monitoring. Technological infrastructures of call-centre operations provide an opportunity for managers to electronically monitor the behaviour and performance of their workers, such as what tasks they are currently performing, the number of calls they have taken, the number of calls in their queue, the average time handling a customer inquiry, and the time between breaks (e.g., paperwork after call, drink breaks, or restroom breaks). If a call-centre worker is spending too much time on one call, a supervisor may listen in, identify what the problem is and sometimes help solve the problem. In many cases, call centre workers are not told when a call is listened to or taped. The widespread use of electronic monitoring increases the levels of stress, depression, and anxiety that call-centre workers experience at work (Sprigg and Jackson, 2006).

According to our survey, the use of electronic monitoring varied widely across different types of centres. Table 7.7 reported these results. The use of electronic monitoring was most intensive in call centres hiring contingent workers only, where managers on average reported that 67 per cent of all employee activities were electronically monitored, regardless of how the information was used. In contrast, workers in companies hiring only regular workers were monitored 46 per cent of their work time, while the level of electronic monitoring was about 55 per cent in companies with mixed uses of regular and contingent workers. Furthermore, managers reported the extent to which they used information collected via electronic monitoring for different purposes on a Likert scale of 1 (not at all) to 5 (a great deal). We found that companies hiring contingent workers were most likely to use information from performance monitoring to support disciplinary actions (4.05) and least likely to do so in order to enhance employee performance (3.21). In contrast, performance monitoring as a basis for disciplinary action was lowest for workers in companies hiring regular workers only (3.68), while performance monitoring as a way to improve performance was highest for regular workers in companies that hired both regular and contingent workers (3.64).

We also find that regular workers are exposed to greater electronic monitoring than contingent workers in companies that use a mixture of both employee groups. Two possible reasons may explain this

Table 7.7 The use of electronic monitoring in call centres

	Companies using regular employees only	Companies using both regular and contingent employees		Companies using contingent employees only
		Regular	Contingent	
Percentage of time electronically monitored	45.56	56.57	54.68	66.84
Purposes of electronic monitoring				
In order to support disciplinary decisions	3.68	3.84	3.72	4.05
In order to improve performance	3.49	3.64	3.46	3.21
Number of companies	125	72		21

Establishment surveys conducted by the authors in 2012

observation. First, some call centres tend to assign more complicated and value-added tasks to regular workers. This will then lessen the need for performance monitoring and close supervision for contingent workers on more routine jobs. Second, in order to reduce administrative costs, some call centres invite employment agencies to get involved in the on-site management of contingent workers. By doing so, they shift the responsibilities of supervision and monitoring to the employment agencies.

Worker Turnover. Contingent workers are much more likely to leave both voluntarily and involuntarily (see Table 7.8). On average, managers reported that 16 per cent of workers in call centres that hired regular workers left their jobs voluntarily in the past 12 months, which was significantly lower than a quit rate of 26 per cent in centres only using contingent workers. At call centres with a combination of both regular and contingent workers, the voluntary quit rates were 13 per cent for regular workers and 28 per cent for contingent workers. Higher levels of voluntary turnover among contingent workers may reflect higher levels of employee dissatisfaction toward the jobs – as shown in our analysis and other studies, contingent workers tend to fill jobs that are routinized and repetitive, provide limited training and developmental opportunities, offer relatively low pay levels, and generally lack employment stability. As a result, contingent workers have a stronger tendency to leave the call centres than regular workers.

We also measured the dismissal rates, or the percentage of workers who were terminated by employers. At call centres that hired both groups of employees, 6.43 per cent of contingent workers were dismissed, which was more than twice as high as the dismissal rate for regular workers (2.55 per cent). Two important factors may account for the

Table 7.8 Employee turnover in call centres (measured in percentage)

	Companies using regular employees only	Companies using both regular and contingent employees		Companies using contingent employees only
		Regular	Contingent	
Voluntary quits	15.85	13.23	27.26	25.75
Dismissals	3.42	2.55	6.43	2.18
Number of companies	125	72		21

Establishment surveys conducted by the authors in 2012

high dismissal rate of contingent workers. First, as contingent workers generally had lower job-related skills than regular workers before filling the positions (as indicated by our analysis on initial training), they might experience high levels of difficulties in reaching productivity targets set by their employers. Workers who fall short of performance targets therefore face high risks of dismissal. Second, labour laws in China require employers to pay severance to dismissed workers based on the length of tenure. For example, to fire a worker with ten years of employment in this organization, an employer is obligated to make a severance payment that is at least ten times this worker's monthly salary. Therefore, in case of low customer demand or financial distress, call centres are more likely to fire contingent workers as a low-cost strategy to adjust employment levels.

Companies using only contingent employees report the lowest dismissal rates among the three types of call centres. Workers often find it easier to reach the performance targets in these companies, as the skill requirements are generally lower than the other two types of call centres. It is less common for these companies to eliminate workers for performance reasons. Besides, since the turnover rate in these call centres is extremely high, managers need to constantly search for new hires to fill the vacancies. As a result, managers tend to retain existing workers, unless they lag far behind in terms of job performance or exert negative influences on the workplace.

Summary

This study explored the characteristics of contingent work in Chinese call centres and discussed the institutional and organizational factors that have driven its recent growth. Our analysis indicates that the dramatic rise of contingent work in call centres is associated with employers' incentives to seek labour-market flexibility in view of strict employment protection regulation. Chinese employers view contingent work as a cost-saving way to increase flexibility because the length of short-term and fixed-term contracts allow employers to terminate employment relationships without incurring severance payments or limitations imposed by employment rights rules. This phenomenon is similar to Spain and France, where restrictive employment protection reforms have resulted in a rapidly expanded contingent workforce (Booth, Dolado, and Frank, 2002; Kahn, 2007). Furthermore, labour laws that regulate contingent work in China remain vague and ambiguous. Therefore, companies have sought to exploit regulatory loopholes and gain benefits. For example, although the law restricts the use of dispatched workers to only 'auxiliary' jobs, the scope of these jobs varies significantly across industries. Therefore it is practically difficult to implement this rule. Similarly, although the Social Security Law requires employers to make contributions to pensions and medical insurance, some temporary help companies register their businesses in low-income areas as a way to reduce their contribution costs.

Prior literature has presented contradictory arguments related to the effect of contingent employment on worker outcomes (Kalleberg, Reskin, and Hudson, 2000; Booth, Francesconi, and Frank, 2002). While some researchers argue that the flexibility of temporary jobs provides a stepping-stone mechanism for workers to enter the labour market and acquire skills, other researchers view contingent work as dead-end jobs associated with negligible job security, low wages, and little job autonomy. Our analysis based on call-centre jobs advances this debate by showing that although contingent workers received lower pay and were exposed to greater unemployment risks, they did have an opportunity to enhance career skills through initial training and ongoing training provided by the employer. Moreover, our analysis provides mixed support for existing arguments on the impact on regular workers. On one hand, we found that regular workers in companies combining regular and contingent workers in the same positions were least likely to leave their jobs voluntarily or involuntarily, which supports the core–periphery hypothesis that employers hire contingent workers as a cushion to protect the employment security of regular workers (Atkinson, 1984). On the other hand, our analysis provides support for Cappellie and Neumark's (2004) external churning argument that the use of contingent work as a way to incorporate market-mediated employment into an organization poses a threat to the work conditions of regular workers. As reported by managers in our survey, regular workers consistently received lower pay, were monitored more intensively, and were more likely to receive workplace punishment based on performance monitoring data in companies that hired some contingent workers than those in companies hiring regular workers only.

A notable trend in recent years is that companies have experimented with various forms of triangular employment relationships and business process outsourcing in order to change, obscure, or disguise the substance of employment relationships. A noticeable example is 'reverse labour dispatch' (Fan Xiang Pai Qian). In a typical triangular employment situation such as labour dispatching, a temporary help agency hires a worker to perform special work assignments at the user firm under a commercial contract. When the special assignment ends, the worker then moves from one placement to another. The agency plays an active role in hiring, wage setting, training and development, and even firing. In return, the only relatively stable employment relationship that the worker has is with the agency. In the reverse labour dispatch situation, however, the employer asks incumbent workers who already have a legal employment relationship to sign labour contracts with labour dispatching agencies. The employer thus becomes a client organization and shifts all legal and social responsibilities as the employer to the staffing agency. In this latter situation, the major service provided by the agency is 'payrolling', instead of helping the client organization to identify, recruit, or train workers with special skills. Another noteworthy form of contingent work is 'reciprocal subcontracting' (*Shuang Xiang Wai Bao*) or 'on-site outsourcing' (*Zhu Chang Wai Bao*). Typically, business process outsourcing involves an organization's decision to subcontract non-central business operations to a third party in order to focus on its core competences. However, due to the new legal rule that the proportion of temporary agency workers cannot exceed 10 per cent of the workforce in all companies by 2016, some have sought to use reciprocal subcontracting to disguise an employment relationship or at least make it ambiguous. For example, in order to bring business in compliance with the labour rules, a major bank brought in 803 employees through reciprocal contracting while hiring 139 dispatched workers (Zhang, 2015). In another large-scale study of over 4,000 companies conducted by FESCO (2013), less than one-third of companies with 10 per cent or more contingent workers reported that they re-hired these workers as regular staff, while 40 per cent reported that they turned to subcontracting for such personnel needs. It is important for researchers to examine these changes in depth and systematically evaluate their impact on workers.

In spite of the emergence and development of workplace collective bargaining in China (e.g., Chan and Hui, 2014), the roles that state-led trade unions may play in regulating contingent work are politically contested and yet to be examined. Although the ACFTU has strongly and successful pushed for more restrictive employment protection rules including the Labour Contract Law and its recent amendments, the central government has vested limited power in unions. Based on the laws, trade unions can only serve in monitoring and consulting roles. In the case of labour dispatching, for example, unions have the right to monitor whether the user organization and the staffing agency comply with the laws and the right to report violating activities to a local labour bureau. In addition, the user organization may consult and determine jointly with unions about the scope of 'temporary, auxiliary, and substitute' jobs. However, the laws do not provide a valid ground for trade unions to be involved in the employer's decision making in regards to the hiring, managing, and firing of contingent workers. Meanwhile, although contingent workers have equal legal rights to join trade unions, their understanding and participation in union activities are particularly low. For example, So (2014) reported that over 70 per cent of dispatched workers either did not know or were not convinced of the representative function of trade unions. Moreover, many temporary help companies do not have unions, which further reduces the opportunities for dispatched workers to join a union.

Note

1 China's rural and urban labour markets are disparate social systems due to a combination of administrative controls such as the household registration, rural commune controls, and food rationing. This chapter focuses on the transformation of labour arrangements in urban industrial settings; changes of the rural labour market are beyond the scope of this chapter.

REFERENCES

Ashford, S. J., George, E. and Blatt, R. (2007) 'Old assumptions, new work', *Academy of Management Annals*, 1(1): 65–117.

Atkinson, J. (1984) 'Manpower strategies for flexible firms', *Personnel Management*, 16 (August): 28–31.

Autor, D. H. (2001) 'Why do temporary help firms provide free general skills training?' *Quarterly Journal of Economics*, (November): 1409–1448.

Batt, R., Doellgast, V. and Kwon, H. (2006) 'Service management and employment systems in U.S. and Indian call centres', in S. Collins and L. Brainard (eds), *Offshoring White-Collar Work*, Washington, D.C.: Brookings Press.

Beijing Bureau of Labor and Social Security (2007) 'A report on the implementation of labor contracts in Beijing', available at https://114.247.102.35/article/1/7732 (accessed 9 December 2015).

Benner, C. (2003) 'Labour flexibility and regional development: the role of labour market intermediaries', *Regional Studies*, 37 (6–7): 621–633.

Bhattacharya, M. and Wright, P. M. (2005) 'Managing human assets in an uncertain world: applying real options theory to HRM', *International Journal of Human Resource Management*, 16(6): 929–948.

Bloomberg. (2012) 'Why China's Factories Are Turning to Temp Workers', Reported on March 8, 2012. Available at: http://www.bloomberg.com/bw/articles/2012-03-08/why-chinas-factories-are-turning-to-temp-workers. (accessed 9 December 2015).

▶

Booth, A. L., Dolado, J. J. and Frank, J. (2002) 'Symposium on temporary work: introduction', *The Economic Journal*, 112(June): 181–187.

Broschak, J. P. and Davis-Blake, A. (2006) 'Mixing standard work and nonstandard deals: the consequences of heterogeneity in employment arrangements', *The Academy of Management Journal*, 49(2): 371–393.

Cappelli, P. (2000) 'A market-driven approach to retaining talent', *Harvard Business Review*, 78(1): 103–111.

Cappelli, P. and Neumark, D. (2004) 'External churning and internal flexibility: evidence on the functional flexibility and core-periphery hypotheses', *Industrial Relations: A Journal of Economy and Society*, 43(1): 148–182.

Chan, C. K. C. and Hui, E. S. I. (2014) 'The development of collective bargaining in China: from 'collective bargaining by riot' to 'party state-led wage bargaining'', *The China Quarterly*, 217: 221–242.

Chen, Y. F. and Funke, M. (2009) 'China's new labour contract law: no harm to employment?' *China Economic Review*, 20(3): 558–572.

Elfstrom, M. and Kuruvilla, S. (2014) 'The changing nature of labour unrest in China', *Industrial and Labour Relations Review*, 67(2): 453–480.

FESCO (2013) 'As the use of dispatched labor in 70% companies has reduced to 10%, the demand for HR business process outsource will increase', available at: http://www.fesco.com.cn/296/2013_11_13/1_296_57282_0_1384333358140.html (accessed 9 December 2015).

Foote, D. A. and Folta, T. B. (2002) 'Temporary workers as real options', *Human Resource Management Review*, 12(4): 579–597.

Frenkel, S. and Kuruvilla, S. (2002) 'Logics of action, globalization, and changing employment relations in China, India, Malaysia, and the Philippines', *Industrial and Labour Relations Review*, 55(3): 387–412.

Holman, D., Batt, R. and Holtgrewe, U. (2007) *The global call centre report: International perspectives on management and employment*, Ithaca, NY: Authors.

Gramm, C. L. and Schnell, J. F. (2001) 'The use of flexible staffing arrangements in core production jobs', *Industrial and Labour Relations Review*, 54(2): 245–258.

Hoskisson, R. E., Hitt, M. A., Turk, T. A. and Tyler, B. B. (1989) 'Balancing corporate strategy and executive compensation: agency theory and corporate governance', *Research in personnel and human resources management*, 7: 25–57.

Houseman, S. N. (2001) 'Why employers use flexible staffing arrangements: evidence from an establishment survey', *Industrial and Labour Relations Review*, 55(1): 149–170.

Houseman, S. N., Kalleberg, A. L. and Erickcek, G. A. (2003) 'The role of temporary agency employment in tight labour markets', *Industrial and Labour Relations Review*, 57(1): 105–127.

Hu, A. G. and Zhao, L. (2006) 'Informal employment and informal economy in the economic transformation in the process of urbanization in China (1990—2004)', *Journal of Tsinghua University (Philosophy and Social Sciences)*, 3(016).

International Labour Organization. (2014a) '*Global Employment Trends 2014: The Risks of a Jobless Recovery*', available at: http://www.ilo.org/global/research/global-reports/global-employment-trends/2014/lang--en/index.htm. (accessed 9 December 2015).

International Labour Organization. (2014b) 'Employment Protection Legislation Database', available at http://www.ilo.org/dyn/eplex/termmain.home.

Jacoby, S. (1985) *Employing Bureaucracy*, New York: Columbia University Press.

Jasmand, C., Blazevic, V. and de Ruyter, K. (2012). 'Generating sales while providing service: a study of customer service representatives' ambidextrous behavior', *Journal of Marketing*, 76(1): 20–37.

Kahn, L.M. (2007) 'The impact of employment protection mandates on demographic temporary employment patterns: international microeconomic evidence', *Economic Journal*, 117(521).

Kalleberg, A. L. (2000) 'Nonstandard employment relations: part-time, temporary and contract work', *Annual Review of Sociology*, 26(1): 341–365.

Kalleberg, A. L., Reskin, B. F. and Hudson, K. (2000) 'Bad jobs in America: standard and nonstandard employment relations and job quality in the United States', *American Sociological Review*, 65(2): 256.

Lee, C. K. (1998) 'The labour politics of market socialism: collective inaction and class experiences among state workers in Guangzhou', *Modern China*, 24: 3–33.

Lee, C. K. and Tierney, R. (2008) 'Against the law: labour protests in China's rust-belt and sunbelt', *Labour history*, 95: 258–259.

Liu, X. (2015) 'How institutional and organizational characteristics explain the growth of contingent work in China', *Industrial and Labour Relations Review*, 68: 372–397.

Masters, J. K. and Miles, G. (2002) 'Predicting the use of external labour arrangements: A test of the transaction costs perspective', *Academy of Management Journal*, 45(2): 431–442.

McGrath, R. G., Ferrier, W. J. and Mendelow, A. L. (2004) 'Real options as engines of choice and heterogeneity', *Academy of Management Review*, 29(1): 86–101.

Nee, V. (1992) 'Organizational dynamics of market transition: hybrid forms, property rights, and mixed economy in China', *Administrative Science Quarterly*, 37(1): 1–27.

Ngok, K. (2008) 'The changes of Chinese labour policy and labour legislation in the context of market transition', *International Labour and Working-Class History*, 73(1): 45-64.

Organization for Economic Co-operation and Development (2014) 'Indicators of employment protection', available at: http://www.oecd.org/employment/emp/oecdindicatorsofemploymentprotection.htm. (accessed 9 December 2015).

Park, A. and Cai, F. (2011) 'The informalization of the Chinese labour market', in S. Kuruville, C. K. Lee and M. Gallagher (eds.) *From Iron Rice Bowl to Informalization*, Ithaca, NY: Cornell University Press, pp. 17–35.

Peck, J., Theodore, N. and Ward, K. (2005) 'Constructing markets for temporary labour: employment liberalization and the internationalization of the staffing industry', *Global Networks*, 5(1): 3–26.

Polivka, A. E. (1996) 'Contingent and alternative work arrangements, defined', *Monthly Labour Review*, 119(10): 3–9.

Puglia, S. E. and Tikiwala, P. A. (2013) 'Slow and steady: Payroll employment grew moderately in 2012', *Monthly Labour Review*, 136 (22).

Reuters (2013) 'Wal-Mart's everyday hiring strategy: Add more temps', Reported on June 13, 2013. Available at: http://www.reuters.com/article/2013/06/13/us-walmart-hires-temps-idUSBRE95C05820130613. (accessed 9 December 2015).

▶

Russell, B. (2008) 'Call centres: A decade of research', *International Journal of Management Reviews*, 10(3): 195–219.

So, J. (2014) 'Exploring the plight of dispatch workers in China and how to improve their conditions: a preliminary study', *WorkingUSA*, 17(4): 531–552.

Sprigg, C. A. and Jackson, P. R. (2006) 'Call centres as lean service environments: job-related strain and the mediating role of work design', *Journal of occupational health psychology*, 11(2): 197–212.

USA Today (2013) 'Temporary jobs becoming a permanent fixture', Reported on July 7, 2013. Available at: http://www.usatoday.com/story/money/business/2013/07/07/temporary-jobs-becoming-permanent-fixture/2496585/ (accessed 9 December 2015).

Wall Street Journal (2013) 'China Begins to Lose Edge as World's Factory Floor', Reported on January 16, 2013. Available at: http://www.wsj.com/articles/SB10001424127887323783704578245241751969774.

Wang, H., Appelbaum, R., Degiuli, F. and Lichtenstein, N. (2009) 'China's new labour contract law: is China moving towards increased power for workers?' *Third World Quarterly*, 30(3): 485–501.

Warner, M. (2004) 'Human resource management in China revisited: introduction', *The International Journal of Human Resource Management*, 15(4–5): 617–634.

Whyte, M. K. and Bian, Y. (1995) 'Work and Inequality in Urban China', *Contemporary Sociology*, 24(4): 342.

Zhang, W. (2014) 'Suggestions for the scientific development of Chinese call center industry', available at: http://www.sic.gov.cn/News/459/3257.htm. (accessed 9 December 2015).

Zhang, Y. (2015) 'Number of dispatched workers reduced by 84.3 thousand in four major banks last year', *Securities Daily*. April 28, 2015. Available at: http://finance.chinanews.com/fortune/2015/04-28/7238115.shtml. (accessed 9 December 2015).

Zhao, S. and Du, J. (2012) 'Thirty-two years of development of human resource management in China: Review and prospects', *Human Resource Management Review*, 22(3): 179–188.

Zhou, Y. (2013) 'The state of precarious work in China', *American Behavioral Scientist*, 57(3): 354–72.

Power, Space, and Subjectivity in a Transnational Garment Factory in China

8

Jaesok Kim

Introduction

The shop floor of Nawon,[1] a South Korean transnational garment factory in Qingdao, north China, always carried a strong, rancid odour. Foreign buyers, who were not accustomed to the aroma, expressed acute embarrassment when they visited: 'I can only stay in the workshop for a short time', a woman buyer from the United States complained. 'The odour makes me nearly sick.' Korean-Chinese employees, whom the Korean management of the factory hired as interpreters and middle managers, claimed that the source of the odour was the Han-Chinese workers in the production lines. In the factory, a small number of Korean-Chinese (an ethnic minority known as *Chaoxianzu*)[2] held privileged positions in the office, while nearly 600 Han-Chinese (*hanzu*) occupied every rank-and-file position on the shop floor. The Korean-Chinese often called the offending aroma 'Han-Chinese odour' (*Hanjok naemsae* in Korean), regarding it as an expression of their inferior ethnic characteristics. 'Han-Chinese don't have any idea of what the word clean means', said Hyesook, a Korean-Chinese woman interpreter. 'This explains why the shop floor and workers' dormitories reek with that strange odour – like something fermenting or rotten'.

In summer months, the temperature of the shop floor and the workers' dormitories often rose to nearly 38 degrees centigrade. This level of heat, combined with poor indoor ventilation and non-existent showers, meant that the workers worked and lived literally soaked in sweat. The Korean-Chinese at Nawon, however, thought that the odour was not simply caused by the poor working and living conditions. The story of the shop-floor odour reveals how spatial divisions, here experienced through human perceptions of bodily cleanliness, served foreign management in its efforts to control Chinese labour. The Korean-Chinese often contrasted their 'odourless' air-conditioned factory office with the smelly shop floor dominated by Han-Chinese, which overlapped the hierarchical division of labour between white- and blue-collar employees. The divided factory space, built upon ethnic and hierarchical differences, reinforced the Korean-Chinese notion of their ethnic superiority over the Han-Chinese and thus justified the unequal power relations among Korean, Korean-Chinese, and Han-Chinese personnel.

In this chapter, I show how factory space helped generate the pervasive controlling effects of managerial power by forging workers with high productivity. Management utilized space to integrate individual human bodies – in this case those of employees – into systems of efficient labour control and high productivity. I expose the connections between spaces, subjects, and power as they were articulated in managerial discourses and embedded in the factory landscape. Modern disciplinary power is visually and spatially organized, and its operations cannot be separated from specific spatial arrangements (Foucault, 1980: 140). The factory is an optimal place to address questions of space, power, and subjectivity because it 'centre[s] on the body as a machine' (Foucault, 1990: 139) and puts the human body under the disciplinary gaze of management. Though management's panoptic control of workers could not completely remove agency from workers, my research found an unusual instance where management achieved a high degree of labor control and minimized shop floor instability.

At Nawon factory, the pervasive effect of disciplinary power went beyond the workshop and extended into the living space of factory employees. As a response to global just-in-time production that requires a high flexibility of labour (Black and Chen, 1995), management implemented a policy of collective living that required almost all factory employees, including Korean managers and Chinese workers, to live on the factory premises.[3] Under this policy, mundane practices of daily living transformed the different 'structures of feeling' among factory residents, defined by Raymond Williams (1977: 128–29) as sets of perceptions and values that 'operate in the most delicate and least tangible part of activities'. Despite its intimate and private nature, the factory residents' structures of feeling were subject to managerial power and eventually served as frameworks for moulding multiple subjectivities, differentiating Korean managers, Korean-Chinese intermediaries, and Han-Chinese (hereafter Han) rank-and-file workers.

Nawon management established its shop-floor authority by adopting the allegedly universal or modern principles of 'scientific management'. Historical memories and localized experiences, however, underlay the managerial discourse on the modern and the global, affecting the actual realization of abstract principles. This discrepancy reveals an imaginary dimension of modernity as a 'vast ensemble of universals' (Hostettler, 2012: 13). Modernity, which is often associated with universal values such as progress, science, and rationality, in fact has its own localized origins, carrying the historical baggage of class, ethnicity, gender, and religion (Comaroff and Comaroff, 1991; Dirks, 1990). I approach the three-tiered residential division of Koreans, Korean-Chinese, and Han as part of the inevitable 'localization' strategy employed by transnational capital (Clark et al., 1986: 23–24). Spatial separation supported powerful disciplinary effects since it invoked the factory residents' images of the Korean War (1950–53), concerns over China's rapid economic development, and ethnic divisions and hierarchies in post-Mao China.

Modern disciplinary power can never be total, and resistance may break out at different points in the capillary-like chain of power that reaches the lowest rung of localities or organizations (Knights and Vurdubakis, 1994). The normalizing gaze of management has never achieved the totality of panoptic control, as it failed to remove worker recalcitrance from the shop floor (cf. Smith and Thompson, 1998; Thompson, 2003; Thompson and Ackroyd, 1995). If the potential of resistance exists inside the realm of modern disciplinary power (Foucault, 1990: 95–96), one can expect problems for management – and this was exactly what happened at Nawon. The histories and personal sensibilities of factory subjects at Nawon set limits on the power of management to forge docile labour. Most Han employees at Nawon came from remote villages in Pingshan, a poor and underdeveloped region (*pinkundiqu*) of Shandong province. The management put them under its close surveillance on the shop floor and located them at the lowest level of the three-tiered spatial hierarchy of everyday living. The separated dwellings with poor living conditions brought the Han workers into a status similar to 'the abject', which equated with the uncivilized, the disgusting, and the abominable (Kristeva, 1982: 2). The Han workers' bodies, however, were not blank objects to be imprinted with the disciplinary power. Their nostalgic memories of 'home' (*jia* or *wojia*) and a sense of Sino-centrism[4] raised the workers' critical awareness of an all-inclusive managerial power and set a limit on its disciplinary effects. The separated space of the factory dormitories, which the management created for high labour flexibility, was transformed into a space of labour resistance as the workers appropriated the spatial design in their efforts to express their discontent with management.

Fieldwork at Nawon Qingdao Apparel

The global headquarters of the Chinese factory under investigation is Nawon Korea, located in Seoul, South Korea. During the time of study, Nawon Korea had two production facilities in Korea and China. The corporation functioned as a typical contract manufacturer that made and shipped products to foreign buyers. Established in 1993, Nawon Qingdao was one of the oldest Korean-owned businesses in the Qingdao region. Thanks to its geographical proximity to Korea and low labour costs, Qingdao has been the largest investment destination for Korean corporations in China since 1992.[5] Intensive fieldwork in the corporation was undertaken from 2002 to 2003.[6] I conducted follow-up research to 2007 and interviewed managers and workers of the corporation. Nawon was a medium-sized garment manufacturing corporation that hired about 700 employees, including three expatriate Korean managers, 16 Korean-Chinese interpreters, and more than 600 Han workers. The management employed the Korean-Chinese as bilingual interpreters and cultural brokers between Han and Koreans, because the Korean managers were unable to speak Chinese and lacked the local knowledge of cultural and social conditions.

My South Korean nationality put me in an ambiguous position during fieldwork. At Nawon Qingdao, I had to maintain good relationships with the Korean management as well as the Chinese employees. My personal connection to the management initially helped me to conduct research in the factory. I was allowed to interview Korean managers and access corporate documents and managerial memos. The same connection, however, initially hampered my efforts to establish close relationships with the Chinese employees. At the early stages of my research, many employees suspected that I was an agent of management. Only after I started working with the ordinary labourers on the shop floor as a novice employee, doing overtime with them, and participating in after-hours socialization, did they gradually drop their suspicions. It took two months for workers to talk to me about their feelings, ideas about labour, and life in the factory.

Power and Subjectivity on the Factory Shop Floor

Since Frederick Taylor argued that a clear hierarchical difference between management and labour should be the precondition of 'scientific management' (Taylor, 1947 [1911]: 54), space has been used as a means of maintaining factory hierarchies and disciplining labour. Under the tenets of Taylorism and later Fordism, management ranked workers spatially and specified their individual operations to record every move on the shop floor and discern anomalies in the production process. On the assembly lines of textiles and automobiles, management placed machineries, tools, and workers in a spatial sequence of operation, allowing each component part to travel the least possible distance in the process (Shiomi, 1995: 1–6).The normalizing gaze of Bentham's Panopticon has been built into the space of factories, while combining techniques of record-keeping, visibility, and social control (Foucault, 1977 [1975]: 200–204; McKinlay, 2006).

The use of space as a method of labour control and surveillance was also widespread in socialist countries such as the former Soviet Union and China. Socialist governments officially promoted workers' rights over those of management and initially attempted to create an 'equal and cooperative' management–labour relationship (Kim, 2013: 39). When adopting Taylorism and Fordism to increase productivity, however, factories inevitably introduced principles of professional management, according to which managers, distinct from workers, 'scientifically' administer the corporation. This adoption reestablished the superiority of management over rank-and-file workers, which was expressed in the wide use of observation windows, stop-watches, and bookkeeping (Berliner, 1957; Burawoy, 1985; Lee, 1995; Priestley, 1963).

After a brief disruption of managerial authority during the Cultural Revolution (1966–76), the post-Mao government launched a nationwide campaign of the 'Four Modernizations' (industry, agriculture, military, and science and technology), which advocated the universal efficacy of science, progress, and rationality. The campaign aimed at achieving fast economic development and high productivity, which, on the shop floor, reinforced management's authority over labour (Lee, 2007: 15–20). Lisa Rofel observes how a factory's space reflects Chinese management's double efforts to maintain hierarchical work structures and increase productivity (Rofel, 1999: 257–76). At a state-owned silk factory in Hangzhou, China, management divided the factory space to enhance the separation of management and labour. Rofel shows that the post-Mao factory regime was preoccupied with implementing minute control over workers' bodies under the slogan of 'scientific management' (Rofel, 2009: 96).

The shop-floor space of Nawon embodied the principles of the 'modern and scientific' management. The Korean managers came to understand the importance of the spatialized hierarchy through their experience of shop floor management in South Korea. Nawon Korea, the corporate headquarters of Nawon Qingdao, began its operation as a contract factory during the early 1980s. As a factory located at the low end of the global chain of garment production (Bonacich et al., 1994), Nawon Korea adopted the basic factory architecture common to foreign garment factories, expressed in separate workplaces of managerial staff and rank-and-file workers. Nawon Korea designed Nawon Qingdao according to a pre-existing pattern: in the main factory building, sound-proofed thick walls divided the indoor space into two areas, one assigned to the office and the other to the production area. The observation windows installed on the wall between the shop floor and the main office created a clear hierarchy between the two spaces. The windows gave Korean managers a commanding view of the shop floor, while placing the workers on the shop floor under a disciplinary gaze of management.

This arrangement was intended to transform workers' bodies into production machines, as it integrated the high visibility of the shop floor with minute tracking of individual workers' productivity. Management attached numbered stickers on every garment part, which allowed them to track unfinished clothes through the entire manufacturing process. If a finished garment proved defective, the management, by referring to the numbers, easily tracked the workers who were responsible for the faulty product. 'The numbers [on the garment parts] are like our eyes', a Korean manager remarked. 'They watch the workers and let us know who did clumsy work.' In addition, the observation windows allowed management to track workers' bodily movements at the worktables. Workers on the shop floor felt the constant pressure of observation, never knowing when the managers would appear from the opposite side of the windows and watch them. They particularly feared meeting the Korean managers' eyes because the Koreans regarded workers who frequently returned their gaze as 'bad workers'. Therefore, the workers had to produce while feeling, as one put it to me, the managers' watchful eyes on the backs of their necks. 'It's a strange situation', Yanli, a woman worker complained. 'I can do nothing except work while a person who may be hostile to me stares at me from above and behind.'

Beyond the Shop Floor: Spatial Practices of Everyday Living and Subject-Making

The pervasive effect of disciplinary power went beyond the workshop and extended into the living space of Nawon employees. The management ordered almost all factory employees, including Korean managers, Korean-Chinese intermediaries, and Han workers, to live on the factory premises and thus increased the flexibility of labour. Since the late 1980s, the advancement in electronic point-of-sale technology using bar codes has greatly increased the command of retailers over garment factories. With this technology, retailers now make a real-time monitoring of consumer purchases and promptly reorder products just-in-time to restock their shelves (Black and Chen, 1995). Under the 'just-in-time' or 'quick response' system, many garment factories, including Nawon, felt increasing pressure to deliver smaller orders in less time to meet tightly planned shipping schedules (Kim, 2013: 49–51). Because of the volatile and unpredictable nature of orders, the management of Nawon frequently required its employees to work overtime. If the Chinese employees had lived in rental houses scattered outside the factory, it would have been difficult for the management to arrange for a large number of employees to show up on the shop floor on short notice. The management could put its employees within easy reach by locating the dormitories on factory premises.

A glaring division of living space lay between management and labour, which was similar to that of the workplace. The location of factory dormitories, where most Han workers lived, clearly reflected the hierarchical differences: six-foot-high concrete walls separated the Han workers' dormitories from the main factory area, where the Korean living quarter was located. The management further enhanced the spatial separation by installing two check points that controlled the workers' movement between the dormitories and the main factory. With the check points, the management made it very clear that no Han worker could pass through the gates unchecked. Every time the workers returned to the dormitories through the factory main gate, two female staff from the Personnel Affairs Division checked their bodies for any contraband owned by the factory, such as finished clothes and garment parts. This strict regulation repeatedly reminded the workers that they were members of a distrusted category.

The living quarters of Nawon, however, did not simply reflect the division between management and labour: The Korean managers lived in the innermost area, Korean-Chinese lived in-between, and Han were relegated to the margins of the factory premises. The ethnicized spatial division, as well as the three-tiered factory hierarchy of Koreans, Korean-Chinese, and Han, was unique to South Korean factories in China. At Nawon Qingdao, Korean-Chinese took most of the intermediary managerial positions thanks to their bilingual skills, Korean cultural background, and relatively high educational level. Korean managers, who could not speak Chinese, had no choice but to work through the Korean-Chinese.[7] Conversely, the management placed the Han workers' living space outside the main factory premises, a place it considered proper for not only their low status but also their 'backward' nature.

Spatial arrangements affect the body, as well as self-presentation and consciousness, establishing an intimate relationship between physical bodies and the symbolic order of significant distinctions (Bourdieu, 1984 [1979]: 170–87). Basic amenities provided by the management, which varied according to detailed guidelines of what should and should not be given to factory residents, also conditioned the three groups' perceptions of their differences. This allowed managerial power to operate through the most intimate dimension of everyday living and enhanced the power effect of separated living space. It demonstrates how, through practices of everyday routines, individual bodies are made into particular kinds of bodies that can be habitualized into domination (Bourdieu, 1977 [1972]: 177–78; 1984 [1979]: 85–86).

Korean residential area: a fortress of national superiority

As the living space for the most high-ranking Korean managerial staff and their families, three Korean houses on the main factory premises had distinctive architectural and spatial characteristics. The interior residential area formed an exclusive space only open to Koreans. Thanks to the four-foot high foundations, the residents of these houses had a near-complete view of the factory from their windows, while people outside could not see into the interior spaces of the residences. The architectural design of the Korean houses was highly distinguished from other factory buildings. Factory employees called the three dwellings 'German houses' because they resembled the German colonial architecture in Qingdao, built when the city was a German concession (late-nineteenth and early-twentieth centuries). In contrast to the grey-coloured factory buildings of simple rectangular design (scornfully called 'matchboxes' by the Chinese workers), the managers' houses had sloping red slate roofs, large viewing windows in the living room, and outer walls decorated with small gravel-inlay bricks.

Korean managers who lived in these 'German houses' knew well how their commanding view over the factory contributed to maintaining their high status in the factory hierarchy. The Nawon president said that his morning routine of drinking tea and contemplation helped him to focus on business activities and reaffirm his authority in the factory. Sitting deep in his armchair and sipping tea, he 'looked down at' all factory buildings through his private windows. Korean managers, including the president, argued that people who gave orders should maintain a superior position in every respect. 'It is hard to imagine', a Korean manager insisted, 'that a Han worker can look down at me... It would be a completely upside-down situation because we give orders and the workers obey our orders'.

The houses were the testimony to the Korean management's effort to maintain its superiority over Chinese employees by establishing their spatial centrality and reproducing their 'modern' Korean lifestyle in 'backward' China. According to their recollection during the time of my research, the Korean managers, who came to China following Nawon Korea's quest for cheap labour in the early 1990s, thought that they had unexpectedly encountered their past. When they first arrived in Qingdao in 1993, what they saw at the factory site was not neatly levelled ground ready for factory construction, but an expanse of swamp filled with mud, foul water, and garbage. Even during the time of my research in the 2000s, the Korean managers superimposed the images of Korea during the 1960s on the images of China in the 1990s. The managers, all in their late fifties at the time of my fieldwork, pointed out that the landscape of the Chinese countryside was similar to that of the Korean countryside of their childhood memories. Having grown up in the poverty-stricken Korean society after the Korean War (1950–53), the managers believed that they noticed signs of China's 'premodernity' (*Jeongeundae seong* in Korean) in the abandoned swampland, backward rural villages, and low living standards. The fact that most Han workers at Nawon were recruited from Pingshan County, one of the poorest regions (*pinkundiqu*) in Shandong province, reinforced the images of backwardness. This attitude denied the local workers' coevalness (Fabian, 1983: 32) – their existence in the same time with the Korean managers – and reinforced notions of managerial superiority.

The spatial separation between the main factory premises and factory dormitories greatly contributed to the near complete absence of social relations between the Korean residents and Han workers. Though having lived in the factory for almost a decade, the family members of the Korean managers could not remember even a single personal moment when they met workers. They were, in fact, bewildered by my inquiry because they could not understand why they should be interested in workers or their lives. Two Korean mothers – the wives of the factory president and the plant manager – argued that they needed to protect their children from the 'bad' influence of the Han workers. 'Living close to the backward [Han] workers from the countryside', one of the Korean mothers remarked, 'presents many disadvantages to raising our children here'. [8]

Korean-Chinese living quarter: expressions of ethnic excellence and desire

The management's spatial positioning of the factory residents and its minute regulations regarding the provision of amenities generated a privileged living space exclusively designed for the Korean-Chinese interpreters. The management provided a separate living place, which fostered a sense of intimacy that made the Korean-Chinese employees feel close to the Korean management – an attitude considered indispensable to the smooth operation of the factory. The location of the Korean-Chinese living quarter – near the managers' houses – clearly reflected a managerial strategy of using living space to create pro-management attitudes. The Korean-Chinese quarter was exempt from the night-time curfew imposed on the Han workers' dormitories. Korean-Chinese at Nawon Qingdao were free to move around the premises; they passed the gatehouse at the main factory entrance without being checked by the security guards – a freedom the Han workers most envied.

Management offered to the Korean-Chinese a list of housing benefits that were similar to those given to the visiting Korean managers. Other than sharing their rooms with two or three other Korean-Chinese interpreters, the basic living arrangement was similar to that of junior-level Korean managers. Thanks to their large personal space, the Korean-Chinese rooms always looked well organized and far less crowded than those in the Han dormitories. Korean-Chinese employees took warm showers in the 'Western-style' bathrooms that were attached to each room. They used washing machines located in their living area, saving time and effort. Korean-Chinese employees also enjoyed commensality with Korean managers, eating in the Korean dining hall that was separated from the factory canteen where the Han workers ate.

Differences in living space reflected management's effort to treat Korean-Chinese employees, in every aspect, as superior to the Han workers. Management believed that it was important to reinforce Korean-Chinese authority on the shop floor, which was, in management's view, constantly threatened by the Han workers' discontent with the superior status of the interpreters. A small number of Korean-Chinese occupied most of the intermediary managerial staff positions, while the majority of Han employees bore the heavy burden of sweatshop labour on the shop floor as rank-and-file workers. The Korean-Chinese predominance in the middle-manager positions completely overturned the dominant ethnic power relationships in China, in which the Han-Chinese prevail as the dominant ethnic majority and occupy the 'centre' of Chinese life in historical, social, and economic terms.

From the start of Nawon Qingdao, this overturned ethnic hierarchy encouraged Han workers to question the privileged status of Korean-Chinese employees. They argued that the Korean-Chinese assumed such an exceptional status not because of their individual skills but because of their bilingualism and Korean cultural attributes. A Han section leader on the shop floor proclaimed:

> The Korean-Chinese in this factory happened to be born in a Korean-Chinese household. They made no effort to learn the language because every day they speak Korean with their family. This is why we can't accept their privileged status in the factory... We spend lots of time and energy to learn skills on the shop floor. The Korean management, however, doesn't recognize our efforts and skills because it needs employees who can speak Korean.

Many Han workers tried to depreciate the Korean-Chinese high status by noting that their authority was effective only within the factory walls. 'The Korean-Chinese can behave as our superiors', a worker insisted, 'only thanks to the Korean management's support for them. They're just like the foxes that borrow the tigers' fierceness' (*hujiahuwei*). When Han workers expressed their anger, they did not consider the high educational level of the Korean-Chinese as a factor in their privileged status. The management, according to a Han senior worker, would have hired Korean-Chinese instead of Han, even if the latter had excellent credentials and bilingual competence.

The Korean managers believed that spatial closeness to Koreans and superior living conditions would alter the Korean-Chinese self-image of themselves as an underprivileged ethnic minority and transform them into quasi-Koreans. This transformation would make them more confident when they needed to control Han-Chinese workers. 'Once the Korean-Chinese [at Nawon] believe that they're like Koreans', a manager insisted, 'they feel more comfortable in dealing with the Han on the shop floor'. Another Korean manager recalled a past managerial policy that had ordered the Korean-Chinese employees not to speak Chinese on the shop floor. During the first year of Nawon's operation in China, the management ordered the Korean-Chinese staff to hide their identity of an ethnic minority and behave like Koreans. Exclusive use of Korean language was part of that policy. The management, however, gradually discontinued the use of this 'Koreanization' (*hanguk saram mandeulgi*) policy, once Korean-Chinese superiority was established.

The privileged living space of the Korean-Chinese greatly increased their consciousness of ethnic distinction. The Korean-Chinese at Nawon often linked the factory dormitories' poor physical conditions to the Han workers' degenerative physical and moral condition, assuming that Han ethnicity was inferior to their own. While Korean-Chinese discourse about dormitories focused on overcrowding and sanitation – material conditions that threatened the physical body – they often associated these problems with the Han workers' lack of proper moral qualities such as diligence, obedience, and self-discipline. Many Korean-Chinese of the factory assumed that the Han workers' dirty clothes and crowded rooms reflected their inferior ethnic nature, which they contrasted with their own clean and well-organized rooms – and by extension their ethnic superiority.

The vision of the 'clean' Korean-Chinese and the 'dirty' Han found its most dramatic expression in the differing condition of toilets. Nawon management built two kinds of toilets, one for the managerial staff and the other for the Han workers. The facilities differed in their basic amenities and arrangements: managerial staff had bright, white-tiled rooms with individual basins, toilet bowls, mirrors, and a box of tissues. Workers' toilets lacked such arrangements, and had poor lighting and bare concrete walls; they were equipped with neither walled space between individual toilet bowls nor basins. Because more than five hundred workers had to share the small toilets, it was impossible to keep them clean. According to the Korean-Chinese at Nawon, however, the conditions of toilets reflected a 'fundamental' ethnic difference between the ethnic groups: 'You can't imagine how dirty the Han toilets are', Hyesook, a Korean-Chinese office worker remarked. 'Everywhere on the floor you can see spit... You see it everywhere, the mix of the spit and toilet paper with shit!' She argued that, just like the pungent odour of the workshop, the unhygienic toilet expressed the inferior qualities of the ethnic Han.

Korean-Chinese and Korean revulsion against Han workers was founded upon visceral reactions to dirt and contagion, which were highlighted by the reactions to the pungent shop-floor odour, unhygienic toilets, and accidental encounters with the workers. Separate dwelling and living conditions of Han workers reinforced their status (in Korean and Korean-Chinese eyes) as 'the abject', a spatial concept that establishes and maintains social distinctions between self and other by determining 'the place where I am not and which permits me to be' (Kristeva, 1982: 2–3). At Nawon Qingdao, ideas of separating, demarcating, and punishing transgressions were omnipresent – which exaggerated differences within and without.

Factory dormitories: space of labour subjugation

The establishment of a 'dormitory labour regime' (Pun and Smith, 2007: 30–33) further explains the Han workers' spatial marginality and virtual incarceration in their separate living space. The formation of factory dormitories extended the length of work day by eliminating the physical and social limits of labour reproduction (Harvey, 2001: 18). In post-Maoist China, the provision of dormitories for migrant workers helps management to secure access to fresh rural labour reserves, increase labour productivity, and depress the wage demands of workers. This regime also distanced the working and living spaces of labour from the effects of existing local cultural norms and labour practices. The Han workers, as rural-to-urban migrants, did not feel comfortable in the local community of Qingdao. Their non-local, migrant status made it difficult for them to form permanent labour communities and, through such organizations, demand improvements in their working and living conditions (Kim, 2015; Nash, 1993: 87–120; Taussig, 1991: 93–139).

The widespread managerial assumption about women's 'nimble fingers' and their relative docility (Lee, 1998; Lynch, 2007; Ong, 2010; Pun, 2005) made the factory dormitories at Nawon highly gendered spaces. The management believed that women were mentally and physically suited to making garments, work that is highly repetitive and labour-intensive. Nawon management also considered women to be more patient than men. In fact, the space within factory dormitories reflects a key feature of the dormitory labour regime in China: unmarried, young, and female workers predominate in labour-intensive manufacturing sectors (Pun and Smith, 2007: 33). Labour studies on south China demonstrate that the labour regime contributed to reproducing a young and predominantly female working class, though it did not completely exclude relatively old and married women or men workers from the workforce (Lee, 1998; Pun, 1999). The Nawon factory is an extreme case of this pattern: the management, with its strong preference for women workers, kept the production lines and dormitories completely female, while a growing shortage of young female labour forced other factories nearby to recruit a small number of men to work alongside women.

Management utilized the space of the dormitories to reproduce workers' bodies as machines (Foucault, 1990: 139), by making them appear at the factory gate on time in order to produce garments of high uniformity. Surveillance methods such as a gatehouse, floodlights, evening roll calls, and night-time curfew applied to the dormitories, placing workers under the relentless gaze of management. Women labourers were controlled even after work hours, a time that management considered idle and, for this reason, potentially wasteful and dangerous. The wide, near-360 angle observation windows of the gatehouse allowed guards to have an unobstructed view of the workers going in and out of the dormitories. The guards, who were all male locals, also conducted the roll calls and imposed curfews. When they finished evening roll calls, guards shut off all lights in the dormitories, which made the indoor space of the buildings pitch-black. This evening blackout made movement within the dormitories nearly impossible and did more than anything else to reinforce managerial control over subordinate workers.

Local government officials cooperated with the Korean management to control labourers who were almost entirely of migrant origin and thereby suspect. Control of the two gatehouses at the factory and the dormitory entrances was delegated to local men who owed their positions to local party officials. Nawon was one of the 19 transnational corporations operating in the region and made major contributions to the development of the region by generating considerable tax revenue. Local officials also believed that it was necessary to reduce the possibility of social unrest that might be provoked by undisciplined workers from the 'backward' (luohou) countryside; hence, they cooperated to confine them to the managed space of the factory dormitories. When workers were hired, local government collected their original residence cards and issued temporary cards. They recorded changes in the number of migrant workers at Nawon factory and reported them to the governments of the workers' home villages. They even controlled the women's reproductive systems by regularly conducting pregnancy tests. Local officials thus combined modern techniques of surveillance and record-keeping with traditional means of social control (Foucault, 1977 [1975]: 205), as they operated gatehouses, kept statistics on hiring and migration, and monitored women workers' bodies.

Managerial power, however, operated not simply in obviously oppressive ways. Perhaps the most subtle means of controlling workers was through manipulating the spatial practices of eating, washing, and even 'easing nature', thereby transforming their ideas of individual and collective selves. Pierre Bourdieu argues that the seemingly normal practices and spatial properties of a living place – such as its orientation, layout, and arrangement of furniture – can serve to maintain social order (Bourdieu, 1970). Space embodies power, he argues, when people are performing everyday routines while assigned to distinctive places (Bourdieu, 1977 [1972]: 177–78; 1984 [1979]: 85–86). In the dormitories, routine practices of daily living gradually transformed the workers' structure of feeling, especially their intimate ideas of discomfort, inconvenience, and uncleanliness. This transformation, which inscribed stigmas

of hierarchical differences and social distinctions into their consciousness and bodies, reveals that the structure of feeling is highly susceptible
to the effects of managerial power.

Each floor of the dormitories had nine different-sized rooms and
one shared toilet. Depending upon room size, management installed
four to six bunk beds and assigned seven to ten workers to each room.
The high room density made the rooms look perpetually crowded,
which contrasts with the spacious quarters of the Korean-Chinese
employees. Because of the limited space, the workers described their
rooms as 'hopelessly dirty and disorganized'. To make matters worse,
the workers' dormitories lacked heating and the public lavatories on
each floor did not have showers. In the absence of washing machines
workers had to launder clothes by hand, which was especially difficult during the cold winter. Despite management regulations requiring
a thorough cleaning of the toilets once a day, the overpowering foul
odour persisted.

Workers also had to endure low room temperatures and relied on
blankets for warmth; as a result, many workers suffered from chilblains
during the winter months. Their rough hands and faces negatively
affected self-perception and contributed to a sense of social inferior-
ity. The women workers often contrasted their 'dark and rough' hands
with the 'white and fair' hands of Koreans and Korean-Chinese in the
factory. At Nawon, the hands of most Han workers were far from the
feminine ideal that appeared in the women's magazines they occasionally read. They complained that, as they were exposed to the cold temperature of the dorm rooms and the shop floor for extended periods,
their hands and faces looked 'old' and 'ugly'. Several workers compared their hands with those of Korean male managers: 'Did you see
the hands of that Korean manager?' Haiyan, a Han worker said. 'His
hands are even fairer than mine, a young woman's hands'. As they saw
no possibility of improving their living conditions, the workers gradually accepted their rough hands as part of routine factory life. This
acceptance, however, was almost always accompanied by a small sigh,
conveying their discontent with the uncomfortable spatial order of
the factory.

Conditions of Labour Resistance

The Han workers' bodies were not entirely 'the inscribed surface of
events', or blank pages to be imprinted with the disciplinary power
(Foucault, 1984 [1971]: 83). Far from inert subjects that waited to be

classified and segregated into the divided factory spaces of difference, they bore historical experiences that derived from the conditions of their spatial origin – the rural villages. These historical experiences enabled the workers to be keenly aware of the pervasive effects of the managerial power. The women workers often contrasted their factory living with the idealized rural life in their memories. Crowded dorm rooms and 'strange and unexpected' schedules of overtime repeatedly frustrated the workers, while reminding them of the 'relaxed and idyllic' life back in the countryside. 'These dorm rooms are too crowded', Chunli, a woman worker, said. 'I hate the rooms but I can't live outside. There's nowhere to go. What can I do?' Migrant workers increasingly prefer living outside of management's gaze, as the low-cost private accommodation expands and the wages increase (Smith 2003; Siu 2015). Women workers at Nawon, however, could not follow this trend because living in the dormitories was enforced by their labor contract with management.

The nostalgic memory of home (*jia* or *wojia*) raised the workers' critical awareness of their entire experience of the factory. 'I can't escape', another worker, Haiyan, argued. 'I go to work and I'm in the factory. I have meals, all in the factory. I come back to take some rest, still in the factory'. Several workers mentioned that the floodlights outside the dorm buildings were too bright and irritated their eyes at night. It was a completely strange situation, they argued, because at home 'indoor space is bright and outside is dark at night'. Home, to the workers, is more than a physical space encompassed by four walls. It is a place from which one leaves and to which one returns each day, a private space protected from the outside (Levinas, 1969:152). The factory dormitories lacked this distinction between inside and outside, and failed to establish a separation from the workplace (Levinas, 2000: 207–12). It allowed the workers to recognize their virtual incarceration in the factory and eventually set certain limits on the effect of managerial power to forge docile subjects out of free-spirited young women.

Some workers drew on xenophobic, Sino-centric ideas to express their discontent with management. The process involved also exemplifies how, although in vague and crude forms, the historical consciousness of particular subjects sets limits on the effects of the all-inclusive managerial power. Many Han, who represent the ethnic majority of China, believe that they are the rightful and obvious inheritors of Chinese imperial power and history. They also argue that ethnic Han constitute the most cultured, and therefore most advanced, ethnic group in East Asia (Fairbank, 1968; Hsiao, 1967; Kang, 2010). At Nawon, several Han workers expressed their discontent with the management by drawing physical contrasts between China and Korea:

Worker A: How big is Korea? Is it bigger than our country?

Worker B: [to worker A] You really don't know? Korea is much smaller than China. [With hands] China is this big and Korea is this small.

Worker C: Really? Then, how can people from such a small country control us?

Worker B: Once we become powerful and rich, China will crush this small country [humorously, crushing gesture with hands].

The workers' critical awareness and discontent, however, failed to develop into any form of open resistance. Their complaints about the poor working and living conditions usually ended with remarks about the inevitability of their factory labour. Chunmei, a sewing machine operator in her early twenties said:

We have lived in the factory for more than three years and we've been accustomed to (*xiguanle*) our current living... We know that our living and working conditions are bad. But it's not particularly bad. It's just as bad as those of other factories nearby... We came to this factory not to enjoy urban life but to make money. Insofar as we can get our wages on time, we don't care much about the living conditions.

The local government officials' collaboration with Nawon management in labour control further discouraged the workers from openly express-ing discontent. The workers thought that the ethnicized spatial divisions were fundamentally unfair because management obviously privileged Korean-Chinese employees. At the same time, however, they argued that it was not only useless but dangerous to publicly express their dis-content. The workers suspected, no doubt correctly, that local govern-ment officials would side with the management during labour disputes. Considering their lack of political leverage, the workers recognized their spatial and social marginality as inevitable.

Other studies on women migrant workers in China have found that, through factory jobs, many have tried to escape the countryside and aspired to participate in the cosmopolitan consumption of distant cit-ies (Lee, 1998; Pun, 1999, 2005; Chang, 2009). Most women workers at Nawon, however, thought that their factory jobs would neither 'liber-ate' them from rural villages nor help them to join the dazzling arena of urban consumption. Their low wages, combined with discriminatory policies, meant that workers could not realistically expect to settle in the cities and achieve the legal status of urban residents. Their single-minded focus on wages derived from their awareness of the temporary or transient nature of their current jobs. The workers were keenly aware of the disposable nature of their labour, having observed the management's preference for the flexible and cheap labour of young, unmarried rural women. Most women workers at Nawon, except those in section and line leader positions, had to quit their jobs and return to their hometowns when they married. They believed that earning a steady income and saving as much as possible before marriage was their only viable option.

The women workers' high savings rate inadvertently deepened the existing spatial division at Nawon. Their suppressed consumption originated from practical considerations of savings for future weddings, their siblings' educations, and the living expenses of aging parents. More than 90 per cent of Nawon workers said that they rarely shopped in downtown Qingdao – in most cases no more than twice a year. The small, run-down retail shops near the factory were occasionally visited. Workers confined their leisure activities to the space provided by the factory dormitories, effectively separating them from the world outside. This pattern of saving contrasts with the growing interest in consumption among migrants in other parts of China where a 'new-generation' (*xinshengdai*) of workers is emerging.[9]

Nawon management's exceptional ability to pay wages on time further contributed to maintaining the workers' wage-first world views, diverting their attention from poor working and living conditions. Even during the low-order seasons, the management secured subcontract orders that met the workers' expectation of a 'decent' (*shidangde*) wage. Nawon's close business ties with foreign buyers and other factories, established during the factory's decade-long operation in China, explains the guaranteed delivery of wages. The situation at Nawon was radically different from that of other factories in the region. Most factories that specialized in manufacturing garments, shoes, or toys for foreign buyers suffered from frequent labour unrest because they failed to find subcontract orders to secure 'decent' wages. During my fieldwork in 2003, the Qingdao area experienced several cases of work stoppages as the workers – frustrated and angered by late or non-existent wages – refused to work. The Nawon workers were keenly aware of these developments and had heard the miserable stories of workers in other factories. As one Nawon worker, Chunli, once said:

> The managements of the nearby factories often fail to pay wages to the workers on time. Their wage is also lower than ours because they

do less overtime. You can never know how miserable workers feel if they can't get their money after they have worked day and night... We're lucky to have the management that gives us wages on time.

On-time delivery of wage, however, is not the entire story. The improbability of the workers' immediate resistance does not deny their agency. Following Saba Mahmood, I regard agency not as a synonym for resistance to domination, but as 'a capacity for action that historically specific relations of subordination enable and create' (Mahmood, 2001: 203). Although Nawon workers did not organize what appeared to be obvious forms of resistance, they maintained their own motivations, desires, and goals. Utilizing the savings that they earned through their factory jobs, they were effecting subtle changes in existing gender relations and may eventually destabilize the traditional patriarchal structure of their rural communities. The women workers of Nawon frequently proclaimed that, with their contributions to household economies back in the countryside, they have stronger voices in deciding key familial issues such as their own marriages and large expenditures on home renovations and agricultural innovation (Kim, 2015).

Nonetheless, if – for any reason – management failed to pay decent wages to Nawon workers, the unusual stability of the workshop would be undermined. Managers often boasted that they had not experienced any large-scale labour disputes during its decade of operation in Qingdao, but there were always seeds of instability. The factory was exposed to the unpredictable and fickle demands of distant consumers and, most of all, the incessant demands for reducing production costs. These factors constantly threatened management's ability to generate profits and guarantee decent wages. In 2003, the Han workers at Nawon Qingdao launched an unprecedented strike against a new plant manager who had previously worked at a Korean-owned garment factory in Guatemala, a country that Nawon management considered more globalized in production efficiency and labour control. Under a slogan of a 'higher level of global production', he had increased work speed and enhanced labour control, while repeatedly failing to deliver decent wages. Intensifying price competition with other contract factories, weak overseas market demand due to recessions, as well as the new manager's relative inexperience of managing a shop floor in China explained his failure to maintain Nawon's good record of on-time wage delivery.

The strike also showed how the workers appropriated the factory's spatial divisions established by management. During the strike, women workers locked the steel gate between the main factory area and their dormitories. No one was able to open the gate because an obstruction had been hammered into its keyhole. This small but decisive act high-lights the workers' subversive use of spatial division and unveiled the hidden vulnerability of managerial power. Factory dormitories could be sites of labor resistance as well as managerial surveillance, as the collective mode of living enabled workers to establish networks of solidarity (cf. Siu 2015; Smith and Pun 2006). As a result of the strike, Nawon Korea, the headquarters of Nawon Qingdao, replaced the troubled plant manager with a Korean who had worked at Nawon Qingdao as a junior manager for a long time. They considered that the junior manager, through his long-term employment in China, had the experience and understanding to calm the workers' unrest and restore managerial authority. No single worker had been individually punished by management because the wildcat strike had no recognizable leader, while the workers were delighted to secure a more able plant manager.

Conclusion

At Nawon factory, the mandates of the global just-in-time production contributed to the creation of a specific dormitory labour regime, thereby enabling management to control the living space of factory employees and guide the reproduction of labour. Following the insights of Michel Foucault, this case demonstrated how the connections between space, subjects, and managerial power interacted in a twenty-first century transnational factory in China. Managerial power enhanced its subtle but pervasive disciplinary effects by creating different dwelling conditions within separated and bounded living spaces. My research shows in detail how the human body and human consciousness are vulnerable to disciplinary power, though the normalizing gaze of management could never completely remove the seeds of labour resistance. This case study has demonstrated what David Harvey has called the 'porosity of human body', the close relationship between body, self-image, and the surrounding world (Harvey, 1996: 218–19). My analysis of the factory residents' spatial practices reveals that the most private and intimate human practices of eating, washing, sleeping, and eliminating were vulnerable to the power arrangements controlled exclusively by management.

Space explicitly and implicitly reflects and establishes the larger economic, historical, cultural, and political orders wherever people are situated (Gupta and Furguson, 1997: 6). The transnational nature of Nawon factory exposed its shop floor to the vagaries of globalized production and competition. My own approach highlighted the historical dimension of space and how it affected the actual formation of factory landscapes and their resulting subjectivities. Despite their self-assertions as agents of the modern, the scientific, and the progressive, Nawon managers' actual practices were rooted in historical and cultural specificities, which were expressed in the factory's three-tiered spatial division. Korean-Chinese as *de facto* Koreans dominated the Han workers, while the workers – a category the management deemed backward – suffered from abject living and working conditions. The management envisioned its workshop as a space of high efficiency and rapid responsiveness to the demands of the global market. The same management, however, located the factory dormitories and the Han workers outside the space of real-time production, effectively recognizing them as marginal in space and backward in time. The managerial discourse of modernity and its discriminatory policy of separate working and living spaces reflects a form of 'ethical variability' (Petryna, 2005: 192), which deems certain people to be located at different evolutionary stages and therefore deserving of differential treatment.

The historicity of factory space and its connectedness to larger structural orders exposed Nawon to changes over time, which undermined the legitimacy of its spatial order. Especially since the mid-2000s, the rapidly increasing cost of labour in China, a consequence of the Chinese government's pro-labour polices, significantly reduced the management's capacity to maintain low production costs and survive fierce global competition (Kim, 2013: 228–33). The government's policy of 'upgrading' (*chengji*) its industry from labour-intensive production with low technology to capital-intensive units with high technology (Yu, 2012) also adversely affected the Korean transnationals in China that specialized in manufacturing low-end products such as textiles and garments. Under this policy, local-level governments reduced or even stopped benefits once offered to these factories, such as reduced tax rates, expedited customs services, and participation in labour control.

Under these increasingly unfavourable business conditions, the Nawon management began to consider relocation, this time to a country that had lower labour costs than China and offered pro-management policies. The impending relocation reflects the deterritorialization process of capital, which seeks to overcome the deterioration of profits through incessant geographical transfers (Brenner, 1999: 64; Lefebvre, 1976: 55–57). Much like its previous relocation from Korea to China in 1993, the management intended to build its new factory as a near replica of Nawon Qingdao. It maintained what was essentially an evolutionary view that deemed the workers of host countries, in this case Vietnam and possibly Bangladesh, to be backward and underdeveloped – paralleling their view of China in the 1990s. Most of all, management planned to maintain the three-tiered factory hierarchy under which an intermediary group, such as the Korean-Chinese, would act as middle managers, assisting Korean managers in controlling workers who were citizens of foreign country.[10] It still remains undecided exactly how management would insert itself into the new location of production, which is embedded in its own historicity. Existing political, economic, and social relations of production would set certain limits on the management's original plan of relocation and generate tensions between foreign management and local labour, which are likely to force management to modify its vision of ideal factory hierarchy and methods of labour control. The inevitability of globalized production cannot eliminate the local historicity and contingencies, which makes the story of Nawon by no means over. Just as global capital relentlessly pursues high productivity, so too the new formation of factory space and labour subjectivity must proceed.

Notes

1 The name of the factory is fictitious, as are the place names below city and provincial level and all personal names.
2 Korean-Chinese (Chinese nationals of Korean ethnic origin) are one of the 55 legally recognized ethnic minority groups in China. Han-Chinese (or simply Han) are the largest ethnic group, constituting about 92 per cent of China's population. The Korean-Chinese in this study came from the Korean-Chinese Autonomous Prefecture that is located in northeast China.
3 The exception was the eight Han male workers who lived in rented rooms outside the factory. See Kim (2015) for a detailed discussion on this group.
4 Sino-centrism refers to an idea shared by many Han-Chinese. It assumes that the Han-Chinese, the ethnic majority of China, should occupy the centre of China and the world in political, cultural, and geographical senses, because they are the most cultured and the most advanced in material and moral senses (Fairbank 1968; Hsiao Kang 2010).
5 As of the year 2000, the average hourly wage of a Korean worker in the textile industry was 5.32 USD, while that of its Chinese counterpart was only 0.69 USD (Werner International, 2001).
6 My book, *Chinese Labor in a Korean Factory* (Kim 2013), also originated from this research.

7 Among the Korean-Chinese at Nawon, 15 were high school graduates and one other graduated from a college. In contrast, most Han workers had not finished junior high school.

8 Despite the problems, there were advantages such as low living costs and daily exposure to Chinese language environment. Nawon Korea's additional financial supports also contributed to their decision to live in China. The Korean cultural norm that families should live together also had a strong influence.

9 The workers of the 'new-generation' (*xinshengdai*) were born in the countryside during the late 1970s and 1980s, and entered the urban labour market in the late 1990s and 2000s (Pun and Lu, 2010: 495). They are more highly educated and willing to spend their income (Yan, 2008), and less patient about workplace mistreatment and more attentive to their rights than the first-generation migrant workers (Chan and Pun, 2009; Wu, 2009). At Nawon factory, more than 80 per cent of the Han workers were in their twenties or born in the 1980s, which indicates that they were in the same age group of the new-generation. Except for similarities in basic demographic data, however, they possessed characteristics more similar to those of the first-generation, who saved their income for economic purposes and tended to endure hardships in the workplace. Their background of rural poverty, low-level education, and relative inexperience of factory labour made them similar to first-generation workers.

10 The Korean managers planned to bring several of the Korean-Chinese middle managers of Nawon Qingdao with them to the new production location, not simply because their labour was cheaper than that of Koreans, but also because the Korean-Chinese were considered to have been 'perfectly tailored' to perform their intermediary role.

REFERENCES

Berliner, J. S. (1957) *Factory and Manager in the USSR*, Cambridge, MA: Harvard University Press.

Black, J. T. and Chen, J. S. (1995) 'The role of decouplers in JIT pull apparel cells', *International Journal of Clothing and Technology*, 7: 17–35.

Bonacich, E, Cheng, L. and Chinchilla, N. (eds) (1994) *Global Production: The Apparel Industry in the Pacific Rim*, Philadelphia, PA: Temple University Press.

Bourdieu, P. (1970) 'The Berber house or the world reversed', *Social Science Information*, 9(2): 151–170.

_____ (1977) [1972] *Outline of a Theory of Practice* (trans R. Nice), Cambridge, UK: Cambridge University Press.

▶

▶

_____ (1984) [1979] *Distinction: a Social Critique of the Judgment of Taste* (trans R. Nice), Oxford: Polity Press.

Brenner, N. (1999) 'Beyond state-centrism? Space, territoriality, and geographical scale in globalization studies', *Theory and Society*, 28: 39–78.

Burawoy, M. (1985) *The Politics of Production: Factory Regimes under Capitalism and Socialism*. London: Verso.

Chan, C.K.C. and Pun, N. (2009) 'The making of a new working class? A study of collective actions of migrant workers in South China', *China Quarterly*, 198: 287–303.

Chang, L. T. (2009) *Factory Girls: From Village to City in a Changing China*, New York: Spiegel and Grau.

Clark, G. L., Gertler, M. and Whiteman, J. E. M. (1986) *Regional Dynamics: Studies in Adjustment Theory*, Boston: Allen & Unwin.

Comaroff, J. and Comaroff, J. (1991) *Of Revelation and Revolution: Christianity, Colonialism, and Consciousness in South Africa* (Vol 1), Chicago, IL: University of Chicago Press.

Dirks, N. B. (1990) 'History as a sign of the modern', *Public Culture*, 2(2): 25–32.

Fabian, J. (1983) *Time and the Other: How Anthropology Makes its Object*, New York: Columbia University Press.

Fairbank, J. K. (1968) *The Chinese World Order: Traditional China's Foreign Relations*, Cambridge, MA: Harvard University Press.

Foucault, M. (1977) [1975] *Discipline and Punish*, New York: Vintage Books.

_____ (1980) *Power/Knowledge: Selected Interviews and Other Writings, 1972–1977*, Brighton: Harvester Press.

_____ (1984) [1971]. 'Nietzsche, genealogy, history', in P. Rabinow (ed) *The Foucault Reader*, New York: Pantheon, pp. 76–100.

_____ (1990) *The History of Sexuality* (Vol. 1), New York: Random House.

Gupta, A. and Ferguson, J. (1997) *Culture, Power, Place: Explorations in Critical Anthropology*, Durham, NC: Duke University Press.

Harvey, D. (1996) *Justice, Nature and the Geography of Difference*, London: Blackwell.

_____ (2001) 'Globalization and the 'spatial fix'', *Geographische Revue*, 2: 23–30.

Hostettler, N. (2012) *Eurocentrism: a Marxian Critical Realist Critique*, London: Routledge.

Hsiao, K. C. (1967) *A History of Chinese Political Thought* (trans F. W. Mote), Princeton, NJ: Princeton University Press.

Kang, D. C. (2010) *East Asia before the West: Five Centuries of Trade and Tribute*, New York: Columbia University Press.

Kim, J. (2013) *Chinese Labor in a Korean Factory: Class, Ethnicity, and Productivity on the Shop Floor in Globalizing China*, Stanford, CA: Stanford University Press.

_____ (2015) 'From "country bumpkins" to "tough workers": the pursuit of masculinity among male factory workers in China', *Anthropological Quarterly*, 88(1): 159–188.

Knights, D. and Vurdubakis, T. (1994) 'Foucault, power, resistance and all that', in M. J. Jermier, D. Knights and W. R. Nord (eds) *Resistance and Power in Organisation: Critical Perspectives on Work and Organization*, London: Rutledge, pp. 167–198.

▶

▶

Kristeva, J. (1982) *Powers of Horror: An Essay on Abjection* (trans L. S. Roudiez), New York: Columbia University Press.

Lee, C. K. (1998) *Gender and the South China Miracle: Two Worlds of Factory Women,* Berkeley, CA: University of California Press.

——— (2007) 'The unmaking of the Chinese working class in the northeastern rust-belt', in C. K. Lee (ed) *Workings in China: Ethnographies of Labour and Workplace Transformation,* London: Routledge, pp. 15-37.

Lee, C. (1995) 'Adoption of the Ford system and evolution of the production system in the Chinese automobile industry, 1953–93', in H. Shiomi and K. Wada (eds) *Fordism Transformed: The Development of Production Methods in the Automobile Industry,* Oxford: Oxford University Press, pp. 297–314.

Lefebvre, H. (1976) *De 'etat: l'etat dans le Monde Moderne* (Volume I), Paris: Union Général d'Editions.

Levinas, E. (1969) *Totality and Infinity: An Essay on Exteriority* (trans A. Lingis), Pittsburgh, PA: Duquesne University Press.

——— (2000) *God, Death, and Time* (trans B. Bergo), Stanford: Stanford University Press.

Lynch, C. (2007) *Juki Girls, Good Girls: Gender and Cultural Politics in Sri Lanka's Global Garment Industry,* Ithaca, NY: Cornell University Press.

Mahmood, S. (2001) 'Feminist theory, embodiment, and the docile agent: some reflections on the Egyptian Islamic revival', *Cultural Anthropology,* 16: 202–236.

McKinlay, A. (2006) 'Managing Foucault: genealogies of management', *Management and Organizational History,* 1(1): 87–100.

Nash, J. (1993) *We Eat the Mines and the Mines Eat Us: Dependency and Exploitation in Bolivian Tin Mines,* New York: Columbia University Press.

Ong, A. (2010) *Spirits of Resistance and Capitalist Discipline: Factory Women in Malaysia,* Albany, NY: State University of New York.

Petryna, A. (2005) 'Ethical variability: drug development and globalizing clinical trials', *American Ethnologist,* 32(2): 183–197.

Priestley, K. E. (1963) *Workers of China,* London: Holywell.

Pun, N. (1999) 'Becoming *Dagongmei*: the politics of identity and difference in reform China', *The China Journal,* 42: 1–19.

——— (2005) *Made in China: Women Factory Workers in a Global Workplace,* Durham, NC: Duke University Press.

Pun, N. and Lu, H. (2010) 'Unfinished proletarianization: self, anger, and class action among the second generation of peasant-workers in present-day China', *Modern China,* 36(5): 493–519.

Pun, N. and Smith, C. (2007) 'Putting transnational labour process in its place: the dormitory labour regime in post-socialist China', *Work, Employment and Society,* 21: 27–45.

Rofel, R. (1999) *Other Modernities: Gendered Yearnings in China after Socialism,* Berkeley, CA: University of California Press.

——— (2009) 'Rethinking modernity: space and factory discipline in China', *Cultural Anthropology,* 7(11): 93–114.

▶

Shiomi, H. (1995) 'Introduction', in H. Shiomi and K. Wada (eds) *Fordism Transformed: The Development of Production Methods in the Automobile Industry*, London: Oxford University Press, pp. 1–10.

Siu, K. (2015) 'The working and living conditions of garment workers in China and Vietnam', in A. Chan (ed) *Chinese Workers in Comparative Perspective*, Cornell University Press.

Smith, C. (2003) 'Living at work: management control and the dormitory labour system in China', *Asia Pacific Journal of Management*, 20(3): 333–358.

Smith, C. and Pun, N. (2006) 'The dormitory labour regime in China as a site for control and resistance', *The International Journal of Human Resource Management*, 17(8): 1456–1470.

Smith, C. and Thompson, P. (1998) 'Re-evaluating the labour process debate', *Economic and Industrial Democracy*, 19: 551–577.

Taussig, M. (1991) *Shamanism, Colonialism, and the Wild Man: A Study in Terror and Healing*, Chicago: University of Chicago Press.

Taylor, F. W. (1947) [1911] 'The principles of scientific management', in F. W. Taylor, *Scientific Management*, New York: Harper & Row, pp. 5–144.

Thompson, P. (2003) 'Fantasy island: a labour process critique of the 'age of surveillance', *Surveillance and Society*, 1(2): 138–151.

Thompson, P. and Ackroyd, S. (1995) 'All quiet on the workplace front?: a critique of recent trends in British industrial sociology', *Sociology*, 29(4): 615–633.

Werner International (2001) *Spinning and Weaving: Labor Cost Comparisons 2000*, Reston, VA: Werner International Management Consultants.

Williams, R. (1977) *Marxism and Literature*, Oxford: Oxford University Press.

Wu, Y. (2009) '*Lun xinshengdai nongmingong de tedian* (A discussion about the characteristics of the new-generation migrant workers)', *Dongyueluncong*, 30(8): 57–59.

Yan, H. (2008) *New Masters, New Servants: Migration, Development, and Women Workers in China*. Durham, NC: Duke University Press.

Yu, M. (2012) 'Industrial structural upgrading and poverty reduction in China', Paper prepared for the UNIDO project, China Center for Economic Research, Beijing: Peking University.

Labour Market Institutions: Unions and Collective Bargaining

Employer Responses to Labour Shortage in China: The Case of the Knitwear Industry

9

Hao Zhang

Introduction

The labour shortage prevalent in the coastal areas of China ever since the mid-2000s has been well documented by both mass media and scholarly literature. What is obviously absent in the literature, however, is an examination of firms' responses to this issue, that is, what strategies firms have adopted in order to tackle the problem of labour shortage. Drawing on ethnographic field research in two knitwear industrial clusters respectively in Zhejiang and Guangdong, this study embarks on an initial effort to address this topic.

I identify, in this study, two strategies that firms devise and use to deal with labour shortage. The first one is labour substitution, which seeks to eventually reduce firms' reliance on manual production labour as well as labour costs, by engaging in labour-substitution projects including automation, climbing the value chain to engage in more value-added production procedures such as designing, branding, and marketing, and industrial relocation to Western China, the labour 'low lands' relatively speaking. The second strategy is labour upgrading, which aims to attract and retain workers through improved working conditions. While employers may improve working conditions individually and unilaterally, this chapter focuses on a specific mechanism of labour upgrading, that is, multi-employer wage coordination or industry-level collective bargaining. The two strategies are not mutually exclusive as employers may possibly take both. However, at any given time one strategy tends to dominate the other.

Further, I examine antecedents of these different strategies that firms employ. I argue that work organization and labour process, the role of local state, as well as several employer characteristics are important factors that may shape firms' responses to labour shortage. Firstly, work systems with a low level of automation, a high degree of production-process reliance on skilled manual labour, and the use of piece-rate wage system seem to be associated with firms' adoption of the labour-upgrading strategy. Because it increases the level of automation, decreases the production-process reliance on manual workers, and replaces piece-rate positions with hourly ones, labour substitution in the long run tends to undermine firms' motivation to pursue labour upgrading (the reverse does not hold though). Secondly, the local state plays important roles in guiding firms towards different approaches. In particular, labour-substitution approaches are relatively costly, where state support is often crucial. Finally, the origin of investment, inter-firm relations, and firm size are also likely to affect firms' strategic choices in response to labour shortage via shaping the viability or ease of implementing different strategies.

My main contribution to the literature is twofold. First, I bring firms back to the centre of analysis by looking into their strategic choices in response to labour shortage. This firm-centric approach is dominant in Western industrial relations frameworks, but under-utilized in China labour studies. Second, I offer a labour-process perspective to complement the dominant economic or institutional analysis on labour shortage and industrial wage coordination in China.

Literature Review and Argument

Labour Shortage in China

Labour shortage has emerged in China since the mid-2000s especially in the Pearl River Delta and Yangtze River Delta regions, where there are high concentrations of migrant workers and clustered industries. Demographic data earlier suggested signs of exhaustion of rural surplus labour, prompting some economists to argue that China's development had met the Lewis turning point (Cai, 2007). The classic Lewis model predicts that with the exhaustion of rural surplus labour, wage gaps between the rural and urban areas will be closing, which, however, does not seem to have happened in China. The rapidly increasing minimum wages (and wages in general) in urban Eastern China – particularly in the post-2009 financial crisis period – seems to contradictorily coexist with the enduring labour surplus in rural Western China (Chan, 2010; Golley and Meng, 2011) – in other words, wage gaps are indeed widening while surplus labour still exists in the secondary market.

This paradox implies a market failure. Later studies have therefore engaged in providing explanations for this paradox of why workers are reluctant to go to Eastern/urban areas that still provide better wages. Institutional barriers are a popular explanation. For instance, Knight, Deng, and Li (2011) argue that institutional discriminations – regarding child education, housing, and other social welfare – associated with the *hukou* (household registration) system against rural migrant workers have discouraged them from working in the cities. Although migrants, especially the younger generation, show increasing intention to seek a permanent residence in cities (Cao, Li, Ma, and Tao, 2015; Tang and Feng, 2015), these institutional barriers at times impede them from doing so – they often have to make compromises and go for suboptimal solutions such as returning to their hometown but working in the non-agricultural sector (Yue, Li, Feldman, and Du, 2010), and their sense of identity (Frenkel and Yu, 2015), is still mostly associated with the rural areas. Zhang (2013) provides an alternative explanation by looking at workers' social reproduction processes and argues that hometown communities provide workers with both economic and non-economic support which have artificially reduced labour costs, so that increasingly more workers prefer to stay and work close to their hometowns (rural and Western China) as opposed to the Eastern and urban areas where they have to pay much more for social reproduction. In addition, Chan (2010) argues that, instead of being permanent, the current labour shortage in China is a short-term structural mismatch of supply and demand, as well as being affected by the cyclical effects of the world economy.

In any case, scholars have reached the consensus that the phenomenon of labour shortage is prevalent in Eastern China, and pressures on firms are real. Firms have felt the difficulty in hiring workers, demonstrated by the growth of both real wages and labour demand-supply ratios (Chan, 2010; Lüthje, Luo and Zhang, 2013). Furthermore, the labour shortage has empowered workers by providing them with more labour-market opportunities. Workers therefore are more inclined to quit for better pay elsewhere. Workforces in some industrial clusters, including the garment industry, have become extremely unstable with astonishingly high worker turnovers and disorganized labour poaching (Lüthje et al., 2013). Other studies suggest that workers now are more and more willing to demonstrate their growing bargaining power against employers and go on strikes more often and more aggressively than ever before (Elfstrom and Kuruvilla, 2014).

What obviously lacks in the literature, however, is an investigation of how firms respond to the labour shortage, which is the focus of the study. My fieldwork finds that there are two general employer strategies for dealing with labour shortage and the ensuing workforce instability. The first is labour substitution, that is, firms may embark on efforts to reduce the production-process reliance on manual skilled labour, or simply reduce the labour costs. They may initiate programmes of either industrial upgrading to increase the importance of other production factors such as capital via automation, or industrial relocation to places where labour is cheaper. The second employer strategy is labour upgrading which may be done by employers individually or collectively, the rationale being to seek relatively uniform wage standards in order to stabilize the local workforce and reduce employee turnover and labour poaching. Next, I will briefly review the literatures on both employer strategies.

Industrial Upgrading

Classic economic theory suggests that as capital (both human and physical) becomes more abundant relative to labour, industrial restructuring and upgrading tends to emerge (Porter, 1990). This in reality consists of two common approaches that are often simultaneously used: on the one hand relatively low-end workshops are shut down in places where labour costs are increasing, and transferred to 'lower lands' where labour is comparatively cheap. This cheapness does not mean lower wages only, but also looser labour, environmental, and other social regulations. On the other hand, some establishments that stay are upgraded in various ways, such as automation, moving up the value chain to integrate more value-added production procedures (e.g. designing, branding, and marketing), and establishing more efficient and flexible local production networks (e.g. the flexible specialization production model (Piore and Sabel, 1984)).

Specific to the garment industry, Gereffi (1999) has identified a typical approach of industrial upgrading in East Asian countries such as Hong Kong, South Korea, and Taiwan in the late 1980s and early 1990s. The approach features a shift of the production mode from original equipment manufacturing (OEM) to original brand name manufacturing (OBM), where firms started to climb up along production chains and incorporate the capacities of design and sale into their businesses. In China, Zhang (2011) has found, however, that the OEM model and the buyer-driven regime of production are still dominant in the textile and garment industry. A later and more comprehensive examination of the industry indicates that OEM production is still prevalent, while some firms have succeeded in climbing production chains, taking up the designing (but not branding) procedures, and adopting a model called original designing manufacturing (ODM) – somewhere in between OEM and OBM. Very few of them, however, are engaged in real OBM production (Lüthje et al., 2013).

Industry-Level Wage Coordination

The second employer strategy that theoretically serves to retain and stabilize the workforce is labour upgrading – particularly multi-employer wage coordination – which seeks to impose relatively uniform wage standards across firms or even industries in order to reduce workers' incentive to quit for better pay. This coordination can be formal such as multi-employer collective bargaining, or relatively informal such as wage coordination among employers. Centralized wage coordination used to exist widely in the West, but has experienced a decentralization process since the late 1980s and early 1990s, partly due to the decline of the union movements and the neoliberal globalization (Katz, 1993). Various informal forms of wage coordination have emerged in many sectors, and are favoured by employers due to the flexibility they can provide. An emergent model in several European countries is called 'coordinated' or 'organized decentralization', which seeks to set a general framework agreement at a relatively central level and, in contrast to formal centralized bargaining, gives more flexibility to the lower levels in negotiating their own compromises (Sisson and Marginson, 2002).

In China, most studies on industry-level wage coordination focus on relatively centralized formal collective bargaining (see Kuruvilla and Zhang, 2015 for a comprehensive review). Multi-employer bargaining is typically institutionalized at the regional-industry level, because it provides favourable conditions for centralization, that is, roughly similar production and wage systems across firms. The well-known Wenling case – which existing studies see as an exemplar of successful regional-industry-level bargaining (Pringle, 2011; Wen and Lin, 2015) – is a case I revisit here. In contrast to prior studies, however, I use it as a case to illustrate the employers' response to labour shortage, that is, initiating spontaneous wage coordination projects. Indeed, there is already notable, though limited, evidence that employers actively engage in informal wage coordination within regional industries in China. Zhang (2014) found that in Tianjin's auto industry, for example, although formal collective bargaining was institutionalized at the workplace level, firms as well as unions engaged in informal coordination even without the presence of employer associations or industry-level unions.

As shown, although scholars have found evidence of both industrial upgrading and industrial wage coordination in China, we need a more systematic understanding of how firms respond to labour shortage, and probably more importantly, why firms adopt different strategies. This study makes an initial effort to answer these questions. Specifically, I have identified two strategies that firms have been using to tackle the problem of labour shortage, that is, labour substitution and labour upgrading. I argue that the dominant approach firms tend to employ is associated with various factors in relation to work organization and labour process, the role of the local state, and employer characteristics. These factors may affect firms' intentions, capacity (particularly financial and infrastructural), and the cost (both financial and temporal) regarding their adoption of specific strategies. To begin with, the labour process may be important – the way that work is organized may provide incentives for or impose constraints on firms' adoption of different strategies towards addressing labour shortage. In particular, a low automation level, a high degree of production-process reliance on manual skilled labour, and the use of the piece-rate wage system seem to be favourable conditions for employers' adoption of the labour-upgrading strategy. Second, local states, through their various policies, often guide firms towards divergent approaches to dealing with labour shortage. This role of the local state is particularly important for initiating labour-substitution programmes because these programmes are relatively costly and the state can sometimes provide firms with subsidies as well as relevant infrastructures and institutional support, and facilitate the reach of economy of scale at the industry level. Last, employer characteristics, including the origin of investment, inter-firm relations, and firm size, may affect the viability of different employer strategies to deal with labour shortage. In general, bigger firms and firms with non-local investments tend to favour labour substitution, while smaller and locally funded firms with closer inter-firm ties are more likely to take the strategy of labour upgrading.

Methodology

I choose two industrial clusters in the knitwear sector to illustrate the two employer strategies toward labour shortage. I choose this sector because it is the most labour intensive and therefore highly sensitive to labour shortage, and one can expect to observe both employer strategies of labour substitution and labour upgrading in this industry. Theoretically, on the one hand the knitwear industry and the garment industry in general adopt the mass production model extensively (Lüthje et al., 2013). Skills are extremely transferable – workers can easily hop across firms or even across regions, especially when the demand for labour is fast increasing relative to the supply. On the other hand, production technologies and the typical division of labour are simple and standardized across firms relative to other industries, and wage structures across firms are largely similar, if not identical, with heavy employment of the piece-rate wage system, therefore providing favourable conditions for potential wage coordination. As for labour substitution, in fact, the garment industry, in most cases, is hard to upgrade via automation – the skills of sewing are just too difficult to be imitated by automatic robots. So a workshop that manufactures shirts, for instance, that we see nowadays looks largely the same as fifty years ago. However, the fact that the knitwear industry is an exception to this doctrine strategically avoids this problem – nowadays automatic knitting machines have been invented and put into use in mass production (Lüthje et al., 2013), therefore providing opportunities for the knitwear industry to be upgraded. All in all, the knitwear industry serves as a case that is both highly vulnerable to labour shortage, and likely to adopt either or both labour upgrading and labour-substitution strategies.

I choose two typical industrial clusters in the knitwear industry, each representing one of the two employer strategies. I firstly revisited the well-known Wenling case, which was regarded as an paradigm of industry-level collective bargaining in China but fell significantly behind in industrial upgrading and relocation. I then chose the knitwear industrial cluster in Dalang, Guangdong Province that had neither institutional nor informal arrangements for wage coordination, but firms actively engaged in various labour-substitution projects.

I carried out ethnographic field research in these two clusters several times from 2009 to 2013. I conducted a total of 46 in-depth interviews and additional informal talks with workers, employers, and officials from local governments, unions, and employer associations. I also did non-participant observation on the production processes and working conditions in all of the four firms that I visited, two in each cluster (see Table 9.1 for basic information on the four firms). In addition, media reports, official documents, and publicly available statistics are also employed as a supplement to the first-hand data.

Table 9.1 Basic information of the case study firms

		Production Mode	Workforce						Average Wages (yuan per month)	
			Total	Workers		Staff			Knitting	Jointing
					Migrant workers		Full-time Designers			
Dalang	A company	ODM/OBM	2,000	80%	Mostly	20%	2%		Approximately 3,000	3,000-4,000
	B company	ODM/OBM	300	67%	Mostly	33%	2%		Approximately 2,500	Approximately 2,800
Wenling	C company	OBM	180	97%	Almost none	3%	0		Approximately 2,500	Approximately 2,500
	D company	OEM/ODM	60	92%	46%	8%	0		Approximately 2,500	Approximately 2,500

Employer Responses to Labour Shortage

Dalang: Labour Substitution

The town of Dalang is located in Dongguan in Guangdong Province. Centred on Dalang, there are about 10,000 knitwear firms, over 3,000 of which are located within Dalang and currently employing 100,000 workers. The entire industrial cluster is one of the largest knitwear clusters in China, producing more than 1.2 billion pieces of knitted garments. Two-thirds of them are collected and distributed in Dalang, 60 per cent of which are exported to international markets (Xiao and Liang, 2010).

The first knitwear firm was established in 1979. With investment from a boss from Hong Kong, the factory soon attracted local peasants. Working there was something to be proud of at that time. Many local workers in the factory later, however, bought manual knitting machines and yarn, hired a few helpers, and started their own businesses. The industrial cluster grew fast, to more than a thousand family workshops at its peak. Dalang thus soon became a known knitwear cluster in the global market. With China's entrance to the WTO, Dalang received its first international order from Russia in 2001.

The growing knitwear industry also started to attract more and more workers from outside the city and the province. The total amount of migrants reached 200,000 by 2003 and 300,000 by 2010, way more than the local population of 60,000 by 2003 (Liao and Ye, 2003) and 65,000 by 2010.

Some migrants started their own businesses later. In one of the firms – denoted by B company – that I visited, the boss originally came to Dalang as a migrant worker. After many years of work, he gained intimate knowledge of the industry, accumulated considerable savings, and established a solid network in the industry, including brokers, customers, and local government officials. He ultimately started his own business in 2002. B company now manufactures for several French and Italian brand name companies and retailers, including one of the world's largest retailers of fast-moving consumer goods. The firm currently receives 40 per cent of its contracts via brokers based largely in Hong Kong, and exports 80 per cent of its products to Europe and the US.

B company has developed labour-substitution approaches to address labour shortage in recent years, which are largely seen in other firms in Dalang as well. These include climbing the value chain, replacing increasingly expensive labour with automatic machines, and relocating low-end production to inland China. It is important to note that the first two approaches were not new, as they had already been taken by Dalang firms before labour shortage emerged to serve the goal of industrial upgrading (which can increase profits). Over the years, the first two approaches of industrial upgrading or labour substitution have transformed work organization in the knitwear industry of Dalang. First, the firm has gone through a transformation of its production mode from OEM to a mixture of ODM and OBM, partly motivated by the state's stimulation projects. In recent years, the local government has started a brand-building project for the purpose of local economic upgrading, encouraging firms to create their own brands rather than stick to OEM production that simply provides labour-intensive knitting and processing services. The government has announced to award 300,000 *yuan* for the creation of a provincial 'Top Brand' and a million *yuan* for a 'China Top Brand'. The outcomes of the project were significant. By 2012, provincial and national 'Top Brands' in Dalang had numbered 17. Eighty per cent of companies with annual main business revenue equal to or more than five million *yuan* had set up a designing department, hiring over 1,300 designers, producing about 300,000 patterns each year (Dong and Liang, 2012).

Although B company has not been able to win a prize so far, it is on its way, hovering between ODM and OBM, equipped with designing and some branding capacities. Employing six designers, the firm can now work more closely with wholesalers and brand name garment companies, providing them with products with original designs. In addition, it also has its own brands and can label the products with those brands whenever necessary. Mostly, however, contractors require having their own brand names put on the labels.

The second approach of labour substitution that is employed by firms and promoted by the local government is technological upgrading, that is, automation. Indeed, substitution of manual labour via automation has not gone as far in the garment industry in general as some other sectors like automobile and electronics. Even the Fordist assembly line has not been successfully transplanted into the garment industry so far (Lüthje et al., 2013). The knitwear sector, however, is somewhat exceptional to this general scenario as noted. For one thing, the typical production process in this sector is relatively simple. It only takes two steps – knitting and jointing – in order to transform yarn to a piece of knitwear (see Figure 9.1 for a simple illustration of the organization of production in B company). For another, knitting is relatively easy to be mechanically imitated. The most up-to-date auto-knitting machines are capable of combining both knitting and jointing procedures and getting them done simultaneously.

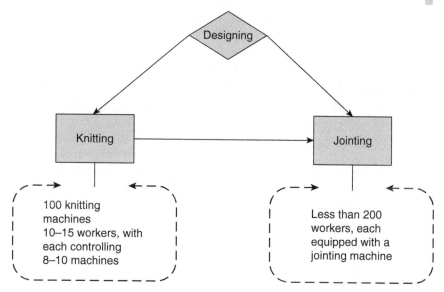

Figure 9.1 Organization of production in B company's Dalang factory

The knitting machines most commonly used in Dalang, however, only knit, leaving jointing to manual workers equipped with a traditional jointing machine. This choice is based on a cost–benefit calculation. The latest machines, being able to joint as well as knit, can only produce single-color patterns. And most importantly, such a machine costs five to ten times the price.

Automatic knitting machines have completely eliminated the traditional knitting jobs in B company. Before this, firms largely employed knitting workers, each one working on a semi-auto machine. On these machines, knitting used to be performed stitch by stitch and line by line. A needle, under the worker's operation, goes through the stitches of a line to form a new line, and backwards to form another. Today, automatic equipment works based on a similar logic, but completely frees human hands from the production – a worker no longer needs to control the size and knitting tightness, or to change the needle when a special pattern needs to be made. Moreover, these machines are able to work 24 hours a day, and can actually produce many complicated patterns.

The productivity of an automatic knitting machine is much higher than that of a traditional one. One such machine is able to replace at least eight traditional manual machine workers. According to my own observation of the knitting workshops in Dalang, a machine works with more than twenty spindles of yarn, possibly in different types and colours. The more spindles available, the more complicated patterns a machine is able to produce. When the machines are working automatically, a worker simply monitors it and fixes errors when they come up, such as repairing yarn breaks and replacing used-up yarn spindles. Only 10 to 15 workers control the 100 or so knitting machines in B company, each of whom monitors eight to ten machines at the same time. To monitor the 24-hour running machines, more workers are employed to work in shifts. The workers are mostly males between 20 and 25 years old. They have received one week pre-job training on machine operation and one to three months' on-the-job training. It is noteworthy that unlike most other types of production workers in this industry, these machine operators earn hourly as opposed to piece-rate wages, simply because the knitting speed depends on machine capacity rather than worker skills.

The local government also encourages firms to use more automatic machines in order to reduce reliance on increasingly expensive labour. They have announced a subsidy of 2,000 *yuan* for firms acquiring each machine, which equals about 1 per cent of the price of a brand new machine in the market. Some enterprises choose to buy second-hand machines from other factories, however, which cost about half the price or even less.

Dalang has thereby become the region with the highest concentration of knitting machines in the world (Wu, 2011). Thirty thousand knitting machines are running in the town nowadays, whereas this number used to be only about 1,000 in 2005. In addition, over a hundred domestic or foreign knitting machine producers have set up production or sales bases in Dalang.

The third labour-substitution approach adopted in B company consists of an ongoing plan of gradually relocating production to inland China where migrant workers traditionally come from, in order to seek new sources of cheap labour. The firm has so far established three factories. In addition to keeping the original one in Dalang, B company has set up two establishments in a small county in Sichuan Province, a traditional labour-sending area and the hometown of the employer.

Low-end production is now put in the factories in Sichuan, whereas only orders that are urgent and/or require relatively high-tech machines are processed in the old factory in Dalang. The level of automation in the Sichuan factories is much lower. In recent years, the workforce of its factory in Dalang has shrunk from approximately 1,500 to slightly over 300 workers (including management), while the Sichuan factories have already employed around 300 workers, who however only receive 50–60 per cent of the pay in Dalang. The whole production relocation process is supposed to be completed within 3–5 years. Under this plan, the factory in Dalang will ultimately turn into an R&D (research and development) and marketing centre, capitalizing on its proximity to the global market as well as brokers that are mostly based in Hong Kong.

This approach too is commonly employed in the industrial cluster in general. A company that I have studied in Dalang also has the agenda of production relocation to the west on their table. At the time of my field research, about 80 per cent of the production had been done in the Dalang factory, while it had already built up establishments in Guangxi Province (a province that is next door to Guangdong) that were producing for 20 per cent of the orders. Furthermore, A company had bought land in Guangxi to build two new factories of jointing and finishing – the most labour-intensive procedures of the production process for knitwear.

This production relocation approach used by firms has an equivalent at the industry level, where the local government has planned to transform Dalang into a multi-function centre – a collecting and distributing, marketing, and R&D centre – from a sole production base. Relevant policies indeed date back to the early 2000s. The yearly International Woollen Knitwear Fair, as part of this agenda, started in as early as 2001, aiming at propagating Dalang as a trading centre of knitwear at the national level, which also has an influence over the Asia-Pacific regions. I personally participated in the ninth fair in 2010. The entire production chain in the knitwear industry found itself in the fair, that is, from the most advanced knitting machines in the world, to varieties of final knitted products; from world-renowned brand name garment companies and retailers, to brokers, and producers. Although some interviewed bosses commented that the fair served more as propaganda than to promote the achievement of new contracts – thanks to modern technology, most orders are nowadays placed online – Dalang's status as a centre of knitwear production, many interviewees agreed, was clearly conveyed to participants. In addition, the government has established a factory store centre that seeks to connect producers directly with the market, and a fashion industrial park of knitwear that attracts designers and designing offices around the country.

Wenling: Labour Upgrading

The Wenling case represents the second strategy firms adopt in China's knitwear industry in response to labour shortage, that is, labour upgrading or, more specifically, industry-level collective bargaining.

Wenling is a town in South Zhejiang Province. Most knitwear firms in Wenling are clustered in the town named Xinhe, with a population of 120,000. In 1994, there were more than 130 knitwear firms, with 20 to 200 workers. By 2002 – the year before the first industry-level union contract was signed – 12,000 workers were working in the cluster, 85 per cent of whom came from other provinces.

Knitwear is a seasonal industry, and in peak seasons – usually starting from July and August – the workforce used to be short by 30–40 per cent in the cluster in Wenling. This labour shortage intensified employer competition for workers and therefore worker job-hopping, because it was easy for workers to communicate across factories about wages, given that the factories were agglomerated within only a few areas.

Existing studies see the Wenling case as a paradigm of successful regional industry-level bargaining (Pringle, 2011; Wen and Lin, 2015) as noted, while the stage of its development prior to 2002 is overlooked or downplayed, which I found particularly interesting as it illustrates how employers actively engaged in spontaneous wage coordination in response to labour shortage even before the state or the official union started to intervene. Local employers initiated informal wage coordination in 2000 in order to deal with labour shortage. Bosses from several major firms came up with the first local wage framework agreement in an informal meeting. In 2001, an employers' association was established and the framework agreement was made more meticulous. This apparently had not effectively solved the problem of job-hopping, however, as the framework agreement somehow 'lacked authority, since it was just the enterprises' unilateral decision' (interview, July, 2012) according to the Chairman of the Wenling Knitwear Industry Employer Association.

The local government, in particular the labour bureau and the official union, started to intervene in the process in 2002, turning the framework agreement into a formal collective contract between the employer association and the industrial union, which was created in the same year for the sake of collective bargaining. The contract has been renewed every year since then, and serves as a uniform standard for the piece-rate wage system that the industry exclusively employs. The 2011 contract, for instance, has specified up to 72 procedures involved in producing a knitted garment. Each procedure was given a standard amount of working time after timing a few skilled workers practising the procedure. Wage negotiation was then conducted based on the unit price of each standard working time, that way the unit price for each production procedure was determined. All the 72 unit prices constitute the main part of the collective agreement.

As a result of the wage coordination, workers in Wenling receive largely similar wages across firms as well as occupations, as shown in Table 9.1, while it is less so in Dalang. As for the wage level, Dalang workers in general receive higher nominal wages than Wenling. This difference is likely attributed to the different levels of living costs in the two areas – living in Dalang is more costly than in Wenling. Even so, employers in Wenling complained to me about losing workers to other knitwear clusters in China, likely including Dalang. But this study does not seek to address these dynamics.

Wenling has fallen behind in labour substitution. Firms seem to lack incentives or capacity to resort to industrial upgrading – abandoning the labour-intensive production and pushing up along production chains – when initially faced with a shortage of labour. The D firm that I have studied here engages in both OEM and ODM production, while the C firm has only OBM production, referred to by the local government officials as the best knitwear company in town. These claimed OBM and ODM models are suspicious, however, as neither of the firms has a full-time designer team. Production workers constitute 92 per cent and 97 per cent of the workforces in the two firms respectively, suggesting that firms in Wenling still heavily rely on manufacturing instead of designing and branding for profit (see Table 9.1). Neither of these firms has considered an expansion or relocation strategy. When asked about this, the senior manager of the C firm gave me a resolute answer of no.

In 2003 when the industry-wide bargaining just started, firms rarely employed automatic knitting machines in Wenling. Manual workers performed 80–90 per cent of the production. Labour intensity in Wenling's knitwear industry was greater than that in Dalang even at the time of my visit. The larger firm has not even fully eliminated the traditional manual knitting machines. In one of the workshops, I saw several dozen workers – mostly women – working on these manual machines, each controlling one. A worker was quickly adjusting the needles on a really old machine, strictly following the freehand-drawn pattern design on a piece of paper in front of her face. Most of the workers were apparently very experienced, but obviously the productivity of the machines is much lower than that of automatic ones.

Antecedents of Employer Responses to Labour Shortage

The two cases are too different to constitute an ideal matched-case comparison. So firms' divergent responses to labour shortage in these two areas cannot be ascribed to any single dimension. One way of addressing this problem is to examine factors that may have directly affected firms' strategic choices – the antecedents of the strategies that they chose, either labour substitution or labour upgrading. I find that work organization and labour process, the local state's role, and several employer characteristics have shaped firms' responses to labour shortage, which I examine in turn in this section. It should be borne in mind that although I at times discuss how firms in these two clusters vary according to these three factors, it is not through case comparisons that these factors are identified.

Work Organization and Labour Process

As noted, the labour process in the knitwear industry, as in the garment industry in general, is typically Taylorist mass production. Firms have not developed practices such as teamwork like in the automobile industry or Fordist assembly lines in the electronics manufacturing industry (Lüthje et al., 2013). In the four firms that I have studied, production procedures – knitting, jointing, finishing, and packing – are placed in different functional workshops. In other words, organization of production in firms largely replicates the model depicted in Figure 9.1.

The following section discusses why work organization in Dalang does not meet the conditions for labour upgrading, in particular, industry-level collective bargaining. Before doing that, however, we need to know why the conditions in Wenling are favourable. When labour shortage emerged in Wenling, labour process and work organization in the local knitwear industry featured low-level automation, a high degree of production-process reliance on skilled manual labour, and the prevalent use of the piece-rate wage system, which were favourable conditions for firms' adoption of the labour-upgrading strategy to address labour shortage. To begin with, the low level of automation and, relatedly, the high degree of production-process reliance on skilled manual labour increase firms' incentive to retain workers and stabilize the workforce via labour upgrading, particularly, collective wage coordination across firms. In the early 2000s, there was only very limited, if any, adoption of automatic machines and the slow move towards ODM and OBM production had not begun in Wenling. This low automation and the over-reliance on production instead of designing and branding for profit positioned manual production workers in a vitally important position in the production system. '*Workers create the wealth of the firms*', said the chair of the industry association in Wenling, '*No workers, no wealth; no workers, no success*' (interview, July 2012).

Moreover, as opposed to hourly wages, the piece-rate wage system may likely contribute to the development of multi-employer wage coordination for three reasons: first, piece-rates are more accurate and fair measures of work effort for manual workers particularly in the garment industry. Second, it is easier to establish industry-wide standards on the piece-rate of each production procedure than on the hourly wage of each occupation which may not be comparable across firms. Third, particularly for the garment industry, piece-rate workers are more skilled and therefore more crucial to the labour process than hourly wage workers. Since skilled piece rate workers cannot be easily replaced, employers may find it necessary to retain them through collective bargaining. As such, collective bargaining on piece-rates can achieve a better balance between equity (fair, standardized wages) and efficiency (motivation for high productivity) and therefore it is more acceptable to both employers and workers/unions. These factors, among others, make the piece-rate system a favourable condition for industry-level wage bargaining. Particularly for emergent models of multi-employer bargaining, it lays the foundation for wage standardization across firms in the same industry. In the early 2000s, firms in Wenling exclusively employed the piece-rate wage system and initiated wage coordination when they started to feel the labour shortage.

In Dalang, however, such favourable conditions regarding the labour process and work organization have been largely undermined by previous industrial upgrading programmes, which discouraged firms from pursuing labour upgrading when faced with labour shortage in the mid-2000s, but encouraged their continual adoption of the labour-substitution strategy. First, the work system in Dalang's firms replaced the piece-rate wage system, the foundation of the Wenling model of centralized bargaining, with hourly wages.

Second, and probably more importantly, the organization of work that the Dalang firms adopted reduced the reliance of the labour process on manual labour. To begin with, the automatic knitting machines deskilled manual knitting workers – a traditionally skilled workforce – and changed them into adjunctive operators of knitting machines, so that skilled workers were no longer an indispensable factor in the remodelled production process. These workers are now employed with simple and unskilled tasks, such as changing the yarn and fixing minor machinery problems. As a result, the speed of production no longer depends on workers' experience and skills, but rather on machinery. The deskilling of knitting workers via automation is directly reflected in their training process. In C firm in Dalang, for instance, a knitting worker receives 1 to 3 months' on-the-job training in order to be able to operate an automatic machine, whereas a jointing worker whose work is still labour intensive – that is, working on manually-controlled jointing machines – needs to receive at least 3 months' on-the-job training before being qualified to carry out the work under the formal piece-rate wage system.

Furthermore, the way work is organized in the Dalang firms has decreased both labour cost and its share in total production cost – or, in other words, labour intensity – further reducing the importance of manual production workers in the generation of firm profit. The automatic knitting machines, for example, successfully reduced labour costs and increased productivity. As shown in Table 9.1, knitting workers on average receive about 10–15 per cent lower pay than jointing workers in the same firm, because the jobs of monitoring knitting machines are not as skilled as operating jointing machines according to one interviewed boss. Also, the total employment size in knitting workshops was significantly reduced – one machine replaced eight traditional knitting workers. In addition, the transformation from OEM to ODM and OBM production has allowed firms to engage in more value-added production procedures, that is, designing, branding, and marketing, and thus to rely less on manual operators for profit.

Consequently, the firms in Dalang do not have as much incentive to retain workers through collective wage coordination as the firms in Wenling. In addition, the experience of Dalang suggests that the implementation of the labour-substitution strategy, over time, discourages firms from taking the labour-upgrading strategy. That said, the reverse may not hold, that is, firms' adoption of the labour-upgrading strategy may not prevent them from adopting the labour-substitution strategy given ever-changing market competition and technology. As evidenced by the Wenling case, although the firms initiated labour-upgrading programmes such as the industry-level wage bargaining, they have recently adopted automatic knitting machines to replace manual labour. In fact, recent bargaining developments in the Wenling knitwear industry has provided further evidence for the argument that industrial upgrading tends to undermine industry-level wage coordination. Having lasted for over ten years, industry-level bargaining in Wenling has recently encountered a bottleneck, according to my conversion with the chair of the employers' association:

Me: What is the proportion of automatic knitting machines today, cluster-wide speaking?

Chair: 80%. It was introduced only in recent years. Manual labour accounts for only 20% now (in comparison with 80-90% before). Workers are secondary (to the machines). They do not play a major role.

Me: How do these machine operators get paid? Still piece-rate?

Chair: Some piece-rate, some monthly pay. Piece-rate (has a problem)…as the work does not take as much manpower as before.

Me: So for those that still get piece-rate, is their pay following the industry-level contract's pay scheme?

Chair: Eh…you know, this has happened only recently, and we are still trying to figure it out.

Me: So it's not in the bargaining?

Chair: No, it's not. We are still working on this. But if there's no controversy within enterprises, union and other parties will not take a part in it any more. If there is no controversy and workers work hard, the union and the association would not like to get themselves involved. Most importantly, the automation level is relatively high now, employers are hence not as enthusiastic about wage (bargaining) as before'. (Interview, July, 2017)

All in all, a low level of automation, a high degree of production-process reliance on manual skilled labour, and the prevalent use of the piece-rate wage system are favourable conditions for employers' adoption of the labour-upgrading strategy. The labour-substitution strategy, once implemented, tends to undermine the possibilities of labour upgrading by reorganizing work and labour process in a way that weakens these favourable conditions. The focus on work organization and labour process, however, cannot fully explain why the knitwear firms in Dalang chose to go for labour substitution when labour shortage was becoming an issue while their counterparts in Wenling did not. Therefore, it is important to examine another factor at play: the role of the local state.

The Role of the Local State

As pointed out earlier, the Dalang government offered various infrastructures and economic stimulation to facilitate industrial upgrading, which was a key incentive for the local knitwear firms to opt for the labour-substitution strategy in response to labour shortage. The state's support is important, however, not only because of the calculable economic subsidies but also due to the economy of scale that the state is able to facilitate. That is, a few firms who initiate industrial upgrading programmes by themselves may not be able to reach optimal outcomes, while local industry-wide upgrading can potentially reduce various tangible and intangible costs through economy of scale and therefore generate efficiency gains for all of the local firms. For example, industrial upgrading programmes restructure firms' production processes, which at times entails an entirely new set of workforce skills (e.g. the ability to control automatic machines, and to design and market in the ODM and OBM production). If only a few firms engage in industrial upgrading, they may have to bear all the costs of retraining the workforce, while latecomers can be free riders who poach workers trained by these pioneer firms without paying for the costs. If all firms in an industry upgrade their production and the state also provides infrastructures for the formation of relevant skills (e.g. through public vocational schools and training programmes who adjust their curricula accordingly), all players may reach economy of scale and share the relatively low costs. Another example is that, if only a few firms in an industry climb the value chain and offer designing services, they have to bear all the costs of marketing. But if the entire industrial cluster becomes well known for its firms' capacity to offer ODM and OBM production (as in the knitwear industry propagated by the Dalang government via the international fair), additional commercial spending of individual firms may not be necessary. These economies of scale and the need to avoid the free-rider problem cast the local state in the role of promoting industrial upgrading at the local industry level.

This local-state role, however, is apparently absent in Wenling. The local government did not actively engage in promoting industrial upgrading and/or relocation, while its role lies solely in the labour bureau and official union's later intervention in employers' spontaneous wage coordination in response to labour shortage. As a result, although some knitwear firms in Wenling eventually started to adopt automation, they were not only left behind by their counterparts in Dalang and elsewhere in China, but also unable to reach economy of scale. As for industrial relocation, employers in Wenling are even more reluctant. This is likely explained by the third factor: employer characteristics.

Employer Characteristics

The social composition of employers is different between Dalang and Wenling. Employers in Wenling seem to be less outward thinking because they are mostly from the local area, whereas a significant proportion of bosses in Dalang are from outside Guangdong. It is likely that the latter are more willing to relocate their production to other areas – for instance, the boss of B company transferred part of the production to his hometown in Sichuan – while those in Wenling are very reluctant to do so. In addition, because most of them are from the local area, Wenling employers are closely connected to each other, leading to stronger inter-firm relations than those in Dalang, a favourable condition for multi-employer coordination. We need more evidence and systemic examination to support these speculations, however, which is beyond the scope of this study. But they are largely consistent with Friedman's (2014) conception of local entrepreneurialism, which features locally funded investment, low capital mobility, and high employer associability, and is therefore linked to the emergence of a similar multi-employer bargaining case in the sunglasses industry in Rui'an, Zhejiang. Finally, firm size may be an important factor shaping firms' responses to labour shortage. Small firms may have less resources and capacity (particularly financial resources) to engage in industrial upgrading or relocation than large firms. Because firms in Wenling are in general much smaller than those in Dalang in terms of employment size (e.g. as indicated in Table 9.1, even the large firm in Wenling is much smaller than the small firm in Dalang), they may face more constraints to pursue the labour-substitution strategy which usually requires a substantial investment of capital and time.

It is worth noting that the association between work organization and firms' responses to labour shortage may be possibly confounded by firm size, as small firms, due to their various constraints, tend to have low level automation, a high degree of reliance of the production process on manual skilled labour, and piece-rate wages on the one hand and lack the resources and capacity to choose the labour-substitution strategy on the other. However, the earlier analysis on the favourable conditions for firms' adoption of the labour-upgrading strategy suggests that work organization and labour process may indeed have an independent influence.

Conclusion

In this study, I have identified two strategies firms in China's knitwear industry have adopted in response to labour shortage. On the one hand, the Dalang knitwear industrial cluster represents the labour-substitution strategy, which features replacement of manual labour with machinery, transformation of the production model from OEM to ODM and/or OBM to engage in more value-added capacities such as designing, branding, and marketing, and industrial relocation to inland China where labour is simply cheaper. On the other hand, the Wenling case represents the labour-upgrading strategy that aims at retaining and stabilizing the local workforce by establishing a uniform piece-rate system at the local industry level.

In addition to filling the gap in the literature, my examination of firms' strategic choices in reaction to labour shortage brings firms back to the centre of analysis in work and employment studies in China, which is a dominant approach in the Western labour and employment relations sphere (Kochan, Katz and McKersie, 1986). Moreover, I have revealed, by revisiting the well-known Wenling case, that employers' informal coordination actually laid the foundation for the later centralized bargaining. Existing studies, however, have focused only on this latter and formal part of the Wenling model, leading to the view of the industry-level collective bargaining in Wenling as an outcome of either the state's actively restructuring the local industrial relations system (Wen and Lin, 2015) or the official union's engaging in experimental reforms (Pringle, 2011). The informal stage prior to the formalized bargaining, unfortunately, has been largely overlooked.

That being said, a firm's strategic choice, being constrained and shaped by its internal and external contexts, is likely an outcome of a set of factors; work organization and labour process, the state's role, and several employer characteristics seem to all contribute to the different development paths of the two industrial clusters in this study. To begin with, a low level of automation, a high level of production-process reliance on manual skilled labour, and the prevalent use of the piece-rate wage system seem to be associated with firms' adoption of the labour-upgrading strategy. Second, the local state plays an important role in guiding firms towards different approaches, particularly in encouraging firms to engage in labour-substitution programmes by providing economic stimulation as well as infrastructures and institutional support. Finally, several employer characteristics seem to play a role. In particular, the different social composition of employers potentially contributes to the divergent responses of firms to labour shortage, consistent with Friedman's (2014) comparison between the local entrepreneurialism and global integration models, respectively in Zhejiang and Guangdong.

The main limit of this study lies in the methodology. Without a matched-case comparison, I am unable to make strict causal claims. The factors that I have identified, while significant, are neither sufficient nor necessary conditions. There are likely more factors at play, such as the targeted product market (international vs. domestic). In addition, although I find two major strategies that firms tend to use to deal with labour shortage, it is by no means an exhaustive list. Future research might look for other firm strategies and extend this study to other industrial and institutional domains.

REFERENCES

Cai, F. (2007) 'Zhongguo jingji mianlin de zhuanzhe jiqi dui fazhan he gaige de tiaozhan (The turning point faced by the Chinese economy and the challenge it presents to development and reform)', *Zhongguo Shehui Kexue (Social Sciences in China)*, 2007(3): 4–12.

Cao, G., Li, M., Ma, Y. and Tao, R. (2015) 'Self-employment and intention of permanent urban settlement: evidence from a survey of migrants in China's four major urbanising areas', *Urban Studies*, 52(4): 639–664.

Chan, K. W. (2010) 'A China paradox: migrant labour shortage amidst rural labour supply abundance', Eurasian Geography and Economics, 51(4): 513–530.

Dong, Z. and Liang, L. (2012) 'Zhicheng Dalang: maozhi yu shishang tongxing (Knitwear city Dalang: knitting and fashion hand in hand)', *Zhongguo Fangzhi (China Textile)*, 2012(10): 140–143.

Elfstrom, M. and Kuruvilla, S. (2014) 'The changing nature of labour unrest in China', *Industrial and Labour Relations Review*, 67(2): 453–480.

Frenkel, S. J. and Yu, C. (2015) 'Chinese migrants' work experience and city identification: challenging the underclass thesis', *Human Relations*, 68(2): 261–285.

Friedman, E. (2014) 'Economic development and sectoral unions in China', *Industrial and Labour Relations Review*, 67(2): 418–503.

Gereffi, Gary. 1999 International trade and industrial upgrading in the apparel commodity chain. *Journal of International Economics*, 48: 37–70.

Golley, J. and Meng, X. (2011) 'Has China run out of surplus labour?' *China Economic Review*, 22(4): 555–572.

Knight, J., Deng, Q. and Li, S. (2011) 'The puzzle of migrant labour shortage and rural labour surplus in China', *China Economic Review*, 22(4): 585–600.

Kochan, T. A., Katz, H. C. and McKersie, R. B. (1986) *The Transformation of American Industrial Relations*. New York: Basic Books.

Kuruvilla, S. and Zhang, H. (2015 forthcoming) 'Labour unrest and incipient collective bargaining in China', *Management and Organization Review*.

Liao, Z. and Ye, H. (2003) 'Guangdong Dalang: jueqi de zhongguo yangmaoshan mingzhen (Dalang in Guangdong: emerging knitwear city in China)', *Guangming Ribao (Guangming Daily)*, December, 12.

Lüthje, B., Luo, S. and Zhang, H. (2013) *Beyond the Iron Rice Bowl: Regimes of Production and Industrial Relations in China*. Frankfurt and New York: Campus Verlag.

Katz, H. C. (1993) 'The decentralization of collective bargaining: a literature review and comparative analysis', *Industrial and Labour Relations Review*, 47(1): 3–22.

Piore, M. J. and Sabel C. F. (1984) *The Second Industrial Divide*. New York: Basic books.

Porter, M. E. (1990) *The Competitive Advantage of Nations*. New York: Free Press.

Pringle, T. (2011) *Trade Unions in China: The Challenge of Labour Unrest*, London and New York: Routledge.

Sisson, K. and Marginson, P. (2002) 'Co-ordinated bargaining : a process for our times?' *British Journal of Industrial Relations*, 40(2): 197–220.

▶

▶

Tang, S. and Feng, J. (2015) 'Cohort differences in the urban settlement intentions of rural migrants: a case study in Jiangsu Province, China', *Habitat
International, 49*: 357–365.

Wen X. and Lin, K. (2015) 'Reconstituting industrial relations: the experience of
Wenling' *Journal of Contemporary China,* 24(94): 665–683.

Wu, X. (2011) 'Dalang maozhi xie chuanqi, shinian shenghui zhu huihuang
(Dalang's knitwear legend, and its ten years' successful fairs)', *Zhongguo Fushi
Bao (China Apparel Weekly),* November, 18.

Xiao, L. and Liang L. (2010) 'Dalang: zhicheng zhuanshen (Dalang: the knitwear
city's transition)', *Zhongguo Fangzhi (China Textile),* 2010(10): 96–99.

Yue, Z., Li, S., Feldman, M. W., & Du, H. (2010) 'Floating choices: A generational
perspective on intentions of rural-urban migrants in China', *Environment &
planning A, 42*(3): 545–562.

Zhang, H. (2011) 'Hegemonic authoritarianism: the textile and garment industry',
in C. Scherrer (ed.) *China's Labour Question,* München u. Mering, Germany:
Rainer Hampp Verlag, pp. 117–32.

Zhang, H. (2013) 'Domestic integration and east-west dualism regime of labour:
production, relocation, and migrant workers working at-home in China', in J.
D. Krein, E. T. Leone and P. H. E. Duarte (eds.) *Sustainable Growth, Development
and Labour: Progressive Responses at Local, National and Global Level*, Campinas,
SP: Curt Nimuendajú, pp. 83–106.

Zhang, H. (2014) *Informality in China's Collective Bargaining,* Unpublished master
thesis, Cornell University, Ithaca, NY.

Collective Consultation in China: A Comparative Study of Two Auto Companies

10

Fuxi Wang and Mingwei Liu

Introduction

Since its introduction in the 1994 Labour Law, collective consultation, a Chinese version of collective bargaining, has gradually evolved at different levels and into different forms with strong sponsorship of the state that aims to maintain social stability. At the national level, the number of collective contracts and employees covered by the contracts have both risen dramatically, reaching 2.44 million and 276 million respectively in 2013 (Chen, 2014). However, the remarkable achievement in terms of numbers is just one side of the story. On the other hand, collective consultation at the workplace is widely viewed as a formality or meaningless to workers (Liu 2013; Clarke, Lee and Li, 2004; Warner and Ng, 1999; Chan, 1998).

The formalistic nature of collective consultation is largely due to its top-down implementation without much involvement from workers (Lee and Liu, 2011). Yet, starting in the 2000s, cases from a few state-owned enterprises (SOEs) and international joint-ventures (JVs) as well as econometric evidence of the effects of collective consultation have accumulated in the belief in the somewhat effectiveness of collective consultation in improving workers' welfare (Friedman, 2014; Liu and Li, 2014; Yao and Zhong 2013; Lee and Liu, 2011; Liu, 2010; Tong, 2005; Zhang, 2009). For instance, Liu and Li (2014) found that a union established in a Sino-Japanese JV out of political necessity had a certain voice – it won increased wages and reduced working time for workers through collective consultation. Moreover, more genuine collective bargaining initiated by workers' industrial actions has emerged recently and shown a higher potential to safeguard workers' interests (Lee et al., 2014; Chan and Hui, 2013). However, given the control of authoritarian state agencies and union oligarchy (Friedman, 2014), the Party-state has continued to dominate the development of collective consultation in China, turning 'collective bargaining by riot' into 'Party-state led collective bargaining' (Chan and Hui, 2013).

This chapter aims to contribute to this literature by providing a deep look into the top-down implemented collective consultation. We seek to address the following questions: Is there any variation in the top-down implemented collective consultation? If so, what causes such variation? Can the better cases of top-down implemented collective consultation make a difference in terms of workers' welfare and the development of trade unions?

To answer these questions we paid four visits to two auto companies C and J from 2011 to 2015 to conduct the fieldwork. These two companies were located in the same economic development district of a central Chinese city, affiliated to the same state-owned group company D, produced similar products (passenger cars, engines, and automobile parts), targeted the same market, but had different ownership status: C was a SOE while J was a JV between the state-owned group company D and a Japanese auto company with both parties owning 50 per cent shares. Both companies were local models with their low records of labour disputes, relatively high wages, decent working conditions, and good health and safety records. The comparison of these two similar cases may allow us to better discover the underlying causes of variation in collective consultation, if any. In addition, the vast majority of Chinese labour studies have been conducted in coastal areas. By focusing on collective consultation in inland China, this chapter contributes to a more comprehensive understanding of Chinese labour relations.

Our field work involves in-depth interviews and informal talks. More specifically, in C, we conducted interviews with the human resource (HR) director, the vice secretary of the Party committee, one middle manager, one department-level union chair, one part-time union staff, three supervisors, and seven rank-and-file workers; in J, we interviewed two union staffers, one HR manager, two supervisors, and 14 rank-and-file workers. We approached these interviewees through either personal relations or visits to the workers' dorms. Some of the interviewees were sought for information more than once on different occasions. In J, thanks to the arrangement of the union, we also conducted interviews with a focus group of department managers, the union chair and staffers, and worker representatives. In addition, with the assistance of the two enterprise unions, we collected survey questionnaires from 526 randomly chosen frontline workers and managers in the two companies (166 from all of the eight workshops of C Auto and 360 from all of the 14 workshops of J Auto, with 20–50 employees sampled in each workshop). Finally, we collected internal documents of the two companies, media reports, and worker comments in online forums to supplement our interview and survey data.

We find that there are significant differences between the two auto companies in terms of process and outcome of collective consultation. While C had typical, formalistic collective consultation, collective consultation in J seemed to be more genuine with significant worker involvement in the process, confrontation with the Japanese-led management, and substantial gains for the workers. The seemingly more authentic collective consultation in J, we argue, is largely an outcome of J's organizational politics that involves the 'fight for control' between the two equal equity Chinese and Japanese partners. Given the strong control of corporate operation by the Japanese side, particularly the Japanese management's rejection of the normal workplace functions of the Chinese Communist Party, the Chinese side, including the Party committee, management, and the union, unite to confront the Japanese management when conflicts arise. The workplace union, given its status and various activities endorsed by laws, is mobilized by the Chinese side to challenge the Japanese management. In particular, collective consultation is strategically utilized and substantialized by the Chinese side as leverage for their negotiation with the Japanese management on issues related to both labour and business operation. In addition, to enhance their legitimacy and bargaining power vis-à-vis the Japanese side, it is highly important for the Chinese side to gain the workers' support. As an institution that can involve workers to resolve their complaints as well as show unions' (as well as the Party's) concern for worker interests, collective consultation is thus also used by the Chinese side as a mechanism to mobilize worker support, though in a way under their control. The JV partner's country of origin seems to moderate the relationship between the partnership politics and effectiveness or authenticity of collective consultation. On the one hand, Chinese nationalism against Japan plays a role. It not only may intensify the conflict between the Chinese and Japanese sides and at times strengthen the Chinese side's determination to gain control or influence, but also may make the Chinese side more cautious and responsive to worker demands than their counterparts in many other companies such as C because of the potential of these unmet demands in turning workers' anger into radical actions in the name of nationalism. As such, the anti-Japan nationalism may heighten the Chinese level of confrontation with the Japanese during collective consultation. On the other hand, the popularity of enterprise-level collective bargaining in Japan makes substantial collective consultation acceptable to the Japanese management. However, although collective consultation in J carries some features of authentic collective negotiation seen in the West, it is intrinsically different from worker-led collective bargaining. It is not so much labour–management consultation as negotiation between the Japanese and Chinese partners with the latter manoeuvring workers' power to serve their own interest. Below we will illustrate our argument with detailed case studies of collective consultation in the two auto companies.

Collective Consultation in C and J

C was founded in 2007 by its parent company D who made a strategic move to launch passenger cars of its own brand to seek sustainable development rather than to heavily rely on the brands of its renowned foreign partners. The management team and core technicians were sent directly from D, taking with them the culture and management practices of D. Hence, C was operated and managed as a typical SOE, with its management and Party committee having the paramount decision-making power. In 2012 C had an annual production capacity of 160,000 automobiles and 1,670 employees. Among the production workers 174 were dispatch workers and 250 were technical school student interns, the so-called labour dualism often seen in auto factories in China and elsewhere in the world.

J was founded in 2003 jointly by D and a Japanese auto company. To ensure the transfer of advanced technologies and managerial practices, 50 per cent of shares were given to the Japanese partner, the maximum a foreign auto company could procure in China. Transforming from a state-owned auto parts factory and affiliated to D, J was under strong influence of SOE culture and management practices which were often in conflict with Japanese corporate culture and managerial practices. Because both partners wanted decision-making power but neither could take dominance due to the agreements they reached in the cooperation contract, they often had to fight for control over important issues. Compared to C, J Auto was bigger in size, with 6,325 employees and an annual production capacity of 340,000 cars in 2013. Different from C, all production workers in J were regular employees with direct employment contracts.

Our fieldwork finds that collective consultation in C was remarkably different from that of J in terms of both process and outcome.

Different collective consultation processes

C had its first collective contract soon after its establishment in 2007. However, collective consultation in C was largely a formality, typical among Chinese companies. As C was covered in its parent company D's group-level collective contract, it did not even hold separate collective consultation but directly applied D's collective contract. As the HR director of C put it, 'regarding the so-called collective consultation and collective contract, we just abide by the decisions made by the headquarters [D company]. The HR department of the headquarters is in charge of coordinating the [group-level] consultation. The only thing that we see is this document [collective contract]'. (interview, July 10, 2013) Neither the vice union chair of C nor the head of the HR department knew how collective consultation was conducted in the headquarters. Nor were they sure whether C's workers were involved in this process. Wages in C were solely determined by the management, though C's union occasionally collected workers' demands and opinions on wages and submitted them to the headquarters to serve as the basis of group-level collective consultation. The HR director in C confessed, 'How can the union know how wages should be determined? It is the HR department that makes the proposal. Union involvement just makes the process look more democratic on the surface. In essence, it is all determined by the management'. (interview, July 10, 2013) As a result, the workers of C were largely excluded from the collective consultation process. Although some workers were asked by the union about their demands or suggestions on wages, they thought the information was to be used by the management for decision making rather than collective consultation. More importantly, the workers' demands or suggestions usually did not receive any response.

The conclusion of the first collective contract in J in 2003 was also formalistic without much involvement of the workers in the process. The union chair of J drafted the contract following the group-level collective contract as well as relevant legal documents, which was then co-signed by the general manager and the union chair. However, the formalistic collective consultations started to change when concluding the second collective contract in 2006. Under the pressure of workers' complaints about the Party committee's and union's inability to protect worker rights and interests against the Japanese management, the union chair suggested substantializing collective consultation as a mechanism for wage increase, which was endorsed by the Party committee and Chinese management who viewed collective consultation as leverage for them when negotiating with the Japanese management on various issues. Originally the union requested a three-month salary as an annual bonus, which was accepted by the management after four rounds of consultation between the management representatives and the union chair. However, the Japanese general manager rejected this agreement and asked the union to withdraw its consultation proposal. The union, backed up by the Party committee and the Chinese management, stood its ground and sent a formal request to the Japanese parent company asking for an enforcement of the consultation agreement. This unprecedented tough action caught the Japanese side's attention. After consulting with the head of the Chinese management, the Japanese general manager finally gave in for fear of harming the Japanese parent company's public reputation. Later, the Japanese management agreed with regular wage negotiation after the union chair showed them the legal documents regarding the union's right to negotiate labour issues with the management on behalf of the employees. From then on, substantial collective consultation was conducted annually between the union and the Japanese-led management.

The collective consultation process in J features significant worker involvement and confrontational bargaining. Beginning in 2007, to increase the union's bargaining power, 14 worker representatives jointed the union chair to bargain with the Japanese-led management. These worker representatives came from a pool of candidates who were first nominated at the department/sector level and then were elected anonymously by all of the department union chairs and the company union chair. How worker representatives were nominated at the department/sector level varied slightly. In some departments/sections workers were asked to vote for a fixed number of candidates from a list hand-picked by the section chief (all section chiefs were Chinese managers). In other departments/sections, workers could vote for any number of candidates on the list provided by the section chief. The department/sector lists of candidates included front-line workers, supervisors, and higher-level managers. It was implicitly promised that front-line workers who could make contributions at the bargaining table would have an opportunity to be promoted to management positions (such as deputy supervisor). However, it is clear that the nomination of worker representative candidates was under the discretion of section chiefs. Moreover, some workers we interviewed were not involved in the nomination process at all, suggesting the great limitation of worker involvement in J's collective consultation. Nonetheless, the final lists of union negotiators were comprised of both rank-and-file workers and lower-level managers. The negotiators later held meetings with front-line workers without the presence of managers to elicit suggestions and complaints on wages, benefits, and other working conditions. In addition, these union negotiators were heavily involved in deciding on bargaining issues and developing negotiation strategies. As a former union negotiator put it:

> Before each round of negotiation, we, the worker representatives, proposed several issues. Then, we were split into several discussion groups, discussing about how to negotiate and what counterarguments the management would make. Of course, we considered the situation of the company. For example, if the situation was bad, it would be unreasonable for us to ask for a wage raise. So one should be fully prepared and think about what the opposite side would say. If we wanted to reach one goal in a year, we would make a proposal on three related issues. You (the management) could not veto all of them! So we emphasized that [the negotiation] should aim at the goal that we really wanted to achieve... If the goal was 7 months' salary [as annual bonus], we would ask for 10 months; and we would achieve 7 months eventually ... Before negotiation, we practiced and discussed about how to achieve our negotiation goals. (interview, June 26, 2012)

At the bargaining table the union negotiators often confronted the Japanese management with palpable arguments and expressions of anger. A former union negotiator described his bargaining experience proudly:

> I taught Sato (a pseudo name of the Japanese vice general manager) a lesson. Our compensation was low and we wanted a raise. The Japanese said we should primarily be concerned about spiritual life, followed by material life. So I taught them a lesson by talking about one problem. Back then, the air conditioner was just installed. He (Sato) raised an argument: we didn't have air conditioners in the workshops, but later they were set up. After we improved the working condition, everyone's mental outlook was improved. But a wage rise is out of the question. In response, I talked to him, 'Such improvement has mainly enhanced productivity but has nothing to do with workers' primary welfare and material life'. Later, he asked me how much I earned. I said my salary was even lower than my wife's. He then

asked whether I had a car. I said I had a car, but my wife bought it. So my wife drove the car, but I didn't. I was using examples to make my point. (interview, June 26, 2012)

One repeatedly occurring story in our interviews in J was that during the negotiation with the Japanese management some worker representatives 'punched the table'. A worker representative who did this said, 'Sato didn't talk to me for over half a year after I punched the table in front of him' (interview, June 26, 2012). Although the Party committee and the union had great control over who could be drawn into the bargaining team, quite a few production line workers who dared to speak for workers were recruited. Moreover, the union chair protected these worker representatives from the Japanese management's retaliation. For instance, the Japanese management once came to the union chair asking him to fire two worker representatives who appeared most aggressive at the bargaining table and seemed to be unsatisfied with the company, but the union chair defended them by claiming that they 'couldn't be removed because they were elected by the workers' (interview, July 17, 2013). Indeed, our interviews suggested that the Party committee and the union intentionally recruited workers who were willing to speak for the workers and promised them job security. The confrontational nature of collective consultation in J can also be reflected from the multiple rounds of negotiation – at least three rounds and the maximum to date is 13 rounds.

The comparison above clearly shows the significant differences in the collective consultation processes in C and J, which are summarized in Table 10.1.

Different collective consultation outcomes

Outcomes of collective consultation in C and J also differ significantly. Our requests for the detailed records of each round of collective consultation were politely denied, but our contacts in each firm gave us access to the latest collective contracts as a personal favour, though with some hesitation. Based on these contracts and our interviews, collective consultation in J resulted in an average annual wage increase of more than 12 per cent for all employees between 2008 and 2012, and more than 30 per cent for core employees between 2010 and 2012. In C's collective contracts, the annual wage increase was merely 3 per cent between 2010 and 2012, less than a quarter of the annual wage increase in J. Collective contracts in J also include a wide range of welfare beyond

Table 10.1 Differences in collective consultation process in C and J

	J Auto	C Auto
Whether workers are involved	Yes	Rarely
How workers are involved	Information and suggestions were collected from workers. Negotiators included worker representatives who were first selected in each department and then voted by all of the department union chairs	Information and suggestions were collected from workers as routine work of the union while workers were not aware of their involvement in collective consultation
Whether there is confrontation in the bargaining	Yes. Palpable arguments and anger expression (punch the table); the union chair defended the worker representatives	No. The union chair did not challenge the decisions made by the HR department
How many rounds of bargaining	Maximum 13 rounds; at least three rounds in recent years	Unconditional acceptance of the group-level collective contract without firm-level consultation

legal requirements such as complementary health insurance, short-term paid vacation, and free physical examination for all employees. The only provisions beyond legal requirements in C's collective contracts are annuities of no more than six months contingent on firm performance and employment preference given to laid-off workers whose labour contracts are terminated. Conversely, J's collective contracts have several notable pro-labour terms. First, article 58 of J's collective contract in 2012 states that worker representatives who participate in the negotiation of this collective contract cannot be dismissed during the contract term. Second, article 47 states that decisions on large-scale layoffs cannot be made without the union's permission. Third, article 50 states that the union has the right to call for a meeting with the management at any time beyond the institutionalized communication mechanism between the union and the management. These differences in outcomes of collective consultation in the two companies are summarized in Table 10.2.

One may argue that the higher annual wage increase in J may be due to the fact that wages in J are much lower than those in C. In other words, J's higher wage increase may just compensate for the existing wage gaps between the two companies. Therefore it is necessary

Table 10.2 Differences in collective consultation outcomes in C and J

	J Auto	C Auto
Wage increase rate	Ave >12% (2008–2012)	3% (2010, 2011, 2012)
	Core >30% (2010–2012)	
Provisions beyond legal requirement	Complementary health insurance	Annuity contingent on firm performance
	Short-term paid vacation	Laid-off employees (within six months after their labour contracts are terminated) are given preference for job openings
	Free physical examination for all employees	
	Paid day-off for off-site training tests	
	Worker representatives can't be fired within the term of collective contracts	
	Large-scale dismissal needs union permission	
	Institutionalized communication mechanism between union and management	
	Labour-management meeting whenever needed	
	Union permission needed for overtime beyond 36 hours per month	

to compare wages, benefits, and other working conditions in the two companies. Table 10.3 presents results of this comparison based on our employee survey. In addition to comparing the mean wage of each company, we performed statistical regression on the working conditions on the company dummy variable controlling for various individual demographic characteristics including gender, age, education, tenure, job position, and employment status. Because the employees were sampled from each workshop of the two companies, we also corrected the clustering effects. We report the OLS (for wages) and Logit (for benefits and other working conditions) regression coefficients of the company dummy as well as their statistical significance in the last column.

As shown in Table 10.3, monthly average take-home wage in J (4,210.36 RMB or 702 US dollars) is significantly higher than that (2,546.51 RMB or 424 US dollars) in C. In addition, J has significantly higher coverage of paid

Table 10.3 Comparsion of wages, benefits, and other working conditions in C and J

	Observations	J Auto	C Auto	t-value	J Auto effect
Ave. Monthly Take-home wages (yuan)	429	4210.36	2546.51	−17.4223***	0.491***
Social Insurance (Basic)	520	96.37%	98.15%	1.0873	−0.56
Social Insurance (Full)	520	77.37%	75.31%	−0.5154	0.558+
Housing Fund	520	91.34%	87.65%	−1.3086	0.45
Paid Vacation	520	90.22%	72.22%	−5.4052***	1.227***
Complementary Health Insurance	520	48.32%	31.48%	−3.6304***	0.732**
Annuity	520	37.99%	74.07%	8.0724***	1.400***
Free Health Examination	520	91.06%	75.31%	−4.9184***	1.212**
Ave. Weekly Working Hours	505	49.09	51.16	2.4397*	−2.104
On-the-job Training	523	91.36%	91.46%	0.0372	−0.199
Company Sponsored Off-line Training	524	49.17%	40.24%	−1.9022+	0.391

Note: ***$p < 0.001$, **$p < 0.01$, *$p < 0.05$, +$p < 0.1$

vacation, complementary health insurance, and more free health examinations than C, though lower coverage of annuity.

Our interviews confirm the higher wages in J. In C the basic monthly income for a full-time, entry-level, regular assembly line worker was 1,690 RMB, or 282 US dollars in June 2012, while the number was 2,200 RMB or 366.7 US dollars in J, about 30.2 per cent difference.

Explaining the Differences in Collective Consultation: The Role of Organizational Politics

Given that collective consultation in both C and J was top-down implemented in the same local context, the account for the differences in collective consultation process and outcome is worth investigation. We argue that organizational politics, or more specifically, partnership politics in J leads to more substantial or seemingly more genuine collective consultation than that in C. As a typical SOE, C featured hegemonic managerial control of labour (Walder, 1986; Lee, 1999) under which collective consultation was nothing but a formality. In J, a Sino-Japanese JV, the goal of both partners to gain control resulted in the division of the management and sometimes disagreements and even conflicts between the two partners. As such, the Chinese side strategically resorted to collective consultation as leverage for their negotiation with the Japanese side on various labour, business, and political issues and as a mechanism for them to gain workers' support to strengthen their legitimacy and bargaining power vis-à-vis the Japanese side. Consequently collective consultation in J was substantialized and the Chinese side were more responsive to workers' demands than normally seen in many other companies such as C. Finally, having a Japanese company as J's partner may also matter, as the anti-Japan nationalism and the Japanese companies' familiarity with decentralized collective bargaining may both play a role in the power dynamics and collective consultation of J.

C Auto: Hegemonic managerial control and formalistic collective consultation

In SOEs such as C both the union and management, in principle, are still under the leadership of the Party committee, though the management has high managerial decision making power and autonomy, with the Party usually assisting the management (Liu 2013). In essence, there is no significant difference between the Party committee, management, and union – they are all cadres or managers in the eyes of workers. As a department union chair put it, 'The management and the union come from the same family. If the union wants to prosper, the company has to be good. Everyone knows that...' (interview, July 11, 2013)

In C, because of its subordination to the management and Party committee, the union's capacity and willingness to perform substantial collective consultation, if any, was very low. In fact, the union had never seriously challenged managerial decisions, which, according to the union chair, was normal. Instead, the union's job was to explain managerial policies and decisions to the workers and persuade them to comply. When asked about what role the union played in handling workers' complaints and suggestions, a department union chair commented:

[The union is like] lubricant, a messenger between the management and workers. It would be unrealistic to expect the union to do something to increase workers' wages. It does not have the power. The union only serves as a transmission belt, a bridge between the management and labour, because there is a huge difference between the Chinese union and Western union ... we will explain the labour policies when workers come to us to complain. (interview, July 11, 2013)

The union had done almost nothing to back the workers' demands. According to many workers we interviewed, the union 'exists in name only' or 'is never heard of' (interview, July 14, 2013). If the workers had conflicts with the company, they believed that the union would 'speak for the state-owned company and won't consider others, because the union belongs to the company'. (interview, July 14, 2013)

Regarding collective consultation, both the vice union chair and a department union chair we interviewed had no idea how collective consultation was conducted at the group level (i.e. in D) and both admitted that they had no influence at all on the group level collective contract. As far as they were concerned, the collective contracts were simply documents no different from other labour-related policy documents issued by the management or the Party committee.

Although the union did collect demands and suggestions from the workers once a year before the workers' congress, it was merely a 'formality'. As confessed by a worker:

It is just a formality. We were brought to an office sitting in squad and they took down what we said to keep records of what we demanded. After that, some company documents were distributed to each squad. We all read them. We read the company newsletter, we waited, but none of the issues we raised were resolved. (interview, July 14, 2013)

Another worker put it, 'How could our wages be negotiated? They are totally determined by the management' (interview, July 13, 2013).

The Party committee, management, and union in C did not feel the need to substantialize collective consultation as a way to maintain harmonious labour relations since they had not met any strikes or strong resistance from the workers. The majority of the workers in C were local urban workers who still had high dependence on this SOE for their various political, economic, and social needs (Walder 1986). Most of the workers we interviewed were willing to endure the low pay in exchange for job security, guaranteed social insurance, or career opportunities implicitly promised by SOEs. Moreover, the managerial use of dispatch workers and student interns in C (more than one-quarter of the workforce) raised the regular workers' fear of being replaced by contingent labour, further repressing the workers' demands and willingness to fight for wage increase or improvement of other working conditions. In addition, when deemed necessary, the management could respond to worker demands by changing its HR policies. Such HR policy change, however, was mainly to motivate the workers to work harder.

J Auto: Conflictual JV partnership and confrontational collective consultation

Different from the 'three-in-one' relationship among the Party committee, management, and union in C, the governance structure of J was more complicated due to the JV partnership. Because of the clear division on the management side along the line of the partnership, the 'three-in-one' relationship just existed on the Chinese side, who at times had conflicting goals or interests with the Japanese side. Moreover, the partnership agreement compromised both sides' discretion on business operation. In the board of directors, both sides occupied four positions with equal power. The top management team was also composed of an equal number of managers from each side. In addition, at the operation level, J had an inter-tangled managerial structure that compromised the control of either side of the partnership. Specifically, the general manager and the middle managers were Japanese, while frontline managers and sector chiefs were Chinese. Frontline managers reported to the middle managers who were supervised by sector chiefs. The general manager, the head of J, was in charge of sector chiefs. *Hence, the daily operation of J was under the absolute control of neither side.* As a manager put it, 'unlike in SOEs, the [Chinese] leaders in J can't decide on their own. They will have to provide valid reasons; otherwise, it won't be approved by their Japanese supervisors'. (interview, June 26, 2012) The same was largely true for the Japanese managers, though to a lesser extent since the general manager was from the Japanese side. In addition, the Party committee in J was not recognized by the Japanese side. A particular function of the Party committee in SOEs and JVs is managing cadres (i.e. Chinese managers and union officials), which falls into the territory of the HR department in JVs. Although the Chinese management firmly executed any decisions made by the Party committee, the Japanese management cast doubts on the legitimacy of the Party's decisions. As a union staff commented, 'The Party committee takes charge of cadres. The Party committee in a JV is in a weak position, and usually the Party committee is on the side of Chinese management. There are Party members in the company, including the top managers (on the Chinese side) who are in charge of annual goals and strategy.

But the Japanese don't recognize it'. (interview, June 26, 2012) According to a department union chair, Party activities in J were even 'held in private' and the Japanese avoided attending these activities:

> The Japanese actually avoid contacts with the Party. If you mention the Party committee, they will respond, 'the Party committee has nothing to do with me, and I won't attend [the activities]'. (interview, July 17, 2013)

Given that the Party committee had an important role in decision making on the Chinese side, the failure to recognize its status in J greatly challenged the authority of the Party. On the other hand, however, the Japanese management acknowledged the status and power of the union. As a department union chair put it, 'The Japanese are not afraid of the Party committee, not afraid of the [Party's] discipline committee, but afraid of the union' (interview, June 26, 2012). Another department union chair said the Japanese 'will avoid activities held by the Party committee, but they will be willing to attend union-organized activities'. (interview, July 17, 2013)

Therefore, the union in J was viewed by the Chinese management and Party committee as an instrument to leverage bargaining power for the Chinese side in its negotiation with the Japanese side on various issues. As a major function of the union, collective consultation was thus strategically promoted by the Chinese side as a legitimate platform confronting the Japanese management. In particular, because its workplace status and political activities were greatly restricted by the Japanese management, the Party committee gave its strong support to the union in initiating and developing substantial collective consultation, counting on the latter to organize Party activities and to gain resources for the Party committee. As a union staffer put it when asked why substantial collective consultation could develop in J:

> (It is because of) the Party committee. The Party committee won't talk to the Japanese; only the union can negotiate with the Japanese. (interview, July 17, 2013)

The major issues negotiated in collective consultation were those related to wages, benefits, and other working conditions, which are clearly stated in various laws regulating collective consultation. Through supporting the union to take a tough position in collective consultation, the Chinese management could also leverage some power when negotiating with the Japanese management on important or even daily business and operation issues, which was pointed out by several managers we interviewed as a major incentive for the Chinese management to support and promote substantial collective consultation.

Because workers' support was often crucial for them to confront the Japanese side, the Chinese side also strategically used collective consultation to mobilize workers' support in order to strengthen their legitimacy and bargaining power vis-à-vis the Japanese side. A union staff member who had been working in J since its establishment said, 'If you track our history, lots of things are clear. Why do the senior Chinese managers keep speaking for the employees? [Because] the Japanese don't support the Party's work...Whatever the Party wants to achieve, it is way too difficult... The Party thus needs workers' support' (interview, July 17, 2013). In the minds of the union and Party leaders of J, one effective way to gain workers' support was to institutionalize substantial collective consultation to involve workers in corporate decision making and to win gains for workers. Indeed, some workers of J we interviewed had started to get to know the union and Party committee as well as their work in the process of collective consultation; and they were relatively satisfied with what the union and Party committee did for the workers.

The strong support of the union and collective consultation by the Chinese management and Party committee can also be seen from their appointment of Mr Chen (pseudonym) as the union chair of J who played a pivotal role in coordinating the interests of different parties and leading confrontational collective consultation. In China, the regulations on collective consultation are often subject to the interpretation and discretion of union leaders (Friedman, 2014). Workplace union leadership is thus an important factor that shapes the effectiveness of collective consultation. Chen had for a long time held managerial positions in the Chinese parent company D before he was promoted as the vice general manager and secretary of the Party committee of the predecessor of J. When J was established, Chen was appointed as the union chair and vice chair of the Party committee, stepping off his management position. Chen's work experience allowed him to understand well the agenda and objectives of both the management and union, and equipped him with the knowledge of various managerial tricks and leadership skills needed to confront the Japanese management. As Chen put it, 'it is important [for a union chair] to see the situation clearly, set priorities, and choose the right time to speak for the workers and strive for their interests'. (Zou, 2010)

Chen's joint appointment as the vice secretary of the Party committee was instrumental for him to unite the Party committee, Chinese management, and union effectively working towards the Chinese side's common objectives. He frequently communicated with the Chinese managers and Party committee members in informal occasions and at Party committee meetings, soliciting what they wanted the union to do, conveying them the workers' demands, and gaining their support for the union's work, particularly collective consultation. As a department union chair commented, 'Union's work is not constrained by the management, unlike SOEs where we usually say unions are the puppet of the management' (interview, July 17, 2013).

Chen's belief in the importance of striking a balance between company development and workers' interests was critical to the establishment of collective consultation in J. It is Chen who initiated collective consultation in J and recommended it to the Party committee and Chinese management as a key platform and leverage for the Chinese side to negotiate with the Japanese side. Later, to improve the effectiveness of collective consultation and to show the Japanese managers the union's power, Chen drew 14 worker representatives into his negotiation team, making collective consultation more confrontational. He believed that 'union's image [among workers] is built amid confrontation and stalemate with management' (Zou, 2010). Additionally, Chen purposely maintained a certain degree of antagonism between his negotiation team and the Japanese management during collective consultation rather than avoiding confrontation. In the face of the Japanese management's request to fire the worker representatives who fought most fiercely during negotiation, Chen defended those workers by arguing that they could not be fired because they were elected by the workers. Later, all of those worker representatives were promoted to managerial positions as a reward for their contribution to collective consultation. When we asked a union staffer who had witnessed the development of collective consultation in J about the role of Chen in collective consultation, he said, 'Personally speaking, more than 50 per cent of the work [is done by him]'. (interview, July 17, 2013) Therefore, it is clear that Chen's strong leadership is an important factor underlying the more substantial collective consultation in J.

The country of origin of foreign JV partners seems to moderate the relationship between partnership politics and effectiveness of collective consultation. In other words, the fact that the JV's partner is a Japanese company may contribute to the confrontational collective consultation we see in J. First, a radically anti-Japanese popular nationalism (He, 2007) might strengthen the Chinese side's willingness and determination to fight with the Japanese side on important disagreements. A middle manager told us during our focus group interview '... the nationalistic sentiments historically are different [in the two countries]. Thus, cooperation with a Japanese company is extremely difficult' (interview,

July 13, 2013). In addition, the anti-Japanese nationalism further divided the management in J along the national line and resulted in an uneasy relationship between the Chinese and Japanese managers. As admitted by an HR manager, many Chinese managers indeed were affected by the anti-Japanese nationalistic sentiments and developed hostile attitudes towards the Japanese managers, especially when they were treated harshly by the latter (interview, June 26, 2015).

Second, the Chinese public's anti-Japanese nationalism made the Chinese side of J confront the Japanese management on some labour issues that could potentially harm the Chinese parent company's reputation. For example, some Japanese managers used to insult their Chinese subordinates using curse words. The union suggested that the Japanese management forbid such behaviour during collective consultation, but the latter did not think it was an issue in the Japanese culture. The Chinese side thus had to threaten the Japanese management that such abusive treatment of Chinese employees, if not corrected, would be reported to the Japanese parent company. A key reason why the Chinese side insisted on resolving this issue, according to the HR manager we interviewed, was that they were afraid that once such abusive treatment was exposed to the media, the public's anti-Japanese nationalism would greatly damage the reputation of J and its Chinese parent company. (interview, June 26, 2015)

Third, the anti-Japanese nationalism made the Chinese side more responsive to the workers' demands and complaints, which, if unmet or unresolved, could easily turn workers' anger into radical collective actions under the influence of nationalistic sentiments. As Friedman (2014, p. 148) pointed out, when Chinese workers were not satisfied with their working conditions in a Japanese company, their anger would be expressed in nationalistic directions. A discussion among J workers in the Badu Tieba (an online forum) supported such nationalistic emotional outburst:

yu7019 (user name): Insider information: J Auto decided on our bonus as 3 months' salary ... 3.5 months was proposed by the Chinese side, but the Japanese devil eventually approved 3 months.

yu7019: Every year, it has to be approved by the Japanese Devil, and every year, it is less than proposed.

C2311: The passion is running high over this in the internal forum, but the Chinese senior leaders are indifferent. Ah, pathetic Chinese! The nation's anti-Japanese people stick together!!!!!

Amitoto: Grandpa Mao, we are oppressed by the Japanese Devil!

The strong anti-Japanese nationalism among the workers required the Chinese side to respond in a timely and effective manner to any potential labour conflict, which sometimes had to be done through tough negotiation with the Japanese side. For instance, after the Diaoyu Islands Dispute emerged in 2013, to stabilize the workforce, the Chinese side held an emergency meeting with the Japanese management and persuaded the latter to agree that wages would not be cut despite the dramatic decline of sales that year (interview, June 26, 2015).

On the other hand, having a Japanese company as a JV partner may facilitate the institutionalization of collective consultation since collective bargaining on wages and benefits is common in Japanese companies. This was confirmed by our interview with a union staff in J:

Q: Are the Japanese used to negotiating wages and benefits with the union?

A: Yes, they are, because they have a strong union back in Japan. The workers there rely on their unions to negotiate wages.

Q: Is the fact that they are willing to negotiate with our union influenced by their practice back in Japan?

A: Absolutely! (interview, June 26, 2015)

In short, collective consultation in J was more substantial and genuine than that in C, which can be explained by J's internal partnership politics that led to the Chinese side's strategic use of collective consultation to leverage their influence in corporate affairs and to gain support of workers to strengthen their legitimacy and bargaining power vis-à-vis the Japanese side.

Discussion and Conclusion

This chapter presents two case studies of top-down implemented collective consultation in China. We find significant differences in collective consultation processes and outcomes in two auto companies that are similar in many aspects but different in ownership. While collective consultation in C (a SOE) was largely a formality, it was more substantial and confrontational in J (a Sino-Japanese JV). Based on our study and the existing literature, we suspect that such substantial collective consultation may exist in some other JVs (particularly Sino-Japanese JVs) as well. While the Chinese and Japanese partners have equal shares in our case, equal equity of JV partners may not be a necessary condition for such substantial collective consultation.

We attribute the seemingly more genuine collective consultation in J to its internal organizational politics rooted in the JV partnership. Such partnership politics, or more specifically, the two partners' fight for control in the firm's operation, motivated the Chinese side including the Party committee, management, and union to substantialize collective consultation as their leverage to gain more influence vis-à-vis the Japanese management on various labour, business, and political issues. In addition, the Party committee, management, and union in J strategically made use of substantial collective consultation as a mechanism to gain worker support for their legitimacy and negotiation with the Japanese side. Having a Japanese company as the JV partner also contributed to the institutionalization of substantial collective consultation in J, thanks to the anti-Japanese nationalism in China and the Japanese management's familiarity with collective bargaining in Japan.

In spite of palpable arguments, expression of anger, and confrontation between the workers and Japanese management at the bargaining table, collective consultation in J was intrinsically different from worker-led collective bargaining in the West. First and foremost, the institutionalization of collective consultation in J was driven by the Party committee, Chinese management, and the union under their control, rather than by the workers or their independent representative. The major goal of the Chinese side in developing substantial collective consultation was to use it as their leverage when negotiating with the Japanese side. As such, collective consultation in J was not so much labour–management consultation as negotiation between two business partners. Indeed, a union staff member confessed that, 'In J Auto, the nature of collective consultation is different. It is not consultation between labour and management, but one between the Chinese side and the Japanese side' (interview, July 17, 2013). While such business negotiation may possibly advance the worker agenda, it may also sacrifice some worker interests in exchange for business or political gains for the Chinese side. Moreover, both the Chinese and Japanese sides, as the employer, have a common interest in efficiency, which fundamentally determines that workers' gains through such collective consultation, if any, are deemed to be very limited. As a union staff member in J said, '... surely the Party protects production first...Ours [Party] will protect worker interests if production is already guaranteed' (interview, July 17, 2013). In addition, without substantial worker mobilization and involvement, the sustainability of such collective consultation is questionable. Most of the workers we interviewed were not familiar with collective consultation or collective contracts, although many did know their existence through watching J's internal TV programmes, reading J's newsletters, surfing J's website, and so on. As such, once the underlying partnership politics driving substantial collective consultation disappear because of ownership change, collective consultation may become formalized as seen in C.

Second, as mentioned above, the union in J was not an independent representative of the workers but an instrument of the Party and Chinese management. While there were elections of worker representatives at the department level, the nomination of candidates was controlled by the union. Despite the strong leadership of Chen, it was at best a functioning transmission belt between the workers and the Chinese management and the Party committee. It was still a typical Leninist dual functioning union that faced great limitations in promoting the workers' interest. Moreover, this union served relatively well as the Party's tool of labour incorporation. A telling example is that the union purposely selected active workers to confront the Japanese management during collective consultation and later promoted these workers to managerial positions (with the support of the Party committee and Chinese management). Such labour incorporation may negatively affect the development of genuine unionism in J in the future.

Finally, this chapter contributes to the literature in two important ways. First, we discover significant variation in the top-down implemented collective consultation in China through two comparative case studies. We show that in China enterprise-level collective consultation without independent unions can be substantial and meaningful for workers, though with great limitations. As enterprise-level Party committees play an important role in such collective consultation, we call on future research to pay more attention to the role of the Party in shaping workplace employment relations and outcomes. Secondly, to our knowledge, our study is the first that links organizational politics with the development of trade unions and labour relations in the workplace. More studies on how power dynamics within organizations affect employment relations, particularly in the Chinese context, are needed in the future.

REFERENCES

Chan, A. (1998) 'Labor relations in foreign-owned ventures: Chinese trade unions and the prospects for collective bargaining', In G. O'Leary (ed.) *Adjusting to Capitalism: Chinese Workers and the State*. Armonk, NY: M.E. Sharpe, pp. 122–149.

Chan, C. K. C. & Hui, E. S. I. (2013) 'The Development of Collective Bargaining in China: From 'Collective Bargaining by Riot' to 'Party State-led Wage Bargaining'', *The China Quarterly*, 217: 1–22.

▶

▶

Chen, J. (2014) '2.42 million collective contracts signed national-wide and 287 million employees covered' Available from: http://paper.people.com.cn/rmrbhwb/html/2014-10/13/content_1487175.htm. (Accessed: 27th Aug 2015).

Clarke, S., Lee, C. H., & Li, Q. (2004) 'Collective consultation and industrial relations in China', *British journal of industrial relations*, 42(2): 235–254.

Friedman, E. (2014) *Insurgency Trap: Labour Politics in Postsocialist China*, Cornell University Press.

He, Y. (2007) 'History, Chinese nationalism and the emerging Sino–Japanese conflict', *Journal of Contemporary China*, 16(50): 1–24.

Lee, C. H. & Liu, M. (2011) 'Collective bargaining in transition: measuring the effects of collective voice in China', In Hayter, S (ed.) *The Role of Collective Bargaining in the Global Economy: Negotiating for Social Justice*. Cheltenham, UK: Edward Elgar Publishing.

Lee, C. H., Brown, W. & Wen, X. (2014) 'What Sort of Collective Bargaining Is Emerging in China?', *British Journal of Industrial Relations*.

Lee, C. K. (1999). From organized dependence to disorganized despotism: Changing labour regimes in Chinese factories. *The China Quarterly*, 157, 44–71.

Liu, M. (2010) 'Union Organizing in China: Still a Monolithic Labor Movement? ' University Dissertation (Cornell University, NY). *Industrial and Labor Relations Review*, 64 (1): 30–52.

Liu, M. (2013) 'China.' In Frege, Carala and John Kelly (eds) *Comparative Employment Relations in the Global Political Economy*, London: Routledge, pp. 324–347.

Liu, M., and Li, C. (2014) 'Environment pressures, managerial industrial relations ideologies and unionization in Chinese enterprises', *British Journal of Industrial Relations*, 52(1): 82–111.

Tong, X. (2005) 'Labor unions in enterprises: proactive actors, taking the operation of the labor union at B Corporation, a Sino-foreign joint venture in Beijing, as an example', *Chinese Sociology & Anthropology*, 37(4): 52–71.

Walder, A. (1986) *Communist Neo-Traditionalism*. Berkeley, CA: University of California Press.

Warner, M. & Ng, S. H. (1999) 'Collective contracts in Chinese enterprises: A new brand of collective bargaining under 'market socialism'?', *British journal of industrial relations*, 37(2): 295–314.

Yao, Y., & Zhong, N. (2013) 'Unions and workers' welfare in Chinese firms', *Journal of Labor Economics*, 31(3): 633–667.

Zhang, X. (2009) 'Trade unions under the modernization of paternalist rule in China', *Working USA*, 12(2): 193–218.

Zou, M. (2010) 'How to balance interests of both parties in labor-capital game? *Zhonggong Net*. http://character.workercn.cn/c/2010/06/29/081526477975302. html. (Accessed: 27th Aug 2015).

Direct Elections of Workplace Trade Unions in China: Implications for the Changing Labour Regime[1]

11

Chris King-chi Chan and Elaine Sio-ieng Hui

Introduction

While migrant workers' strikes are not a new phenomenon in China (Chan, 2010), the Nanhai Honda workers' strike in 2010 has exerted unprecedented pressure on the party-state (Chan and Hui, 2012). Many China labour experts have placed hope on the institutional reform implemented subsequent to the Honda strike (Friedman, 2013; Chang, 2013), some even considering it a turning point for Chinese labour relations. Since 2010, the party-state and its subordinate official trade union, the All-China Federation of Trade Unions (ACFTU) has made a greater effort to promote trade union elections and collective consultations in factories wherein strikes are prevalent (Chan and Hui, 2014; Hui and Chan, 2015). Chang Kai (2013:91), one of the leading labour scholars in China, writes: 'The Chinese labour relations are transforming from individual based into collective based...There are two forces and paths which supplement each other: one is the state-led, top-down process of construction; the other is the workers-initiated, bottom-up process of reinforcement'.

Five years after the Honda workers' strike, it is time to revisit the possibilities and limitations of the transformation of workplace relations. In 2015 the China Labour Bulletin (CLB), a labour rights watchdog based in Hong Kong, interviewed workers from Nanhai Honda.

A worker whose name was quoted as Jiang told CLB researchers that his salary increased from 1,500 yuan in 2010 to 3,300 yuan presently.

The trade union committee in the factory has been re-elected and collective wage bargaining has been organized regularly after the provincial level trade union sent a delegation to train workers in the factory. Jiang, however, was unsatisfied with the work of their trade union leaders (CLB, 2015):

> I know that the process is always more important than the result and I want to be part of the process. As a union member, I need more than just getting fed with information and giving useless feedback on a deal that has already been done. I want to cast my vote and directly elect the union chairman.[2]

The CLB reports called for theoretical reflections and empirical inquiries over the new conditions of workplace relations in factories wherein significant strikes resulted in state intervention to promote trade union reform. To what extent are the trade union elections, currently promoted by the ACFTU and the party-state, democratic? What is the implication of such union reform for the transformation of labour relations in China? As a labour law expert, Chang's (2013) optimistic view on the changing form of labour relations in China is based on his review and observation of the changes of the government's labour policies. However, the authors argue that sociological studies focusing on the workplace level and the views and perceptions of workers are essential to answer the aforementioned questions.

The tradition of industrial sociology in the West offers us insightful concepts and methods to study workplace issues in China. However, the dramatic changes in labour politics in China has provided evidence to challenge, reconstruct, or develop the Western-centred theory. In this chapter, we bring in a concept – labour regime – put forward by Michael Burawoy, a Neo-Marxist industrial sociologist, to analyse the potential and limitations of workplace trade-union reform in China. The authors contend that the 'contested despotic' labour regime in China has not progressed into a 'hegemony', though a legal framework suitable for this transition is available and direct trade union elections have been conducted in some factories.

The regulatory role of the state in workplace relations was illuminated by Burawoy (1979; 1985) in his conception of 'politics of production' or 'labour regime'. Burawoy (1979; 1985) categorizes two types of labour regimes in capitalist industries: 'market despotism' and 'hegemony' depending on the extent of intervention from the state. And he suggests that 'bureaucratic despotism' was practiced in the authoritarian socialist state. Burawoy (1985: 12) defines the market despotism labour regime as being when 'the state is separated from and does not directly shape the form of the factory regime', and hegemonic regime as being when 'the state shapes the factory apparatuses by stipulating, for example, mechanisms for the conduct and resolution of struggle at the point of production'.

Burawoy's conceptualization of the categories of labour regimes in capitalist development has ignited debates and critique within the fields of industrial sociology and industrial relations (Littler, 1990). Recently, Thompson and Brork (2010: 9) pointed out that Burawoy's (1985) idea of 'factory regimes' is 'problematic ... to generate conceptions of whole epochs of capitalist development ... from ... small scale ethnographies'. Littler and Salaman (1982: 265) commented earlier that 'there is always a mixture of modes of production and managerial strategies at any one time'. Hyman (1987) argued that management has different strategies to control workers, but no single strategy will be successful ultimately due to the 'contradictions within capitalist enterprise'. Responding to Burawoy's (1985) claim that the economic crisis had given rise to a new form of labour regime – 'hegemonic despotism', Hyman (1987: 52) commented that 'the emerging pattern of labour control contains its own emerging contradictions. The new disciplines imposed on workers can be expected ... to provoke unpredictable and disruptive forms of revolt'. In other words, management strategies are always changing and responding to different patterns and levels of workers' resistances throughout the history of capitalist development.

Following the tradition laid down by Burawoy, Lee (1998) conceptualizes the factory regime in foreign-owned factories in South China as 'localistic despotism'. Lee's intention is to introduce a cultural dimension to labour process theory. In the Chinese sweatshops, the local state was absent in protecting the rights of young female migrant workers, the management was highly disciplinary, and the politics of 'locality' (the place of origin or *jiguang*) had been employed as a strategy of control (and resistance). In recent years, however, the Chinese state has become increasingly active in intervening in workplace relations. The Labour Law which took effect in 1995 has been better enforced since the wave of worker strikes starting from 2004 (C. Chan, 2010). In 2007, three significant laws were legislated, namely the Employment Promotion Law, the Labour Contract Law, and the Labour Dispute Mediation and Arbitration Law. The second law strengthens workers' individual and collective rights while the last law intervenes more actively in the resolution of labour conflicts through workplace reconciliatory or judicial mechanisms. Does the legal reform mean that the labour regime in China is becoming 'hegemony'? Our previous research has shown that without effective workplace trade unions and strong shop steward culture, 'effort bargaining', which Burawoy (1979: 161) defines as 'the monetary reward for labour expended or the reward for effort', took the form of industrial conflict while coercion is still a dominant form of management and control in factories (C. Chan, 2010). We therefore contend that the labour regime in China is more despotic than hegemonic. That said, due to the increasing pressure imposed by the state's intervention and workers' collective actions on the management, C. Chan (2010) considers the factory regime in China a form of 'contested despotism', which may give way to a new form of balance of power in the future. While Burawoy's notion of 'labour regime' is a point of departure for our analysis, we consider the labour regime in contemporary China as a changing rather than static process.

As will be elaborated in the following sections, state intervention on factory regimes has escalated significantly and state policies have addressed trade union democratic reform. Meanwhile, worker struggles have been radicalized in recent years. What are the implications of these changes on the conception of labour regime in China? This article tries to address this question.

The Transformation of Labour Relations in China

Industrial relations in China have undergone substantial changes since 1978, as the country has shifted from a command economy to a market economy and has been gradually incorporated into global capitalism. With the large-scale privatization of state-owned enterprises and the increasing inflow of foreign investment in the private sector, Chinese workers have become vulnerable in the labour market, and have been subjected to unfair and often illegal treatment at work (A. Chan 2001; C. K. Lee 1998). The party-controlled trade unions have failed to protect workers against unscrupulous employers. This has induced widespread extra-trade union activism in the country. Specifically, strikes bypassing official trade unions have become a vital means through which Chinese workers safeguard their interests in the face of capitalist exploitation (A. Chan 2011; C. K. C. Chan 2010). In 2010, the Honda workers' strike sparked a country-wide wave of strikes in China (Hui 2011; K.-C. C. Chan and Hui 2012).

In China, union officials at the enterprise level are generally appointed, not elected (Taylor and Li 2007). Furthermore, chairpersons of enterprise trade unions are usually concurrently Chinese Communist Party (CCP) cadres, or senior managers of the enterprises. Increasing labour militancy has created huge pressure on both the Chinese government and the official trade unions to promote at the enterprise level what is officially called 'direct elections' (*zhixuan*) (Jingbao 2012; Zhongguo Caifu 2012) or 'democratic elections' (*minzhu xuanju*) (Yangcheng Evening News 2010; Nanfang Daily 2012b, GDFTU 2012b), especially in the Pearl River Delta (PRD) of Guangdong Province. At the national level, on 5 June 2010 the AFCTU issued a document entitled 'Reinforcing the building of workplace trade unions and giving them full play' (ACFTU 2010), which states that workplace trade union elections should be conducted in accordance with the law. In August 2010, the then Vice-Chair of the ACFTU, Mr Wang Yu Pu, noted in a national meeting on trade unions' grassroots organizing that trade unions 'in enterprises that have mature conditions should explore the possibility of holding direct election of trade union chairs; they should ensure that the elections truly reflect the preferences of members and that the elected chair represents workers, speaks out for them and acts for them' (Liaowang 2012). In March 2012, the ACFTU sent an investigation team to Guangzhou to study the implementation of 'democratic elections' in enterprises and in June it extended this research to Shenzhen (GDFTU 2012). At the provincial level, the then Deputy Chair of the Guangdong Provincial Federation of Trade Unions (GDFTU), Mr Kong Xiang Hong, confirmed in June 2010 that the federation would speed up the democratization of plant trade unions and he announced that a pilot scheme for the 'democratic election' of workplace trade union chairs would be conducted at ten factories (Takungpo 2010). At the city level, the Deputy Head of the Shenzhen Federation of Trade Unions (SZFTU), Mr Wang Tongxin, announced a plan to organize union elections in 163 enterprises in Shenzhen in 2012 (Liaowang 2012). In August 2012, the SZFTU issued the 'Opinions on Further Strengthening the Organizing of Enterprise Trade Unions', which states that democratic elections should be organized in enterprises (Nanfang Daily 2012c). In Guangzhou, the 'Measures on the Candidates for the Elections of Guangzhou Enterprise Trade Union Chairperson and Interim Measures on Appointing Trade Union Inspectors to Instruct the Elections of Grassroots Trade Union Chairperson' were issued in 2011 to guide enterprise trade union elections (Nanfang Gongbao 2011). And the new Chair of the Guangzhou Federations of Trade Unions (GZFTU), Ms Zhao Xiao Wei, highlighted that enterprise union elections should be organized in accordance with the laws.

This study investigates the post-2010 wave of trade union elections that resulted from this revived attention to 'direct elections' or 'democratic elections' in enterprise trade unions[3] by examining closely two factories: Autoco, an automobile spare part factory in Fushan, and Eleco, an electronic factory in Shenzhen.

Workers' Strikes-Driven Elections in the PRD

The new type of union elections in the PRD reflects a new socio-political and economic context. At the level of industrial relations, despite the attempts of the ACFTU and the party-state to contain labour unrest, exploitative working conditions, skyrocketing inflation, the widening income gap, and the failure of the unions to represent their members' interests continue to fuel workers' strikes, as exemplified by the country-wide waves of strikes ignited by the Honda workers in 2010. At the economic level, serious labour shortages have compelled the Guangdong government to allow higher minimum wages and better labour policies, including union elections, to stabilize employment relations (interviews with a provincial trade unionist, 27 December 2012). Furthermore, the plan to upgrade the industries in Guangdong from low end to high end has freed the government from concerns about small-scale and uncompetitive enterprises, which usually cannot afford organized labour in the form of trade unions. In other words, union elections, as a means to overhaul the Chinese trade unions, are now seen by the party-state and the union federations as a way to mitigate the intensifying labour conflicts without imposing significant negative effects on the labour market or the economy. (To a certain extent, the strategy is also regarded as helping to drive the bad apples out.) Against this larger socio-economic background, we examine the new type of elections using two in-depth case studies.

The Autoco case

The Autoco workers staged an extra-trade union strike in May 2010, which involved over 1,800 workers and lasted for 17 days. In addition to higher wages and better welfare, the workers demanded democratic union elections. They argued that the trade union chair, who was the deputy head of the business management department, represented the management's interests rather than the workers'. In the end, the workers' wages were raised from 1,544 yuan to 2,044 yuan, and the then vice president of the GDFTU arranged a number of meetings in June and July 2010 with some of the strike leaders to discuss union elections (interviews with a strike representative 1 August 2010). He revealed that there were plans to organize union elections and collective bargaining in Autoco. However, he denied the request of the strikers' representatives to remove the existing union chair and insisted that the chair should be given 'a chance to correct himself'. In addition, he warned the strike representatives that independent trade unionism is not allowed in China and that trade union reform in Autoco should be carried out within the legal framework. He also reminded one of the key strike leaders not to have any contact with any foreign forces, as he probably knew that she was in touch with some outside supporters during the strike (interviews with a strike representative, 1 August 2010).

Subsequently, union elections were held in Autoco from September to November 2010. Figure 11.1 shows how the Autoco trade union structure was reformed after the strike.

Before the strike, only the trade union members' representatives existed (less than a hundred in number), union executive committee members (seven in total) and the union chair. However, many workers, including those who had worked in the company since its establishment in 2007, were unaware of the existence of the union members' representatives before the strike, which suggests they were not properly elected by the workers. As part of the trade union reform, the union organization was expanded to include union division representatives (*gonghui xiaozu daibiao*) and a union branch committee (*gonghui fenhui weiyuan*). The former were elected at the division level (*ban*), whereas the latter were elected at the departmental level (*bu*). The overarching

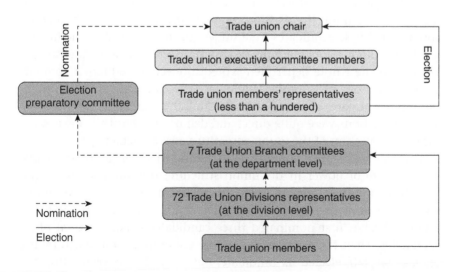

Figure 11.1 The union elections in Autoco in 2010

trade-union structure was broadened to improve union-worker relations. Moreover, the post-strike elections had two other purposes: the election of five more union executive committee members and two vice-chairs. To prepare for these elections, an election preparatory committee was established to decide the electoral rules and regulations. This committee comprised the existing seven union committee members, whom our worker interviewees said were not elected through proper elections (if there were any at all), two trade union members' representatives and two staff and workers' representatives (*zhigong daibiao*), whom workers were not aware of before the strike, and two strike representatives. Among these 13 people, only one was a rank-and-file worker (*yixian yuangong*) and two were lower-level supervisory workers; the others were managerial staff. One of the election preparatory committee members told us that the district and town-level trade union officials attended all of their meetings, giving suggestions and commenting on the electoral procedures (interviews with workers, December 2010).

There were seven departments in Autoco, each consisting of several divisions. Altogether there were 72 divisions in the company. At the first stage of the union reform, workers in each division elected their division representatives in a 'sea election', meaning there were no candidates for the position; workers just put down the name of the person they supported on the secret ballot paper. The worker who got the most support from his/her colleagues became the division representative. At the second stage, the elections for the seven union branch committee members were held at the departmental level. The elected division representatives in each department first used the sea election method to elect four candidates from among the division representatives to run for the branch committee. These candidates were subject to the approval of the higher-level trade unions, including the provincial federation. Subsequently, the workers in the whole department voted to elect three branch committee members out of the four candidates. The candidate with the highest number of votes in this election became the branch chair. These two levels of elections were quite direct and democratic, but this was not the case in the election of the union committee and vice-chairs.

The union executive committee, including the chair and vice chairs, is the centre of power in the union structure; the union division and branch committees merely serve as subordinate consultative units. For the elections of the union executive committee, each of the seven union branches first nominated three candidates making a total of 21 candidates. Then the election preparatory committee, dominated by the managerial staff, elected six candidates out of the 21. Following this, the trade union members' representatives (whose existence most workers were unaware of before the strike) elected five union committee members out of the six candidates. The two newly elected committee members with the highest votes then became the vice-chairs. At this stage most newly elected division representatives and the union branch committee members could not vote in the elections because they were not the union members' representatives. Excluding the majority of the workers from the elections of the executive committee members and the vice-chairs was highly controversial (if not completely undemocratic), not to mention the fact that the legitimacy of those who had been granted the privileges to vote was in grave dispute.

Despite the claim that the elections held in Autoco were 'direct elections' and 'democratic elections', when assessing the new wave of elections we must pay serious attention to who had the right to run in the elections, who had the right to nominate candidates, who had the right to vote, and who were actually elected. In the case of Autoco, the elections of the division representatives and the union branch committee were quite direct and democratic; however, the direct participation of workers stopped at this level. Only the branch committee and the election preparatory committee, dominated by the managerial staff, had the right to nominate candidates for the union executive committee. Furthermore, only the disputed union members' representatives had the right to vote in these elections. If the purpose of workplace union elections is to make those who govern the union accountable to their members and to subject them to monitoring to ensure their allegiance to the members, then it should be clear that most of the 1,800 workers at Autoco were deprived of the right to nominate the candidates for the union vice chairs and committee members, the right to run in these elections, and the right to vote in these elections. These rights were granted to less than a hundred union members' representatives, whose legitimacy was in dispute. It is worth noting that according to the Trade Union Law (article 9), Provisions on the Work of Enterprise Trade Unions (thereafter Provisions on Trade Unions, article 11) and Trial Measures on the Election of Enterprise Trade Union Chairman (thereafter Measures on Trade Union Chairman, article 14), the union executive committee and chair can be elected in either the trade union members' congress or trade union members' representatives' congress; in the former case, all of the members can vote in the election, whereas in the latter only a handful of members can vote. According to our research, the 'direct elections' taking place in the PRD seem to have taken an easy route from the authority's point of view, but it definitely is not an inclusive approach from the democratic-participatory perspective. When most union members cannot vote directly in the elections of the union executive committee members and chairs, the accountability of the officials to the rank-and-file members may be weakened, and the chances that companies or higher-level trade unions will manipulate the elections may increase.

In addition to the controversy over the lack of democracy in the Autoco elections, there were complaints about the management's manipulation of the process. For example, one of the key strike leaders obtained the same number of votes as her rival during the election of division representatives making a second round of voting necessary. Before the second round, a division head (*ban zhang*) tried to persuade his subordinates not to vote for the strike leader. In the end, she got only eight votes compared to her rival who received more than 20 votes. Some of her colleagues apologized to her after the election, saying that they were pressured by the division head not to vote for her (Interview with a strike leader, 28 September 2010). The enterprise's desire to influence the election by excluding the worker activists was evident. Under this type of quasi-democratic and partly manipulated election, who was actually elected in Autoco? In the end, two vice chairs were elected in February 2011 – one of them was a department head and the other was the deputy department head. Most of the newly elected executive committee members (with only one exception) were from the managerial or supervisory levels. An election preparatory committee member revealed to us that the then vice president of the GDFTU promised them before the elections that at least 50 per cent of the union committee members should be from the rank-and-file, but after the elections he said that lower-level supervisory staff were counted as rank-and-file workers.

The term of the union executive committee ran out at the end of 2011 and elections were held to elect the new committee for a new 3-year term – 2012 to 2015. Shortly before this election, the election for the new term of trade union members' representatives was held. Replacing the old representatives that were unknown to most workers, the new union members representatives were elected by the members. For the election of the new union executive committee, as in the previous selection, there were restrictions on who had the right to nominate the candidates and who had the right to vote in the election. This time the outgoing union committee members, who came largely from the managerial level, had the sole privilege of nominating the candidates after consulting with the union division representatives and the union branch (see Figure 11.2).

Before putting forward their nominations, the outgoing committee had to first seek approval from the Autoco Party branch (which together with the Chinese Communist Youth League branch was set up shortly after the strike) and the town-level trade union (Lau 2012). According

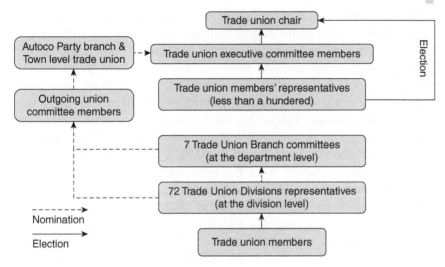

Figure 11.2 The union elections in Autoco in 2011

to the Measures on Trade Union Chairman (article 7), the enterprise party branch, together with the next level up of the trade union and the union members' representatives, are responsible for the nomination and election of the enterprise union chair. After all of these steps were accomplished in November 2011 the union member representatives' congress was held to elect the new union committee members. Following this, the union chair was elected from among the new committee members. In short, the majority of the rank-and-file members were denied the chance to elect those who were supposed to govern the trade union on their behalf. The newly elected union members' representatives were the only people granted voting privileges but they were only allowed to choose from the preselected options offered by the outgoing committee members who were under the leadership of the party-state and the higher-level trade unions, and the influence of the management.

Who were elected under such highly manipulated circumstances? A union branch chair told us that 'the higher level trade unions suggested that the position of the enterprise union chair should be taken up by the mid-level management, such as the department head. This will make the work of the union easier and smoother' (interview with a union branch chair, 26 September 2012). The results concurred with this suggestion. The newly elected chair was a department head, and was simultaneously the Secretary of the Party branch in Autoco. In other words, he was someone to whom both the company and the party-state could entrust the trade union. In fact, it is stipulated by the Measures on Trade Union

Chairman (article 20) and Provisions on Trade Unions (article 51) that an enterprise union chair should be under the leadership of both the enterprise party branch and the higher-level unions, with the former playing a more important role; in enterprises without any party branch, the union should be under the sole leadership of the higher-level unions.

In brief, the union elections in Autoco were initiated by the large-scale workers' strikes. The actual elections, however, were shaped by various actors. The higher-level trade unions established the rules for the elections: the vice president of the GDFTU ruled out the possibility of electing a new chair in 2010; cumbersome procedures were designed to deprive most rank-and-file members of the opportunity to elect the union committee members and a union chair; and the SS town trade unions (and the Party branch) had the final say over the candidates for union executive committee members and the chair. The enterprise manipulated the results of the elections by pressuring workers not to vote for 'troublemakers'. The party-state tried to maintain control by establishing a Party branch and a Youth League branch in Autoco shortly after the strike. The Party branch was a gatekeeper that ensured that all of the candidates for the union executive committee and chair positions were acceptable to the Party. The fact that the newly elected union chair was simultaneously the secretary of the Party branch revealed the tight link between the union and the Party.

The trade union election was meant to be a means to heighten the enterprise unions' representational capacity. However, can the current practice of indirect and quasi-democratic elections be a solution to the problems facing the Chinese trade unions? Before the 2010 strike, there was no collective bargaining in the factory. However, after the strike the company had taken the initiative to bargain wages with the trade union; this had led to wage increases greater than those in the years before the strike. Many workers informed the authors that their employment conditions had improved in the post-strike period. However, in March 2013 more than 100 Autoco workers went on strike because they were dissatisfied with the enterprise trade union's performance in the ongoing wage negotiation. In 2011 and 2012, the average wage increase for the Autoco workers was about 30 per cent and 15 per cent respectively (interview with a worker, 29 April 2013; CLB 2013). In the collective wage negotiation in 2013, the trade union proposed a wage increase of 388 yuan for the rank-and-file workers, who constituted over 80 per cent of the factory's total workforce; but the company rejected this proposal and offered to increase their pay only by 10.2 per cent (i.e. 220 yuan). The company at the same time proposed to increase the salaries of the second-ranking staff by 12.4 per cent, the third- and fourth-ranking staff by 19.8 per cent, and the fifth-ranking staff by 18 per cent. Many rank-and-file workers found the company's counter-proposal unsatisfactory and voiced their suggestions, but the enterprise union elected through 'democratic elections' accepted the company's offer after a number of negotiations. Many rank-and-file workers criticized the union for its compromising attitude and for failing to represent and defend their interests. One of them noted that 'the company's proposal is biased towards the higher-ranking staff. Many union's executive committee members are not rank-and-file workers; therefore they do not fight for our interests' (interview with a worker, 29 April 2013).

Discontented with the newly elected trade union, some workers from the assembling division staged an extra-trade union strike to demand a higher pay rise. Shortly after the strike broke out, the management rushed to the open space inside the factory premises to persuade the strikers to resume working; but the strikers did not move. Later, the union chair and the union branch committee members came to persuade the strikers to talk to the management in the meeting room. In this meeting, the union chair broke into tears, saying that the union had tried its best to advance workers' interests and he was surprised to see the workers going on strike. Instead of supporting the workers' strike, the elected trade union acted as the company's mediator to halt the strike. Despite this pressure from the union chair, the strikers clearly expressed their dissatisfaction with the 10.2 per cent wage increase of 220 yuan and requested a pay rise of at least 300 yuan. The management responded that it would give them a reply the next day. On the second day, workers from two other divisions joined the assembling workers in their industrial actions; they either stopped working or worked slowly. The strike imposed huge pressure on the management, who quickly restarted the wage negotiation with the union. In the new round of negotiations, the management agreed to raise the wages of the rank-and-file workers by 14.4 per cent (i.e. 310 yuan). This incident shows that if elections are a formality or fail to transform the pro-capital and pro-party-state enterprise unions into a truly representative body of workers, workers' struggles may continue nonetheless, exposing the unrepresentative character of the unions.

The Eleco case

In April and May 2012, elections were held in the Japanese-owned Eleco, after workers went on strike in March to demand higher wages, better benefits, and the democratic election of trade union officials.

The factory employed about 850 workers (Liaowang 2012, Southern Metropolis Daily 2012). The little-known enterprise union was first established in 2007. The last chair, who was a department head, noted in a newspaper interview that 'the enterprise trade union was arranged by the higher-level trade unions; it was established for the mere sake of establishing and its officials were not selected through elections'. At the time of the strike, all of the union executive committee members came from the managerial and supervisory level (Southern Metropolis Daily 2012) and they did not support the strike. During the strike, the workers issued an open letter with seven demands; trade union elections were at the top of these requests. The strike forced the company to loosen its grip on the union and after the strike, the company agreed to organize a union election. Furthermore, the company agreed to give an annual operational fee of one hundred thousand yuan to the union and that the CEO would have two meetings with the union chair each year (Southern Metropolis Daily 2012b).

The key issues in the Eleco elections were again who had the right to run for office, to nominate candidates, and to vote, and who were actually elected (see Figure 11.3).

As in the case of Autoco, a trade union preparatory committee was first set up to decide on the electoral procedures. Little was known about the composition of this preparatory committee; it was not reported by the media nor revealed by our interviewees. The Eleco workers first elected union committee members for the seven branches, altogether 75 in number, who were at the same time elected as the union members' representatives. This was different from the Autoco case in which the branch union committee members (and the division representatives) were not necessarily the same as the union members' representatives. Our interviews with workers revealed that different departments deployed different election methods at this level. For example, in

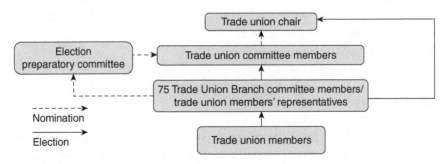

Figure 11.3 The union elections in Eleco in 2012

some departments workers nominated the candidates, whereas in others the managers designated the candidates (Interviews with workers, 22 November 2012). According to a newspaper report, 65 out of the 75 (87 per cent) union members' representatives were rank-and-file workers (Liaowang 2012). The second stage of the elections selected the 11 union executive committee members. The 75 union members' representatives first elected 14 candidates from among themselves for the union executive committee. The trade union preparatory committee, which had an unclear composition, was given the power to approve these candidates (Economic Observer Daily 2012). Once the candidates were approved, the union members' representatives elected 11 of the 14 to be union executive committee members. In other words, only the 75 union members' representatives, out of the 850 workers in Eleco, had the right to nominate candidates and vote in the election of union executive committee members. According to our interviews with workers, among the 11 newly elected officials, only one was a rank-and-file worker; the others were department heads, section managers (*ke zhang*), team leaders (*zu zhang*), and so forth. The third stage of the process was to elect the union chair and vice chair. The 11 elected executive committee members elected among themselves three candidates for the union chair and vice-chair, and then the 75 union members' representatives voted for their preferred candidate. In this stage, the right of nomination was restricted to an even smaller number of people. After numerous rounds of voting, a new chair, who was the section head of the production department, was elected (Nanfang Daily June 2012).

A number of features of the Eleco elections deserve our critical attention. First, as in the Autoco case, the entire election process was not direct, but rather highly cumbersome. Furthermore, the elections were only quasi-democratic. The higher the level of the positions being filled, the more exclusive was the election process and the fewer the number of workers who had the right to nominate and vote in the election. Moreover, the higher the position within the union structure, the lower the number of the rank-and-file workers who were elected. This indirect election system had a strong filtering mechanism that not only excluded the rank-and-file workers from the top positions, but also excluded them from nominating and voting for candidates for the higher positions. However, this election system allowed most workers to vote at the lowest level of the union elections giving them a minimal sense of control. This type of indirect election system reflects the reservations that the city-, provincial-, and national-level unions have about direct democratic elections; they are afraid that they will lose control over the workplace unions if workers directly elect the union chair because workers may nominate or elect somebody who is deemed 'untrustworthy' by the higher-level unions.

The second issue that should draw our attention is the role of the higher-level trade unions in these elections. As in the case of Autoco, their influence was conspicuous in Eleco. The elections were initiated and guided by the SZFTU, and the district- and town-level trade unions (China Business Media 2012, Southern Metropolis Daily 2012 b, Shenzhen Overseas Chinese News 2012). The electoral procedures were designed by the SZFTU (interview with a labour scholar, 10 October 2012). They gave 'guidance' to the last chair on how to carry out the elections and sent officials to attend the elections (Longang District Trade Union 2012). Their involvement was not restricted to procedural issues; they were also involved in matters of real significance. They kept a tight grip over the nomination of candidates, as revealed by the then vice president from the GDFTU in a newspaper interview on the Eleco elections:

No matter what elections method is used, the most critical thing lies on the nomination and confirmation of the candidates; this is the most fundamental procedure ... Candidates should not be casually proposed by any individuals or organisations; instead they should be proposed by workers on the condition that they are approved by the higher-level trade unions. (Nanfang Daily June 2012)

This demonstrates that the higher-level unions want to be gatekeepers. Only candidates who were deemed trustworthy and qualified in the eyes of the government apparatus were allowed to run in elections. In fact, according to Measures on Trade Union Chairman (article 9), the higher-level trade unions and enterprise party branches are required to review the candidates for the enterprise union chair and readjust those candidates who are not qualified. Under the system of democratic centralism, it is stated clearly that the lower-level unions must obey the higher-level unions (Constitution of the Chinese Trade Unions article 9). The higher-level unions should guide the enterprise union elections (Trade Union Law article 11; Measures on Trade Union Chairman article 4) and all of the elected officials and candidates for union chair should be subject to the approval of higher-level unions and the enterprise party branch (Provisions on Trade Unions article 11 & 24; Measures on Trade Union Chairman article 11). In other words, on the surface, workers or their representatives have been given the right to vote, but in fact they are only allowed to fly within the cage, so to speak.

The third issue that needs to be considered is the action of the company. As explained earlier, in some departments the managers selected the candidates who would run in the election of the union members' representatives; this was certainly an improper managerial manipulation. In addition, it was reported that after the union elections a number of strike activists were removed from their original job positions. Some workers regarded this as revenge by the company. The Eleco trade union tried to seek help from the SZFTU but did not get a positive response. The SZFTU told the trade union that 'this is about the development needs of the enterprise and the trade union should not intervene' (China Fortune 2012). It was obvious that although the company had agreed to hold the union elections, it was far from tolerant of strike activists. The suspected revenge on the strike activists and the tacit consent given by the SZFTU has overshadowed the future development of the fledgling trade union.

The fourth issue is that the current indirect election system not only deprives the majority of workers of the chance to elect the top governing body of their own organization, it has also defeated its original purpose of making the unions more legitimate and representative. Most of the workers we interviewed participated in the elections of the union members' representatives and they had positive comments about those elections and how they were conducted. However, they knew little about the elections of the union committee members and chair, as they were not union members' representatives and could not cast a vote. Therefore, these elections were a black box to most workers. Some workers remarked that they did not know what the union executive committee members were doing and found them irrelevant to the workers. Unless the intention was to create such a gap between the union and its members, the election system should be made more inclusive and transparent.

Similar to the case of Autoco, the newly elected enterprise trade union in Eleco failed to advance workers' interests and thus provoked workers to undertake extra-trade union actions to safeguard their own well-being. On 28 Feb 2013, 106 Eleco union members signed a joint letter requesting the recall of the newly elected chair from office (interview with workers, 7, 8, 10, and 11 March 2013; Guangzhou Daily 2013; Yangcheng Evening News 2013). These Eleco workers were dissatisfied with the chair because he did not support workers who had labour disputes related to their labour contracts. According to the Labour Contract Law, once workers have completed two consecutive fixed-term contracts, employers should offer them a permanent contract. However, Eleco did not renew the contract of 22 workers who had finished two contractual terms; instead it offered them a compensation amount to their monthly salary times their total years of service, and asked them to sign a settlement agreement. After signing the agreement, the workers found out that the compensation offered by Eleco was just half of the legal requirement. Workers wrote in their letter to the public that they had sought help from the enterprise union numerous times, but 'the union did not take any measures, and thus we were deceived by the company, and signed the settlement agreement ... we asked the union to intervene in the dispute afterwards; it did not offer any help and the chair even kicked us out of the union office'. The company renewed the contracts of another 13 workers and offered them a pay rise of 10 per cent in 'the letter of intent on renewing the labour contract'. However, the new contract the company later offered these workers did not contain the pay rise. A joint letter signed by 106 workers said that in this case the union chair did not defend workers' interests, but rather persuaded the 13 workers to accept the revised contract.

Eleco workers' request to recall the enterprise union chair was not approved by the enterprise trade union committee, which has been given the right by the Trade Union Laws to make decisions concerning the recall request (Chinese workers 2013). And a labour scholar told us that the SZFTU found the workers' recall request irrational and unreasonable. Because of the hindrance created by the enterprise- and city-level unions, the recall request was turned down. This incident has two implications for the implementation of democratic trade unionism in China. First, it again illustrates that if 'direct elections' are largely a formality and the newly elected unions cannot prioritize workers' interests over the concerns of the party-state and business interests, or be truly accountable to workers, then aggrieved workers are likely to defend their own interests through extra-trade union actions. Second, workers taking action to recall an enterprise trade union chair had not been common in China; thus Eleco workers' recall request reflected the growing trade union consciousness of the Chinese workers. However, their assertion of the associational rights and their attempt to make their trade unions accountable to them has met resistance from the quasi-democratic enterprise union and the higher-level unions that have been incorporated into the party-state.

Conclusion

As elaborated, workers' strike is one of the crucial driving forces for the current wave of union elections in Guangdong. To alleviate the labour unrest that has increasingly targeted the unions' lack of representativeness, the party-state and the ACFTU must not only grant economic concessions to workers, but also loosen their grip on unions and promote 'direct' and 'democratic' elections at the enterprise level. Workers' strikes have not only led to elections in the companies where the strikes have occurred, they have also compelled the Shenzhen and Guangdong unions to initiate elections in companies where no strike has been staged.

Coming back to our conceptual reflection of the changing labour regime in China, obviously neither Burawoy's (1985) concepts of market despotism, bureaucratic despotism, or hegemony nor Lee's (1998) concept of 'localistic despotism' are able to grasp the conditions of factory regimes in China.

Burawoy (1979: 179) highlights that there are two 'motor[s] of change': 'class struggle' and 'capitalist competition' in the transition of a labour regime in capitalism. The deepening of capitalist competition since China's entry into the WTO is one of the main factors contributing to the transformation of workplace relations in recent years. Both enterprises and local states competed for workers with other enterprises or cities under the phenomenon of 'the shortage of labour' (C. Chan, 2010). Therefore, 'capitalist competition' remains a valid factor to explain the transformation of the labour regime in globalized China. Burawoy (1979: 179) adopted a narrow definition for 'class struggle' as 'between the organized representatives of capital and labour – namely management and union'. In China, the official trade union, especially at the workplace and the local levels, so far does not represent workers in the same way that its Western counterparts do. Although direct elections have been introduced into some enterprises as we have elaborated in this chapter, the elections are not fully democratic and have created conflict between trade union leaders and rank-and-file members. While internal conflicts within unions exist in democratic capitalism (Hyman, 1975), the collusion between elected trade union leaders and the state or the management in China has weakened their function of representing workers. The associational power of the Chinese workplace trade union (Wright, 2000) is also hindered by the lack of rights to strike and independent organization.

Burawoy (1979) highlights three levels of 'class struggle': economic, political, and ideological. For him, economic and political struggles 'reshape or maintain the distribution of economic rewards ... and the relations in production' respectively, while ideological struggles 'take us beyond capitalism' (Burawoy, 1979: 177, 179). Ideological struggle of workers was not witnessed in our case studies and their political struggle was not very potent, but Chinese workers' struggle has exerted a sound impact on the policies of local authorities, the reform of trade unions, and the labour legislation made by the central government. All these have in turn reshaped 'the distribution of economic rewards'. To underline the specificity of class struggle in post-socialist China, Chan (2010) calls it 'class struggle without class organization'. The limitation of this form of class struggle is that it is more effective with regard to the economic aspect of effort bargaining around the issue of wages, but less effective on political struggles related to 'the relations in production' (Burawoy, 1979: 179). A proactive strategy of gaining greater control or autonomy in production was absent, not to mention an internal labour market and internal state that the post-war US workers achieved through trade union's participation in collective bargaining (Burawoy, 1979). In the CLB's report mentioned at the beginning, a worker, Tan, said this:

> I have not been promoted and my salary has remained stagnant since 2013. Many of my colleagues think that the company is punishing me for my involvement in the strike. I think it is a clear message telling me to back off.

It further accounts for why a 'contested despotic' labour regime has not advanced into 'hegemony', although a legal framework for this transition is available (C. Chan, 2010). Direct trade union elections and collective bargaining without freedom of association (Chan and Hui, 2014) are the new strategies that the state and management have adopted to control workers and dampen their militancy (Hyman, 1987). To what extent will workers be tamed by this new strategy? What is the new form of resistance staged by labour? These questions are to be examined in the future.

List of Abbreviations

Name	Abbreviation
All-China Federation of Trade Unions	ACFTU
Chinese Communist Party	CCP
Guangdong Federation of Trade Unions	GDFTU
Guangzhou Federation of Trade Unions	GZFTU
Measures on the Election of Enterprise Trade Union Chairman	Measures on Trade Union Chairman
Provisions on the Work of Enterprise Trade Unions	Provisions on Trade Unions
Shenzhen Federation of Trade Unions	SZFTU

Notes

1 This chapter is based on Hui, E. S. I. & Chan, C. K. C. (2015) 'Beyond the Union-Centred Approach: A Critical Evaluation of Recent Trade Union Elections in China'. *British Journal of Industrial Relations*, 53(3), 601–627. The approach of understanding the Chinese changing labour regime has been developed in Chan's book (2010). The authors would like to thank the Research Grants Council (RGC) of Hong Kong (project no.: CityU 140313), Chiang Ching-kuo Foundation for International Scholar Exchange, and the College of Liberal Arts and Social Sciences of the City University of Hong Kong for their financial support to this research.

2 See http://www.clb.org.hk/en/content/five-years-nanhai-honda-workers-want-more-their-trade-union-0. Accessed on 30 May 2015.

3 Although we argue that a new wave of trade union elections in Guangdong is emerging, we are well aware that many company trade unions officials are still not democratically elected. In fact, some workers' attempts to push for elections have met with resistance from the higher-level trade unions or their employers (see, for example, China Fortune 2012, iSun Affairs 2012).

REFERENCES

ACFTU (2010) *Further Strengthen the Building of Workplace Trade Unions and Give Them Full Play [jinyibu jiaqiang qiye gonghui jianshe congfen fahui qiye gonghuii zouyong]*. China: ACFTU.

Burawoy, M. (1979) *Manufacturing Consent: Changes in the Labor Process Under Monopoly Capitalism*. Chicago: The University of Chicago Press.

Burawoy, M. (1985) *The Politics of Production*. London: Verso.

Chan, A. (2001) *Chinese Workers under Assault*. Armonk, N.Y.: M.E. Sharpe.

Chan, A. (2011) Strikes in China's Export Industries in Comparative Perspective. *China Journal, 65*, 27–52.

Chan, C. K. C. (2010) *The Challenge of Labour in China: Strikes and the Changing Labour Regime in Global Factories*. New York/London: Routledge.

Chan, C. K. C., & Hui, S.-I. E. (2012) The Dynamics and Dilemma of Workplace Trade Union Reform in China: The Case of the Honda Workers' Strike. *Journal of Industrial Relations, 54*, 653–668.

Chan, C. K. C., & Hui, S.-I. E. (2014) The Development of Collective Bargaining in China: From 'Collective Bargaining by Riot' to 'Party State-led Wage Bargaining' *China Quarterly* (217), 221–242.

▶

Chang, K. (2013) The transformation of labour relations into a collective form and the betterment of the government's labour policies (*laodong guanxi de jitizhuanxing yu zhengfu laogong zhengce de wanshang*) *China Social Sciences* (*zhongguo shehui kexue*) 6, 91–108 [In Chinese]

China Fortune 2012. After the direct elections of trade unions, http://money.eastmoney.com/news/1583,20120918251427566.html (accessed 7 June 2013).

Chinese Workers 2013 http://www.chineseworkers.com.cn/_d276227433.htm. (Accessed 2 January 2014)

Clarke, S., Lee, C. H., & Li, Q. (2004) Collective Consultation and Industrial Relations in China. *British Journal of Industrial Relations, 42*(2), 235–254.

CLB (China Labour Bulletin) 2013 http://www.clb.org.hk/schi/content/clb%E4%B8%93%E5%AE%B6%E7%82%B9%E8%AF%84%E5%8D%97%E6%B5%B7%E6%9C%AC%E7%94%B0%E5%9C%A8%E9%9B%86%E4%BD%93%E8%B0%88%E5%88%A4%E8%BF%87%E7%A8%8B%E4%B8%AD%E5%8F%91%E7%94%9F%E7%9A%84%E5%81%9C%E5%B7%A5%E4%BA%8B%E4%BB%B6. (Accessed 10 December 2015)

CLB (China Labour Bulletin) 2015 http://www.clb.org.hk/en/content/five-years-nanhai-honda-workers-want-more-their-trade-union-0. (Accessed 10 December 2015)

Economic Observer Daily 2012. Elections of enterprise trade unions in Shenzhenfollow legal regulations. http://finance.sina.com.cn/roll/20120601/224012205745.shtml (accessed 18 June 2013)

Friedman, E. (2013) Insurgency and Institutionalization: The Polanyian Counter-movement and Chinese Labor Politics. *Theory and Society*. 42(3):295–327.

GDFTU 2012 http://www.gdftu.org.cn/ghyw/mzgl/201208/t20120815_308215.htm. (Accessed 10 November 2012)

GDFTU 2012b http://www.gdftu.org.cn/zghd/xxlgjy/lgld/201209/t20120912_317813.htm. 2012-09-12. (Accessed 10 October 2012)

Guangzhou Daily, 1 March 2013 http://gzdaily.dayoo.com/html/2013-03/01/content_2165723.htm. (Accessed 10 December 2015)

Hui, E.S.I. & Chan, C. K. C. (forthcoming) 'Beyond the Union-Centred Approach: A Critical Evaluation of Recent Trade Union Elections in China'. *British Journal of Industrial Relations*. Article first published online: 1 DEC 2014 DOI: 10.1111/bjir.12111.

Hyman, R. (1975) *Industrial relations: a Marxist introduction* London: Macmillan.

Hyman, R. (1987) Strategy or structure? Capital, labour and control. *Work, Employment & Society, 1*(1), 25–55.

iSun Affairs, 18 June 2012 http://www.isunaffairs.com/?p=7263. (Accessed 20 July 2012)

Jingbao, 18 June 2012 http://news.sohu.com/20120618/n345877143.shtml. (Accessed 10 December 2015)

Lau, R. (2012) Restructuring of the Honda Auto Parts Union in Guongdong, China: A 2-year Assessment of the 2010 Strike. *WorkingUSA: The Journal of Labor and Society 1089–7011 Volume December pp. 15*, 497–515.

Lee, C. K. (1998) *Gender and the South China Miracle: Two Worlds of Factory Women*. Berkley: University of California Press.

▶

Liaowang, 2 June 2012 http://news.xinhuanet.com/local/2012-06/02/c_123226461
.htm. (Accessed 30 August 2012)

Littler, C. R. (1990) The labour process debate: a theoretical review 1974–1988.
Labour process theory, 46–94.

Littler, C. R., & Salaman, G. (1982) Bravermania and beyond: recent theories of
the labour process. *Sociology*, *16*(2), 251–269.

Longgang District Trade Unions, 9 Sept 2012 http://www.lgzgh.org/detail.
aspx?cid=8318. (Accessed 21 December 2012)

Nanfang Daily, 2012b, 25 May 2012 http://epaper.nfdaily.cn/html/2012-05/25/
content_7087709.htm. (Accessed 23 July 2012)

Nanfang Daily, 5 June 2012 http://epaper.nfdaily.cn/html/2012-06/05/con-
tent_7090697.htm. (Accessed 21 December 2012)

Nanfang Daily 2012c, 2 August 2012 http://www.21cbh.com/2012/
nfrb_802/240451.html. (Accessed 23 July 2012)

Nanfang Gongbao, 2 April 2011 http://www.nfgb.com.cn/NewsContent.
aspx?id=16571. (Accessed 3 May 2012)

Shenzhen Overseas Chinese News, 10 April 2012 http://www.sz-qb.com/
html/2012-04/10/content_36443.htm. (Accessed 10 December 2015)

Southern Metropolis Daily, 3 April 2012 http://news.sina.com.cn/c/2012-04-
03/081124217070.shtml. (Accessed 10 December 2015)

Southern Metropolis Daily, 2012b, 6 April 2012 http://news.sina.com.cn/c/2012-
04-06/093424229620.shtml (Accessed 10 December 2015)

Taylor, B., & Li, Q. (2007) Is the ACFTU a Union and Does it Matter? *Journal of
Industrial Relations*, *49*, 701–715.

Thompson, P., & Van den Broek, D. (2010) Managerial control and workplace
regimes: an introduction. *Work, Employment & Society*, *24*(3), 1–12.

Wright, E. O. (2000) Working-Class Power, the Capitalist-class Interests, and Class
Compromise. *American Journal of Sociology, 104*(4), 957–1002.

Yangcheng Evening News, 3 July 2010 http://www.ycwb.com/ePaper/ycwb/
html/2010-07/03/content_867517.htm. (Accessed 9 August 2010)

Yangcheng Evening News, 1 March 2013 http://bbs.hangzhou.com.cn/
thread-9677278-1-1.html. (Accessed 10 December 2015)

Zhongguo Jingying Bao 8 June 2012 China Business Media. http://biz.cb.com.
cn/12716612/20120608/384366.html (Accessed 19 August 2012)

Strikes and Labour Activism

A Pathway to a Vital Labour Movement in China? A Case Study of a Union-Led Protest against Walmart

12

Chunyun Li and Mingwei Liu

Introduction

In 2006, all Walmart stores in China became unionized, which came as a big surprise to the international labour community. However, except for the first batch of several store unions which were established by the All-China Federation of Trade Unions (ACFTU) through the direct mobilization of workers, the vast majority were set up jointly between Walmart and the ACFTU with limited or nominal involvement of workers. This pattern of union organizing, according to Liu (2010), tends to result in management-controlled or co-opted workplace unions, which indeed was supported by later empirical studies (Chan, 2011; He and Xie, 2011).

Yet, in 2014, a union in a Walmart store in Changde City, Hunan Province (Changde store hereafter), led a 97-day protest against Walmart's policy of store closure, the longest labour protest in China in the past decade. It came as an even bigger surprise as Chinese unions are generally not allowed to lead collective actions. Why did a management-co-opted union choose to confront the employer in such a radical way? How did the union sustain the protest? What were the responses of the state and the ACFTU? And what are the implications for the future development of Chinese trade unions and the labour movement? This chapter attempts to address these questions through an in-depth analysis of this unique case.

Interest in Chinese trade unions has been increasing in the past decade. Despite its growing membership, collective contract coverage, and influence in labour legislation, a critical challenge confronting the ACFTU has been the impotency of its branches in the workplace (Liu et al., 2011). Incapable or malfunctioning workplace unions, the ACFTU's main interface with workers, directly lead to the ACFTU's illegitimacy and obscurity among workers. Prior efforts of the ACFTU to revitalize workplace unions, for example direct election of workplace union committees and professionalization of union staff, have largely failed due to the ACFTU's various structural constraints (Howell, 2008; Liu et al., 2011; Pringle, 2011). The ACFTU has almost never relied on rank-and-file mobilization as a source of power (Liu et al., 2011, p. 294) and the organizational logic of Chinese unions remains that of the Party-state (Friedman, 2014a, p. 30).

As such, the dominant view is that there is no organized labour movement in China (Blecher, 2002; Elfstrom and Kuruvilla, 2014; Chen, 2015). Without breaking away from the Party, Chinese trade unions are unlikely to transform into genuine representatives of workers. However, Clarke and Pringle (2009) challenge this view by comparing trade unions in China, Vietnam, and Russia. They argue that it is not so much the Party leadership as the inertia of the trade union apparatus and the dependence of primary union organizations on management that prevent the transformation of unions. Further, several scholars (e.g. Liu, 2010; Liu et al., 2011; Pringle, 2011) examine a pathway for the transformation of Chinese trade unions under the existing political regime, that is, through gradual reforms of the regional federations of trade unions (FTUs). These scholars find that regional FTUs have become the focus of change in the hierarchy of the ACFTU and attribute the progressive changes of some regional FTUs to their administrative power granted by the Party-state and capable, pro-labour union leaders. However, taking a dialectic view, we contend that the strength of regional FTUs may also be their weakness as dependence on the Party-state may impose great constraints on their reforms and thus fundamentally prevent the unions' transformation. Conversely, the weakness of workplace unions – that is, their lack of administrative power or support from the Party-state – may, under some circumstances, increase their representative potential relative to that of regional FTUs.

In this chapter, we argue for another potential pathway to a vital labour movement in China that consists of two interconnected parts: the transformation of workplace unions into rank-and-file representatives and civil society actors' support of workplace unions. Despite being controlled or co-opted by management or the Party-state, workplace unions may possibly transform into genuine representatives of workers when employer policies greatly affect all of the employees including the union leaders. Of course, employers may continue to buy off union leaders by treating them differently from rank-and-file workers, which is typical in the Chinese context. Yet the strategy of 'divide and conquer' may not always work for two reasons. First, under some circumstances such as corporate restructuring, particularly corporate relocation and closure, the interests of union leaders (and low- and mid-level managers) may still be significantly affected even with better treatment than that of rank-and-file workers. In fact, managers, some of whom are union leaders, have played a critical role in many strikes in China (Harney and Ruwitch, 2014). A notable example is the workplace union-led protest against Kraft Foods Inc. for its relocation of China headquarters from Beijing to Shanghai in 2008 (Shen, 2008). Second, workplace union leaders may still choose to side with rank-and-file workers, though this may be very rare. The possibility of transformation may be even heightened if workplace unions have been elected more or less democratically which may significantly improve the workers' awareness of unions and the unions' accountability to their members. Further, the transformed workplace unions may possibly organize and lead workers' collective actions or strikes. Although strikes are still sensitive and sometimes suppressed by the government, no Chinese law clearly forbids workplace unions or workers from engaging in industrial actions to protect their rights and interest.

The transformed workplace unions have two notable advantages in developing a labour movement in the Chinese context. First, as grassroots unions established following the legal procedures and ACFTU rules, they enjoy institutional legitimacy in representing workers which various informal worker organizations and labour non-governmental organizations (NGOs) sorely lack. Second, largely outside the Party-state's administration system, they have higher operational autonomy from the Party-state than regional FTUs. However, the transformed workplace unions may lack bargaining power due to the weak workplace and marketplace power of Chinese workers (Lee, 2007). Moreover, given the enterprise-based nature of workplace unions, it is difficult to diffuse such transformation to other workplaces or to link the transformed unions with each other. Therefore it is necessary for workplace unions to gain support from civil society actors such as labour NGO staff, lawyers, and scholars who can provide technical, financial, or network resources for the unions' struggle and help link the otherwise fragmented labour movements. With the help of social media, these civil society actors may form informal groups which could magnify their impacts. The major obstacle for this pathway, however, is the suppression of transformed workplace unions and civil society groups by various levels of FTUs and the Party-state. Nonetheless, we contend that this pathway, by integrating the actions of institutionalized workplace unions with civil society activism, has a potential to develop a vital labour movement in China.

This study is based mainly on participatory observation of this union-led protest and interviews with union officials and workers in the Walmart Changde store and civil society actors involved in this protest. We visited the store in March 2014, met three store union committee members and a worker at a workshop in April, and followed the discussions and events in the workers' online discussion group. In addition, we draw on secondary data from various sources including the store union's blog, a worker's diary, and news reports.

Antecedents of Union Revitalization

Critical challenges facing trade unions in the developed world and some unions' renewal practices have prompted intensive research on union revitalization since the mid-1990s (e.g., Fosh, 1993; Clawson and Clawson, 1999; Voss and Sherman, 2000; Hurd et al., 2003; Frege and Kelly, 2004; Connolly, 2012; Serrano, 2014). Defined as various attempts to tackle and potentially reverse problems confronting union movements (Frege and Kelly, 2003, p. 9), union revitalization means many different things for scholars and practitioners. Some scholars have identified six prominent union renewal strategies in major developed countries: union organizing, organizational restructuring, coalition building, labour-management partnership, political action, and international links (Frege and Kelly, 2003, p. 9; Hurd et al., 2003). For some other scholars, revitalization involves member participation and mobilization, internal union democracy, and direct action circumventing institutional procedures (Fosh, 1993; Clawson and Clawson, 1999; Voss and Sherman, 2000). Studies on non-Western countries underline how particular forms and internal dynamics of union renewal vary historically and in different socio-political contexts (Ost, 2002; von Holdt, 2002; Dibben, 2010; Lee and Trappmann, 2014). For instance, Ost (2002) shows that the often prescribed social movement unionism (e.g., embracing social justice goals and coalition building), which is popular in the US context, has been detrimental to labour in Eastern Europe, and that economic unionism or serving the members has helped revive some unions in the post-communist context. Focusing on emerging economies, Dibben's (2010) study of union renewal in Mozambique emphasizes improvement in employment rights and engagement with the informal sector.

An increasing number of scholars (e.g., Hyman, 2004; Connally, 2012; Serrano, 2014; Engeman, 2015) advocate an understanding of union revitalization as regenerative initiatives along two interwoven dimensions, that is, an institutional dimension and a movement dimension. Trade unions are characterized by a constant tension between a movement dimension that features social combat or direct action on one hand, and an institutional dimension that features participation in industrial relations machinery and negotiation of order on the other (Hyman, 2001, p. 61; von Holdt, 2002, p. 298; Fantasia and Stepan-Norris, 2004, p. 557). While institutional practices work by bringing the weights of legal rules, regulations, and the 'proper channels' down on an opponent, movements or extra-institutional tactics compel by the use or threat of disruption and the circumvention of prescribed channels (Fantasia and Stepan-Norris, 2004, p. 558). The success of organized labour depends on a delicate balance and synergy between institutional and movement dimensions, and this balance differs in different situations (Heckscher, 2006, p. 316). A focus on the interaction between continuous movement and institutionalization and their manifested forms sheds light on different union renewal initiatives in changing situations (von Holdt, 2002, p. 298; Serrano, 2014, p. 234).

There is a body of research on the antecedents of union revitalization (Frege and Kelly, 2003; Heery, 2005). Drawing on the social movement literature, Frege and Kelly (2003) elaborate a general framework identifying five predictive variables on union revitalization strategies: social and economic change, institutional context such as the political system and industrial relations regulations, state and employer strategies, union structure, and framing processes. In the British context, Heery (2005) specifies six potential factors pressing for regenerative union change: three internal push factors, rank-and-file activism, national union leadership, or specialist change agents within particular unions; and three external pulling factors: political opportunity, receptive employers, or active civil society groups. Particular to the revitalization of the American labour movement, strategic union innovation is driven by top-down influence from national or international union support, bottom-up activism from active local leadership, or outside influence from activists with non-union activism backgrounds (Voss and Sherman, 2000; Hurd et al., 2003).

In general these studies emphasize the critical role of actors in pressuring for or driving union revitalization. These change agents range from grassroots unions and national unions, to non-union actors including government, employers, and civil society groups such as community, faith, identity, advocacy, welfare, and campaigning organizations working on various issues (Frege et al., 2004). Moreover, there is an emerging consensus that effective integration of movement and institutional elements, or more specifically, coalitions between two types of change agents, that is, social movement activists or organizations and trade unions, is key for union revitalization in contemporary capitalism.

Chinese Unions in Motion? Potential Change Agents and Forms

Who are the potential change agents of the Chinese labour movement? As a state-assigned monopoly of worker representation, the ACFTU has a double identity of being a state apparatus and a labour organization, although the later representative function is largely incapacitated by the state (Chen, 2003). Responding to various internal crises and external pressures, the ACFTU at different levels (i.e., national, regional [provincial, municipal, district], and workplace) has engaged in different activities and experienced varying degrees of change since 2000 (Liu at al., 2011). At the top of the pyramidal organization, the national ACFTU wields the highest political power with its head joining the political Politburo; but it is more conservative (keeping to the tight Party-state control) than some progressive regional FTUs (Friedman, 2014a). At the regional level, various union innovations such as the establishment of sectoral unions, sectoral collective consultation, and trade union legal-aid centres have received increasing attention (Friedman, 2014b; Pringle, 2011; Liu, 2010; Chen, 2004). The effects of these innovations, however, have been mixed to date. Even for those with initial success, the sustainability is questionable. At the workplace level, recent changes to energize workplace unions (e.g., direct union elections) have been found to be insufficient (Howell, 2008; Pringle, 2011, p. 162). As a result, workplace unions are still widely viewed as the weakest link of the ACFTU.

However, we argue that, in the hierarchy of the ACFTU, workplace unions are most likely to engage in 'regenerative' initiatives in the near future, although support from upper-level unions is important for the success and sustainability of these initiatives. There is a rupture between FTUs at various levels and workplace unions owing to different organizational logics. FTU officials are selected from civil servants, paid by government, and can change jobs across FTUs, Party, and government agencies; while workplace union officials are usually selected by employers or workplace Party committees from workers (most often managerial workers), paid by employers, and can hardly take a position in FTUs,

Party, or government agencies. This organizational rupture brews the potential of workplace unions to become a major agent of change in the Chinese labour movement.

First, it is very difficult for FTUs or the Party-state to influence the operation of workplace unions which are outside the government administration system. Without the status of government officials or civil servants, workplace union leaders, even if they are Party members (which is common in state-owned enterprises and has become increasingly common in the private sector), are essentially workers who are more likely to represent the interests of workers (including themselves) than that of the Party-state. Although they are often controlled or co-opted by their employers, workplace union leaders may form solidarity with their fellow workers and even lead collective action when their own interest is seriously affected by employer policies. Second, compared to FTUs, workplace unions' proximity to workers means that they are more likely to encounter direct pressure from workers for change and that they have a higher potential to successfully mobilize workers. This may be particularly true if the workplace unions are established in a more or less democratic way. Finally, workplace unions enjoy the legitimacy of worker representation which, through various labour and trade union laws and regulations, grants legal or institutional support to a wide range of union activities such as collective consultation, dispute resolution, and representing workers in work stoppages. Such legitimacy can help transformed workplace unions defend against employers or government, a critically important factor for developing a sustainable labour movement in the Chinese context.

Workplace unions' activism may take several forms. They may take means within institutional boundaries to advance workers' rights and interests, including leveraging the voice function of workplace unions, that is, raising workplace issues or workers' demands to management directly or through collective consultation; mobilizing legal rules or channels, for example reporting workplace issues to government labour agencies or helping workers fight legal battles; and resorting to FTUs who may compel management with their administrative or persuasive power. Transgressing institutional boundaries, workplace unions may also mobilize rank-and-file workers for collective action or ally with civil society groups. Such transgressions have been extremely rare in China. However, drawing on the resource-based view of union action which suggests that unions engage in various activities to access resources needed for their purposes (Frege et al., 2004), we argue that activated workplace unions may engage in extra-institutional activities when they lack institutional support or effective institutional means to reach their goals.

A related potential agent of change in the Chinese labour movement are civil society groups or organizations, particularly labour NGOs. Prior research generally arrives at pessimistic conclusions regarding the impacts of civil society groups on the Chinese labour movement. For instance, labour NGOs are found to shepherd individual worker grievances into legal channels and shun workers' collective action (Lee and Shen, 2011), let alone stimulating independent unionism or political change in China (Franceschini, 2014). However, several labour NGOs have begun mobilizing workers and promoting collective bargaining over the past few years. In a few cases they helped workers obtain their pension contribution arrears and overtime pay through collective petitions and strikes (China Labour Bulletin, 2014). These solidarity-building-oriented labour NGOs also coordinate several online and offline networks linking labour activists across China including labour lawyers, labour NGO staff, worker activists, and scholars. Thanks to their technical, financial, and network resources, these informal groups of labour activists not only provide great support to the transformed workplace unions, which often have poor resources and weak bargaining power, but also help diffuse and link workers' action across workplaces. Therefore, the alliance of the two agents of change, that is, workplace unions and civil society groups, has the potential to develop an energized labour movement in China.

However, the pathway identified above may be blocked by the suppression of the two agents of change by the Party-state. Neither the transformed workplace unions nor civil society groups aim to form worker organizations independent from the ACFTU or challenge the ruling of the Party-state. Instead, they target employers for workplace justice by utilizing the existing organization (i.e. workplace unions), channels (e.g. collective bargaining), and workers' own bargaining power backed up by their collective actions, which may help promote industrial peace in the long run. However, presently the Party-state seems to be obsessed with short-term social stability and has a deep fear of any social organizations out of its control. As such, the Party-state has been very cautious of the development of workplace unions and kept a close eye on labour NGOs and activist groups. To serve the Party-state, FTUs tend to draw red lines for transformed workplace unions aiming to prevent any collective action of workers. Yet, given the rupture between FTUs and workplace unions, the constraints imposed by FTUs on workplace union activities may be challenged or even ignored by the transformed workplace unions. The threats and repression of government, however, are severe, which may dissolve the transformed workplace unions and greatly weaken labour NGOs. The viability of the above identified pathway for a vital Chinese labour movement, therefore, to a large extent depends on the openness of the political space for economic-interest-centred labour activism.

Below we will illustrate our argument with the case of a union-led protest against Walmart.

A Union-Led Protest in the Walmart Changde Store

Walmart opened its first store in China in 1996. After gradual development in the initial years, Walmart accelerated its expansion in 2008 through acquisitions and opening new stores. On average, 38 new stores were opened yearly between 2009 and 2013. However, without rigorous deliberation, some new stores failed to generate profit for Walmart (Xie, 2014). The new Walmart China president and CEO, who took charge in 2012, re-oriented the expansion strategy to include improving the profitability of existing stores and closing 9 per cent of poorly-performing stores. The Changde store, which had been running deficits since its opening in January 2009, was one of the poorly-performing stores to be closed.

The main point of contention between Walmart and its Changde store workers revolved around the way the store's closure was handled. On March 5, 2014, Walmart suddenly and unilaterally announced that the Changde store would be shut down on March 19 and posted their provisions of worker settlement: workers either agreeing to be relocated to stores in other regions or accepting the legally defined severance pay, that is, [N years of service +1] months' salary. However, Walmart's application of the legally defined [N+1] severance pay was contended by the store workers who believed that because Walmart failed to provide the mandatory one-month notice of layoffs to the store union, another punitive legal standard, that is, 2 [N+1] severance pay should be applied. In addition, Walmart brought in substitutes to replace the workers immediately after the announcement, which further incited the anger of many workers. Indignant at the store's abrupt closure, 120 workers staged a protest outside the store in the afternoon with banners saying 'Firmly Resist Walmart's Non-legal Store Closure' and 'We Want Jobs; We Want to Live'. Later Walmart announced that it would reward an extra half months' salary to the workers accepting its settlement before March 19. As a result, 50 workers accepted the settlement package by March 19. The rest continued to protest until mid-June, after which the dispute evolved into a year-long legal fight. This case is unique in many ways. The most prominent feature is that the protest was led by a workplace union which transformed into a genuinely representative union.

The transformation of the store union

The Walmart Changde store union was established in 2009 through a 'democratic election'. According to the store union chair Mr Huang, 'the general manager of this store is relatively open-minded (*kai ming*) and willing to go through a public [union] election' (Interview, March 18, 2014). The elections were relatively democratic – all of the workers voted unanimously to elect nine union committee members who then elected the union chair and vice chair. There was no obvious intervention of the top management in the election process, but departmental managers were eligible for union positions. Because of their daily publicity among ordinary workers and higher capability, managers were often elected into the union committee. For instance, in the 2013 election, the elected union committee comprised of mainly managers; the union chair (Mr Huang) who won the votes of all of the workers was an administrative manager in charge of customer complaints and public relations; and the vice chair was an asset protection manager.

The store union performed its dual functioning role (i.e. promoting production and protecting worker interests) quite well before the 2014 protest. Because the Changde store had been running a deficit for several years, Mr Huang thought that it was important to help the store improve efficiency and overcome economic difficulties so that jobs could be protected. To him, many workers stayed in Walmart with low wages simply because they had a conviction that a giant corporation like Walmart would guarantee job security. In addition, with the union funds contributed by Walmart (about 3,000 RMB per month), the store union actively engaged in a number of welfare activities such as providing holiday benefit and organizing outdoor sports and entertainment. It had also coordinated a social donation campaign for a worker who passed away from leukaemia. Finally, the store union participated in the annual collective wage consultation initiated by Walmart under the ACFTU's pressure in 2008. Given the store's operational deficits, Huang's consultation team had never asked for a high wage raise during the consultations. Yet, Huang did show a sense of accountability to the workers which is very unusual for most Chinese workplace union chairs (Chen, 2009; Liu and Li, 2014). For instance, in 2013, the store union asked for a 5 per cent wage raise which Huang viewed as a decent '*report back*' [*jiao dai*] to its members. Another example is the store union's efforts to help the laid-off workers search for jobs in several local companies after the store closure was announced.

The organizing and functioning of the store union make it fall into one of the typical types of workplace unions in China, that is, a managerial tool with a constrained voice (Liu and Li, 2014, p. 104). While the 'democratic election' did not result in a genuinely representative union but a management co-opted union, it made the elected union committee members relatively popular among the workers and more or less concerned with worker interests. In addition, the management-sanctioned union activities helped build solidarity among the workers. These are all important conditions for the later transformation of the store union into a genuinely representative union.

The critical event that eventually transformed the store union, however, was the store closure that united the union commissaries and workers who were both seriously affected and urged the union to play its representative role. In the union committee, the vice chair and the publicity commissary had served Walmart for more than ten years, much longer than the others who usually had no more than five years of tenure. Because longer tenure meant a higher stake in the severance pay which was linked with years of service, the two had been active in plotting collective resistance since late February upon hearing the rumours of closure. Although supporting this collective resistance plan, Huang originally chose the relocation option when the top management contacted him informally before the announcement of the store closure promising him promotion after relocation. Later, however, Huang changed his mind, deciding to lead the collective protest after observing the department managers being forced to meet the top management team for their settlement plan. Several managers resisted the meetings by running away from the top managers. Being caught up by the top managers, a manager of the reception department even burst into tears and screamed which not only enraged Huang but also showed him how helpless and vulnerable the mid-level managers were when facing a ruthless employer. Huang started to wonder whether Walmart's promise to him would be kept. Another employer practice that angered Huang was the sudden replacement of all of the workers with substitutes. Huang explained his change:

Actually I wanted to work for Walmart. It provides me many opportunities and I became a manager in just a few years. But why [am I standing with workers]?... It deprives the workers' jobs in a discriminative, insulting, and brutal manner. This infuriates me. Normally, we are close like sisters and brothers; when employees encountered this problem, I chose to stand up as a union. I want to act worthily of the workers' trust in electing me as the union chair. I also want to fulfil the responsibility of a union chair. (Interview, March 19, 2014)

Huang then called for a union committee meeting to discuss details of collective resistance on March 4. During the meeting, the participants selected a nine-person 'rights-defence team' (seven union commissaries and two worker activists) with three negotiators (Huang, the vice union chair, and the publicity commissary), drafted an 'authorization letter of collective rights-defence', and laid out plans to take custody of the goods in the store to mount bargaining power. Thanks to the workers' internal solidarity which was built by their common interest in the store closure as well as past union activities, the store union soon collected signatures from 120 workers who authorized it to lead the collective resistance on March 5. The union's strength in worker mobilization was immediately felt by Walmart. In the afternoon, the store union coordinated a successful resistance to a 'store closure meeting' where the top management had planned to announce its decision. Only five workers showed up to the meeting. The top management had to resort to the store union to coordinate another meeting on March 14, which all of the workers attended following Huang's notice.

The store union used various tactics to mobilize the rank-and-file, among which the most helpful was developing platforms for both internal and external communication. The union set up two WeChat (an instant messaging software in China) groups to facilitate internal communication, one for the union committee and the other for all participating workers. A female manager was assigned to document and report every action of the store union and post on internet bars. Through these online outlets, the store union posted calls for cross-store alliance and sought social support.

The store union also combined negotiation initiatives with various disruptive tactics including protesting on the street, occupying the store's delivery depot, and blocking the trucks that attempted to transport the goods out of the store. It aggregated 15 demands from the workers and requested negotiations with Walmart. The core of these demands was to double the severance pay according to the law to compensate the workers for Walmart's failure to provide the mandatory one-month notice of layoffs to the store union. To press Walmart for negotiation, Huang and the vice union chair frequently gave speeches in front of the workers to mobilize them for collective action, making a unique scene in China where unions generally refrain from worker mobilization and collective action. It is also worth noting that the store union abandoned the term 'rights-defence team' after receiving a warning from the Changde City FTU (CCFTU) who deemed it illegal and always identified the nine team members as union commissaries. The legitimacy and unique strength of workplace unions in representing workers in China can be clearly seen from the words of a union commissary, 'if [we did these] in other names, [we] would have been cracked down very early' (Liu and Zhu, 2014).

In early March, the store union sought support from the local government and upper level unions. Huang presented letters to the CCFTU, the labour bureau, the labour disputes arbitration committee, the public security department, and the letters and visits bureau (LVB). None of these agencies took the workers' issue seriously. Yet, these agencies became alerted immediately after receiving a police report on the workers' protest on the street. The chief of the LVB organized an urgent meeting where officials from the CCFTU and relevant government departments listened to Huang's presentation of the case. The government officials demanded Huang to stop the public protest. Huang agreed but maintained worker gatherings in and around the Changde store.

In the following days, several labour-management conciliatory meetings were organized by local government and FTU officials. The meeting on March 7, with the CCFTU as the coordinator, was described by Huang as turning from a 'debate' into a 'criticism session' (*pi pan da hui*) where the labour bureau officials criticized the store unions' claim of Walmart's misconduct in the process of layoff as having no legal grounds. The meeting on March 14, chaired by the LVB, ended unhappily when the workers who wanted to win economic interests and respect left the scene due to the officials' endless talk about harmony and stability. On March 18, the district mayor, who chaired another conciliatory meeting, followed the labour bureau officials' claim warning Huang that 'Walmart didn't violate any laws. So, your protest is illegal. Police may arrest you. And you as the union chair will be responsible for any consequences!' (Interview, March 19, 2014).

Confronting the local government's hostility and threats, Huang started to question himself and the legality of their collective protest:

I, as a grassroots union chair, had not received any professional training. The only thing we had was a training note I got three years ago from a workshop for enterprise union chairs organised by the provincial FTU. This was my rights-defense talisman. I read it again and believed that the note still supported our claim. Several union commissaries and I went to the Xinhua bookstore for relevant legal materials. We bought labour law and corporate law books. We read them again and again but found no new grounds. The old grounds were already refuted. This landed us in an unfavorable position. (Interview, April 3, 2014)

The local government's threats and the store union's limited legal knowledge and experience of contention prompted the store union to seek and appreciate support from external labour activists. A call from a Walmart worker (activist ZJ hereafter) in Shandong Province who was also a director of a labour NGO lifted Huang from helplessness and desperation:

> At this time there was a call from heaven. It was from Yantai [a city in Shandong Province] but I didn't recognize it. It was very timely! His explanation empowered me. At that moment, we would give up without his call. When all the legal articles I could find were refuted, I felt very helpless and desperate. I thought we should end our action. However, I still believed that there was something wrong with Walmart. After his call, I felt that we were not subaltern [*ruo shi qun ti*], [and that] we were not a lonely army. He gave us the guts and reason to fight. Moreover, he was very resourceful and found many external resources and support for us. (Interview, April 3, 2014)

Solidarity-Building Labour Activist Groups

Activist ZJ introduced Huang into a WeChat group consisting of more than 100 labour activists across China who had frequent online communication and offline interaction. Intrigued by a union-led collective protest, these labour activists were eager to provide help, particularly technical, financial, and network resources, to the store union. Moreover, they played a pivotal role in linking the store union with contentious workers in other Walmart stores.

Technical Resources

Upon finding out about the union-led protest from the WeChat group, a leading labour activist in Shenzhen, Lawyer Yi Duan, together with five other labour activists, visited the Changde store on March 19. Lawyer Duan gave a mobilization talk to the rallied workers, confirming the legality and legitimacy of their demands. Further, the activists helped the union draft a formal 'collective bargaining request' letter, reframing the workers' demands around Article Four of the Labour Contract Law which sets the general principle of equal, collective consultation on significant employment issues. Based on the vaguely-defined right of consultation, this reframing helped turn the dispute on legal terms into interest-based bargaining on severance pay. Huang and the workers were strongly encouraged by this new legal ground and the support from those external labour activists. After Duan's visit, the female manager wrote in the union blog:

> Not wavering anymore; colleagues now feel solid. We finally realize that we are not lonely fighters, with so many warm-hearted people from many circles visiting us and supporting us behind the scenes. These strangers moved us! Shocked! A group of unmet people traveled thousands of miles to support our action. A larger group of people from all corners showed sympathy and support to us. What can stop us from persisting? (Changde store union blog, March 19, 2014)

Following the information in the labour activists' WeChat group, Professor Kai Chang of Renmin University of China, who had represented workers in the Nanhai Honda strike in 2010, visited the store to support the protest on March 21. After being authorized as the union's legal consultant, Professor Chang lobbied the provincial and city/district-level labour bureau and FTU officials, interpreting relevant laws in favour of the workers. In addition, Professor Chang helped the union re-draft the 'collective bargaining request' letter, adding two more legal articles that support the worker's demands. Responding to Walmart's refusal to bargain, Professor Chang helped the union draft an arbitration request, hoping that the arbitration committee would force Walmart to accept mediation which had been a preferred labour dispute settlement method since 2008 (Liu, 2014; Zhuang and Chen, 2015). Professor Chang's legal expertise and reputation encouraged the store union and the workers. In addition, Chang's lobby neutralized many officials' attitudes and even led some to appreciate the store union's position, expanding the political space of the protest.

Besides personal visits and frequent online communication, Lawyer Duan coordinated a workshop in Dengfeng City of Henan Province on April 3–4 to discuss the Changde store protest. More than 20 labour activists, including labour lawyers, scholars, and labour NGO staff, met with Huang and his three colleagues to explore and debate potential action strategies. Drawing on their experiences and expertise, these activists shared comments and contention tactics. The core debate concerned the path forward: arbitration (promoted by local government and FTU officials and Professor Chang) versus collective bargaining (advocated by Duan and several other activists). A story shared by a labour NGO staff from Guangzhou resulted in a laugh among the participants, but it was revealing and persuasive:

> I just received my verdict several days ago. It had been two years since I was dismissed due to layoffs in my department, a situation similar

to this Walmart case. I can show you my verdict which tells you how the arbitration-litigation system drags a worker in a simple dispute for such a long time. I strongly recommend you insist on collective bargaining at this stage, leaving arbitration as the last resort since we have one year till the due date to file an arbitration request. (CHH, Dengfeng, April 3, 2014)

After fierce debates on the de-collectivization effects of the arbitration process (which requires workers to file separate, individual applications), a consensus was reached that the store union and workers must unite as a collective to bargain with Walmart and that the store union should not rely on arbitration but use it as a pressure tactic complementing workers' collective action. After setting this tone, participants examined potential means to press Walmart to sit at the bargaining table. Three pathways emerged during the discussion. The first was suggested by Lawyer Duan and several activists: petition the ACFTU centre in Beijing which may be able to pressure Walmart. Additionally an activist from Jiangsu Province recommended several tactics to persuade and pressure Changde commerce and labour bureaus to block Walmart's store closure until the workers' grievances were solved. As a last resort, a labour dispute arbitrator from Fujian Province suggested filing individual arbitration requests and lawsuits every few days to make more than 200 dispute cases (i.e., 77 persisting workers going through the official three-stage labour dispute resolution process), which would cost Walmart more money than the severance pay demanded by the workers. Another participant who was a human resource manager agreed that so many vicious lawsuits could be a great challenge for top management. At the end of the workshop, Huang said 'we are strongly encouraged by this workshop and will carry out the several packages of action strategies upon returning'.

Activists groups' expertise helped the union and workers find legal space, choose tactics, and clarify the meaning of their struggle. After reading an online report of the workshop, a worker in the Changde store wrote in the worker WeChat group:

I have a strong feeling that our fight carries significant meaning. I read the report from 7 to 9 am and took notes of important points. Please dispel any misunderstanding and unite firmly in this rights-defense group led by Chairman Huang. Hold high morale in fighting against Walmart! .... Win decently in this significant rights-defense battle! Let Walmart remember our names. We are becoming heroes who change history! (Worker WeChat group, April 15, 2014)

Having met in the workshop, several experienced labour activists from Guangzhou, Nanjing, and other cities joined the Changde worker WeChat group where they observed the workers' discussions and provided advice. This is a common mode of coaching practiced by the solidarity-building labour activists: help workers establish mobile discussion platforms and invite activists with relevant expertise to join and coach the groups.

Financial Resources

Solidarity-building labour activists, especially those working in labour NGOs, sometimes coordinate donation campaigns to support protesting workers. Financial support for the Changde protest started after the arrest of two workers on March 21 who had conflicts with policemen sent to help Walmart clear up the store. One worker was jailed for five days, charged with interfering with public administration. To pacify the panic among the workers and their families, Lawyer Duan initiated a donation campaign on March 22, spreading calls for donations in several WeChat groups and on Weibo (microblog in China). Duan explained the significance of social donations: 'Besides making up economic loss to workers' families, social donation also tells workers and their families that they are not criminals and that they are doing right things. Sending money to families of detained workers is a counter-act to government's arrests. It rids workers of worries and makes them braver next time' (Interview, March 22, 2014).

Although Lawyer Duan suggested donating 20 RMB per person in his call for donation, many people chose to contribute 50 RMB or more. Ordinary workers, labour NGOs, civil rights activists, and labour lawyers, one after another, reported their donations in the labour activists WeChat group. Huang reported that he received 3,720 RMB in two days. Nonetheless, on March 25, the campaign was stopped by the CCFTU officials who forced the store union to issue a disclaimer denying any effort to seek social donations. Huang's disclaimer disappointed many labour activists who decided to cease their help, only to be united again after an explanation offered by Huang later that day: 'The disclaimer was to protect our action ... We sincerely apologize for any hurt it caused to sisters and brothers who have helped us. Please understand our situation! We always strive to fight and have never given up' (Activists WeChat group, March 25, 2014).

The store union spent the donated money and remaining union funds to support the detained worker, make big protest banners, and build tents to house the protesting workers who took day and night shifts to occupy the delivery depot. As the protest continued into late April, the workers were increasingly pressed by economic difficulties in supporting their families. Huang thus asked the CCFTU whether he could accept social donations. The answer was 'no'.

Network Resources

The emerging activist groups have sought to help the store union build a wide network of allies, supporters, and sympathizers through mobilizing (1) media, (2) workers in other Walmart stores, (3) Walmart customers, (4) international union organizations, (5) corporate social responsibility (CSR) organizations, and (6) pro-labour individuals and groups within the government. Some of these initiatives ended quickly without significant help for the workers. Mobilization of media and pro-labour officials, however, seemed to expand the political space of the protest.

The labour activists mobilized their media friends to report on the Changde protest. A scholar from Beijing who established the activists WeChat group also operated another WeChat group comprising of journalists and labour activists (which was named as a labour media group). Through this media group, some activists sent protest news and introduced journalists to the protesting workers. Upon finding out about the Changde protest, journalists from the *Financial Times* reported the case on March 24, which kicked off a wave of domestic media coverage with ten reports and references in the next ten days including main stream outlets such as the Southern Weekly. Three journalists (from the *Financial Times* and *Reuters*) were also invited to attend the workshop in Dengfeng city and meet Huang's team in person. These journalists reported widely and sympathetically on the protest. A report by Beijing Business Today on April 9 broke this case into the top media of the central government such as the People Net, Xinhua Net, China Daily, and China Economy. While some reports captured mainly the legal disputes involved in the case, those journalists contacted by the labour activists presented the labour side of the story. One example is Reuters' report titled 'Huang's tale: from Walmart cashier to labour leader in China'.

Extensive media coverage seemed to have an impact on local policing behavior. Policemen sent to help Walmart clear up the store had violent conflicts with the workers on March 18 and 21. With widespread media attention, the police repression weakened from April. For instance, on April 11, the on-site policemen called upon by Walmart stood by without stopping the workers from blocking the trucks attempting to transport goods out of the store. Surprisingly and boosting the workers' morale, the policemen even urged the top managers to solve the labour dispute as soon as possible. Huang wrote excitingly in the activists WeChat group that day: 'Historical victory! The policemen are willing to stand by neutrally. This is a rare victory, an unprecedented step forward'.

Also notable is the use of social media in this case. Activist ZJ learned the importance of social media from his experience of helping a group of female workers establish their workplace union in 2006. Because of the worker-controlled blog, ZJ received several calls from journalists and support from the national ACFTU as well as labour activists in Guangdong. Thus ZJ helped the store union set up a union blog to release daily activities of the protesters from early March to April 30. Huang and a female frontline supervisor wrote these daily summaries and analyses and posted them online and in the WeChat groups, with the goal of encouraging the protesting workers and framing the story to outsiders. A dedicated union blog dispelled potential misreports of the protest and attracted external attention and support. There were 7,226 visits to the union blog within 40 days.

The activists' efforts to mobilize cross-store solidarity and customer resistance did not succeed. Activist ZJ diffused the information on the Changde protest in a QQ (an instant messaging software in China) group consisting of about 170 Walmart workers from more than 100 stores in China, calling for cross-store collective action. Several labour activists also joined in the QQ group to propagate workers' precarious situation under Walmart's abrupt store closures and benefits of cross-store solidary. All of the messages vanished quickly due to a lack of response. Cross-store collective action was not realized, though Huang and some labour activists got in touch with a few protesting workers from two Walmart stores in Ma'anshan City, Anhui Province (this protest lasted only three days in mid-March). Another short-lived campaign was the 'Resist Walmart; Vote with Your Feet!' on Weibo aiming to mobilize customer resistance to Walmart.

The labour activist groups also attempted to elicit support from global unions. Activist ZJ, with the help of a PhD student from the US, wrote a help-seeking letter in English to the American Federation of Labour and Congress of Industrial Organizations (AFL-CIO), Change to Win, and the International Labour Organization on March 23. He also published this letter on Weibo and blogs. However, such international help-seeking made the Changde protest politically sensitive as the ACFTU headquarters was very averse to it. Responding to the ACFTU's negative attitude, the Hunan Provincial FTU (HPFTU) organized an urgent internal meeting on March 24 to discuss the issue and set the Changde protest as a 'political event', usually a negative term that justifies government suppression. The next day the CCFTU called the Changde store union committee for a solemn meeting and closely examined Huang's documents and action. The CCFTU then forced Huang to issue a public notice on the union blog disclaiming any contacts with external organizations or donation initiatives. Although the misunderstanding between supportive activists and Huang's team was soon dispelled by Huang's explanation, a division among the labour activists emerged regarding contacting international organizations. A minority group of activists doubted the merits of global contacts which might justify government repression while a larger group deemed the risk worth taking as it had prompted the ACFTU to take actions and to alert the local officials of the seriousness of the dispute. Nonetheless, contacts with international organizations ended with symbolic statements of support on their websites (e.g., the websites of AFL-CIO and UNI global union) without any substantial help given to the protesting workers.

Attempting to leverage overseas CSR movements against Walmart's notorious anti-labour practices, lawyer Duan, with the help of a PhD student from the US, sent an email in English to Walmart's global ethics office, explaining the legal issues involved and asking for a further investigation of the case. Acknowledging receipt of this complaint, Walmart's internal ethics office did not have any follow-up response or action. In addition, activist ZJ called Students and Scholars against Corporate Misbehavior (SACOM), a CSR organization in Hong-Kong. SACOM then wrote a public letter to the CEO of Walmart and received a response from Walmart top management who insisted on the legality of the store closure package and the approval of local officials.

Efforts to win the support of local government officials turned out to deliver the most benefits in terms of expanding the political space of this protest. Professor Chang's first step in helping the protesting workers was to lobby the officials of the provincial-level labour bureau and FTU. After eliciting their understanding of the workers' position, Professor Chang further lobbied relevant officials at the city level, neutralizing their repressive attitudes. After Professor Chang's visit, the local media (city and provincial level) were allowed to report positively on the protest. Another scholar, Professor Xie of Hunan University, invited the Hunan Provincial Democratic League to visit the Changde store on April 9 conducting an investigation. This investigation was a big event for local officials given the Democratic League's symbolically high status in the Chinese political system. During the visit Professor Xie criticized the local officials' pro-capital approach and recommended labour-management bargaining as the way to solve the dispute. This provincial Democratic League's stance signalled to local officials the significance of the case and that many people were watching how they would resolve the dispute. Huang's team sensed the improved government attitude and wrote in the union blog on April 10:

> Yesterday Hunan Provincial Democratic League came to investigate our case. The CCFTU, labour bureau, and other government departments' attitude changed greatly. This is an outcome of Professor Chang's top-down influence. It is telling from the officials' words.

By providing technical, financial, and network resources to the store union, solidarity-building labour activist groups played a critical role in assisting and sustaining the protest. As indicated by Huang:

> We took up the rights-protection weapon hastily. This weapon is the Provincial Union's training notes. With millet and rifles [a metaphor indicating primitive weapons], we have been fighting with Walmart's professional legal team. We have not failed because we have so many teams supporting us. (Interview, April 3, 2014)

Constraining FTUs

While the store union broke away from its double identity to mobilize and represent the rank-and-file workers and to ally with civil society activists groups, the upper level unions, that is, FTUs at various levels, still prioritized their institutional role as a Party-state instrument in containing labour unrest. As such, the FTUs were intolerant of the store union's movement-like activities and attempted to constrain its activities within institutional boundaries. Specifically, while the FTUs supported the store union's legal demands and action, they imposed restrictions on its extra-legal action and blocked social extra-legal support to the store union.

The CCFTU's support for the store union varied with its perception of the legal strength of the workers' claims. On the first day of the protest when Huang's team visited the CCFTU, a few officials from the legal department enthusiastically expressed that they would help the workers and introduced several legal-aid lawyers to assist the store union. The main rationale for this support was the CCFUT's perception that Walmart had violated laws as argued by Huang's team. However, the

CCFTU officials also demanded that the store union could not contact any media so as to protect the city's business environment and good image. Nonetheless, while Huang's team kept their promise of staying away from media in the first few weeks, the CCFTU officials reduced their support after the legal-aid lawyers commented that the store union's claims lacked legal support and that Walmart's store closure procedures were in accordance with laws. Later the CCFTU officials suggested Huang compromise and stop the collective action if Walmart made any small concession. Although the CCFTU pointed out some potentially illegal practices of Walmart during the store closure in its report to the local government, it became silent after the local government preferred the local labour bureau's report which endorsed Walmart's practices. Yet, the CCFTU welcomed Professor Chang's legalistic approach and became more active after Chang persuaded some local government officials. As the protest evolved, the ACFTU headquarters asked for internal reports on the case. The CCFTU wanted to show off and thus followed Professor Chang's advice to issue an official notice on March 31, urging Walmart to engage in collective bargaining with the store union. However, after being ignored by Walmart, the CCFTU, a resource-poor agency within the Party-state, lacked means to further pressure Walmart.

The FTUs' approach to this protest was revealed by a professor teaching at the HPFTU's College (April 3, 2014), according to whom the HPFTU arrived at a five-point instruction to the CCFTU after an urgent meeting: guide the workers to defend their rights according to laws and through legal channels; the term of 'rights-defence team' is problematic; according to the administrative jurisdiction, the Changde City Party committee and CCFTU, rather than the HPFTU, should be in charge of resolving the dispute; trade unions *must* have political sense (*zhengzhi xing*) and should not be taken advantage of by others, especially foreign forces; and trade unions should not support any worker demands beyond legal standards.

To carry out this instruction, the CCFTU asked the store union to stop using the term of 'rights-defence team' and contacting with external labour activists except Professor Chang who advocated a legalistic approach for dispute settlement and enjoyed legitimacy among government officials. What the CCTFU actively offered were legal-aid lawyers and coordination of the workers' labour dispute arbitration application. After the arbitration committees at various levels refused to take the workers' applications for reasons such as no jurisdiction or inappropriate claims, the CCFTU persuaded the city-level arbitration committee to accept the case. In addition, the CCFTU sent a legal-aid lawyer to help the store union after Professor Chang's team withdrew in mid-June.

Beyond these legal aids, the CCFTU refused to grant any economic assistance to the protesting workers. The CCFTU expressed symbolically in a notice that workers in economic difficulties may apply for its financial assistance. But after the workers submitted applications, it refused to make any award. Moreover, the CCFTU disapproved of the workers' extra-legal collective action, that is, occupying the store as a bargaining chip, and commanded Huang to stop blocking Walmart's transporting goods out of the store. It argued that Walmart's dealing of its goods was protected by laws and that the workers' dispute should be resolved through official mediation or arbitration. If the occupation continued, the CCFTU officials threatened Huang that the store union would have to take the responsibility for any consequences.

The FTUs at all levels opposed and severed external, extra-legal support to the store union's protest. This is shown vividly from the ACFTU's strong opposition to the involvement of Lawyer Duan who was perceived by the ACFTU as an ally of foreign forces. As soon as the ACFTU headquarters detected Duan's team's social donation initiatives, and the foreign help-seeking letters on March 24, it urged the HPFTU to cut off the store union's link to Duan. Ironically, a few days prior to March 19, Duan was invited by a professor of the HPFTU's college to give a two-hour lecture on collective bargaining to more than 200 workplace union chairs. Upon sensing the ACFTU headquarters' negative view of Duan, the HPFTU decided to ban any future lectures by Duan. Claiming its linkage with foreign forces, the CCFTU blocked the social, extra-legal support to the store union with the rhetoric of law. The notice of the CCFTU to the store union on May 15 stated that they: 'Strongly oppose collecting social donations to sustain rights-defence. Fundraising for rights-defence does not conform to laws ... Strongly oppose workers' help-seeking contacts with external organizations. According to the Trade Union Law ... primary union members' unauthorized contact with foreign organisations violates laws'.

Coercive Local Government

Local governments in inland China tend to be less open, more eager to please capital, and more likely to repress labour protests than their counterparts in coastal areas, due partly to lower economic development levels and weaker labour activism in inland cities. The Changde Walmart protest, in the eye of the local government, was a 'stability maintenance' event that had to be controlled and dissolved immediately. Thus both the government stability maintenance machinery led by the local Party's political-legal committee (the Party's organ overseeing domestic security operations and police) and industrial relations machinery such as the CCFTU and labour bureau intervened trying to absorb or dissolve the protest. Constraints imposed by FTUs were, to some extent, contested by the store union due to the merely symbolic authority of FTUs over workplace unions. For instance, the store union rejected the CCFTU designated legal-aid lawyers and issued a store union notice refuting the CCFTU's request to cease store occupation. However, the local government's repressive practices, including threatening the store union and workers, use of force, and relational repression, were fatal to the union-led protest. At last the government-controlled labour arbitration and litigation channels absorbed and dismantled the protest.

Huang used the term 'encirclement and suppression' (*wei jiao*) to describe the government repression. After several conciliatory meetings coordinated by the CCFTU and LVB in early March failed, the government's threats and use of force escalated. On March 18, the district mayor called for a multi-party meeting during which he warned Huang of potential arrest. On that day, a dozen policemen appeared in the store and had physical conflicts with the occupying workers. On March 19, Huang received a call from the district police bureau, attempting to dissuade the store union from protesting as well as notifying him of a warning (*jing shi xing*) meeting the next day. On March 20, the Party's political-legal committee called Huang and the other two key coordinators (the vice union chair and the union publicity commissary) for a warning meeting. Three of them were interrogated separately, with the publicity commissary being intimidated the most. Huang was interrogated for three hours, being asked about whether the workers had collaborated with overseas organizations and the legality of their demands, and forced to go through relevant laws that punish contenders. On March 20, the chief of the Changde business and commerce bureau led his 20 subordinates to the store to warn the protesting workers. On March 21, several dozen policemen went to help Walmart transport goods out of the store and arrested two occupying workers (one female worker was released immediately after she claimed that she was pregnant).

The local government has also taken the approach of relational repression to demobilize the workers, that is, using their social ties to pressure them not to protest (Deng and O'Brien, 2013). After mid-May, the workers' residential neighbourhood committee (*ju wei hui*) officials were tasked to persuade or harass the persisting workers. These officials' visits and calls sometimes frightened the workers' families. After the arbitration hearing on May 27, the labour arbitrators joined the harassments: calling frequently to pressure the workers to accept Walmart's settlement of paying the workers an additional 3,000 RMB as 'legal expenses'. The frequent harassments put high pressure on the workers. Huang said on June 9 during an interview:

> I confronted great pressure, firstly from the government. And secondly, they tried to persuade my family. My mother's brother who worked in the government was approached by the officials. They [officials] hinted that Chang was involved in a foreign undertaking and asked me to be cautious of Chang.

Neighbourhood committee officials' harassments culminated on June 11 when about 200 policemen escorted Walmart trucks transporting its goods out of the store. These officials visited the homes of the persistent 69 protesting workers, carrying pictures of the workers and conveying a simple message to them and their families: do not interfere in Walmart's removal of goods from the store and accept Walmart's settlement offer. The local government's suppression put an end to the workers' daily gathering at the delivery depot and all extra-legal actions.

The local government insisted that labour disputes should be resolved though legal channels and considered the store unions' other actions unreasonable. However, the legal channels excluded the contending workers from the decision-making process and isolated them from each other. The workers used to have face-to-face communications when they rallied at the delivery depot where Huang's team also gave daily briefings and mobilizing talks. Such communications enabled the workers to discuss managerial responses and protest tactics. After their being trapped into legal channels without collective action, however, the main platform of communication was the WeChat group where only a few workers left messages. The store union did not have much new information to post either because Huang's team did not know any updates from the arbitration panel. With fewer and fewer messages in the WeChat group, the workers became increasingly uncertain about who were still persisting and the arbitration outcomes. With pressures from the government and various uncertainties, most of the workers, one by one, accepted Walmart's settlement offer. By the time of the arbitration decision on June 25, only 18 workers were left. Six of them filed litigation in early July. The protest was finally dissolved into a labour dispute purely on legal terms.

Discussion and Conclusion

To tackle various problems facing labour movements, labour schol-ars frequently prescribe union renewal strategies. Based on a case of a union-led protest against Walmart, this chapter examines a potential pathway to a vital labour movement in China. We find that workplace unions, which are usually regarded as the weakest link of the ACFTU, may potentially become an agent of change for a genuine labour move-ment. Although workplace unions are often controlled or co-opted by employers, some employer policies or practices, such as store closure in this case, may negatively affect all employees including union leaders leading to solidarity among union leaders and rank-and-file workers and their strategic use of workplace unions as an institutionalized platform for contention. Moreover, as suggested by this case, the gradual expan-sion of democratic union elections in recent years, albeit with various flaws, may help increase workers' awareness of unions and union lead-ers' accountability to the members, which may facilitate the later trans-formation of workplace unions.

This case also illustrates the unique advantages of workplace unions in developing a vital labour movement in China. First and foremost, as a legitimate representative of workers, workplace unions can engage in both institutional means of contention such as collective bargaining, arbitration, litigation, and petition to FTUs and government, and extra-institutional means such as mobilizing rank-and-file workers for collec-tive action or allying with civil society groups. These tactics were used by the Changde store union. The fact that this protest was led by a work-place union with endorsement of its members dramatically enhanced the legitimacy of this radical action. In addition, workplace unions' proximity to workers may facilitate worker mobilization and formation of solidarity, as seen in this case. Both the institutional legitimacy of the Changde store union and its proximity to the workers contributed to the unusual length and great influence of this protest. Finally, compared to FTUs, workplace unions may have higher operational autonomy from the Party-state. In this case, the store union was able to take radical col-lective actions, using a grey area in China's labour laws, while the local and provincial FTUs had to strictly follow the Party-state, unable to pro-vide substantial support to the store union and workers.

Workplace unions' limited resources and lack of support from upper-level unions and government may prompt them to ally with civil society groups, another potential agent of change in the Chinese labour move-ment. Newly emerged solidarity-building labour activist groups may provide technical and financial resources to workplace unions and help them elicit support from various domestic and international individuals, groups, and organizations. These labour activist groups may even help connect and link the otherwise fragmented, struggles of workplace unions, though such efforts failed in the Changde case. Given the complementary strengths of workplace unions and labour activist groups, the coalition of the two agents of change may be promising in advancing the Chinese labour movement.

Nevertheless, both agents of change have their own weaknesses. First of all, it is extremely difficult for workplace unions to transform into genuinely representative unions due to various structural constraints. Such transformation often requires both a crisis confronting all employees and strong union leadership. Yet, paradoxically, these two conditions may also negatively affect the sustainability of such transformation, as crises such as factory closure and relocation may make transformed workplace unions lose their structural power and eventually their status as trade unions, and strong workplace union leaders as employees may be easily sanctioned or fired by employers. In this case, after the store closure finished, the store union was disbanded. Secondly, given their affiliation with the ACFTU, workplace unions face various institutional constraints on their actions which may significantly reduce their resources and bargaining power. For instance, the store union was not able to receive social donations due to the instruction of the local FTU.

As to the nascent labour activist groups, they are loose, informal, and small which prevents them from supporting workplace unions on a large scale. Moreover, labour activist groups and labour NGOs are vulnerable to government repression. First, the government may closely monitor or even possibly block the online communication platforms of these labour activist groups, making it difficult for these groups to function. Second, labour NGOs supporting worker collective actions have been frequently harassed or even cracked down upon by government. Third, help from labour NGOs or activists who are on government blacklists, while valuable for workplace unions and workers, may possibly have a downside, that is, making the workplace contention more politically sensitive and therefore increasing the chance of government repression.

Moreover, building connections between workplace unions and labour activist groups, who are largely segregated by the ACFTU's top-down structure and the Party-state's tight social control, is a great challenge. Even if the two change agents manage to form a coalition, they may have to face the deep doubt or fear of the Party-state about their alliance, and therefore strong government repression.

The weaknesses of the two agents of change are mainly caused by the negative approach of the Party-state and ACFTU towards labour activism, which may not reverse in the coming years. However, neither the Party-state nor the ACFTU is monolithic. In some coastal areas the local Party-state and ACFTU are more open to economic-interest-based labour activism. In Guangdong Province, the top Party-state and ACFTU officials have promoted democratic elections of workplace unions and have endorsed collective bargaining as an efficient method to solve labour disputes since 2010. There is evidence suggesting that workplace unions directly elected after strikes in Guangzhou tend to perform some meaningful union activities including representing workers in collective bargaining (Chen, 2014; Chapter 13 of this book). These union activities may help strengthen workplace unions' legitimacy and build solidarity between union leaders and rank-and-file workers, cultivating a condition for the transformation of workplace unions. In addition, a few labour NGOs have been tolerated in Guangdong for helping workers engage in collective bargaining and organizing donation campaigns for worker protestors over the past few years. As a result, the number of solidarity-building labour NGOs has gradually increased in Guangdong. Moreover, these labour NGOs may promote the transformation of workplace unions through mobilizing existing workplace union leaders, helping worker activists enter workplace union committees, and providing resources to support workplace unions' activities. In short, while the transformation of workplace unions and the development of solidarity-building labour activist groups may be potentially blocked by the repression of the Party-state and ACFTU, there are also opportunities for the two agents of change to grow.

The Changde protest is unique in at least two respects. First, it is very rare for a workplace union to lead a protest against the employer in order to protect worker interests. Huang's strong pro-labour position and the high stake of the vice union chair and publicity commissary in the store closure are critical but unusual conditions. Second, owing to its notorious image of being anti-union, the employer, Walmart, is able to attract wider attention from labour activists who provide critical support to the store union. Although a single, unique case does not allow us to infer any generalized causal relationship, it provides a rare opportunity for us to discover a potential pathway to a vital labour movement in China. The viability of this pathway, however, remains to be seen.

REFERENCES

Blecher, M. (2002) Hegemony and Workers' Politics in China. *The China Quarterly* *170*: 283–303.

Chan, A. (2011) Unionizing Chinese Walmart stores. In *Walmart in China* (Chan, Anita (ed.), pp. 199–216). Ithaca: Cornell University Press.

Chen, F. (2003) Between the State and Labour: The Conflict of Chinese Trade Unions' Double Identity in Market Reform. *The China Quarterly*, *176*: 1006–1028.

Chen, F. (2004) Legal Mobilization by Trade Unions: The Case of Shanghai. *The China Journal*, (52): 27–45.

Chen, F. (2009) Union Power in China Source, Operation, and Constraints. *Modern China*, *35*(6): 662–689.

Chen, F. (2015) China's Road to the Construction of Labour Rights. *Journal of Sociology*, first published on June 5, 2015 doi:10.1177/1440783315587414.

Chen, W. (2014) The sustainability of collective bargaining in China: A survey of collective wage consultation in the auto industry of Guangzhou City. *Chinese Workers*, *2*: 10–14.

China Labour Bulletin (2014) Searching for the Union: The workers' movement in China 2011–13. http://www.clb.org.hk/en/content/searching-union-workers%E2%80%99-movement-china-2011-13-0 (accessed 9 December 2015).

Clarke, S., & Pringle, T. (2009) Can Party-Led Trade Unions Represent Their Members? *Post-Communist Economies, 21*(1): 85–101.

Clawson, D., & Clawson, M. A. (1999) What Has Happened to the US Labour Movement? Union Decline and Renewal. *Annual Review of Sociology, 25*: 95–119.

Connolly, H. (2012) Union renewal in France and Hyman's universal dualism. *Capital & Class, 36*(1): 117–134.

Deng, Y., & O'Brien, K. J. (2013) Relational Repression in China: Using Social Ties to Demobilise Protesters. *The China Quarterly, 215*: 533–552.

Dibben, P. (2010) Trade union change, development and renewal in emerging economies: the case of Mozambique. *Work, Employment & Society, 24*(3): 468–486.

Elfstrom, M. & Kuruvilla, S. (2014) The Changing Nature of Labour Unrest in China. *Industrial and Labour Relations Review 67*(2): 453–480.

Engeman, C. (2015) Social movement unionism in practice: organisational dimensions of union mobilization in the Los Angeles immigrant rights marches. *Work, Employment & Society, 29*(3): 444–461.

Fantasia, R., & Stepan-Norris, J. (2004) The Labour Movement in Motion. In D. A. Snow, S. A. Soule, & H. Kriesi (Eds.), *The Blackwell Companion to Social Movements* (pp. 555–575). Malden, MA: Blackwell Publishing.

Fosh, P. (1993) Membership Participation in Workplace Unionism: The Possibility of Union Renewal. *British Journal of Industrial Relations, 31*(4): 577–592.

Franceschini, I. (2014) Labour NGOs in China: A Real Force for Political Change? *The China Quarterly, 218*: 474–492.

▶

Frege, C., Heery, E., & Turner, L. (2004) The new solidarity? Trade Union coalition-building in five countries. In *Varieties of Unionism: Strategies for Union Revitalization in a Globalizing Economy* (Frege, Carola and Kelly, John eds, pp. 137–158). Oxford: Oxford University Press.

Frege, C. M., & Kelly, J. (2003) Union Revitalization Strategies in Comparative Perspective. *European Journal of Industrial Relations*, 9(1): 7–24.

Frege, C. M., & Kelly, J. E. (2004) *Varieties of unionism: strategies for union revitalization in a globalizing economy*. Oxford: Oxford University Press.

Friedman, E. (2014a) *Insurgency Trap: Labour Politics in Post-socialist China*. Ithaca: Cornell University Press.

Friedman, E. D. (2014b) Economic Development and Sectoral Unions in China. *Industrial & Labour Relations Review*, 67(2): 481–503.

He, B., & Xie, Y. (2011) Wal-Mart's Trade Union in China. Economic and Industrial Democracy, 33(3): 421–440.

Harney, A. and Ruwitch, J. (2014) In China, Managers are the New Labor Activists. *Reuters*, May 31, 2014. http://www.reuters.com/article/us-china-labor-strikes-idUSKBN0EC10420140601#7A28WqZ6tcPbGUZ0.97 (accessed 9 December 2015).

Heckscher, C. (2006) Organisations, Movements, and Networks. *New York Law School Law Review*, 50(2): 313–336.

Heery, E. (2005) Sources of change in trade unions. *Work, Employment & Society*, 19(1): 91–106.

Holdt, K. von. (2002) Social Movement Unionism: the Case of South Africa. *Work, Employment & Society*, 16(2): 283–304.

Howell, J. A. (2008) All-China Federation of Trades Unions beyond Reform? The Slow March of Direct Elections. *The China Quarterly*, 196: 845–863.

Hurd, R., Milkman, R., & Turner, L. (2003) Reviving the American Labour Movement: Institutions and Mobilization. *European Journal of Industrial Relations*, 9(1): 99–117.

Hyman, R. (2001) *Understanding European Trade Unionism: Between Market, Class and Society*. SAGE.

Hyman, R. (2004) Labour History Symposium. *Labour History*, 45(3): 340–347.

Lee, A. S., & Trappmann, V. (2014). Overcoming post-communist labour weakness: Attritional and enabling effects of multinationals in Central and Eastern Europe. *European Journal of Industrial Relations*, 20(2):113–29.

Lee, C. K. (2007) *Against the Law: Labor Protests in China's Rustbelt and Sunbelt*, Berkeley: University of California Press.

Lee, C. K., & Shen, Y. (2011) The anti-solidarity machine? Labour nongovernmental organisations in China. In *From Iron Rice Bowl to Informalization: Markets, Workers, and the State in a Changing China* (S. Kuruvilla, C. K. Lee, M. Gallagher (eds), pp. 173–187). Ithaca: Cornell University Press.

Liu, M. (2010) Union Organising in China: Still a Monolithic Labour Movement? *Industrial & Labour Relations Review*, 64(1): 30–52.

Liu, M. (2014) Conflict Resolution in China. In *Oxford handbook of conflict management in organisations*. (William K. Roche, Paul Teague, Alex Colvin (eds), pp. 494–519). Oxford, UK: Oxford University Press.

▶

Liu, M., & Li, C. (2014) Environment Pressures, Managerial Industrial Relations Ideologies and Unionization in Chinese Enterprises. *British Journal of Industrial Relations, 52*(1): 82–111.

Liu, M., Li, C., & Kim, S. (2011) Chinese trade unions in transition : a three-level analysis. In *China's changing workplace : dynamism, diversity and disparity.* (Shelton Peter, Sunghoon Kim, Yiqiong Li, and Malcolm Warner (eds), pp. 277–300). London: Routledge.

Liu, Z., & Zhu, Z. (2014) The War between the Strongest Union and Walmart: Rights Protection vs. Stability Maintenance. *South China Weekend*, April 4, 2014.

Ost, D. (2002) The Weakness of Strong Social Movements: Models of Unionism in the East European Context. *European Journal of Industrial Relations, 8*(1): 33–51.

Pringle, T. (2011) *Trade Unions in China: The Challenge of Labour Unrest.* Taylor & Francis.

Shen, S. (2008) Kraft's China Union Says Relocation Violates Law. *Reuters*, March 25, 2008. http://www.reuters.com/article/us-kraft-china-dispute-idUSPEK33478 320080325#pDKFQMcVuKRd4pWk.97 (accessed 9 December 2015).

Serrano, M. R. (2014) Between accommodation and transformation: The two logics of union renewal. *European Journal of Industrial Relations, 20*(3): 219–235.

Voss, K., & Sherman, R. (2000) Breaking the Iron Law of Oligarchy: Union Revitalization in the American Labour Movement. *American Journal of Sociology, 106*(2): 303–349.

Xie, Y. (2014) Walmart store closure has hurt whom? *Chinese Workers, 5*: 35–38.

Zhuang, W., & Chen, F. (2015) 'Mediate First': The Revival of Mediation in Labour Dispute Resolution in China. *The China Quarterly, 222*: 380–402.

Strikes and Workplace Collective Bargaining in the Auto Parts Industry in Guangzhou

13

Yunxue Deng

Introduction

On 17 May 2010, a strike broke out in Honda Auto Parts Manufacturing Co., Ltd (CHAM) in Foshan. After two strike leaders pressed the emergency 'Stop' button on the production line, hundreds of workers walked out of work. Chanting slogans like 'Without a wage raise, we will fight to the end', they marched in the factory campus and demanded a wage increase of 800 yuan. The CHAM strike quickly became the spotlight of domestic and international media because (a) it lasted 17 days which suspended four vehicle assembly plants of Honda and cost huge daily production losses; (b) workers asked for an 800 yuan wage raise which was significantly beyond the legal standard; (c) additionally, strikers requested a democratic reform of the workplace union; and (d) more importantly, it had a profound knock-on effect – a strike wave swept the auto parts industry in the Pearl River Delta (PRD) in the summer of 2010. In Guangzhou alone, over 100 strikes broke out in the auto parts manufacturing industry and vehicle manufacturing industry in two months (from May to July 2010) (W. G. Chen, 2011).

The strike wave has brought two important changes to Guangzhou's auto parts industry: it exposed the vulnerability of the auto parts industry and demonstrated the autoworkers' remarkable workplace bargaining power. It was evident that workers' collective action in one factory could possibly paralyze the entire auto manufacturing production chain, causing great production loss to global capital. Secondly, it also underlined the importance of democratizing workplace trade unions and establishing an effective collective bargaining system. In the 2010 strike wave, the workers bypassed their workplace trade unions and elected their own delegates to bargain with their employers. The workplace unionists were only called later and played a marginal role in the tripartite collective consultation. After the strike wave, the Guangzhou Federation of Trade Unions (GZFTU) re-organized some workplace trade unions and introduced or strengthened the collective consultation system, a Chinese version of collective bargaining. Compared to formalistic collective consultation prevailing in the Chinese workplace (Clarke, Lee and Li 2004; Lee, Brown and Wen, 2014; Kuruvilla and Zhang, 2015), the 'new' system in Guangzhou emphasizes active involvement of workplace trade unions and workers in the collective consultation process. In practice it has been backed up by re-elected workplace unions and autoworkers collective actions in an increasing number of cases. Although the local state's intention was to absorb labour disputes in a controllable way, neither the state nor capital could fully control the process and outcome of workplace collective bargaining. Workers in some factories, by electing representatives and taking collective action, actively participated in the bargaining process. As such, collective consultation has opened a new space for the workers to forge solidarity and fight for their interests collectively.

Studies have shown that, distinct from worker-led collective bargaining in the West, the vast majority of Chinese collective bargaining is largely a formality (Clarke et al., 2004; C. Chan and Hui, 2013). It is ineffective for two main reasons. Firstly, the state-sponsored trade union, which is the only legitimate representative of workers, is generally weak and tightly controlled by the party-state or the management. As a result, the representativeness of this trade union in collective bargaining is quite problematic. Secondly, neither unions nor workers have a legitimate right to lead or organize strikes, which deprives them of the most effective bargaining chip. On the other hand, recent studies have illustrated that responding to workers' activism, the All-China Federation of Trade Union (ACFTU) has made more efforts to promote collective bargaining (Chen, 2010; Liu, 2010; Pringle, 2011; C. Chan and Hui, 2013; Friedman, 2014; Lee et al., 2014; Kuruvilla and Zhang, 2015). For example, Pringle (2011) argued that sectoral collective bargaining is a strategy of the ACFTU to increase workers' income and alleviate their grievances without establishing independent unions or mobilizing rank-and-file workers. C. Chan and Hui (2013) found that after the strike in 2010, a collective bargaining system was established in the CHAM. However, it was a Party-state-led collective bargaining instead of a worker-led one, as it was mainly backed up by the local government and upper-level trade union.

In general, previous studies tended to emphasize the role of the state, especially the ACFTU in collective bargaining, while workers' own voices and actions, as well as the interactions between worker activism and collective bargaining, were largely missing. Therefore, this chapter attempts to illustrate the recent development of workers' protests and collective bargaining in the auto parts industry in Guangzhou. Moreover, it will put autoworkers at the centre of analysis and concentrate on their collective actions, especially with regard to how they activate and push forward collective bargaining through strategic strikes. The key questions of this chapter are: what is the process of the newly strengthened collective bargaining in the auto parts industry in Guangzhou? How effective is the collective bargaining? More importantly, how do rank-and-file workers participate in collective bargaining and fight for their collective interests?

In contrast to the largely symbolic enterprise-level collective bargaining found in the previous literature, I find that the newly established collective bargaining in the auto parts factories has indeed improved worker incomes. I argue that the improved effectiveness of collective bargaining mainly comes from workers' active involvement in the process. In particular, autoworkers' strong workplace bargaining power and their capacity to take collective actions are the most crucial force in squeezing employer concessions in bargaining.

Methodology

The auto industry is one of the pillar industries in Guangzhou. In 2013, 2.2 million automobiles were produced in Guangzhou, accounting for 8.16 per cent of the total automobile output in China. In addition, the value of the auto industry output accounted for 19.3 per cent of the total industrial output in Guangzhou (Li and Yang, 2014). In the year of 2012, there were 216 automobile manufacturing enterprises with annual revenues of more than 20 million yuan and a total workforce of about 107,200 (Wang, 2013). In general, there are four major auto industrial zones in Guangzhou, and most auto parts factories are suppliers of three Japanese auto brands including Toyota, Nissan, and Honda (see Table 13.1).

In order to explore the power of Chinese autoworkers, I conducted ethnographic research in the four auto-industrial zones in Guangzhou

Table 13.1 Four major auto industrial zones in Guangzhou

Name of the Industrial Zone	Location	Number of Auto Suppliers
Nansha International Auto Industrial Zone	Nansha District	Over 20 auto parts suppliers. Majority auto parts are supplied to Toyota.
Guangzhou Economic and Technological Development Zone	Luogang District	118 auto parts suppliers. Majority auto parts are supplied to Honda, Toyota, and Nissan.
Huadu International Auto Industrial Zone	Huadu District	Over 200 auto parts suppliers. Majority auto parts are supplied to Nissan.
Zengcheng Economic and Technological Development Zone	Zengcheng District	13 auto parts suppliers. Majority auto parts are supplied to Honda and Nissan.

Li J. T. and Yang, Z. G. [Eds.]. (2013) *Guangzhou Lanpishu: Guangzhou Qiche Chanye Fazhan Baogao 2013* [Blue Book of Guangzhou: Annual Report on Guangzhou's Automobile Industry 2013]. Beijing: Social Sciences Academic Press.

from November 2013 to May 2015, during which 89 in-depth interviews were conducted. Interviewees included rank-and-file workers, worker activists, strike leaders, lower-level supervisors, enterprise-level trade-union activists and presidents, and city-level and district-level trade-union officials. Ethnographic data were also collected by observing worker activists' gatherings, enterprise-level trade-union elections, trade unions' meetings, and training programs.

The Introduction of Workplace Union Reform and Collective Bargaining

Before the strike wave in 2010, there were trade unions and symbolic collective bargaining in most auto parts factories in Guangzhou. However, these workplace unions were usually staffed by high-level management and distant from rank-and-file workers. It was common that workers regarded workplace unions as a corporate department representing the management. Moreover, the previous workplace collective bargaining system was largely formalistic. Due to the inactive trade union and collective bargaining system, workers' wages were highly disconnected from the relatively high profit of the auto parts industry. For years, it was not unusual that autoworkers' basic wage adhered to or be only slightly higher than the local minimum wage.

In 2010, the CHAM strike had a strong domino effect in the Guangzhou auto parts industry. In factory after factory, the autoworkers stopped work, launched sit-in strikes, and demanded wage bargaining with their employers. Since these conflicts were interest-based (rather than legal-rights based), they could not be settled through legal channels. While the local state attempted to solve the conflicts through tripartite consultation, the workplace trade unions were unable to perform their role of transmission belt between capital-labour or state-workers, let alone act as a worker representative in collective consultation. As a result, it was difficult for the local state to settle the conflict in a timely manner. The strike made the upper-level trade unions realize that it was important to reform the workplace union to absorb labour grievances and control industrial conflicts, as mentioned by a GZFTU official: 'An effective (workplace) union is much better than an obedient, inactive one. ... The (workplace) unions should be activated to control workers' militancy. The party and the state would like to see that. If a union president is influential on the shop-floor, and workers listen to him, he could persuade workers to go back to work (in a strike). We need unions like that' (interview, November 30, 2013).

Since 2010, the GZFTU and its branches had reformed a number of workplace trade unions. Among the four districts mentioned above, Nansha and Luogang district-level unions had actively promoted trade union elections, while Huadu and Zengcheng district-level unions had not. For example, in the Luogang industry zone (in Guangzhou) alone, 73 factories had held elections of enterprise-level unions (Huang, 2012). Generally speaking, the elections were conducted at three levels, which included the election of union member representatives, union committee members, and a union president. It seems that most elections of union member representatives were democratic or direct, meaning that the rank-and-file workers had participated in the election process. However, elections of union committee members and chairmen were usually indirect and more likely to be manipulated by the management and the local government.

The workplace union election, on one hand, indeed improved the autonomy and representativeness of workplace unions. Since the election of union representatives was direct, it was possible for worker activists to be elected as union representatives. Besides, as the union representatives accounted for 8 per cent to 20 per cent of the total workforce, it is more difficult for them to be manipulated by management. On the other hand, it must be emphasized that the workplace union reform was not thorough or fundamental, and the newly elected workplace unions were not independent unions. In the first place, as mentioned above, the union elections were only semi-democratic, and most of the union committee members and the union presidents were not directly elected by rank-and-file workers. Secondly, union committee members and presidents were not full-time union officials but full-time employees of the company. As a result, their motivation to represent workers and confront the management was hindered by the fact that their career and income were controlled by their employers. Moreover, the workplace unions are not allowed to collect union funds by themselves. Instead, union funds in Guangzhou (equivalent in many other cities), that is 2 per cent of total wage bills of companies, are collected by the taxation bureau directly and transferred to the GZFTU who then return 60 per cent of the funds to workplace unions. Thus, the workplace trade unions are not economically independent.

In addition to union election, collective consultation was introduced or strengthened in Guangzhou, particularly in Nansha and Luogang districts. Compared to previous formalistic collective consultation, the new system strengthened the implementation of the procedural rules of collective consultation, especially those on the participation of workers and workplace unions, including rules such as: (a) union negotiators should be recommended by workplace unions or elected by workers; (b) before bargaining, workplace unions should collect workers' expectations about wage raises or other demands; (c) collective bargaining outcomes need to be discussed and approved by a majority at a union representatives meeting; and (d) the written collective bargaining agreement needs to be displayed to all employees. Moreover, the GZFTU and its branches provided detailed training and guidelines to workplace unionists about how to elect negotiators, collect relevant information, and bargain with the management. In practice, the upper-level unions persuaded workplace unions to bargain in a harmonious way, and not resort to strikes to pressurize the management. For example, one guidebook edited by the Luogang District Federation of Trade Union (LGDFTU) states that 'during collective negotiation, the enterprise trade union should lay emphasis on presenting facts and reasoning; should communicate instead of challenging and arguing with the management'. Here, we can see that the workplace unions still did not have the right to strike, even though they were encouraged to participate in collective bargaining. As such, they lacked motivation or power to fight with the company on the bargaining table.

Overall, facing intensive labour protests, the local state has made partial compromises on issues related to workers' rights of association and collective bargaining. Although the strengthened collective bargaining system is still systematically constrained by the local state, it provides the autoworkers an opportunity to pursue their interests collectively through participating in the process of collective bargaining.

Strikes and Collective Bargaining in the Workplace

As we mentioned above, the reformed workplace unions are still largely controlled by the employers and the state, and the majority of them could not perform as 'genuine' representatives of workers. Additionally, due to their lack of a strike right, workplace trade unions could not (or were not willing to) organize strikes publicly. As a result, the autoworkers quickly found out that the workplace unions, just by 'communicating' or 'reasoning' with the management, could not win concrete economic gains from their employers. For the autoworkers, they still had to rely on their direct action or show their capacity for collective action to pressurize the management. Indeed, in the past few years, it has become common sense among autoworkers in South China that striking is the fastest and most effective way to increase wages and bonuses.

It is worthy to note that, since the strike wave in 2010, the local state of Guangzhou has implicitly granted a limited strike right to workers. It seems that the local state has been relatively tolerant of workers' economic and non-destructive strikes (Cai, 2006). In most cases, the local state tended to persuade both labour and the management to resolve the conflict through collective bargaining, rather than suppressing workers with violence. Such tolerance provided a significant political opportunity for workers to take collective action. Moreover, the autoworkers developed a set of strategies to guide their actions and decrease the possibility of direct state suppression, such as sit-in strikes, blocking shipment passage or trucks to cut off auto parts supply to assembly plants, and employing anti-Japanese and patriotic discourse to justify their actions. Additionally, most of their actions were peaceful, non-destructive, well-organized, and targeted at the management rather than the local state. Confrontational actions which were frequently taken by migrant workers, like protesting on the street, blocking highways, breaking machines, congregating at the government buildings, or attacking management staff or state officials (Lee, 2007; Leung and Pun, 2009; C. Chan, 2010), were seldom taken by the autoworkers.

Furthermore, the newly established collective bargaining system that strengthens the participation of worker and workplace unions inadvertently facilitates the emergence and escalation of strikes in two ways. In the first place, collective bargaining often centres on important focal issues which can help form solidarity among workers. As a union vice president mentioned, 'In the past, we had various demands which were kind of in a mess. Now the collective bargaining system provides us a coherent demand [which is usually about increasing wages or bonus] and a common goal to achieve' (interview, May 12, 2015). Secondly, union negotiators and union representatives tend to (and sometimes are required to) inform workers about the progress of collective bargaining, which can serve as continuous mobilization. With the sustained attention of rank-and-file workers on the bargaining process, it is also much easier for worker activists to mobilize them to engage in collective action. Consequently, the strengthened collective bargaining system, which was designed to absorb labour activism, also generated new worker militancy.

Though there is no concrete data on the number of strikes in the auto parts industry from 2011 to 2015, it seems that at least in some auto parts factories the workers have consciously influenced the process and outcome of collective bargaining through strikes. Table 13.2 lists

Table 13.2 Selected strikes during collective bargaining in the auto parts industry in Guangzhou (2013–2015)

Factory	Date	Description
Factory Venus: car doors and windows supplier of Toyota and Honda	22 Jan 2013	Causes of strike: The company attempted to delay the process of collective bargaining and proposed a year-end bonus of 1.5 months' basic salary. To push forward the bargaining process, all workers (about 500 people) went on strike.
		Role of the workplace union: The strike was organized by union representatives in the name of the Venus union.
		Role of the state: The state supported workers' demand to resume collective bargaining. One LGDFTU official went to the strike scene, and announced to strikers that 'labourers have the right not to work.' Meanwhile, they attended and observed the following collective bargaining.
		Outcome: After the strike, the collective bargaining resumed. The strike lasted for 5.3 hours (from 10:10 am to 15:30 pm), and the union and management quickly reached a formal agreement: a year-end bonus of 3.5 months' basic salary (at least 7,000 yuan for each worker).
	23–27 Jan 2015	Causes of strike: During the bargaining over year-end bonus, the union asked for 5 months' basic salary, while the company insisted a bonus of 1.5 months' salary. After three days of strike, the workers forced Guangzhou Toyota assembly plant to a production halt. However, the strike faced the joint suppression of Venus company and Guangzhou Toyota.
		Role of the workplace union: Some union representatives informally initiated the strike.

(Continued)

Table 13.2 (*Continued*)

Factory	Date	Description
		Role of the state: The state acted as a neutral mediator. Police came but didn't intervene in the strike. Upper union officials went to Venus and persuaded both sides to reach an agreement soon as possible.
		Outcome: After three more rounds of bargaining, the company proposed a bonus plan, but was rejected by the union representative meeting (50 vs. 19). Then the company announced that the collective bargaining had broken, and refused further bargaining. At last, the workplace union conceded agreeing with 3.4 months of salary as year-end-bonus (at least 7,731 yuan for each worker).
Factory Mars: fuel injection system and shock absorbers supplier of Toyota, Honda, and Nissan	28–29 Jan 2013	Causes of strike: In collective bargaining, workers demanded 5 months' salary as year-end bonus, while the company rejected the demand and only offered a bonus of 1.8 months. All workers (about 1,100 workers) joined the sit-in strike. Moreover, on the second day of the strike, the workers blocked the gateway of shipment to pressure the company.
		Role of the workplace union: Some union representatives initiated the strike informally.
		Role of the state: The state suppressed workers with force. On the second day of the strike, nine workers were arrested by police and then released in one week. But two union negotiators were detained for 37 days.
		Outcome: The workplace union and management resumed collective bargaining and reached a formal agreement: workers gained a 4.3 months' salary bonus at last (at least 8,610 yuan for each worker).
Factory Jupiter: car seats supplier of Honda and Toyota	26 June 2013	Causes of strike: In the collective bargaining over annual wage raise, the workplace union demanded an increase of 600 yuan, while the factory only proposed to increase by 180 yuan. More than 60 out of 800 workers refused to work overtime.
		Role of the workplace union: The strike was organized by some union representatives informally.
		Role of the state: The state didn't intervene. Neither the police nor upper-level trade union showed up in the factory.
		Outcome: The Jupiter union and the management resumed collective bargaining and finally reached a formal agreement: an annual salary increase of 220 yuan. But 26 worker activists were fired after the strike, and the president of the Jupiter union resigned due to pressure from the management in May 2014.

Factory	Date	Description
Factory Saturn: horizontal bars and car springs supplier of Honda, Toyota, and Nissan	17 Dec 2013	Causes of strike: The workplace union demanded 5.9 months' basic salary as year-end bonus. But after four rounds of bargaining, the company only agreed to a bonus of 3.5 months. In order to press the company, all workers (about 500 workers) went on strike.
		Role of the workplace union: The strike was initiated and organized by some union representatives informally.
		Role of the state: The state played a neutral mediator role in the strike. The police didn't intervene during the strike. The LGDFTU persuaded both sides to start a new round of collective bargaining. But a labour bureau official threatened the strikers to go back to work, or he would fire all of them.
		Outcome: The strike lasted for 13 hours (from 16:30 pm to the next day 5:30 am). The workplace union and the management resumed collective bargaining and reached a formal agreement: workers gained year-end bonus of 5 months' basic salary (at least 10,250 yuan for each worker).
Factory Uranus: automobile suspension systems, control sticks supplier of Nissan, Toyota, and Honda	25 Feb 2014	Causes of strike: In collective bargaining, the workers demanded 5 months' salary as year-end bonus, while the company proposed a bonus of 1.7 months' salary. All workers (about 160 people) went on strike.
		Role of the workplace union: The strike was initiated by some union negotiators informally.
		Role of the state: The state didn't intervene. Neither the police nor upper-level trade union showed up in the factory during the strike.
		Outcome: The strike went for 3.5 hours (from 8:00 am to 11:30 am). The collective bargaining resumed and the written agreement showed that workers gained 3 months' basic salary as a year-end-bonus (at least 5,100 yuan for each worker).
Factory Neptune: petrol tanks, front bumper, and exhaust pipes supplier of Toyota	23 April 2014	Causes of strike: During the collective bargaining over annual salary increase, the workplace union asked for a 15 per cent salary increase, while the factory only proposed a 10 per cent increase. All workers (about 700 people) went on strike.
		Role of the workplace union: The strike was organized by some union representatives, union committee members, and union negotiators informally.
		Role of the state: The state acted as a neutral mediator. Nansha district labour bureau came to Neptune and claimed that 'we hope you reach an agreement as soon as possible. As long as you don't break machines, it'll be fine.' Besides, the Nansha district-level trade union attended and observed the following collective bargaining.

Table 13.2 (*Continued*)

Factory	Date	Description
		Outcome: The strike lasted for about 11 hours (from 7:20 am to 18:30 pm) and forced the Guangzhou Toyota assembly plant to halt production, causing a production loss of 200 million yuan. The management and the workplace union continued collective bargaining and reached a formal agreement: a 15 per cent salary increase (at least 267 yuan for each worker). But one strike leader, who was also a union negotiator, was fired by the company after the strike.
Factory Pluto: car wiper systems, washer shutters. Supplier of Toyota	22 May 2014	Causes of strike: In the collective bargaining, workers were dissatisfied about the wage plan of the company. All of the workers (about 200 people) went on strike. They asked for 14 demands, and the three major ones were: a wage increase of 20 per cent; dismiss the manager of the personnel department; and prohibit the personnel department from intervening in workplace union affairs and the general election of the workplace union.
		Role of the workplace union: The strike was initiated by some union representatives informally.
		Role of the state: The state acted as a neutral mediator. The police didn't intervene during the strike.
		Outcome: The strike went on for one day, and workers' salary increased 20 per cent (about 340 yuan for each worker). The work of the personnel department manager was suspended.

The author's field work

eight cases of strikes during collective bargaining. It shows that workers, by backing up collective bargaining with collective actions, indeed increased their salary and bonus.

Due to the limited space, the chapter will not elaborate on all of the strikes listed in Table 13.2, but only those during the collective bargaining process in Mars and Venus factories.

The Mars Factory

Mars, established in December 2003, is a Japanese-owned auto parts supplier for Toyota, Honda, and Nissan. Its main products were fuel injection systems and shock absorbers. There was a workforce of about 1,100 in 2013. In the summer of 2010, the workers in Mars launched a strike and gained a wage raise of 40 per cent (about 600–700 yuan). Additionally, under the guidance of LGDFTU, Mars held a workplace union election, as well as an election of union negotiators in 2011. The election of the workplace union in Mars contained three levels: firstly, workers directly elected about 100 union member representatives; secondly, these union member representatives elected seven union committee members; and thirdly, the union committee members elected a president and a vice-president. However, while the election of union member representatives was direct, the elections of the union committee members and the president were both seriously manipulated by the management. While the candidates for the former were selected by the management, the union president was appointed by the Japanese general manager.

On the other hand, the election of trade union negotiators was democratic: firstly, about 100 union representatives elected 12 candidates; then each candidate gave a speech competing for three negotiator positions; and finally the union representatives voted again and the three candidates who got most votes became the union negotiators. Since the union president and vice-president were assured negotiators, there were five union negotiators in total. Nevertheless, in the collective bargaining process, there were serious conflicts between elected union negotiators and the appointed union president. While the elected union negotiators were determined to fight for workers' interests, the union president remained silent and even sided with management. For instance, the president disclosed the union's bargaining strategy and plans to the management, putting the union in a disadvantageous position in bargaining. What was worse, before the collective bargaining over the year-end bonus of 2012 started, two elected union negotiators were recalled by the president without legitimate reasons. After the recall incident, some worker activists realized that it was essential to re-organize the union in order to have an effective collective bargaining.

Before the collective bargaining over year-end bonus of 2012, the union representatives conducted a survey on workers' expectation of bonus, the result of which showed that the workers asked for five months' salary as bonus. But during collective bargaining, the company only agreed on a bonus of 1.8 months' salary. After three rounds of bargaining, a stalemate occurred and both sides refused to compromise. At this point, the worker activists decided to launch a strike. Their major demand was to recall the union president and reorganize the workplace union. On January 28, one of the elected union negotiators drafted and circulated a petition letter titled 'A Revolution of Mars's Trade Union', which listed four main reasons to reform the union, including '(a) Almost all of the union committee members are high-level managerial staff, who do not stand on the side of workers; (b) As the union president has a Japanese citizenship, he cannot represent Chinese workers anymore; (c) The union has failed to perform its duty in collective bargaining; (d) The union president abused his power and recalled two union negotiators without going through democratic procedures' (interview, March 23, 2013). According to the union negotiator, 'about 90 per cent rank-and-file workers and 50 per cent office staff signed this letter' (interview, April 28, 2013).

On January 28, 2013, a strike broke out in one workshop and quickly spread to the whole factory. Most workers gathered in the factory campus and sang the national anthem. When the managers and government officials came to the strike scene, workers chanted slogans like: 'Fire the trade union president!', 'Increase the year-end bonus, or we will fight to the end!'. Moreover, in order to pressurize the management, about 200 workers blocked the shipment passage to cut off the supply of parts to Toyota's and Honda's assembly plants. During the strike, the district government head, street government officials, labour bureau officials, LGDFTU officials, and riot police came to Mars. The police announced to strikers that: 'According to the Chinese Public Order Management and Punishment Law, you have the right not to work (*nimen you bu gong-zuo de quanli*), but you don't have the right to hinder production (*dan-shi nimen meiyou zu'ai shengchan de quanli*). ...You could go home to rest, or go back to work. For those who don't want to rest or work, you cannot block the shipment passage'. Here, the police clearly pointed out the boundary of strike behaviour: while a sit-in strike was acceptable, blocking the shipment passage was considered illegal. On the second day of the strike, workers still refused to retreat from the shipment passage, and then more than 200 riot and plainclothes policemen suppressed the strike by force. Nine workers were arrested and released in one week, but the two union negotiators were detained for 37 days and then sued by the Luogang district Procuratorate. Later, the two union negotiators were declared innocent for there was no valid evidence showing that they organized workers occupying the shipment passage. Moreover, in the written judgement, the judge claimed that 'the defendants X and Y participated in the strike, and defendant X made written materials and demanded to recall the union president. Both actions were legal ways (*hefa fangshi*) for employees to express their demands'.

Although the strike was brutally suppressed by the government, the company finally agreed to a 4.3 months' salary as the year-end bonus (at least 8,610 yuan for each worker) to placate workers. More importantly, workers won another chance to re-elect the workplace union. After the strike, the Guangdong provincial-level union sent an investigation team to Mars and re-elected the workplace union. This time, the election was much more democratic: workers directly elected more than 90 union representatives, and then the union representatives elected nine union committee members including a president and a vice-president. The newly-elected president was a former union committee member, while the vice-chairman was a female rank-and-file worker who actively participated in the strike.

In the eight strikes listed above, the Mars strike was the only one which was suppressed by the police with force. After the incident, autoworkers in other factories in the same industrial zone quickly learned from the Mars strike. In later strikes, the autoworkers no longer took the strategy of blocking shipment passages. Furthermore, the Mars case shows that workers have developed a certain trade union consciousness. Although workers' initial demand was to increase the year-end bonus, the collective bargaining experience showed them that their economic interests were highly associated with their right of freedom of association: a democratic and representative trade union was crucial to defend and fight for their collective interests.

The Venus Factory

The Venus Factory, founded in 2004, is also a Japanese-owned auto parts factory. It supplied car windows and doors to Toyota and Nissan, and had a workforce of about 530 in 2013. During the strike wave in 2010, the Venus workers also went on strike, demanding a wage increase remarkably beyond the legal minimum wage. After a half day of strike, the company agreed on a wage increase of 450 yuan (from 950 yuan to 1,400 yuan, about a 50 per cent increase). Moreover, with the help of the LGDFTU, the Venus factory held an election in 2011. Workers directly elected 44 trade union representatives and seven trade union committee members, and then the committee members recommended a union president and a vice president. The newly-elected union president, XJ, was an office worker who was famous for his rich legal knowledge and bravery when challenging authority. Knowing XJ was elected as the union president, the company intervened and asked to re-elect the union president on the pretext that XJ did not get more than half of the votes from employees (156 out of 348 workers voted for him). At this point, the LGDFTU organized a direct election for union president, and XJ successfully got more than half of the votes and became the president of the Venus union. As a result, the Venus union representatives, union committee members, and the president were all directly elected by workers.

The Venus union was considered one of the most militant unions in Guangzhou's auto parts industry. For Venus unionists, each collective bargaining was 'like a fight' (interview, November 28, 2013), and they had to rely on workers' support to negotiate with the company. Take the collective bargaining over the year-end bonus in January 2013 as an example. During the bargaining, the company attempted to delay the process. In response, the Venus union called a union representatives meeting to discuss countermeasures, during which it decided to demand that the company announced a bonus plan at 10:00 am, 22 January. Otherwise, the union would take 'substantial actions' (*xiangguan xingdong*). After the meeting, the union representatives went back to the workplace and announced the union's decision to the rank-and-file workers. By the stated time the company failed to bring out the plan. The union representatives then initiated and organized a strike since the union president was out on a business trip. All workers joined the strike by sitting in the staff canteen. After the strike, officials of the LGDFTU were called by the company to mediate the dispute. Nevertheless, a union representative recalled that a LGDFTU official came to the staff canteen where strikers gathered and said to all employees that 'labourers have the right not to work. Hope you could settle the dispute soon through negotiation' (interview, May 5, 2014). Here we can see that, while the company attempted to delay the bargaining process, the LGDFTU supported workers' demand to resume collective bargaining. Additionally, a client from a Toyota assembly plant happened to be in the factory during the strike. The strike made him doubt Venus's ability to supply auto parts on time. The pressure from Toyota made the Venus management anxious to reach an agreement with the workers. Therefore, after 5.5 hours of strike, the workers won a year-end bonus of 3.5 months (at least 7,000 yuan for each worker). It is noteworthy that the strike appeared to be spontaneous. Even though it was actually initiated by the workplace union, it was too risky for the union to organize it publicly. Nevertheless, after the incident, the workplace union still faced severe punishment from the management. Some active union committee members were pressured, and some of them were demoted or transferred to sites in another city.

Another strike occurred in Venus on January 22, 2015, which was also triggered by collective bargaining over the year-end bonus. The company proposed a bonus of 1.5 months' salary, while the trade union demanded five months' salary. Neither side was willing to compromise. On the same day, a strike broke out. One worker explained: 'We had an agreement before they (the union negotiators) went to the bargaining. If the bargaining fails, they will call, and we will have a strike' (interview, January 22, 2015). At the beginning of the strike, the workers walked out of their workshops and gathered in the staff canteen. Several policemen came, but they stayed at the factory gate without going into the workplace. Additionally, two strikers mentioned that one policeman said to them that 'striking is fine. But do not break machines or act recklessly' (interview, May 6, May 9, 2015). After three days of strike, the workers successfully led Guangzhou Toyota and several other suppliers of Toyota to a production halt. However, the strike faced joint suppression from Venus and Guangzhou Toyota. While Venus recruited about 50 temporary workers, Toyota also sent about 80 workers from its assembly plant to assist the production resumption. As a countermeasure, the strikers returned to work and changed their strategy to go-slow. For the Venus workers, it was a way to occupy the workplace and prevent others from working on the line. In the meantime, the production output dropped 90 per cent.

After the strike, eight trade union officials from provincial-level, city-level and district level unions came to Venus and persuaded both sides to have a new round of collective bargaining. In the meantime, they persuaded workers to resume production. However, this turned out to be a bad decision of the workers. After the production returned to normal, the company insisted on a bonus plan of 3.4 months and refused to increase it anymore. The Venus union held a union representatives meeting to vote for the plan, which was rejected (50 vs. 19). Then the company announced that the collective bargaining had broken, and refused further bargaining. The eight upper-level union officials did not pressure the company to make further concessions. Additionally, after one week of strike and go-slow, the Venus workers were too exhausted to hold another strike. At last, the workplace union conceded and workers accepted 3.4 months of salary as a year-end-bonus (at least 7,731 yuan for each worker). This case indicates that in the face of strong global capital, it is never easy for autoworkers to fight for their interests. Moreover, the case also illustrates that the auto assembly plant and the auto parts plant were developing joint actions to suppress workers' collective actions. It might become harder for Venus workers to win considerable economic gains from the company in the future.

The Venus union, according to my observation, is the most active and democratic union in Guangzhou's auto parts industry. In addition to wages, the Venus union actively bargained with the company about working time, the company regulations, and the rights of breastfeeding female workers, and so on. Furthermore, the union held a series of training programmes for union members about labour law, the union's work, and the function of collective bargaining. These training programmes were supported by lawyers and university professors who were concerned about labour rights. Through the processes of collective bargaining and training programmes, the Venus workers gradually developed a deeper understanding of the workplace union and collective bargaining. In contrast to their indifference to the previous workplace union, the Venus workers showed strong belongingness to the newly-elected union. An interesting example was that when workers went out for a trip, they carried the Venus union flag with them, even though the trip was not organized by the union. Moreover, the rank-and-file workers realized that a workplace union elected by themselves could indeed fight for their rights. For instance, when Venus workers had labour disputes with the company, they tended to seek help from the Venus union. What is more, workers became more active in the union's work, such as participating and organizing union activities, paying close attention to collective bargaining, offering suggestions to the union and volunteering. The support of the rank-and-file workers in turn supported the Venus union to go further.

Collective Bargaining as a Contested Terrain

Based on their study of the CHAM union, C. Chan and Hui (2013) argued that the new collective bargaining system was a 'party-state-led collective bargaining'. Compared to formalistic collective bargaining, the new bargaining system 'involves more genuine negotiation between workers and enterprise representatives over wages, and the negotiated pay rises are usually above the legal standards'. However, they suggested that the more 'genuine negotiation' and wage rises were based on the state's authority, especially the active intervention of upper-level unions. While C. Chan and Hui are quite correct in suggesting that the new collective bargaining system was introduced and supported by the state, their analysis is weakened by their failure to capture the dynamics and actions of the autoworkers in the bargaining process. The autoworkers, rather than being voiceless and inactive players, participated in the collective bargaining by taking collective action. For example, some CHAM union representatives from the assembly workshop, in the collective bargaining over the year-end bonus of 2012, declared that if the company refused to concede, they would hold a strike. As a result, the company quickly conceded and agreed a year-end bonus of 3.9 months' salary. Another example was that the CHAM workers had another strike to force the management to make a compromise during the bargaining over a wage increase in 2013.

One of the key strike organizers was a union committee member from the assembly workshop. After the strike, the rank-and-file workers won a wage increase of 310 yuan. Therefore, I argue that the improved effectiveness of collective bargaining and the resultant wage raise are largely based on the autoworkers' strong workplace bargaining power and their capacity to take collective action (instead of the authority of the state and upper-level unions). As such, the new collective bargaining system is more like a contested terrain than a party-state-led one.

Besides, it is worthy to note that while striking is the most forceful form of collective action, there are other forms such as boycotts of overtime work, go-slows, gathering at the playground, and singing the national anthem during lunch time. All of these collective actions are significant ways for rank-and-file workers to forge solidarity and influence the outcomes of collective bargaining. Moreover, even though some factories have not had strikes, the threat of strike remains a powerful bargaining chip for unions or workers, which can be seen from a union negotiator's comment: 'During collective bargaining, when the management refused to take concessions, we told them: "OK. It's fine. But we have to inform workers the outcome. It's not our responsibility if they take action". You know, the company is scared of strikes, so the bargaining is not so difficult' (interview, December 10, 2013). Therefore, it is reasonable to argue that workers' own actions (or their potential to take actions) are an important force for effective collective bargaining.

C. Chan and Hui's study is also limited by their overestimation of the role of upper-level unions in raising wage levels. In their study, they mentioned that the involvement of the vice president of Guangdong provincial-level union was the key that enabled the CHAM management to reach a wage agreement with the workplace union. This is one of the reasons why they called it 'party-state-led collective bargaining'. Nevertheless, it is unlikely for provincial-level unions to directly intervene in workplace collective bargaining on a large scale. In practice, it is usually district-level unions which intervened in workplace collective bargaining. Compared to provincial-level unions, the authority of district-level unions is relatively low, which limits their capacity to pressure management to raise wages. In fact, both the Mars and Venus unions, after a stalemate occurred in collective bargaining over annual wage increase, had once invited the district-level union to attend the collective bargaining. But with the presence of district union officials, the companies only raised their proposed wage increase by 10 yuan. Hence, for the autoworkers, it became clear that they could not simply rely on upper-level unions to gain a concrete wage increase from the management.

It seems that the local government could not fully control the development of workplace collective bargaining. Firstly, while the newly established collective bargaining system was meant to decrease labour protests, it in turn generated new worker activism in the workplace; secondly, although the local government indeed intended to increase the autoworkers' income through collective bargaining, the actual wage increases were much higher than its expectation. District-level unions were afraid that rapid wage increase might hinder the ability of local government to attract capital. A Nansha district-level union official commented: 'The demand of workers becomes unreasonable. They keep asking for wage increase. If workers demand wage increase blindly, it may cause the outflow of capital. We have to avoid that in Guangzhou' (interview, April 3, 2015). District-level unions, therefore, might become more reluctant to pressure companies to raise wages or bonuses in the coming years. Besides, it is worth noting that, since January 1, 2015, the 'Guangdong Province Enterprise Collective Contracts Regulations' have come into effect. This regulation can be regarded as another attempt of the local state to control worker activism during collective bargaining. According to article 24 of the regulation, in the bargaining process, 'employees could not violate their labour contracts or fail to complete job tasks', which means workers' collective action in the bargaining process is officially prohibited. Nonetheless, its impact on workers' collective action and collective bargaining needs to be further investigated.

In the meantime, managements have resorted to various ways to control or influence workplace unions and collective bargaining, such as intervening in the daily work of workplace unions, impeding the progress of collective bargaining, and punishing active union members. What is more, capital has developed more coherent ways to control the collective bargaining process. A recent example was that, from 9 to 10 March, 2015, Toyota recruited human resource managers of its first-tier suppliers in Guangzhou to have a two-day training session on collective bargaining and workers' collective actions. The main training content included: (a) Narrow down the scope of collective bargaining. Management shall not bargain with workplace unions about year-end bonuses; (b) According to the 'Guangdong Province Enterprise Collective Contracts Regulations', if workers launch a strike during collective bargaining, it is legitimate for the company to punish the strikers according to its own rules; (c) Rather than turning a blind eye to enterprise unions, top and middle-level managers should guide and instruct union's work, and gradually penetrate workplace unions; (d) Identify and report troublemakers among workers to the local state. The training signalled that management might take more aggressive and systematic measures to attack and manipulate workplace unions and collective bargaining in Guangzhou's auto parts industry in the future.

Workplace trade unions, as workers' representatives, are key players in the collective bargaining process. As mentioned above, due to incomplete union reform and lack of strike right, workplace unions' capacity to bargain with management is generally weak. It is difficult to win concessions from management without the support of workers' collective actions. The weakness of workplaces unions is the reason why autoworkers still resort to direct actions during collective bargaining processes. On the other hand, the cases of Mars and Venus show that some worker activists are aware of the importance of shop-floor organization, and are consciously fighting for the democratization and autonomy of workplace unions. Moreover, autoworkers are acquiring knowledge about workplace unions by engaging in union activities, collective action and collective bargaining. As the Mars case indicates, in the first union election in 2011, the workers and union representatives were easily manipulated by the management. However, in the second union election after the strike in 2013, they were more aware of the importance of union elections and thus tended to elect their own representatives.

In short, I argue that the newly introduced or strengthened collective bargaining in Guangzhou is not merely a means for the state to control worker activism, but also a mechanism that is creating new workplace militancy. Only when we view it as a contested terrain among the state, capital, and workers, can we capture the dynamics and internal-logic of collective bargaining in the auto parts industry in Guangzhou.

Conclusion

The chapter argues that it is important to view the newly established collective-bargaining system in Guangzhou as a dynamic process rather than a static fact. In the process of collective bargaining, the autoworkers have accumulated valuable experiences and knowledge of strikes and workplace unions. In the first place, by taking collective action in the process of collective bargaining, the workers have sensed their strong workplace bargaining power and capacity to fight for their interests. Moreover, my fieldwork suggests that autoworkers' strikes are increasingly well-organized and strategic. Some effective strike strategies in pressuring management or decreasing the possibility of government suppression have been diffused across factories. Secondly, the newly established collective-bargaining system provides the autoworkers an opportunity to engage in union activities, to awake union awareness, and to learn about the capacity and limitation of workplace unions. It is widely accepted that Chinese workers' demands focus on economic interests such as wages and bonuses, while political rights (in particular the trade union right) are not in their agenda. Nonetheless, the cases of Mars and Venus suggest that the workers have gradually acquired and developed a certain trade union consciousness. With the development of collective bargaining, some worker activists have realized that a democratic trade union is essential for workers, and that the more democratic the trade union is, the more effectively it fights for workers' collective interests. The collective bargaining process, thus, nurtures new forms of solidarity and trade union consciousness among the autoworkers.

REFERENCES

Cai, Y. S. (2006) *State and Laid-Off Workers in Reform China: The Silence and Collective Action of the Retrenched*, London; New York: Routledge.

Chan, C. K. C. (2010) *The Challenge of Labour in China: Strikes and the Changing Labour Regime in Global Factories*, Abingdon, Oxon; New York: Routledge.

Chan, C. K. C. and Hui, E. S. I. (2012) 'The dynamics and dilemma of workplace trade union reform in China: the case of the Honda workers' strike', *Journal of Industrial Relations*, 54(5): 653–668.

Chan, C. K. C. and Hui, E. S. I. (2013) 'The development of collective bargaining in China: from 'collective bargaining by riot' to 'party state-led wage bargaining'', *The China Quarterly*, 217:221–242.

Chen, F. (2010) 'Trade unions and the quadripartite interactions in strike settlement in China', *The China Quarterly*, 201:104–124.

Chen, W. G. (2011) Guangzhoushi zonggonghui di shiliujie weiyuanhui di shiyici quanti huiyi gongzuo baogao [The work report of the Guangzhou Federation of Trade Union on the 11th plenary session of the sixteenth committee meeting] [Online], Available from: http://www.gzgh.org.cn/web/Opens/open1.aspx?lid= 15937c84-e7bb-4b3a-a2eb-9d13f551d03a&iid=41. Accessed 5 April, 2015.

Clarke, S., Lee, C. H. and Li Q. (2004) 'Collective consultation and industrial relations in China', *British Journal of Industrial Relations*, 42(2): 235–254.

Friedman, E. (2014) *Insurgency Trap: Labor Politics in Postsocialist China*, Ithaca, New York: Cornell University Press.

Huang, X. (2012) 'Guangzhou Luogang 73 jia feigong qiye zhixuan gonghui zhuxi' [73 Non-public enterprises directly elected union presidents in Luogang, Guangzhou], *Nanfang Gongbao* April 12, 2012. Available from <http://www. gdftu.org.cn/ghyw/jscx/201206/t20120627_286968.htm>. (Accessed at 28 November 2014).

Kuruvilla, S. and Zhang, H. (2015) 'Labor protests and incipient collective bargaining in China', *Management and Organization Review*, forthcoming.

Lee, C. H., Brown, W. and Wen, X. (2014) 'What sort of collective bargaining is emerging in China?', *British Journal of Industrial Relations*, doi: 10.1111/bjir.12109.

▶

Lee, C. K. (2007) *Against the Law: Labor Protests in China's Rustbelt and Sunbelt*, Berkeley: University of California Press.

Leung, P. N. and Pun, N. (2009) 'The radicalisation of the new Chinese working class: a case study of collective action in the gemstone industry', *Third World Quarterly*, 30(3): 551–565.

Li, J. T. and Yang, Z. G. [Eds.] (2014) *Guangzhou Lanpishu: Guangzhou Qiche Chanye Fazhan Baogao 2014* [Blue Book of Guangzhou: Annual Report on Guangzhou's Automobile Industry 2014], Beijing: Shehui Kexue Wenxian Chubanshe.

Liu, M. W. (2010) 'Union organizing in China: still a monolithic labor movement?' *Industrial and Labor Relations Review,* 64(1): 30–52.

Pringle, T. (2011) *Trade Unions in China: The Challenge of Labour Unrest*, Abingdon, Oxon; New York, NY: Routledge.

Wang, L. S. [Ed.]. (2013) *Guangzhou Nianjian 2012* [Guangzhou Yearbook 2012], Guangzhou: Guangzhou Nianjian She.

Work and Employment in the Overseas Chinese Firm

Foxconn Beyond China: Capital–labour Relations as Co-determinants of Internationalization

14

Rutvica Andrijasevic and Devi Sacchetto

Introduction

Foxconn, a Taiwanese-owned firm, is the world's largest electronics contract manufacturer. Foxconn is best known for being the main assembler of Apple's iPhone and iPad and for the harsh working conditions at its mainland Chinese factories. These have fallen under close activist and scholarly scrutiny, which brought to light the firm's militarized disciplinary regime, unhealthy and unsafe working conditions, worker suicides, excessive and unpaid overtime, forced student labour, and crammed factory dormitories (Chan and Pun, 2010; Pun and Chan, 2012; Chan, Pun and Selden, 2013). This despotic management model prompted scholars to identify Foxconn as the epitome of 'bloody Taylorism' (Lipietz, 1987).

Foxconn's manufacturing centre is in mainland China, where it employs around a million people in 32 factories. In addition it has more than 200 subsidiaries around the world. However, despite Foxconn's expansion into South East Asia, Latin America, Australia, and Europe, there is very little scholarly research on the firm's work regimes outside China. Foxconn's territorial diversification strategy begs certain questions about the firm's internationalization, namely the process by which it expands and subsequently organizes its operations from mainland China to its overseas branch plants. This chapter explores Foxconn's internationalization and transfer of work and employment practices from mainland China to Europe, namely the Czech Republic and Turkey, where it opened subsidiaries in 2000 and 2009 respectively. Although Foxconn is Taiwanese-owned, since its manufacturing headquarters and the bulk of its factories are in China, scholars suggest that its work regime is best understood in relation to labour management in mainland China (Pun, Chan and Selden, forthcoming).

Research into multinational firms and their organization across national borders tends to approach the subject from either an economic perspective typical of international business literature or a sociological perspective developed in organizational studies. An economic perspective is based on considerations of economic efficiency and examines the costs and benefits of opening and operating a subsidiary in a foreign market. It seeks to answer questions about the conditions under which firms pursue overseas expansion, the factors that drive locational decisions, and the sequencing and management of this expansion (for an overview see Heinecke, 2011; Drahokoupil, 2014). A sociological institutionalist perspective, on the other hand, is grounded in the notion of 'national business systems'. This term suggests that a firm is positioned within social, economic, and political institutions on a national level, which jointly produce a nationally distinct way of organizing economic activity. Scholars working within this tradition focus their attention on the home and host country influences on the behaviour of the firm (for an overview see Smith, 2005). Until now, both the economic and the institutionalist strands investigated multinational firm's expansion from mature (US, Western Europe, and Japan) to emerging economies (for an exception see Aguzzoli and Geary, 2014), or alternatively from mature to mature economies as in the case of US firms establishing subsidiaries in Western Europe (see Djelic, 2001; Zeitlin and Herrigel, 2000). As Smith and Zheng show in their chapter in this volume, very little attention is paid to the expansion of firms from emerging to mature economies, in particular how firms operating in mainland China establish and organize their subsidiaries in Europe.

This chapter begins to fill this gap by posing the following questions: first, which work and employment practices is Foxconn exporting from its base in mainland China to its European subsidiaries? Second, are these practices applied consistently across European subsidiaries or are there variations from one country to another? Third, if Foxconn adapts its practices depending on the specificity of a national context, which factors influence this adaptation? In asking questions about the labour regime which Foxconn exports from mainland China to Europe and the factors influencing the adaptation of the firm's practices in different host countries, this chapter contributes a more substantive and less biased account of Chinese investments in Europe than those currently propositioned by scholars and media alike. An example of the current stance characterizing the debate on Chinese multinational firms in Europe is offered by the Greek case, where political forces on both the left and the right, including the trade unions, accuse the Chinese state-owned enterprise COSCO of driving the 'race to the bottom' by importing the Chinese workplace model into the port of Piraeus (Kambouri, 2014; Parsanoglou, 2014).

To offer a more nuanced picture of the work and employment practices that Chinese firms import into Europe, rather than focusing solely on the home country effects, we examine the role of the state and the trade unions in the host countries in order to assess the ways in which host states enable the formation of a particular labour regime. We also undertake a detailed analysis of the workforce in order to show how the specificity of workforce composition shapes the firm's labour management practices. This chapter then investigates the ways in which the role of labour, the state, and the trade unions co-constitute the firm's behaviour and its production politics. In contending that the work and employment practices that Foxconn establishes in its European subsidiaries are engendered by the host state's institutional context and labour as much as by the firm, this chapter aims to capture the overlapping influences of actors, sites, and institutions, as well as the power relations between them that inform the workings of transnational firms across borders.

Chinese Multinationals in Europe

The emerging public debate on Chinese investments in Europe begs an interesting question: what academic work exists to explain how Chinese labour regimes are imported into Europe by multinational firms from mainland China? There is a surprising shortage of research into mainland Chinese multinational firms and the work and employment practices they export to their subsidiaries in Europe. Existing work adopts an economic perspective prevalent in international business literature and studies particular features of Chinese investment in the EU such as location, motivation, and modes of entry (Brennan, 2010; Rios-Morales and Brennan, 2010; Zhang, Yang and Van Den Bulcke, 2012; Zhang, Duysters and Filippov, 2012; Meunier, 2014). Studies of Chinese multinationals in Europe that adopt a sociological perspective typical of organizational studies are extremely rare. Currently there are only a couple of examples of this strand of research. These are Burgoon and Raess' (2014) study of the implication of Chinese FDI for organized labour in Europe and Zhu and Wei's (2014) case study of a Chinese takeover of a motorcycle company in Italy.

While the above research offers some initial insight into localization and management practices in Chinese firms in Europe, its analytical scope remains limited due to two factors, both derived from conventional approaches to internationalization. First, most studies of multinational firms limit their analysis to applications and/or adaptations that the firms operate as they internationalize, and second, the tendency is to investigate the relationship between the headquarters and a single foreign subsidiary. Contrary to the dominant trend of examining the relationship between the headquarters located in the home country and a single subsidiary located in the host country (for an exception see Almond et al., 2005), in this chapter we investigate the firm's labour management regimes in several of its foreign subsidiaries: Pardubice and Kutná Hora in the Czech Republic and Çorlu in Turkey. While we pay attention to the relevance of distinctive national context and, in particular, the role of states in constructing the legal frameworks that regulate employment and industrial relations, we also contend that the notion of distinctive national business systems is restrictive since it overlooks the systemic practices of capital. What is needed instead is a more detailed analysis of why some practices are applied and others are not, and a greater separation between the firm's management practices versus local actors within the subsidiary.

We suggest that a way of achieving this more nuanced outlook on the multinational firm is by integrating labour into the analysis of internationalization. Typically, investigations of internationalization focus on the firm's internal management system and work practices (Morgan, Kristensen and Whitley, 2001), neglecting the role of workers in shaping the firm's strategies of labour management and organization of production. Labour is not an inert 'factor of location' (Herod, 1997) or unvarying input into production but rather a dynamic actor which both intentionally and unintentionally shapes the dissemination of a firm's management practices. By showing the ways in which capital and labour co-determine processes of capitalist expansion, this chapter aims to overcome the limitations resulting from internationalization theories' traditional focus on the firm and its management (Selwyn, 2012; Boussebaa and Morgan, 2014).

Last but not least, this chapter seeks to counter a major weakness in the existing literature on Chinese investment in Europe, which is dominated by the use of quantitative data, statistical methods, and desk research. While studies working within the quantitative tradition provide important insights into trends in Chinese OFDI in Europe, datasets and secondary research are unable to answer questions about how social institutions or labour inform the behaviour of the firm. To counter this weakness, we adopt ethnographic methods with a strong emphasis on participant observation, such as living in the dormitories and sharing workers' facilities, which are best suited to examining the role of labour in informing the firm's behaviour. We did ethnographic fieldwork in the Czech Republic in 2012 and in Turkey in 2013, where we conducted 63 and 29 interviews respectively. While the bulk of the interviews are with workers, we also interviewed managers and key informants in public institutions such as labour ministries, trade unions, labour inspectorates, labour offices, local job centres, vocational schools, and NGOs. All interviews with workers were conducted outside the workplace environment, in bars, parks and dormitories, to guarantee the interviewees' anonymity. In the Czech Republic we stayed in the same dormitories as the workers which, unlike dormitories in mainland China, double up as hostels by taking in paying guests.

Heterogeneity of Labour and Workforce Management Models

Who the workers are and where they come from, in particular if they come from more than one country and possess different citizenship statuses, will influence the mechanisms the firm uses to recruit its workforce, insert it into the labour process, and attach it to the firm (Bauder, 2006). In what follows, we examine this process in Foxconn's plants in the Czech Republic and Turkey.

Workforce composition and turnover of workers

In the Czech Republic, the Pardubice plant employs circa 5,000–6,000 and the Kutná Hora plant 2,500–3,000 workers. The workforce is composed of directly and indirectly employed workers. The former constitute about 60 per cent of the workforce and are predominantly domestic Czech and a small group of Ukrainian, Vietnamese, and Mongolian workers directly employed by Foxconn on permanent contracts. The indirectly employed group is made up of EU workers from the neighbouring countries of Slovakia, Poland, Romania, and Bulgaria, who are hired on short-term contracts through Temporary Work Agencies (TWAs). They make up circa 40 per cent of the total workforce, but at times the agency worker presence peaks up to 60 per cent (Bormann and

Plank, 2010). Contrary to mainland China, where Foxconn does not employ workers over 35, in the Czech Republic the age of workers varies: directly employed workers are aged 30 to 50, agency workers are 20 to 35, and a minority of the latter group are older men and women aged 50 to 65.

In Turkey, Foxconn employs about 350–400 workers. Unlike the Czech Republic where the workforce is split between domestic direct workers and EU migrant agency workers, the labour force in Turkey is more homogeneous. The majority of the workforce is made up of Turkish women and men aged between 25 and 45 who are hired directly on open-ended contracts. There are two key traits to the workforce composition. First, Foxconn employs a large number of women workers because in the area around Çorlu the presence of women in the local labour market is widespread; and second, it employs a high percentage of Bulgarian Turks known as Muhacir Bulgarians who came to Turkey in 1989 to escape ethnic cleansing in Bulgaria. In addition, a small percentage of the workforce is made up of high-school students and unemployed people who are required to complete their internships and/or apprenticeships at the Foxconn plant. Their ages vary, but they are usually under 30.

While at first glance there is little similarity within and between the workforce in the Czech and Turkish plants, what connects them to each other as well as to the plants in China is a considerably high level of turnover. While China presents the highest rate of labour turnover, over 50 per cent annually (Pun and Chan, 2012), in the Czech Republic the labour turnover of direct workers is about 30 per cent and in Turkey about 20–30 per cent per year, in particular among manual workers. The turnover is caused by the high levels of seasonal fluctuation in production, high velocity of tasks, repetitive work, and low wages (McGovern, Smeaton and Hill, 2004):

> Each person has five tasks to perform on the assembly line. That's all we do: take a computer screen and place it in front of us, take a cable and push both ends into the machine, take the cooler and push it inside and then the part moves on. One repeats this the whole time. When I first came here, I worked an eight-hour shift on the assembly line and it was so repetitive that I was no longer thinking straight but instead worked like a machine. (Slovak worker, Pardubice, 10 September 2012)

The hourly wage for direct workers in the Czech Republic is around 3.5 euros, amounting to 600–700 euros per month. Compared to the net wage average in the Czech Republic in 2012 of 700–750 and the minimum wage of 330 euros per month (Czech Statistical Office, 2014; Mysíková, 2012), Foxconn workers earn less than the national average but significantly above the minimum wage. In Turkey, wages for assembly line workers are set just above the minimum wage level fixed by the government, 300–350 euros per month, which is periodically revised.

Agency workers earn less; their wage is 2.5 euros per hour or about 400–500 euros per month depending on the amount of hours they work. Next to being highly dependent on the seasonal fluctuation of production, agency workers' turnover is also prompted by weak identification with their job due to the lack of communication among workers and the limited opportunities for career progression. Given their linguistic differences, assembly line workers of different nationalities may rarely speak to each other and depend on translation by their bilingual foreman to speak to the Czech workers, a situation that produces a sense of isolation as well as divisions among the workers.

In addition, for assembly line workers, in particular those hired through TWAs, there are few opportunities for upward progression to higher positions or more senior roles. At best, those who gain a reasonable knowledge of the Czech language might get promoted to the role of assembly line leader. This is in stark contrast to the domestic directly employed workforce, which predominantly occupies high-level or supervisory posts, and monopolizes the roles of foremen, supervisors, and group leaders. A similar hierarchy is present in the Turkish plant, albeit between male and female workers. Gender plays a large part in the company's hierarchy and men hold the majority of managerial positions. In production there is a clear division of labour between men and women: pre-test is fully staffed by women while the assembly line is mixed. During our fieldwork there was only one woman group leader working in production although in the past there were three, one in the warehouse and another in packing. The majority of women in assembly are in their twenties because managers are prejudiced against women in their thirties or older and consider them too slow to work on assembly jobs.

The turnover of workers in the Czech plants needs to be considered in the context of the common labour market. EU nationals enjoy the right to freedom of movement which entitles individuals to access the labour market across the EU. In fact, Polish, Slovak, Bulgarian, and Romanian workers at Foxconn had frequently worked in another European county before arriving in the Czech Republic. This is the case both for young men and women, aged 20 to 35, working on assembly lines, as well as for older men and women, aged 50 to 65, working in packing. Equally, it is not uncommon for workers from countries like Vietnam to have gained international work experience in South Korea, Taiwan, and Qatar. In Turkey, while the workforce is more homogeneous, many Muhacir Bulgarians have dual citizenship and are therefore more mobile than local Turkish workers, and were considering looking for work in the EU since as Bulgarian citizens they enjoy the freedom to move and work within the EU. Moreover, Muhacir have a more secular worldview and a more 'modern' lifestyle than locals. As women are better educated and generally more free and do not wear headscarves, Muhacir women experience greater labour mobility and are more likely to get hired for factory work than local Turkish women, especially as they are more disposed to working unsocial hours (Nichols, Sugur and Sugur, 2001).

This kind of work experience in different contexts, whether national or international, allows workers to develop job-search strategies and compare wages, working conditions and management practices in various plants and/or countries. This knowledge enables workers to define, at least in part, their own labour mobility and enact exit strategies that challenge employers' expectations about their availability to work irregular hours for low pay:

> I am 28 and I was born in a small city in the south west of Romania. I went to a secondary school specializing in automotive mechanics but I'm not interested in mechanical work. If you asked me to look at a car I could not tell you anything about it. I worked in Romania first as a bartender and a retail assistant in an electronics store. At the moment I work in Foxconn in Kutná Hora. In 2007 I was in England, in 2008 in Italy, and 2009 in Greece and now I am in the Czech Republic. I was in England for three months and worked in Debenhams selling cosmetics. The pay was low because I found work via an agency and they kept a lot of the money. After three months my contract was finished and I went home and then from there to Italy. In Greece I worked in agriculture and harvested peppers. That was small money too: I would get 40 euro cents for 1 kilo of peppers and did 12 hours' work per day, working Monday to Saturday. I did not like it and after three months I came back. Then I found this job in 2011 via a friend of mine. (Romanian worker, Kutná Hora, 9 September 2012)

Heterogeneity and the dynamic nature of labour suggest that the workforce is not always already formed and available in the sites where a transnational firm establishes itself and that workforce mobility is intertwined with the firm's labour management practices. Smith (2006) identifies the expression of high labour turnover as the 'mobility power of labour' and points out that labour scholars judge turnover negatively and as inferior to voice since it is an individual act rather than collective mobilization. Discussions of individual exit are relevant, we argue, because they indicate that mobility generates tension between capital and labour. The high number of indirect workers means that the firm is in a theoretically stronger bargaining position compared with when they have to deal with directly employed labour. We can hence interpret segmentation of the workforce according to directly and indirectly employed status as an example of Foxconn's application of the structural conditions under which workers' bargaining power is reduced. However, our material suggests that indirectly recruited workers accumulate more labour mobility capacity, which puts them in a stronger bargaining role against an employer that is reluctant to establish voice mechanisms, and, as we show in the following section, uses labour market manipulations in the hope of recreating dependency.

Strategies of labour management

Given the heterogeneity of the workforce as well as workers' experience and knowledge of the labour market, Foxconn puts in place different strategies specific to location and workforce composition that enable it to manage turnover and meet the demands of the seasonal just-in-time production and cost-cutting pressure that corporate customers place on the firm. In the Czech Republic, Foxconn relies on TWAs to recruit and manage EU migrant workers. Foxconn started using agency workers in late 2004 when the Czech government introduced the notion of agency employment into the Labour Code, as required by the EU accession process, and set out the rules for temporary work (Hála, 2007). Contrary to the traditional work agencies whose main role is to lease workers to the client firm, international TWAs deployed by Foxconn are small or medium-sized rather than large operators and they focus on recruiting groups of workers. Large agencies, as McLoughlin and Munz (2011) suggest, do not participate in cross-border recruitment since they target individuals rather than groups of workers.

The role of these international agencies is exceptional because they operate a comprehensive management of migrant labour that encompasses recruitment and selection in country of origin, cross-border transportation, work and living arrangements in the country of destination, and repatriation to the countries of origin during periods of low production (Andrijasevic and Sacchetto, 2014). The agencies therefore facilitate workers' mobility but also confine it by signing up workers to short-term contracts. Although they are promised a one-year contract, the initial contract that the workers are put on is 300 hours and it functions as a trial period. The promise of a one-year contract serves as an incentive to complete the 300 hours that, in periods of low production, can take two to three months:

> The agency told us we would work 12 hours a day, every day, and that all we need to do is some operation on the assembly line. They told us we'll work six times 12-hour shifts in a week and have one day off. When we got here they told us we wouldn't do 12-hour shifts but actually alternate one short with one long working week. And then, we went to work today and we were told that there is no work. The scheduling clearly said that we are to work today. I woke up in the morning at 4 am, went to the factory and they sent me back. It's pointless: there was no need for me to wake up that early in the first place. (Slovak worker, Pardubice, 7 September 2012)

Usually, after the initial 300 hours, workers are simply put on another short-term contract. Just as during the 'trial' period workers are not paid their full wages but are given an advance of 1000 CZK (40 euros) per week, the postponing of wages attaches the workforce to the agencies as workers, while they might be frustrated by their working conditions, are unwilling to leave until paid.

TWAs currently play only a marginal role in the labour market in Turkey and cannot operate as a support structure for Foxconn as they do in the Czech Republic. In Turkey, Foxconn's strategy for managing turnover, variations in production and cost-cutting pressure is to rely on a number of fluctuating interns and apprentices. To this end, the management avails itself of two government-run programmes. The first provides internships for high school students and the second, funded by the government through local employment centres (Işkur), involves apprenticeships geared towards unemployed people. Students from vocational and technical schools have to complete a compulsory practical training programme either as a summer traineeship or as training for three days per week throughout their last year of school. Students work alongside the regular workers but are paid only a third of the minimum wage. While in China the student workforce is the structural part of Foxconn's production process (Smith and Chan, 2015), in Turkey Foxconn take only a handful of students. The Işkur scheme for unemployed people is based on a 264-hour apprenticeship lasting about nine weeks. Each year Foxconn staff select a sizeable number of apprentices directly at the Işkur offices and in June 2012 alone Foxconn took on 50 apprentices, paid between 7.5 and 9.3 euros per day by the government for eight to ten hours of work:

> The basic training was for one week only and it took place in the classroom. After that we worked like any Foxconn employee, but got our wages from Işkur. Let me give you an example. When you get to Foxconn the first thing they say is this: 'Işkur may tell you that you will be working eight hours per day, but our working hours are ten hours per day and you have to abide by this'. In other words, Foxconn management sends out the message that Işkur can say whatever they want, but in the end it is Foxconn that decides. (Turkish worker, Çorlu, 11 September 2013)

As well as relying on the temporary workforce, Foxconn in both the Czech Republic and Turkey utilizes the so-called 'hour-bank system' to tie directly employed workers to the firm, while at the same time achieving flexible labour use. In the Czech Republic this set-up requires workers to work a total of 930 hours in six months. Direct workers in production work 12-hour shifts, both day and night, three times a week, and need to be available for any other potential shifts during the same week. The 'hour-bank system' is used to organize the working shifts and has a regulatory function. The management puts to work those who have not accumulated the necessary hours and excludes from production those who have worked a sufficient number of hours. What gets lost in the system is any supplement for weekend working since weekends and weekdays are treated the same and paid at the same flat rate. When there are no orders and workers work only a few shifts, they end up 'owing' hours to Foxconn. Because their hours are calculated over a period of six months, workers on 12-hour shifts are bound to Foxconn both in the company's attempt to get them to 'repay' their hourly 'debt' and in their own attempt to be paid any outstanding overtime at the end of the six months.

A similar practice is in place in Turkey, where the 2003 Labour Act allows Foxconn to average out an individual's working hours to 45 hours a week over a two-month period.[1] Under the 'hour-bank system', companies are allowed to employ workers for up to 60 hours per week, but Foxconn exploits it in a more extreme way than other businesses in the area because working hours can range from 30 to 60 hours per week. Employees work between 10 and 12 hours a day for five or six days a week, but sometimes less if they're not needed. This flexible working pattern permits workers to earn the minimum wage regardless of the amount of the hours they work. But, on the other hand, the extra hours worked in any particular week are not paid as overtime because they are carried over to subsequent weeks so that the average weekly amount of hours worked is always 45. Crucially then, as a result of this averaging practice, workers are not entitled to overtime pay even when, in reality, they have put in more than 45 hours in a week.

Lastly, another crucial practice through which labour is attached to the firm is dormitories. While in Turkey all workers live locally in flats or family houses and travel 20–60 minutes to the factory in the dozen or so buses provided by Foxconn, in the Czech Republic, as in mainland China, the majority of migrant workers are housed in dormitories. While in the Czech Republic dormitories are individual hotels, army barracks, or ex-factory lodgings located off-site and about a 20–30-minute journey from the factory, in mainland China dormitories are part of a larger complex that incorporates the factory, the dormitories, and a number of basic facilities such as beauty parlours, eateries and internet shops. What is similar, however, as Pun and Smith (2007) suggest, is that dormitories facilitate the extension of management's control over labour in a way that intertwines the spheres of life and work. In the Czech Republic that control is exercised by the TWAs which are responsible for controlling the agency workforce:

> I worked for nine months at the plant and then I got sick, went to the doctor and was off for two days. The agency people came saying that that's it, I am fired. We asked if we could stay [in the dormitory] until six o'clock so we could pack our bags and they said that if we wanted to stay longer we needed to pay 400 CZK (16 euros) per person, and so we paid to stay until midday today. (Romanian worker, Pardubice, 8 September 2012)

In the Czech Republic, therefore, as much as in mainland China (Pun, 2007), large-scale factory production relies on migrant labour that is organized so as to combine the spaces of work and residence. However, the use of dormitories is not to be seen simply in terms of Foxconn applying Chinese management practices to the Czech factories as dormitories were in use already during the socialist period. In what used to be Czechoslovakia, the state instituted dormitories with the aim of keeping a large proportion of the population in rural areas and concentrating industries in the major urban centres (Fuchs and Demko, 1978: 178). In this way workers, typically male, young, and low-skilled or manual rural labourers, would live 'at work' during their working week and return to their homes at the weekend. What is different today, compared to the

previous historical process of industrialization, is that in light of fluctuating production, the dormitories permit employers to stand workers
down for several days without risking a shortage of workers. In this way,
dormitories allow Foxconn to avail itself of a pool of stationary workforce, which in the Czech Republic is under the discreet yet constant
control of agencies, and facilitate the 'just in time' model (Smith, 2003)
for the utilization of workers.

Capital relocation and Expansion: The Role of the State and the Trade Unions

In this section we show how the localization of Foxconn in the Czech
Republic and Turkey is largely supported and facilitated by the state in
terms of significant fiscal incentives and provision of land and infrastructure on the one hand, and easing labour-market deregulation via
favourable policies on the other. In addition, we also suggest that capital
expansion is aided by the trade unions since these actively participate in
the segmentation and weakening of labour because of the protectionist
stance they hold towards migrant and agency workers and/or by representing the interests of employers rather than workers.

State-capital alliance

In the Czech Republic, Foxconn first acquired in 2000 a pre-existing
factory in Pardubice, about 100 km from Prague, and later in 2007 it
built a new plant in nearby Kutná Hora.[2] The Foxconn factory in
Turkey is located within the European Free Zone (EFZ) in western
Turkey close to the city of Çorlu in Tekirdağ province.[3] The EFZ is an
enclosed area that houses 150 companies with a total labour force of
around 3,500. The Czech and Turkish factories are a foothold within
Foxconn's strategy of moving closer to its customers' end markets. The
factories in the Czech Republic supply Western European customers and
the Turkish plant supplies Middle Eastern and North African customers,
as well as local ones.

The Pardubice factory is the logistics and management centre for all
of Foxconn's European operations. Due to its pro-foreign investment
policies, the Czech Republic was able to become a 'computer hub for
the Western European market' (Bormann and Plank, 2010: 4). Radosevic
(2004) notes that, among emerging markets, Central and Eastern Europe,
led by the Czech Republic and Hungary, developed into the second-tier

global location in the electronics industry, just after East Asia. The Pardubice region has the highest per-capita exports of goods of all the Czech Republic's regions. FDI attraction is a major developmental strategy of the Višegrad Four region, which includes the Czech Republic, Hungary, Slovakia and Poland. What is distinctive about these four post-socialist countries is that they have put in place what Drahokoupil calls 'investment-promotion machines' (2008) that uphold and foster the competition state through the formation of novel pro-growth coalitions composed of national, regional, and local state actors. One of the common practices to attract capital, as Drahokoupil explains further, is to re-classify the land from agricultural to industrial purposes without a proper legal procedure in order to attract an investor to a region or promote a particular regional development project (206).

Foxconn's case is a good illustration of some of these dynamics. CzechInvest, the investment and business development agency of the Czech Republic's Ministry of Industry and Trade, assisted Foxconn's managing director Jim Chang in finding the most suitable location to set up the manufacturing plant and subsequently Foxconn enjoyed a ten-year tax holiday from 2000 until 2010 (Evertiq, 2007). Locating its plants in the Czech Republic allowed Foxconn to avoid the EU's high tariff barriers, like, for example, the 14 per cent import duty on LCD TVs that are made in China (Taiwan Invest, 2006) and to label their products as 'Made in the EU' rather that the less appealing 'Made in China'. For its second factory in Kutná Hora, Foxconn received support from the City Council, which made it possible for Foxconn's founder and CEO, Terry Gou, to acquire farming land and a castle for the purpose of building a golf course. Gou's exclusive golf resort, Casa Serena, opened in 2008, a year later than Foxconn's factory in Kutná Hora.[4]

The EFZ, established in 1996 on a private basis, is part of the prolonged effort by the Turkish state to attract FDI.[5] Turkey first attempted, albeit unsuccessfully, to set up a free zone in 1928 via an agreement between the Turkish state and the American Ford Engine Company (Organ, 2006). Following another unsuccessful attempt in 1946, the Free Trade Zones Law finally entered into force in 1985 (Kavlak, 2012). With the aim of attracting foreign capital, the military government drove an economic shift from import substitution to market-oriented strategy and put in place subsidies for exporters, a programme of privatization, and restrictions on trade union activities by banning the right to strike in the free zone for the first ten years of its activity (Arnold, 2010: 620). Within the framework of EU negotiations the latter was amended and the government abolished restriction on labour mobilization and trade union's activity.

By locating its plant within the EFZ, Foxconn benefits from various tax breaks including complete exemption from VAT and from taxes on profits and wages, provided that it exports at least 85 per cent of the FOB value of the goods produced. Moreover, since the establishment of the EC-Turkey Customs Union in 1996, exports to the EU from domestic businesses in Turkey have been free of tax. In localizing the plant in the EFZ, Foxconn received support from various state actors. HP and Foxconn managers met with the Investment Support and Promotion Agency of Turkey (ISPAT), a government organization reporting directly to the prime minister and responsible for foreign investments, and subsequently jointly signed the agreement with the ministry. In 2009 Foxconn obtained permission to operate from the Ministry of Finance and started to recruit people at the end of 2010, following a feasibility study involving consultation with members of the government as well as directors of the local schools. This was, as an EFZ manager explains, a novel approach to localizing:

> Before establishing its activity, Foxconn came here and carried out an in-depth analysis of the area in a way that has never been done before. They also met directors from high schools and vocational schools in Çorlu. Schools are important for Foxconn because they hire workers who are graduates from vocational technical schools, mainly from electronics and mechanics branches. (EFZ manager, Çorlu, 9 September 2013)

The role of the state in attracting capital and providing support to the investors in the Czech Republic and Turkey is rather similar, albeit on a smaller scale, to that which Foxconn received from the Chinese government. Following initial localization in the Pearl River and the Yangzi River Delta (South and East China), Foxconn made use of the government's 'Go West' Programme, which encouraged industrial relocation to the western part of the country in order to balance the unequal regional development, and moved to substantially lower-wage regions in development zones in western China. Spurred on by the global financial crisis in 2008, many electronics makers accelerated their production shift to western cities in order to cut labour costs and take advantage of government economic incentives. An example is provided by the State Council's approval in early 2011 of plans for an economic zone aimed at joining together the cities of Chengdu (provincial capital of Sichuan) and Chongqing to further boost the economy of West China. This allowed Foxconn to transfer its workers out of higher minimum-wage areas in the Pearl River and the Yangzi River Delta to Chongqing and other inland cities, where workforce costs are about a quarter to a third lower than in the large metropolises due to the lower legal minimum wage level (Pun and Chan, 2012).

Transnational firms, far from posing a threat to the sovereignty of the state, widen the scope and reach of the state's political and legal structures. If we focus on the juncture between capital and the state, we can observe striking similarities in the state's active soliciting as well as facilitating of capital relocation and expansion. In order to investigate the role of the state's role as guarantor of capitalist expansion, there is a need, we suggest, to separate states and firms so as not to confuse the application of the firm's management practice with the existing structure of the labour market or forms of worker representation that we address in the following section.

Trade union politics and worker representation

Much has been written about China where workers do not enjoy freedom of association, there is no right to strike, and the only legal representative of labour, the All-China Federation of Trade Unions (ACFTU), is subordinate to the Communist Party and an instrument of state control over workers (Friedman and Kuruvilla, 2015). As Anita Chan put it, China's enterprise unions are 'an integral part of factory management' (2011: 42). An occurring phenomena in China, perhaps best exemplified by the strikes at Honda's Nanhai plant in 2010, is the breaking away of workers from the state affiliated union and the formation of a more autonomous base of workers' power (Friedman, 2014).

The situation we encountered in Turkey displays similarities to the one in mainland China. At the Foxconn plant, a number of workers were members of the Turkish Metal Union (TMU), which is active in the automotive, white goods, electronics, iron, and steel sectors. TMU is a member of the biggest Turkish union, Türk-iş, and the links between the two are close because the president of the TMU is also the General Secretary for Organization of Türk-iş. Türk-iş is well known for pursuing a policy of 'class compromise with the neoliberal agenda' (Özuğurlu, 2011:181–2), which has enabled it to survive the military regime in Turkey and gain a significant long-term advantage over other unions such as Disk, the Revolutionary Workers' Trade Union Confederation, which was closed down by the military in 1980 and its leaders prosecuted and imprisoned (Yildirim, Calis, and Benli, 2008). Unions in Turkey operate in a stringent legal environment. Collective bargaining can take place only in relation to an individual establishment or all establishments belonging to the same employer. A union can bargain only if it demonstrates that it has unionized 50 per cent plus one worker in the plant and 10 per cent of all the workers in the industry (Nichols, Sugur, and Demir, 2002).

TMU's unwillingness to side with workers became visible during the recent round of collective bargaining in the automotive sectors which prompted a wave of strikes against the TMU and led to direct negotiations between workers and company representatives. The strikes, as Korkmaz (2015) remarks, are likely to mark the end of the 35-year-old labour relations model in the automotive industry in Turkey. Despite TMU's reluctance to support the workers' struggle, Foxconn did not underestimate the influence of unions or the impact that worker mobilization can have on factory labour. Indeed, the experience of the Korean Daiyang factory in the European Free Zone[6] where workers' attempts to unionize in 2010, and which led to a fierce confrontation with the police, was still fresh in Foxconn workers' minds. Having hired a number of unionized workers during its first few months in Turkey, management soon remedied this oversight and made workers give up their union membership:

> I was a member of Turk Metal Union because I had previously worked at Profilo. When we started to work at Foxconn, the manager came to us and collected identity cards from all those of us who were union members. He threatened us, brought our identity cards to the public notary [who was at the time in the HR office], and through this pressure the manager forced us to leave the union. (Turkish worker/group leader, Çorlu, 8 September 2013)

Foxconn's hostility towards the union is therefore not simply driven by the firm's management practices transferred from mainland China, but is enabled by the Turkish state authorities which are 'intolerant of union activity' (Fougner and Kurtoğlu, 2011: 358).

The fact that unions can facilitate capital expansion and generate vertical divisions among workers is illustrated by Herod's (1997) discussion of the US unions' active participation in dismantling Latin American anti-US and anti-capitalist political organizations so that domestic US workers could continue to enjoy relatively high living standards. The role of the union in creating divisions between the domestic and foreign workforces is clearly discernible in Foxconn's plants in the Czech Republic. Contrary to Turkey, where unions are industry-based, in the Czech Republic the unions are plant-based and the union operating at the Foxconn plant in Pardubice is part of the Metalworkers Federation,

KOVO. While certainly applied by management, the vertical division between direct workers and agency workers is reinforced by the trade union's disinterest in migrant workers' conditions. When it comes to migrant agency workers, the trade unions' position is that they should be employed only on a temporary basis and exclusively as an interim unskilled substitute for domestic Czech workers.

This protectionist stance led critics to argue that Czech trade unions are indifferent to the rights of foreign workers and that their commitment to the principle of equal treatment of the domestic and migrant workforce in terms of remuneration and working conditions is purely rhetorical (Čaněk, 2014). Others suggest that reasons are to be found by considering Eastern Europe's 'transition' from planned to market economy. Following the fall of the communist regimes, skilled and more highly educated workers who headed unions embraced pro-market state policies in the post-1989 years and believed that private firms are best without much union involvement. The interests of this union leadership are then often based on the model of cooperation with management (Kaminska and Kahancová, 2011) and result in little interest in and even exclusion of unskilled workers (Ost, 2009), who in the current context are epitomized by the EU migrant workforce.

By de facto excluding migrant workers, the union protects the interest of domestic workers, who benefit from the presence of migrant agency staff in that the latter absorb the impact of the fluctuating demand for labour:

> The introduction of agency employment into the Labour Code proves a problem for the trade union to look after the interest of core workers and at the same time make sure that agency workers' rights are not taken away from them. If a firm loses an order then the agency workers are being let go first and, although we can tell core workers that we'll protect their place, in reality we are facing the situation where core workers might get punished next. Our representative could also represent agency workers, but the danger then is that we could have a situation where the workforce is 90 per cent agency workers, especially in areas where the job is relatively simple to do. (Czech trade unionist, Prague, 2 July 2012)

It is not surprising therefore that the trade unions in the Czech Republic put pressure on the government to limit migration and maintain strict control over the labour market. However, in ignoring the migrant workforce, the trade unions strengthen the state's hand in deregulating the labour market via relaxed prerequisites in setting up TWAs, lifting the ceiling for limited agency workers to a maximum of 20 per cent of the total workforce, and allowing TWAs to contribute up to 3000 CKZ (115 euros) per month towards agency workers' housing. Similarly to Turkey, then, where recent protests against the dominant trade union are likely to put an end to the existing labour-relations model, the practices currently pursued by the trade unions in the Czech Republic make the unions' future role rather uncertain because, as a former Foxconn worker explains, 'At some moments there were only agency workers in production'.

Conclusions

In this chapter we examined the workforce composition at Foxconn factories in the Czech Republic and Turkey and argued that there are three key elements to be taken into consideration in order to understand the firm's cross-border behaviour. These are the composition of labour, the role of the state, and the position and function of the trade unions. In bringing these three actors to bear on the firm's labour management practices, we broaden the established understanding of host country influence (e.g. Ferner et al., 2005; Léonard et al., 2014) by demonstrating how management, labour, state, and trade unions co-determine the process through which the firm expands and organizes its operations transnationally.

By offering a detailed illustration of workforce composition at Foxconn's factories, we suggest that labour is to be understood not as a static or uniform input into the production process as per the internationalization literature approach (Taylor, 2008), but rather as a dynamic actor whose composition influences the firm's labour management strategies. In China, where the composition of the workforce is more even – over 85 per cent of rural migrant workers are aged between 16 and 29 – and the flow of orders more stable, workers are hired directly by Foxconn on one-to-three-year contracts and work 60 hours per week. In Europe, and in particular in the Czech Republic where the workforce is more varied, Foxconn makes use of the existing legislation on temporary agency work to separate the workforce into directly employed and temporary workers and delegate the recruitment, control, and management of the latter group to the TWAs. Given the sporadic nature of orders, in its Czech and Turkish subsidiaries Foxconn operates the 'hour-bank system' for directly employed workers in order to drive down labour costs and achieve flexible labour use over a prolonged period of time.

In situations where the workforce in composed entirely or partly of migrant workers, such as in mainland China and the Czech Republic, Foxconn avails itself of dormitories. Dormitories operate as devices that temporarily capture and attach a mobile, low-wage workforce to the firm in the context where, in mainland China, the loosening control over *hukou* (household registration system) since the 1980s allows migrant labourers to move either within their own province or outside their own region and, in the EU, where the right to the freedom of movement grants citizens EU-wide labour mobility. We reveal how both the state and the trade unions participate in and support capital expansion and the capture of labour by stimulating FDI and industrial development on the one hand and facilitating greater control over labour through vertical segmentation between domestic and foreign workers on the other. By examining trade union practices in Turkey and the Czech Republic, we suggest that in addition to state policies, trade union interventions play a complementary role in setting the parameters of Foxconn's labour management practices.

The research demonstrates the theoretical relevance of adopting a labour-centred perspective for investigating internationalization, in particular the transfer of the firm's management practices. This is not only because it shows that capital-labour relations co-determine the process of capitalist development but also because it indicates that the conceptualization of the firm's strategies in terms of distinctive national business systems is inadequate to distinguish the systemic practices of capitalism. This means that the Foxconn case cannot simply be interpreted in terms of the 'Chinafication' of work and employment practices taking place in Europe because this reading does not sufficiently take into account the ways in which the firm's modes of labour management are shaped by the interests of various actors in the host country. Understanding that some of these actors or their practices are constituted beyond the boundaries of one nation state either through acts of mobility, as in the case of labour, or via supranational regulatory frameworks, as in the EU directive on temporary work agencies, is pivotal in accounting for the specificities but also the commonalities of contemporary global capitalism.

Notes

1 In Turkey, the legally stipulated working hours are 11 hours per day and 45 hours per week. The two-months averaging period can be extended up to four months by collective agreement.

2 The most relevant customer for Foxconn in the Czech Republic is Hewlett-Packard (HP), even though the plants also assemble desktops, laptops, servers, and printer cartridges for other brands such as Sony, Samsung, Chimei, Innolux, Cisco, and, until a couple of years ago, Apple.

3 In Turkey Foxconn manufactures desktop computers exclusively for HP.

4 http://www.dailymail.co.uk/travel/article-1300046/Golf-holidays-Charmed-Casa-Serena-Czech-golf-course-chateau.html (accessed on 8 December 2014).

5 There are three models of FZs in Turkey: public-public, build-operate-transfer, and build-operate. The European FZ of Çorlu is a build-operate model founded by private actors and established on private land (Kavlak, 2012).

6 http://www.industriall-union.org/industriall-outraged-by-savage-union-busting-in-turkey

REFERENCES

Aguzzoli, R and Geary J. (2014) 'An 'emerging challenge': The employment practices of a Brazilian multinational company in Canada', *Human Relations* 67(5): 587–609.

Almond, P., Edwards, T., Colling, T., Ferner, A., Gunnigle, P., Muller-Carmen, M., et al. (2005) 'Unraveling home and host country effects: An investigation of the HR policies of an American multinational in four European countries', *Industrial Relations: A Journal of Economy and Society*, 44(2): 276–306.

Andrijasevic, R., and Sacchetto, D. (2014) 'Made in the EU: Foxconn in the Czech Republic', *WorkingUSA*, 17(3): 391–415.

Arnold, C. E. (2010) 'Where the Low Road and the High Road Meet: Flexible Employment in Global Value Chains', *Journal of Contemporary Asia*, 40 (4): 612–637.

Bauder, H. (2006) *Labor movement: How migration regulates labor markets*, New York: Oxford University Press.

Bormann, S., and Plank, L. (2010) *Under Pressure: Working Conditions and Economic Development in ICT Production in Central and Eastern Europe*, Berlin: WEED-World Economy, Ecology and Development.

Boussebaa, M., and Morgan, G. (2014) 'Pushing the frontiers of critical international business studies: The multinational as a neo-imperial space', *critical perspectives on international business*, 10(1/2): 96–106.

Brennan, L. (2010) *The emergence of Southern multinationals: their impact on Europe*, Basingstoke: Palgrave Macmillan.

Burgoon, B., and Raess, D. (2014) 'Chinese investment and European labor: should and do workers fear Chinese FDI?', *Asia Europe Journal*, 12(1–2): 179–197.

Čaněk, M. (2014) *The Social and Political Regulation of Labour Migration: the Case of the Czech Republic*, Prague: Univerzita Karlova.

▶

Chan, A. (2011) 'Strikes in China's export industries in comparative perspective', *The China Journal*, 65: 27–51.

Chan, J., and Pun, N. (2010) 'Suicide as protest for the new generation of Chinese migrant workers: Foxconn, global capital, and the state', *The Asia-Pacific Journal*, 8(37): 2–10.

Chan, J., Pun, N., and Selden, M. (2013) The Politics of Global Production: Apple, Foxconn and China's New Working Class, *New Technology, Work and Employment*, 28(2): 100–115.

Czech Statistical Office. (2014) *Statistical Yearbook of the Czech Republic 2013*, Prague.

Djelic, M-L. (2001) *Exporting the American model: The postwar transformation of European business*, Oxford: Oxford University Press.

Drahokoupil, J. (2008) The investment-promotion machines: the politics of foreign direct investment promotion in Central and Eastern Europe, *Europe-Asia Studies*, 60(2): 197–225.

Drahokoupil, J. (2014) 'Decision-making in multinational corporations: key issues in international business strategy', *Transfer: European Review of Labour and Research*, 20(2): 199–215.

Evertiq (2007) *Asian EMS-Firms Discover Eastern Europe*, Available at http://evertiq.com/news/6299.

Ferner, A., Almond, P., and Colling, T. (2005) Institutional theory and the cross-national transfer of employment policy: The case of 'workforce diversity' in US multinationals, *Journal of International Business Studies*, 36(3): 304–321.

Fougner, T., and Kurtoğlu, A. (2011) 'Transnational Labour Solidarity and Social Movement Unionism: Insights from and beyond a Women Workers' Strike in Turkey', *British Journal of Industrial Relations*, 49(2): 353–375.

Friedman, E. (2014) *Insurgency trap: Labor politics in postsocialist China*, Ithaca: Cornell University Press.

Friedman, E., and Kuruvilla, S. (2015) Experimentation and decentralization in China's labor relations, *Human Relations*, 68(2): 181–195.

Fuchs, R., and Demko, G. (1978) 'The postwar mobility transition in Eastern Europe'. *Geographical Review* 68(2): 171–182.

Hála, J. (2007) *Unions Criticise Unequal Treatment of Temporary Agency Workers*, http://www.eurofound.europa.eu/eiro/2006/11/articles/cz0611049i.htm. (accessed 9 December 2015).

Heinecke, P. (2011) 'Theoretical Foundation and Literature Review', in *Success Factors of Regional Strategies for Multinational Corporations*, Berlin: Springer, 13–62.

Herod, A. (1997) 'From a Geography of Labor to a Labor Geography: Labor's Spatial Fix and the Geography of Capitalism', *Antipode*, 29(1): 1–31.

Kambouri, N. (2014) 'Dockworker Masculinities', *Logistical Worlds. Infrastructure, Software, Labour*, 16–23.

Kaminska, M. E., and Kahancová, M. (2011) Emigration and labour shortages: An opportunity for trade unions in the New Member States? *European Journal of Industrial Relations*, 17(2): 189–203.

Kavlak, M. E. (2012) *Economic Impacts of Free Zones in Turkey: A Questionnaire Study conducted with Firms Operating in Turkish Free Zones Regarding the Perception of the firm on the Success of Free Zone,* Ankara: Middle East Technical University.

Korkmaz, E. E. (2015) *Unexpected Wave of Strikes in Turkish Automotive Industry,* Istanbul: Friedrich Ebert Stiftung.

Léonard, E., Pulignano, V., Lamare, R., and Edwards, T. (2014) 'Multinational corporations as political players', *Transfer: European Review of Labour and Research,* 20(2): 171–182.

Lipietz, A. (1987) *Mirages and miracles,* London: Verso.

McGovern, P., Smeaton, D., and Hill, S. (2004) 'Bad Jobs in Britain: Nonstandard Employment and Job Quality', *Work and Occupations,* 31(2): 225–249.

McLoughlin, S., and Munz, R. (2011) *Temporary and Circular Migration: Opportunities and Challenges.* Brussels: European Policy Centre.

Meunier, S. (2014) 'A Faustian bargain or just a good bargain? Chinese foreign direct investment and politics in Europe', *Asia Europe Journal,* 12(1–2): 143–158.

Morgan, G., Kristensen, P. H., and Whitley, R. (2001) *The multinational firm: organizing across institutional and national divides,* Oxford: Oxford University Press.

Mysíková, M. (2012) 'Gender Wage Gap in the Czech Republic and Central European Countries', *Prague Economic Papers,* 3: 328–346.

Nichols, T., Sugur, N., and Demir, E. (2002) 'Beyond cheap labour: trade unions and development in the Turkish metal industry', *The Sociological Review,* 50(1): 23–47.

Nichols, T., Sugur, N., and Sugur, S. (2001) *Immigrant Labour in the Turkish Textile Industry: The Case of Muhacir Bulgarians,* Working Series Paper 15, Cardiff University: School of Social Sciences.

Organ, I. (2006) 'Do tax-free zones create employment? The case of Turkish free zones', *SEER-South-East Europe Review for Labour and Social Affairs,* 4: 127–140.

Ost, D. (2009) 'The Consequences of Postcommunism: Trade Unions in Eastern Europe's Future', *East European Politics and Societies,* 23(1): 13–33.

Özuğurlu, M. (2011) 'The TEKEL resistance movement: Reminiscences on class struggle', *Capital and Class,* 35(2): 179–187.

Parsanoglou, D. (2014) 'Trojan Horses, Black Holes and the Impossibility of Labour Struggles', *Logistical Worlds. Infrastructure, Software, Labour,* 11–16.

Pun, N. (2007) 'Gendering the dormitory labor system: production, reproduction, and migrant labor in south China', *Feminist Economics,* 13(3–4): 239–258.

Pun, N., and Chan, J. (2012) 'Global Capital, the State, and Chinese Workers The Foxconn Experience', *Modern China,* 38(4): 383–410.

Pun, N., Chan, J., and Selden, M. (forthcoming) *Dying for an iPhone: The Hidden Struggle of Chinese Workers,* Lanham, MD: Rowman and Littlefield.

Pun, N and Smith, C. (2007) 'Putting transnational labour process in its place: the dormitory labour regime in post-socialist China', *Work, Employment & Society,* 21(1): 27–45.

Radosevic, S. (2004) 'The electronics industry in Central and Eastern Europe: A new global production location', *Informacion Commerical Espanola: Revista de Economía,* 818: 151–164.

▶

Rios-Morales, R., and Brennan, L. (2010) 'The emergence of Chinese investment in Europe', *EuroMed Journal of Business,* 5(2): 215–231.

Selwyn, B. (2012) 'Beyond firm-centrism: re-integrating labour and capitalism into global commodity chain analysis', *Journal of Economic Geography,* 12, 205–226.

Smith, C. (2003) 'Living at work: Management control and the dormitory labour system in China', *Asia Pacific Journal of Management* 20(3): 333–358.

Smith, C. (2005) 'Beyond convergence and divergence: explaining variations in organizational practices and forms', in: Ackroyd S, Batt R, Thompson P, et al. (eds) *The Oxford Handbook of Work and Organization,* New York: Oxford University Press, 602–625.

Smith, C. (2006) 'The double indeterminacy of labour power: Labour effort and labour mobility', *Work, Employment and Society,* 20(2): 389–402.

Smith, C., and Chan, J. (2015) 'Working for two bosses: Student interns as constrained labour in China', *Human Relations,* 68(2): 305–326.

Taylor, M. (Ed) (2008) *Global economy contested: power and conflict across the international division of labour,* London and New York: Routledge.

Taiwan Invest (2006) *Business Gateway for Europe,* http://taiwantoday.tw/ct.asp?xitem=23580&ctnode=122&mp=9 (accessed 9 December 2015).

Yildirim, E., Calis, S., and Benli, A. (2008) 'Turkish Labour Confederations and Turkey's Membership of the European Union', *Economic and Industrial Democracy,* 29(3): 362–387.

Zeitlin, J., and Herrigel, G. (2000) *Americanization and its limits: Reworking US technology and management in post-war Europe and Japan,* Oxford: Oxford University Press.

Zhang, H., Yang, Z., and Van Den Bulcke, D. (2012) 'Geographical Agglomeration of Indian and Chinese Multinationals in Europe: A Comparative Analysis', *Science Technology and Society,* 17(3): 385–408.

Zhang, Y., Duysters, G., and Filippov, S. (2012) 'Chinese firms entering Europe', *Journal of Science and Technology Policy in China,* 3(2): 102–123.

Zhu, J., and Wei, W. (2014) 'HR strategy and Practices in Chinese Multinational Companies', in C. Julian, Z. Ahmed and J. Xu (eds) *Research Handbook on the Globalization of Chinese Firms,* Cheltenham: Edward Elgar: 162–182.

The Management of Labour in Chinese MNCs Operating Outside of China: A Critical Review

15

Chris Smith and Yu Zheng

China has emerged from being an isolated developing country to a globally networked and dominant internationalized economy. The transition is unprecedented regarding the speed of urbanization, the penetration of the market-oriented reforms, and the scale of restructuring that it has brought to Chinese firms (Cai, 2010). As documented in the previous chapters of this book, three decades of reform have created heterodoxy and diversity that characterizes the nature of work and employment in China. Simultaneously, China-centred research has been puzzled by the question of what constitutes a 'Chinese way of managing people'. We are now witnessing quantum growth in Chinese outward foreign direct investment (OFDI). Some may see this new development as creating further questions about if and why Chinese firms are following 'established' patterns in terms of international company structure (formative or normative), corporate strategy, and management processes. However, the accelerated emergence of Chinese firms onto the global stage also offers an opportunity to reflect on and re-evaluate the nature of the labour process, work and employment in China. This is because, like MNCs from other countries, Chinese firms are likely to carry some home practices with them overseas. And the need to apply such home practices may help Chinese firms articulate, summarize, and legitimate what comprises their work and employment policies abroad *and* at home. There is likely to be some coevolution in practices – revisiting home and foreign practices as these practices are trialled and tested in the domestic and international context (Zhang & Edwards, 2007). We believe that researching work and employment at Chinese firms overseas will be timely and informative to a broader academic and public audience.

This concluding chapter compares what we know about work and employment in China (which, as shown in the previous chapters, is fragmented between continued diluted paternalism, modern human resource management, and coercive forms of labour control) with the situation of Chinese MNCs overseas. The purpose of our comparison is not to draw a few tentative conjectures about the generic features of the Chinese model overseas, but to revisit some existing debates and call for more studies to connect the China-focused research with the wider scholarship of changes in (and issues with) work and employment brought by the emergence and development of new capitalist firms. China, having been the main global manufacturing site (what is often called the 'world's factory' or 'world's assembly line') sucking in international investment in the past three decades, is now exporting not just commodities but also capital and labour. The work and employment implications of the rise of Chinese firms on the global stage is a vital research topic, and yet has been largely absent in the existing literature (Zhu & Wei, 2014). In this sense, this chapter is also a call for a new research agenda to bridge the gap between the context-specific readings of how the introduction of capitalist rules/principles has reshaped working regimes in China and the changes brought by the renewed mobility of capital (and labour) to a more general understanding of work and employment on a global scale.

The chapter is divided into five sections. We start by examining the scale and pattern of Chinese outward foreign direct investment (OFDI), aiming to provide an overview on the growth and character of Chinese OFDI. We then consider the implications of Chinese OFDI for the emergence and development of work and employment as exercised by Chinese firms overseas. With reference to some existing frameworks, we discuss the possibility of adding the experiences of the Chinese firms to theorizing this new wave of work relocation. We do this by identifying three research themes: *revisiting the transfer debate*; *extending the capital mobility vs. labour mobility debate*; and *revitalizing the political agenda on the globalization of work*. We conclude by suggesting future research directions.

Outward Foreign Direction Investment from China: an Overview

Launched in the early 2000s, China's 'Go Global' policy was the state's agenda to promote economic growth through OFDI. This policy has undoubtedly been effective. We have witnessed an unprecedented surge

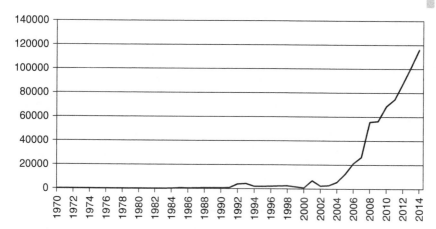

Figure 15.1 Chinese OFDI flows, annual, 1970–2013 (Unit: US$ million)
UNCTAD 2015

of Chinese OFDI since the mid-2000s, with an average growth rate of 40 per cent between 2005 and 2014 (UNCTAD, 2015) (see Figure 15.1).

In relative terms, the share of Chinese OFDI flow among the global OFDI flow has grown rapidly since the mid-2000s as well. According to UNCTAD (2015), Chinese OFDI flow contributed merely 0.5 per cent of the total OFDI worldwide in 2005. This figure went up to 8.6 per cent in 2014, which puts Chinese OFDI at the same level as Japan (8.4 per cent) and Germany (8.3 per cent), after the largest source of global OFDI – the US (24.9 per cent). China also leads OFDI among the developing countries, such as Russia (4.2 per cent), South Africa (0.5 per cent), India (0.1 per cent) and Brazil (0.3 per cent decrease). The three-year moving average of Chinese OFDI flow (see Figure 15.2) indicates the growing trend of China's share among the global OFDI flow. This suggests that China is potentially becoming a new dominant capitalist force, along with the US and Japan.

China's official statistics are sometimes considered biased: Ministry of Commerce (MOFCOM) data, which UNCATD uses to calculate Chinese OFDI, is based on the investment applications approved by the Chinese state and therefore includes round-trip OFDI, which is the investment made by Chinese firms overseas with the objective of reinvesting in China in order to take advantage of tax policies offered exclusively to foreign invested firms in China (Zhou & Leung, 2015). In order to show a comprehensive and more accurate picture of Chinese firms' international presence, we need to deconstruct the official statistics and supplement them with some firm-based data.

Round-trip OFDI has distorted the geographic distribution of Chinese OFDI. A substantial share of Chinese OFDI in Hong Kong is believed to

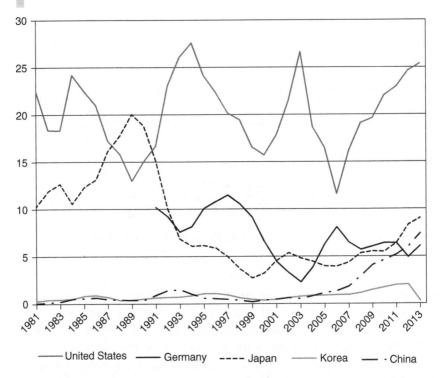

Figure 15.2 Share (%) of global OFDI flow, three-year average, 1981–2013
Authors' calculation based on UNCATD yearly data, 2015

fall into this category (Zhou & Leung, 2015). The World Resource Institute (Zhou and Leung, 2015) calculated a 'de-facto' Chinese OFDI based on MOFCOM's statistics by excluding investment to some offshore financial centres (e.g. Hong Kong, British Virgin Islands, and Cayman Islands) as a measure to take the round-trip OFDI out of the equation. It shows the proportion of Chinese OFDI in developed countries has been rapidly increasing in recent years. Investment into the EU and North America takes up 39 per cent of the total Chinese OFDI by 2013 (Figure 15.3).

MOFCOM's statistics also underrepresent the investment made by private firms, who do not necessarily always report their overseas investment or reinvestment of the earnings made overseas (Wang & Huang, 2012). This has led to some over emphasis on the political agenda of the top-down, state-directed, and central bank-subsidized OFDI (Child & Rodriguez, 2005; Luo, Xue, & Han, 2010). For example, in a report to the International Finance Corporation (IFC) on sustainable and green banking in China, Aizawa (2011) suggests that more than 80 per cent of the Chinese OFDI is funded by the Export-Import Bank of

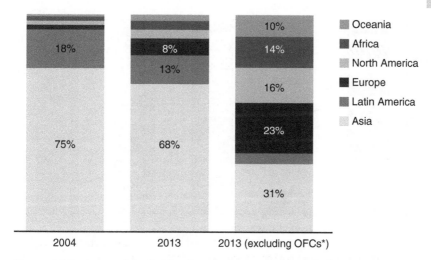

Figure 15.3 Geographic distribution of Chinese OFDI stock, 2004/2013
Zhou and Leung, 2015

China (EXIM) and the China Development Bank (CDB). However, the high level of funding from the state bank is due to the fact that Chinese firms using private funding often will not seek state approval and hence are excluded from the official statistics in Chinese OFDI (Wang & Huang, 2012).

Underrepresentation of investment made by the Chinese private firms in the official statistics of Chinese OFDI also creates an impression that the Chinese firms are predominantly focused on the resource sector. Using firm-based analysis reveals a more realistic picture of the Chinese OFDI, with Chinese firms diversifying into much wider industry sectors. For example, Wang & Huang (2012) compiled a database of the major investment projects approved by the National Development and Reform Commission (NDRC) between 2003 and 2011. This database suggests that the *manufacturing* sector takes up the largest share (42 per cent) of the total number of projects with Chinese investment, although *mining* continuously receives the largest share (52 per cent) of Chinese OFDI in terms of value (Wang & Huang, 2012). Diversification of Chinese OFDI is more evident when analysts use the data from mergers and acquisitions (M&A) projects. For example, EY Knowledge (2015), an established consultancy firm, bases their analysis on the M&A projects conducted by Chinese firms between 2010 and 2014. The results show that investment in the mining and energy sectors is in decline. More investment has gone into the telecommunication, media, and technology (TMT);

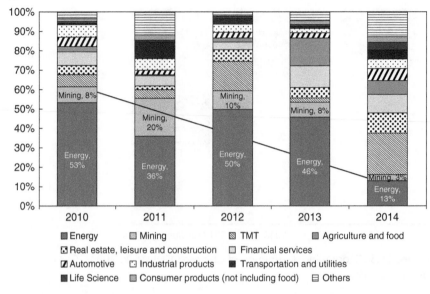

Figure 15.4 Share of Chinese outward M&A projects by sector, value
EY Knowledge, 2015

real estate, leisure and construction; financial services; and agricultural and food sectors over the same five-year period (see Figure 15.4).

We must also note that acceleration of OFDI led by Chinese private firms is not evenly distributed across investment destinations or industry sectors. Compared to the state-funded projects, Chinese private firms are more inclined to invest in developed countries (EY Knowledge, 2015). There is also a clear divide between the central state-owned enterprises (SOEs), local SOEs, and the private firms in terms of the sectors they engaged in (Wang & Huang, 2012) (see Figures 15.5 and 15.6).

Figures 15.5 and 15.6 show variations in industry sectors between investments carried out by the private and the SOE-funded projects, a finding which echoes research using host-country-based data (Ramasamy, Yeung, & Lafor, 2012). The central SOEs are the dominant majority that invested in mining, civil infrastructure (electricity, gas, and water), transport, and information transmission projects, especially when the value of investment is considered. Chinese private firms, in contrast, lead the investment in agricultural and commercial (retail and wholesale) projects. Local SOEs take up the majority of projects in the real estate and leasing sector. This divide, to some extent, reflects the industrial structure as a result of China's state policies favouring the SOEs in resource and infrastructure sectors (Wei, Clegg, & Ma, 2014).

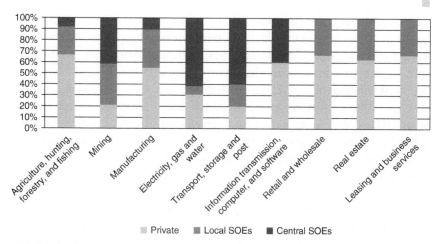

Figure 15.5 Industry distribution of Chinese OFDI by ownership structure based on number of projects

Wang and Huang, 2012

Chinese OFDI's fast growth, its increasing presence around the world, and its gradual penetration into wider industry sectors echo the scenario that we witnessed between the mid-1970 and mid-1990s, when Japanese OFDI, and later Korean OFDI, had started to reshape competition in global industry configurations and affect the nature of work and employment practices. Excluding investments in facilities for processing

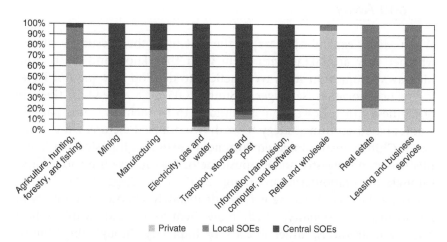

Figure 15.6 Industry distribution of Chinese OFDI by ownership structure based on value of projects

Wang and Huang, 2012

timber and pulp for the Japanese market (which are heavily concentrated in Western Canada), over 85 per cent of all Japanese investments were found in developing countries, although these were considerable service investments in the US (Yoshino, 1974). By 1997, over 50 per cent of Japanese OFDI was focused in Asia (Sakamoto, 1989). Korea, exhibits a similar pattern, which by 1978 had more than half of its OFDI going to Asia. As Korea developed, the distribution of OFDI shifted – following a pattern that China looks likely to reproduce – so that by 1994 Korea's OFDI in Asia had fallen to about 41.9 per cent, with North America hosting 35.3 per cent of Korean OFDI and Europe 12.8 per cent. (MOCFOC 2009, p. 8; 2012, pp. 12,15). The impact on work and employment in China's case is not necessarily comparable to that of Japan or Korea. This is because China's employment regimes were built upon a surplus of relatively inexpensive labour whereas the latter developed their employment practices to address labour shortage in the home societies. And it is too hasty to talk about the 'dominance effect' of Chinese OFDI as we did at the time when Japan overtook the US to become the largest source of global OFDI. However, given the diverse profile of Chinese firms overseas, we believe studying the experiences of Chinese firms will help enrich the way we theorize the management of MNCs in general, and the international transfer literature in particular.

Revisiting the Transfer Debate: Connecting Home and Away

When MNCs expand overseas for the first time, the question is always whether they are taking with them what they know and do, or running away from home-country practices to develop new ways of working in host societies (see Elger & Smith 2005 for a review). In the case of Chinese firms, however, it is difficult to fit them into this pattern. Studies based on firm strategy have shown a mixed picture. On the one hand, China's institutional environment creates high business risk and this has been suggested to be a push factor for Chinese firms to 'escape' through internationalization (Deng, 2009; Wei, Clegg, & Ma, 2014). On the other hand, Chinese firms deliberately choose locations with low institutional stability, which allow them to negotiate with the host country institutions, either directly or indirectly through the Chinese state (Buckley, Clegg, Cross, Liu, Voss, & Zheng, 2007; Kolstad & Wiig, 2012). But to what extent can we say that work and employment practices, which are enabled by China's national institutions, are not tied to

Chinese institutions and therefore applicable elsewhere? To address this question, we need to examine three key issues:

1) Is there a single and integrated 'Chinese model' that can be taken forward to revisit the transfer debate?
2) How will the labour process at firm level be reshaped by increased international mobility of firms and workers?
3) How do the host country's institutional agencies enable and/or resist employment practices brought by Chinese MNCs?

Unpacking the 'China Model'

Some see a rather dominant form of despotic employment relations emerging as the result of China's market-oriented reform since the mid-1990s. Attention has been given to the way labour is attached to employment and organizations, with heavy use of internal migrant labour, an internal passport (hukou) system, casualization of labour contracts, and radical breaks from former long-term bonds between worker and workplace (Friedman & Lee, 2010; Kuruvilla, Lee, & Gallagher, 2011). Many researchers have reported managerial domination inside factories, with unfettered power to discipline workers, and control recreational relations, not just working lives in the factories (Chan & Pun, 2010; Lee, 1998; Lüthje, Luo, & Zhang, 2013; Smith, 2003; Smith & Pun, 2006). These writers argue that the rise of a massive unskilled, rural migrant work force and the lack of properly functioning social institutions providing welfare or representing workers' interests powerfully underpin authoritarian management. Some use 'bloody Taylorism', a term coined by the French regulationist writer Alain Lipietz (1987), to describe primitive accumulation in developing countries led by a profit-driven movement of international manufacturing capital from developed countries where they co-produced deregulated labour markets, labour repression, and detailed divisions of labour (characteristic of Taylorism). In China 'bloody Taylorism' has been best epitomized by one reading of the work regime enunciated by the mega-scale electronics assembly plants of the contract manufacturing firm – Foxconn. Foxconn's labour regime is characterized by military discipline and ideology, task simplification, intensive work, and combining production and reproduction of labour power in huge industrial compounds which function like enclosed cities (Chan & Pun, 2010). Furthermore, such a labour regime can potentially be extended throughout China and exported internationally into other countries. As noted in the work of Sacchetto and Andrijasevic (see Chapter 14), Foxconn in the Czech Republic has used migrant labour from Romania and Bulgaria in order to lower labour costs, and recruited through agencies to segment the workforce and would therefore seem to exemplify the transfer of rigid labour controls that have been found in the Chinese factories. Away from the specific case of Foxconn, more generally Chinese managers, who learnt hard lessons through the neoliberal reforms in China, can also play a role in spreading home employment and work, at least to some less developed regions (Lee, 2009). Here, the emphasis is on a new moral economy of casualized employment and an ethic of hard work and self-sacrifice (also see (Brooks, 2010).

Despite the significance of the above features observed in the workplace in China, we need to be cautious when projecting commonality in the Chinese workplace which then carries some 'transferability' as Chinese MNCs internationalize. Over 30 years of theorizing and empirical engagement with reform and transformation reveals a very mixed picture of labour process, employment relations, and distinctive development patterns (see previous chapters in this collection).

China's move to capitalism has been through several experimental stages, and it therefore embraces a number of sub-national development models. Work organization and employment relations in these regions and cities vary. For example, business models have been observed to be different in Guangdong, Sunan (Southern Jiangsu Province), Wenzhou (Zhejiang Province), Zhongguancun (Beijing 'Silicon Valley'), and Chongqing (City) (Keith, Lash, Arnoldi, & Rooker, 2013; Peck & Zhang, 2013). Lee (2007) compared labour regimes in Northern and Southern China and summarized two industry types: 'sunrise' (export-oriented, contract assembly factories around the coast – what can be referred to as the 'Guangdong model') was contrasted with 'sunset' industries (reforming and declining former SOEs in the North). She suggested that each possesses their own labour regimes, labour supply, and working class politics. Lüthje, Luo, & Zhang (2013) compare production regimes between Chinese firms with different ownership structures. These authors identified four divergent patterns of work organization: SOEs, joint ventures (JV), private export-oriented manufacturers, and low-end subcontractors. The SOEs are characterized by relatively stable conditions of production, compliance with national law, and the presence of a union. The JVs tend to copy traditional Western company styles by paying higher wages and investing in skills and education. While individual labour contracts are commonly used to regulate employment relations, written collective agreements don't exist. The private export-orientated contract manufactures diverge into high-end and low-end producers, which exhibit different labour sub-regimes – with divergent wages, working hours, labour intensiveness, and more or less hostile managerial regimes. And finally, there are low-end subcontractors, particularly in the garments, toys, and shoes manufacturers, where 'modern manufacturing technologies are combined with massive flexibilization of employment and large scale exploitation of migrant workers, including long work hours, violation of legal standards and low wages and usually no presence of unions' (Zajak, 2012, pp. 85–86).

Chinese firms overseas reproduce their 'home' features to some extent. The SOEs, which accounts for three-quarters of Chinese investment overseas, possess complex ownership patterns, including central state-backed, local state invested, and hybrid public–private forms (Goodman, 2014). The Chinese private firms are mostly small family firms – sometimes called the 'Wenzhou model' – and have expanded internationally through social networks (Ceccagno, 2012; 2015; Tomba, 1999; Wei, Li, & Wang, 2007; Wu & Sheehan, 2011). China has become the home base for MNCs from around the world. Chapters by Kim and Zheng in this book discuss Korean and Japanese MNCs management practices in China respectively. Zhang (2015) explores factory regimes in US, German, and Japanese auto makers in China – with an orientation towards the degree of adoption of labour force dualism in the assembly factories. Chan (2011) examines the squeezing of factory and store workers within Walmart supply chains which use elaborate logistical techniques to control suppliers and workers in these 'Walmartized' production chains. MNCs and SMEs from Taiwan, Hong Kong, and Singapore – sometimes referred to as the Greater China – have shaped China's economic growth as well as its distinctive pattern of 'subordinate' employment relations (Henderson, Appelbaum, & Ho, 2013). Again, we can see firms with different ownership origins and structures showing commonalities as well as persistent differences in terms of their work organization and employment relations (Zhu, Zhang, & Shen, 2012).

The value of the China case in reviewing the transfer literature hinges around diversity based on sectors, regions, and companies even within the SOEs and resources sectors. China is linked to the global industrial networks in distinctive ways (Chapter 1) and the growth of Chinese OFDI could well be part of the restructuring of global industry networks. Firm level changes in organizational structure and employment practices may well reflect shifts in economic and power relations between countries as well as transitions in the global division of labour (Edwards & Kuruvilla, 2005).

Firm-based case studies confirm a cross-sector differentiation where Chinese firms internationalize. In the automobile industry, for example, Chinese firms like Geely internationalize to be able to compete in different segments within the industry. We witnessed both international and domestic expansion as production and market competition become more regionalized (Balcet, Wang, & Richet, 2012). There is not necessarily organizational integration so far because the home and overseas units remain relatively independent players in different segments of the automobile industry (Gugler & Fetscherin, 2011). In contrast, the Chinese firms in high-tech industries, such as Lenovo and Huawei have expanded their production and R&D facilities both at home and overseas, which is aimed at enhancing their innovative capacity and moving up segments within the industry (Hanemann & Rosen, 2014). Internationalization is part of their attempt to accelerate the move from OEM suppliers to lead supplier. What should not be neglected is that they are part of the general trend in the PC and mobile-device sectors, where shortened product life cycles and faster technological changes have put pressure on firms to integrate the research and manufacturing functions (Agostino, Giunta, Nugent, Scalera, & Trivieri , 2014). The recent investment in the upstream segment of the agricultural and farming projects in Australia by Yili Group and in the US by Bright Food are believed to be re-exportation driven as a response to the Chinese consumers' concerns for food safety (EY Knowledge, 2015). This move from using a network-based supply chains to ownership-based supply chains is not necessarily China-specific but a trend within the foodstuff industry. The way Chinese firms integrate the overseas outlets with their home units will vary across industrial sectors, but how such variations translate into reorganizing work and employment at home and abroad have yet to be understood.

We must also remember the developmental nature of work and employment regimes in China. In particular, the low-wage export-orientated model faces upward pressure on wages, the rising costs of materials, rise in the value of the Yuan (until recently) and new labour legislation (after the implementation of the 2008/2009 Labour Contract Law), alongside unprecedented external dynamics (e.g. the slackening global demand after the 2008 global financial crisis). Institutional pressures, such as government officials' desire to move up the value chain, have also affected the export-oriented contract manufacturing model to some extent (Zhu & He, 2014). In a systematic study of two sectors (LED lighting and textile & garment industries), Butollo (2014) observes increased use of high-value technology, and declines in labour use as the capital intensity of these industries expands, but he does not observe a corresponding rise in wages and improvement in working conditions. He suggests an underlying 'low cost, low trust, high control' managerial regime across a range of sectors, impervious of typical levers of change, such as labour shortages, upskilling, and rising capital intensity of industry, all of which did not shift Chinese management from its tight wage and labour-control regime. Firms in the export-oriented sectors that did not shut down in the recession moved within China to cheaper productions sites, and new entrants to the export sector 'went west' and not to the coast. Some internationalized to other Asian countries such as Vietnam and Malaysia in order to maintain or prolong the low-cost labour regime (Zhu & He, 2014). Some authors may argue that these firms intend to acquire critical assets to build their competitiveness, whether such assets are 'global brands, new technology and know-how in management and marketing' (Caseiro & Masiero, 2014, p. 246). So what we observe is not a 'successful' model being celebrated and reproduced overseas, which is often the line of argument in the existing transfer literature. Rather, some Chinese firms represent 'less desirable' models that move across borders to perpetuate patterns of labour subordination. The institutional resistance encountered in this kind of transfer and implications to work and employment issues are something that the existing literature rarely picks up. We will come back to this point in the next section.

Any attempt to discuss the Chinese model must also take into account the fact that repressive and authoritarian work and employment practices that have come to characterize China as the 'workshop of the world' (Gao, 2012) might have their origins in foreign firms but have been reshaped through production in China. Foxconn, for example, carries with it imprints from its Taiwanese origins, which sometimes translates into paternalism and managerial dominance. It massively expanded its business and production model honed within mainland China as a contract manufacturer, and its internationalization has dovetailed with generic movements of neoliberalism and more casualized and fragmented labour markets across the world (see chapter by Andrijasevic and Sacchetto). So, the Foxconn case cannot simply be read through its 'Chineseness', but through the perspective of contract manufacturing at a particular juncture in global capitalism. Likewise, foreign invested companies (FICs) in China have driven changes in work arrangement and employment practices of Chinese firms in many other sectors. Several authors have reported dualism in Chinese firms: with directly employed and indirectly employed workers on different labour contracts, benefits, and wages. Such dualism can be interpreted as learning by absorbing and modifying 'advanced' practices and diffusing in the workplace in China (Zheng Y., 2015). Dualistic features of employment can also well reflect what some see as the result of increasing segmentation within a given sector.

Zhang's (2008; 2015) study of the Chinese auto industry suggests there are powerful dual labour management systems, what she called 'lean-and-dual'. While both contract workers and agency workers worked side by side with formally employed direct workers, for formal workers there was 'hegemonic control', with high wages, generous benefits, better working conditions, and relatively secure employment. While for agency, contract and other temporary workers (close to 50 per cent of the workforce) they were under 'despotic labour controls' – lower wages and insecure employment. But this is not especially a *Chinese* pattern. As parts of the auto industry in the UK, the BMW Mini Plant in Oxford, for example, have just such a segmented configuration – with 800 of the 2,500 workers recruited through agencies and on insecure contracts (Macalister & Pidd, 2009). Similarly, Nissan in Canton, Mississippi, in the USA use temporary workers in 40–50 per cent of positions, and are continuing to reduce regular employees (Jaffe, 2014). It seems, therefore, that agency working has become a generic or systemic (not national) feature of employment across many industries – allowing manufacturers to adjust more easily to changes in demand, both up and down – and not something particular to one country or company. This highlights the need for more contextualized research on the transfer of employment and work practices, rather than projecting linear alignment towards either home or host country practices based on one case study research in one sector or firm.

In China the transition from state socialism to capitalism has been accompanied by many attempts to frame the nature of 'home-based' work and employment practices (see Chapter 1). Differences in employment and work systems in China suggest there is not a single dominant labour process model, except perhaps a management focus on tight cost consciousness, competition, and authoritarian control – as Child (1994, p. 158) noted in China 'the use of control and penalties is universally stronger' than in more developed economies. Such mixed features of Chinese firms and their 'home practices' lead us to question the usefulness of a home—away divide, which is prominent in cross-country transfer research. The China case reminds us that whenever newcomers enter a new space (whether a nation or region) there is need for caution about over-valuing nationality, and reading any *new* capitalism through myopic (and blurred) national lenses, when we need to always separate out systemic practices of capitalism, alongside societal differences and dominant lead-country trends in work and employment (Smith & Meiksins, 1995; Smith, 2008).

Extending Capital Mobility vs. Labour Mobility

Internationalization of Chinese firms illustrates the extended mobility of capital and labour. The internationalization of Chinese firms is occurring at a much earlier stage of economic development, compared to most developed countries. Unlike established MNCs, the internationalization of which is triggered by nationally established advantages seeking international outlets to overcome the liability of foreignness (Dunning, 2000). As discussed in the previous section, we have yet to generalize a 'Chinese model' that is more hegemonic when compared to established work regimes. Whether we interpret the 'early' internationalization of Chinese firms as a 'leap-frog effect' (Luo & Tung, International expansion of emerging market enterprises: a springboard perspective, 2007) or 'latecomers effect' (Amsden, 1992; Mathews, 2006), what we see is the extended mobility of capital, independent of the sophistication of technology, saturation of the domestic market, or shortage of labour. This pattern of latecomer internationalization may change the power relations and bargaining dynamics between capital and labour.

Labour power is what workers have to sell to employers. The freedom to choose employers in order to exchange labour time for wages is a vital part of what it is to be a worker. In state-socialist societies, the individual had limited choice, as labour markets were controlled by state agencies which assigned individuals to employers without choice or freedom of movement. In post-reform China there has been an explosion of labour mobility, and high recorded levels of labour turnover and the emerging preference to build careers through movement between multiple employers and movement managed at the discretion of the individual worker. Threats to this mobility persist and new institutional practices of retaining documents, withholding wages, suppressing information, and employer collusions are all expressions of attempts to retain elements of the political interference of labour markets and workers' rights as workers begin to choose where to sell their labour power (Smith & Pun, 2006).

The internationalization of Chinese firms and the increased migration of Chinese workers, demonstrate struggles between employers' attempts to retain coercive controls over the freedom of labour to move around labour markets and workers' attempt to extend their freedom. Lee's (2009) work on Chinese managers and workers working in Africa as extended expatriates within Chinese MNCs, demonstrates patterns of bound or constrained employment (Zheng & Smith, 2015) – not unlike Kafala practices in the Middle East (Khan & Harroff-Tavel, 2011; Roper & Barria, 2014) – all of which translates into unfree labour. Ethnic enclaves of Chinese businesses overseas reinforces home-country habits (Wu & Sheehan, 2011; Wu & Liu, 2014), as do language barriers, lack of awareness of host society practices, or hostility in host societies towards new migrants.

Heavy use of employees sourced from the home country has been reported as a consistent feature of Chinese FDI (Cooke, 2012; 2014; Zheng & Smith, 2015). So for example the Turkish subsidiary of Huawei in Istanbul employed 1,000 employees, but 200 of them were Chinese – a uniquely high expatriate rate (1 in 5), especially given Turkey is also a low not high-wage economy. In other low-waged economies a similar pattern persists – in Huawei India, for example, 30 per cent of the workforce are expatriates (Cooke, 2012, p. 1844). Huawei's domestic employees are more numerous than those working in the 140 overseas subsidiaries, but from 2008 more revenue was generated overseas than in the PRC. Like many Chinese MNCs it has a competitive advantage in having a large pool of inexpensive workers in the home territory, and therefore one of the reasons for OFDI is not to escape the high costs of domestic labour, as is the case with many Western MNCs, and the Chinese MNC will try and create internal employment structures to continue to access labour reserves at home. Expats are there because they follow Chinese firm tenets, they are more focused on work, and, as migrants usually living in company-based industrial dormitories, they are tightly controlled and more likely to focus on work during the contract period and submit to compulsory overtime, which is resisted by local workers, and work flexibly with less voice, which locals shun (Lee, 2009). Here, it is not the nationality of labour which is important, but rather the level of dependency of workers in the overseas location.

Labour dependency is created as firms extend control over international migrant labour. However, national institutional regulations persist to restrain international deployment of labour. Despite its strong preference to labour sourced from China, some SOEs, due to pressure from the local institutions (such as unions), have to use local workers and work with local institutions (Chen & Orr, 2009; Corkin, 2012; Lee, 2009; Mohan, 2013), although the outcome of union opposition varied across countries, sectors, and firms. In the Chinese firms in Bui Dam, for example, most labourers and semi-skilled workers were Ghanaian. The contract with Sinohydro capped the upper limit of Chinese labour on the project at 600. Interestingly, 60 Pakistanis were 'brought in' to operate the heavy equipment. They were treated as 'Chinese' for the 'imported labour' quota but are even cheaper than Chinese workers. (Mohan, 2013, pp. 1,264–5). This would suggest that non-Chinese workers recruited through employment agencies may yield similar levels of dependency to the practices described by Lee (2009) above.

Labour challenges attempts at coercive retention within the boundaries of the firm, and while labour supply may be channelled through firm-level networks, especially for labour capture, workers exercise mobility power by breaking free of these firms and establishing their own companies, moving between employers or acting in concert with Chinese family networks to establish new autonomous firms. In this context simply changing employers or moving out of ethnic enclave employment into the local society employment can be seen as an aspect of class struggle or labour resistance and the assertion of mobility rights by Chinese workers (Wu & Liu, 2014). But Chinese workers are often on indirect contracts, and as such, their mobility threat to the employing firm is constrained, as the employment agency, school, or state agency, can replace one worker who quits with another (Smith & Chan, 2015). But struggles and constraints around the issue of mobility are an important part of the story of Chinese workers' international experience.

A feature highlighted in Wu and Latham's (2014) discussion of Chinese migration is the 'transnationality of Chinese entrepreneurs', which denote the continued strong links to China, bounded ethnic-communities (often characterized by 'closure, segmentation and fragmentation' (ibid: 316) and blend of legal and illegal movements. This is the case in Prato [Italy] where initially local firms imported Chinese workers to compete with Far East producers, only to find these workers leaking out of Italian SMEs and setting up rival businesses, and creating a significant Chinese presence in the town (Baldassar, Johanson, McAuliffe, & Bressan, 2015; Johanson, Smyth, & French, 2009). As a developing country, Chinese people (students, workers, entrepreneurs) move independently of MNCs (Walcott, 2007), and can provide a source of labour for newly arriving Chinese firms (Thunø, 2007). Although the Chinese diaspora has always featured as a significant factor in China's relationship with Asia (and the world) (Pan, 1994), the significant difference between now and the past is that current Chinese migration is coming from a rising global power and not a subordinate, dependent or colonized state within a capitalism dominated by the US, Europe, and Japan. This new economic status of China since the 1980s has been changing patterns of migration, relations between countries, and Chinese identities worldwide (Skeldon, 2007).

We are witnessing changing dynamics between capital and labour brought by the increased international mobility on both sides. The Chinese firms overseas highlight some new developments, such as posted workers, social dumping, and casualization, which allow workers to slip through regulatory cracks, and for new segmented labour markets to be created (Caro, Berntsen, Lillie, & Ines, 2015; Friberg, Arnholtz, Eldring, Hansen, & Thorarins, 2014; Refslund, 2014). These new spaces can create segments for migrant workers, brought from low wages economies through employer, contractor, or employment agency dependent routes, and that means they are living in marginal conditions and institutionally separate from their host society. These new rules and practices for the national, regional and international labour markets mean that when new capital comes – such as Chinese firms – they can utilize these new practices, and reproduce patterns of marginalization and segmentation. A common reaction to these firms – especially new arrivals that stand out in the society, such as the Chinese – is to stigmatize and nationalize/ethnicize the practices they apply as something alien and new, when in fact they are only reproducing (and perhaps extending or adding their own flavour) to what already exists or is emerging in new regional labour market spaces. Therefore when we are assessing the work and employment practices of newcomers we must always be careful not to confuse the application of practices with the new arrival, and not emergent practices with the emerging structure of the labour market itself. The significance of the China case is that it allows us to investigate the contestation between an emerging force of capitalist firms and a wider pool of labour.

Revitalizing the Political Agenda on the Globalization of Work

The political economy of multinationals has long been a key theme in the transfer debate (Edwards & Kuruvilla, 2005). The political agenda that accompanied the Chinese firms overseas has generated much controversy. The arrival of Chinese firms in Europe, America, and the rest of the world has elicited both excitement and anxiety. As the new investors are still relatively unknown and the impact of their investment unclear, the politics behind Chinese firms overseas has generated much fear, scepticism, and speculation, which may have been disproportionally represented as negative by the mass media and some official reports.

There is protectionist rhetoric that Chinese firms represent unfair competition, which is prevalent in the press and popular literature. Typical of these claims is the idea that Chinese investment comes with implicit strings and can act as a 'Trojan horse' (Meunier, 2012, p. 7) affecting established norms and policies, from human rights to labour laws. On labour issues, Chinese firms are accused of breaking rules on working hours and health and safety; using coercive forms of labour control, including withholding wages to inhibit mobility and taking deposits to control migrant workers, whether irregular or regular (Wu & Liu, Bringing class back in: class consciousness and solidarity among Chinese migrant workers in Italy and the UK, 2014); trafficking forced labour (Gao, 2004); ignoring or suppressing trade unions (Burgoon & Raess, 2014); paying wages below subsistence levels, and even employing prison labour on construction and civil engineering projects (Yan & Sautmana, 2012). Although research into Chinese MNCs and their attitudes towards local institutions remains extremely thin, speculation is based on simplistic assumptions about Chinese investment and the willingness of economies to receive this investment alongside concomitant changes to the nature of work and employment they threaten. The reasoning here is based on China being a new capitalist state with money, power, and influence over crisis-ridden and fractured economies in the developing and developed world.

Undoubtedly, Chinese firms are practiced at deploying institutions at home, and potentially doing so in the international arena. Lee (2009) discusses the successful bidding process of Chinese resource and construction companies, who she says consistently outbid other firms for mining contracts by 30 per cent on average. This, she says, is not due to disregarding profitability, and over-valuing of politics (one reading of the Chinese approach informed by seeing the Chinese government behind every investment tree), but rather because of the labour management system, the high and extensive use of Chinese expatriates, and the controls on costs and high performance this delivers. Lee noted these features from her case studies: delayed payment – payment at the end of the (two-year) contract or posting; use of migrant agency workers from surplus reserves of labour in China; what she calls 'bonded management' – men on their own, living at work which reduces the costs of reproduction of expatriate labour which is present without families (something widespread in other expatriate cases); all management and professional jobs being performed by Chinese expatriates; and constrained mobility – as Chinese workers and managers are tied to the firm. These practices which create conditions for dependent or subordinate labour have been characterized as recreating the 'dormitory labour regime' (Smith, 2003; Smith & Pun, 2006) in China for Chinese firms abroad. There is also evidence of state-to-state patronage between Chinese SOEs and African states especially, but with local contestation from workers resisting Chinese deregulation of employment contracts (Lee, 2009).

Chinese MNCs are well capable of embracing locality norms and working with the agencies of local institutions. For example, although 'Chinese firms working on big construction projects tend to insist on importing their own workforce from China, instead of employing local people' (Zheng, 2008, p. 6), they are also found to be rather pragmatic in dealing with the labour market institutions in the host countries. A recent paper on Chinese MNCs in Africa noted 'labour importation varies according to the nature of the project, the Chinese firm involved, productivity levels, and the labour market conditions in Africa' (Chen & Orr, 2009). The Chinese MNC Huawei does not impose an ideological labour policy, but works with the locality in their Asian and African subsidiaries (Cooke, 2012). Zhu and Wei's (2014) recent case study based on a Chinese take-over of an Italian motorcycle company suggests that casualization of employment relations for the skilled workforce was an example of adopting policies of the host country. The newly acquired Italian subsidiary grew by offering technical workers temporary contracts because this was a standard practice in Italy due to a relative surplus of technically qualified labour. Unlike the practice in China, where qualified technical workers were offered long-term contracts as a standard retention measure. We are reminded here that investment by Chinese firms is subject to economic calculations as with other private firms, and it is misplaced to treat China differently and as operating outside of capitalist rationality.

Not all local institutions are hostile to the new capitalist investors, and there is some evidence that Chinese firms have become normal investors, and not deviants. For example, one of the few studies to examine attitudes of trade unionists to Chinese investment notes: '... the labor officials with whom we spoke generally do not perceive Chinese investors differently than other foreign investors, be it American, Japanese, or else [sic]. Union leaders and works councillors do not look upon foreign investors through the prism of the national origin of capital. Instead, two lenses appear to be prevalent, whether the investment is driven by short- or long-term profitability considerations ('finance' vs. 'productive' investments); and how foreign investors take comfort in relation to labor laws and practices' (Burgoon & Raess, 2014, p. 185).

The political economy of MNCs is not new. But there seems to be a wider agenda demonizing Chinese investments, as if emerging MNCs are scarier than other forms of investment (also see Aguzzoli & Geary, 2014) for a similar discourse on Brazilian investment in Canada). American commentators reporting that Chinese investors are hostile to trade unions is a bit rich, when US firms have resisted unionization at home and abroad for decades (Almond & Ferner, 2006; Ferner, Bélanger, Tregaskis, Morley, & Quintanilla, 2013; Royle & Towers, 2001). Such institutional resistance is sometimes voiced by independent agencies and sometimes enacted through collective agencies (Jacoby, 2014). While firms are the key transfer agencies, the role played by relevant parties outside the firm often enable or disable work organization and employment practices (ibid). The Chinese state, as an agency that initiates and enables the internationalization of Chinese firms, has attracted much attention (Cooke, 2014), and the political agenda to restrain China's influence may well be translated into resistance to workplace practices through institutional agencies. Such active roles of agencies beyond firms warrant further investigation as we study work and employment in Chinese firms overseas.

Concluding Remarks

The impact of Chinese OFDI on the global industrial structure, work relocation, and employment practices has yet to be addressed. The practical difficulties of gaining research access are often cited to be the reasons for the lack of workplace-based research in Chinese firms overseas (Wei, Clegg, & Ma, 2014; Zhu & Wei, 2014). However, as discussed earlier, we also see a general disengagement between the underlining discourses of the China-focused research and the international management literature. The China-focused research often features the 'uniqueness' or 'context specificity' of the China experience both at country and firm levels. The international management literature, in contrast, is built upon the assumption that MNCs are the vehicles of disseminating 'best practices', which are deemed to have transnational applicability (Kostova, 1999). A missing link between these two streams of research, to a large extent, has made it controversial when it comes to studying the work and employment issues in the Chinese firms overseas. To be more specific, without any prototype of the 'Chinese model', we seem to have lost the ideological ground to discuss the 'transfer' of 'established practices'. Application of existing comparative paradigms (e.g. the Variety of Capitalism framework) to the China case also becomes problematic, because the capitalism with Chinese characteristics is often a pick-and-mix of different paradigms (Peck & Zhang, 2013). Research into work and employment of Chinese firms overseas is methodologically challenging as well because developing a checklist of the core features of 'Chinese' work and employment (as researchers did at the early stages to understand work and employment issues in the Japanese firms overseas) is not feasible because of the levels of diversity discussed in this chapter.

In the absence of an overarching research agenda, studies of work and employment in the Chinese firms overseas have taken an inductive approach, building from case studies that draw upon theories that range from post-colonialism (Jackson, 2012; Kamoche & Siebers, 2014), socio-history (Lee, 2009; 2014) and neo-institutionalism (Cooke, (2012; 2014). While the number of companies being researched remains limited, these studies have helped to begin to augment our understanding of how Chinese firms may work. However, the problem we suggest may have been that the research focus has been 'country centred' and not 'practices centred'. Given the size and diversity of China, researchers have produced models and ideas that reflect back that diversity, without any clear direction and implications for the evolution of the Chinese firm as it internationalizes.

Following research on Japan, we suggest that through the process of the internationalization of Chinese firms, it might be possible to distil some 'core ingredients' of a Chinese management system. Prior to the accelerated movement of Japanese firms overseas from the 1970s, it was widely presumed that Japanese firms were 'embedded within Japanese society, tied through social networks, national institutions, cultural practices and state policies to the territory of the country' (Elger & Smith, 2005, p. 3). Internationalization allowed for a more complete understanding of the distinct character of the Japanese firm – at home and abroad. We suggest the same strategy could be adopted in understanding the Chinese firm, but with the understanding of fundamental differences between the two cases. We follow (Child, 2009) in questioning the cultural-relativist or country-centred approaches to the problem of transfer and country character, as this starts with the unrealistic claim that China possesses totally 'unique' management practices, rather than analysing the context and meaning of these practices within their local context, inherent diversity, and through comparators from others elsewhere.

REFERENCES

Agostino, M., Giunta, A., Nugent, J. B., Scalera, D., & Trivieri , F. (2014) The importance of being a capable supplier: Italian industrial firms in global value chains. *International Small Business Journal*, doi: 10.1177/0266242613518358.

Aguzzoli, R., & Geary, J. (2014) An 'emerging challenge': The employment practices of a Brazilian multinational company in Canada. *Human Relations, 67*(5), 587–609.

Aizawa, M. (2011) *China's Green Credit Policy:Building Sustainability in the Financial Sector.* Washington: International Finance Corporation (IFC).

Almond, P., & Ferner, A. (2006) *American Multinationals in Europe: Managing Employment Relations Across National Borders.* (P. Almond , & A. Ferner, Eds.) Oxford: Oxford University Press.

Amsden, A. H. (1992) *Asia's Next Giant: South Korea and Late Industrialization.* Oxford: Oxford University Press.

▶

Balcet, G., Wang, H., & Richet, X. (2012) Geely: a trajectory of catching up and asset-seeking multinational growth. *International Journal of Automotive Technology and Management, 12*(4), 360–378.

Baldassar, L., Johanson, G., McAuliffe, N., & Bressan, M. (2015) *Chinese Migration to Europe: Prato, Italy, and Beyond.* Basingstoke: Palgrave.

Brooks, A. (2010) Spinning and weaving discontent: labour relations and the production of meaning at Zambia-China Mulungushi Textiles. *Journal of Southern African Studies, 36*(1), 113–132.

Buckley, P. J., Clegg, J. L., Cross, A. R., Liu, X., Voss, H., & Zheng, P. (2007) The determinants of Chinese outward foreign direct investment. *Journal of International Business Studies, 38*(4), 499–518.

Burgoon, B., & Raess, D. (2014) Chinese investment and European labor: should and do workers fear Chinese FDI? *Asia Europe Journal, 12*(1–2), 179–197.

Butollo, F. (2014) *The End of Cheap Labour? Industrial Transformation and 'Social Upgrading' in China.* Chicago: Chicago University Press.

Cai, Y. (2010) *Collective resistance in China: Why Popular Protests Succeed or Fail.* Stanford: Stanford University Press.

Caro, E., Berntsen, L., Lillie, N., & Ines, W. (2015) Posted migration and segregation in the European construction sector. *Journal of Ethnic and Migration Studies, 41*(10), 1600–1620.

Caseiro, L. C., & Masiero, G. (2014) OFDI promotion policies in emerging economies: the Brazilian and Chinese strategies. *Critical Perspectives on International Business, 10*(2), 237–255.

Ceccagno, A. (2012) The hidden crisis: the Prato industrial district and the once thriving Chinese garment industry. *Revue européenne des migrations internationales, 28*(4), 43–65.

Ceccagno, A. (2015) The mobile emplacement: Chinese migrants in Italian industrial districts. *Journal of Ethnic and Migration Studies, 41*(7), 1111–1130.

Chan, A. (2011) *Walmart in China.* Ithaca: Cornell University Press.

Chan, J., & Pun, N. (2010) Suicide as protest for the new generation of Chinese migrant workers. *The Asia-Pacific Journal: Japan Focus*, http://japanfocus.org/-jenny-chan/3408/article.html. (accessed 10 July 2015).

Chen, C., & Orr, R. J. (2009) Chinese contractors in Africa: home government support, coordination mechanisms, and market entry strategies. *Journal of Construction Engineering and Management, 135*(11), 1201–1210.

Child, J. (1994) *Management in China During the Age of Reform.* Cambridge: Cambridge University Press.

Child, J. (2009) Context, comparison and methodology in Chinese management research. *Management and Organization Review, 5*(1), 57–73.

Child, J., & Rodriguez, S. B. (2005) The internationalization of Chinese firms: a case for theoretical extension? *Management and Organization Review, 1*(3), 381–410.

Cooke, F. (2012) The globalization of Chinese telecom corporations: Strategy, challenges and HR implications for host countries. *International Journal of Human Resource Management, 23*(9), 1832–1852.

Cooke, F. (2014) Chinese multinational firms in Asia and Africa: relationships with institutional actors and patterns of HRM practices. *Human Resource Management, 53*(6), 877–896.

Corkin, L. (2012) Chinese construction companies in Angola: A local linkages perspective. *Resources Policy, 37*(4), 475–483.

Deng, P. (2009) Why do Chinese firms tend to acquire strategic assets in international expansion? *Journal of World Business, 44*(1), 74–84.

Dunning, J. H. (2000) The eclectic paradigm as an envelope for economic and business theories of MNE activity. *International Business Review, 9*(1), 163–190.

Edwards, T., & Kuruvilla, S. (2005) International HRM: national business systems, organizational politics and the international division of labour in MNCs. *The International Journal of Human Resource Management, 16*(1), 1–21.

Elger, T., & Smith, C. (2005) *Assembling Work: Remaking Factory Regimes in Japanese Multinationals in Britain.* Oxford: Oxford University Press.

EY Knowledge. (2015) *Riding the Silk Road: China sees outbound investment boom. Outlook for China's outward foreign direct investment.* Shanghai: EY Knolwedge.

Ferner, A., Bélanger, J., Tregaskis, O., Morley, M., & Quintanilla, J. (2013) US multinationals and the control of subsidiary employment policies. *Industrial and Labor Relations Review, 66*(3), 645–669.

Friberg, J. H., Arnholtz, J., Eldring, L., Hansen, N. W., & Thorarins, F. (2014) Nordic labour market institutions and new migrant workers: Polish migrants in Oslo, Copenhagen and Reykjavik. *European Journal of Industrial Relations, 20*(1), 37–53.

Friedman, E., & Lee, C. (2010) Remaking the world of Chinese labour: a thirty year retrospective. *British Journal of Industrial Relations, 48*(3), 507–533.

Gao, Y. (2004). *Chinese migrants and Forced Labour in Europe.* Geneva: International Labour Organisation.

Gao, Y. (2012) *China as the Workshop of the World.* New York: Rouledge.

Goodman, D. S. (2014) *Class in Contemporary China.* London: Polity Press.

Gugler, P., & Fetscherin, M. (2011) Geely's internationalization and Volvo's acquisition. In I. Alon, M. Fetscherin, & P. Gugler, *Chinese International Investments* (pp. 376–390). London: Palgrave.

Hanemann, T., & Rosen, D. H. (2014) *High tech: the new wave of Chinese investment in America.* San Francisco, CA: The Asian Society and the Rhodium Group.

Henderson, J., Appelbaum, R. P., & Ho, S. (2013) Globalization with Chinese characteristics: Externalization, dynamics and transformations. *Development and Change, 44*(6), 1221–1253.

Jackson, T. (2012) Postcolonialism and orgnizational knowledge in the wake of China's presence in Africa: interrogting South-South relations. *Organization, 19*(2), 181–204.

Jacoby, W. (2014) Different cases, different faces: Chinese investment in Central and Eastern Europe. *Asia Europe Journal, 12*(1–2), 199–214.

Jaffe, S. (2014) *Forever Temp? Once a bastion of good jobs, manufacturing has gone gaga for temps.* Retrieved July 10, 2015, from In These Times: http://inthesetimes.com/article/15972/permatemps_in_manufacturing.

Johanson, G., Smyth, R., & French, R. (2009) *Living Outside the Walls: The Chinese in Prato.* Chicago: University of Chicago Press.

Kamoche, K., & Siebers, L. Q. (2014) Chinese management practices in Kenya: toward a post-colonial critique. *The International Journal of Human Resource Management*, published online first.

▶

Keith, M., Lash, S., Arnoldi, J., & Rooker, T. (2013) *China Constructing Capitalism: Economic Life and Urban Change.* New York: Rouledge.

Khan, A., & Harroff-Tavel, H. (2011) Reforming the kafala: Challenges and opportunities in moving forward. *Asian and Pacific Migration Journal, 20*(3–4), 293–313.

Kolstad, I., & Wiig, A. (2012) What determines Chinese outward FDI? *Journal of World Business, 47*(1), 26–34.

Kostova, T. (1999) Transnational transfer of strategic organizational practices: a contextual perspective. *Academy of Management Review, 24*(2), 308–324.

Kuruvilla, S., Lee, C., & Gallagher, M. E. (2011) *From Iron Rice Bowl to Informalization: Markets, Workers and the State in a Changing China.* New York: Cornell University Press.

Lee, C. (1998) *Gender and the South China Miracle: Two Worlds of Factory Women.* Berkeley: University of California Press.

Lee, C. (2007) *Against the Law: Labor Protests in China's Rustbelt and Sunbelt.* Berkeley: University of California Press.

Lee, C. (2009) Raw encounters: Chinese managers, African workers and the politics of casualisation in Africa's Chinese Enclaves. *The China Quarterly, 199*, 647–666.

Lee, C. (2014) The spectre of gobal China. *New Left Review, 89*(3), 29–56.

Lipietz, A. (1987) *Mirages and Miracles: Crisis in Global Fordism.* London: Verso.

Luo, Y., & Tung, R. L. (2007) International expansion of emerging market enterprises: a springboard perspective. *Journal of International Business Studies, 38*(1), 481–498.

Luo, Y., Xue, Q., & Han, B. (2010) How emerging market governments promote outward FDI: Experience from China. *Journal of World Business, 45*(1), 68–79.

Lüthje, B., Luo, S., & Zhang, H. (2013) *Beyond the Iron Rice Bowl: Regimes of Production and Industrial Relations in China.* Chicago: University of Chicago Press.

Macalister, T., & Pidd, H. (2009) *Uproar in Cowley as BMW confirms 850 job cuts at Mini factory.* Retrieved July 10, 2015, from The Guardian: http://www.theguardian.com/business/2009/feb/16/bmw-mini-job-cuts.

Mathews, J. A. (2006) Catch-up strategies and latecomer effect in industrial development. *New Political Economy, 11*(3), 313–335.

Meunier, S. (2012) *Political Impact of Chinese Foreign Direct Investment in the European Union on Transatlantic Relations.* Brussels: European Parliament.

Ministry of Commerce of People's Republic of China, National Bureau of Statistics of People's Republic of China, State Administration of Foreign Exchange (2009) *Statistical Bulletin of China's Outward FDI.* Beijing: China Statistics Press.

Ministry of Commerce of People's Republic of China, National Bureau of Statistics of People's Republic of China, State Administration of Foreign Exchange (2012) *Statistical Bulletin of China's Outward FDI.* Beijing: China Statistics Press.

Ministry of Commerce of People's Republic of China, National Bureau of Statistics of People's Republic of China, State Administration of Foreign Exchange (2015) *Statistical Bulletin of China's Outward FDI.* Beijing: China Statistics Press.

Mohan, G. (2013) Beyond the enclave: towards a critical political economy of China and Africa. *Development and Change, 44*(6), 1255–1272.

▶

Pan, L. (1994) *Sons of the Yellow Emperor: A History of the Chinese Diaspora.* Oxford: Oxford University Press.

Peck, J., & Zhang, J. (2013) A variety of capitalism ... with Chinese characteristics? *Journal of Economic Geography, 13*(3), 357–396.

Ramasamy, B., Yeung, M., & Lafor, S. (2012) China's outward foreign direct investment: Location choice and firm ownership. *Journal of World Business, 47*(1), 17–25.

Refslund, B. (2014) Intra-European labour migration and deteriorating employment relations in Danish cleaning and agriculture: Industrial relations under pressure from EU8/2 labour inflows? *Economic and Industrial Democracy.*

Roper, S. D., & Barria, L. A. (2014) Understanding Variations in Gulf Migration and Labor Practices. *Middle East Law and Governance, 6*(1), 32–52.

Royle, T., & Towers, B. (2001) *Labour Relations in the Global Fast-food Industry.* London: Rouledge.

Sakamoto, H. (1989) Japan's outward and inward FDI. *The CTC Reporter, 27,* 16–20.

Skeldon, R. (2007) The Chinese overseas: the end of exceptionalism? In M. Thunø, *Beyond Chinatown: New Chinese Migration and the Global Expansion of China* (pp. 35–48). Chicago: The University of Chicago Press.

Smith, C. (2003) Living at work: management control and the dormitory labour system in China. *Asia Pacific Journal of Management, 20*(3), 333–358.

Smith, C. (2008) Work organisation within a dynamic globalising context: a critique of national institutional analysis of the international firm and an alternative perspective. In C. D. Smith, B. McSweeney, & R. Fitzgerald (Eds.), *Remaking Management between Global and Local* (pp. 25–60). Cambridge: Cambridge University Press.

Smith, C., & Chan, J. (2015) Working for two bosses: Student interns as constrained labour in China. *Human Relations, 68*(2), 305–326.

Smith, C., & Meiksins, P. (1995) System, society and dominance effects in cross-national organisational analysis. *Work Employment & Society, 9*(2), 241–267.

Smith, C., & Pun, N. (2006) The dormitory labour regime in China as a site for control and resistance. *The International Journal of Human Resource Management, 17*(8), 1456–1470.

Thunø, M. (2007) *Beyond Chinatown: New Chinese Migration and the Global Expansion of China.* Chicago: The University of Chicago Press.

Tomba, L. (1999) Exporting the 'Wenzhou model' to Beijing and Florence: Suggestions for a comparative perspective on labour and economic organization in two migrant communities. In H. Mallee, & F. N. Pieke , *Internal and International Migration: Chinese Perspectives* (pp. 280–294). Richmond, Surrey: Curzon Press.

UNCTAD (2015) *Foreign Direct Investment.* Retrieved April 25, 2015, from United Nation Conference on Trade and Development: http://unctadstat.unctad.org

Walcott, S. M. (2007) Wenzhou and the third Italy: entrepreneurial model regions. *Journal of Asia-Pacific Business, 8*(3), 23–35.

Wang, B., & Huang, Y. (2012) Industry and ownership structure of Chinese overseas direct investment. *China's Global Investment* (pp. EABER Working Paper

Series, Paper No.75). Canberra: East Asian Bureau of Economic Research (EABER).

Wei, T., Clegg, J., & Ma, L. (2014) The conscious and unconscious facilitating role of the Chinese government in shaping the internationalization of Chinese MNCs. *International Business Review, 24*(2), 331–342.

Wei, Y. D., Li, W., & Wang, C. (2007) Restructuring industrial districts, scaling up regional development: a study of the Wenzhou model, China. *Economic Geography, 83*(4), 421–444.

Wu, B., & Latham, K. (2014) Migration from China to the EU: The Challenge within Europe. In K. Brown, *China and the EU in Context: Insights for Business and Investors* (pp. 303–321). Basingstoke: Palgrave Macmillan.

Wu, B., & Liu, H. (2014) Bringing class back in: class consciousness and solidarity among Chinese migrant workers in Italy and the UK. *Ethic and Racial Studies, 37*(8), 1391–1408.

Wu, B., & Sheehan, J. (2011) Globalization and vulnerability of Chinese migrant workers in Italy: empirical evidence on working conditions and their consequences. *Journal of Contemporary China, 20*(68), 135–152.

Yan, H., & Sautmana, B. (2012) Chasing ghosts: rumours and representations of the export of Chinese convict labour to developing countries. *The China Quarterly, 210*(2), 398–418.

Yoshino, M. Y. (1974) The multinational spread of Japanese manufacturing investment since World War II. *Business History Review, 48*(3), 357–381.

Zajak, S. (2012) *In the Shadow of the Dragon: Transnational Labor Activism between State and Private Politics A Multilevel Analysis of Labor.* Köln: Köln University Dissertation.

Zhang, L. (2008) Lean production and labor controls in the Chinese automobile industry in an age of globalization. *International Labor and Working Class History, 73*(1), 24–44.

Zhang, L. (2015) *Inside China's Automobile Factories: the Politics of Labor and Worker Resistance.* Cambridge: Cambridge University Press.

Zhang, M., & Edwards, C. (2007) Diffusing 'best practice' in Chinese multinationals: the motivation, facilitation and limitations. *The International Journal of Human Resource Management, 18*(12), 2147–2165.

Zheng, C. (2008) China's Investment in Africa: Expanding the 'Yellow River Capitalism' and Its Implications. Melbourne: 31st African Studies Association of Australasia and Pacific.

Zheng, Y. (2015) Building from below: Subsidiary management moderation of employment practices in MNCs in China. *The International Journal of Human Resource Management.* DOI: 10.1080/09585192.2015.1091368

Zheng, Y., & Smith, C. (2015) Overturning the orthodoxy on expatriate use in MNCs: the case of Chinese MNCs abroad. *The 33rd International Labour Process Conference.* Athens, Greece.

Zhou, L., & Leung, D. (2015) *China's Overseas Investment, Explained in 10 Graphics.* Retrieved June 15, 2015, from World Resources Institute: http://www.wri.org/print/42536

▶

Zhu, C. J., Zhang, M., & Shen, J. (2012) Paternalistic and transactional HRM: the nature and transformation of HRM in contemporary China. *The International Journal of Human Resource Management, 23*(19), 3964–3982.

Zhu, J., & Wei, W. (2014) HR strategy and practices in Chinese multinational companies. In J. C. Craig, Z. U. Ahmed, & J. Xu, *Research Handbook On The Globalization Of Chinese Firms* (pp. 162–182). Cheltenham: Edward Elgar.

Zhu, S., & He, C. (2014) Global, regional and local: new firm formation and spatial restructuring in China's apparel industry. *GeoJournal, 79*(2), 237–253.

Name Index

Subject Index